Reading Minds

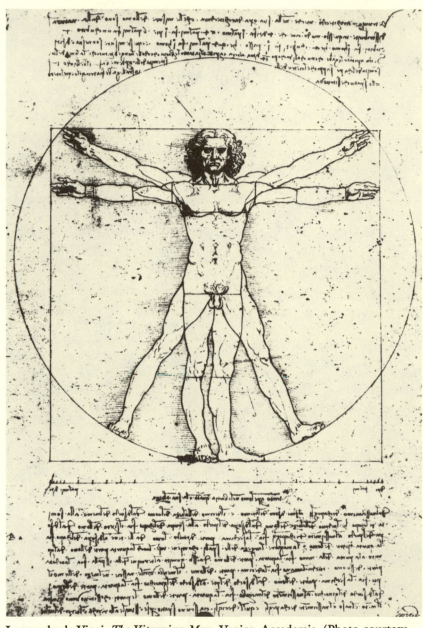

Leonardo da Vinci, *The Vitruvian Man*, Venice, Accademia. (Photo courtesy of Foto Marburg/Art Resource, New York.)

Reading Minds

THE STUDY OF ENGLISH
IN THE AGE OF
COGNITIVE SCIENCE

Mark Turner

PRINCETON UNIVERSITY PRESS

PRINCETON, NEW JERSEY

Library of Congress Cataloging-in-Publication Data

Turner, Mark, 1954–
Reading minds : the study of English in the age of
cognitive science / Mark Turner.
p.   cm.
Includes bibliographical references and index.
1. English philology—Study and teaching (Higher)—
United States.   2. Cognitive learning—United States.
I. Title.
PE68.U5T87   1991   91-16188   420.71'173—dc20

ISBN 0-691-06897-6
ISBN 0-691-00107-3 (pbk.)

This book has been composed in Adobe Galliard
First Princeton Paperback printing, 1994

Princeton University Press books are printed
on acid-free paper and meet the guidelines for
permanence and durability of the Committee on
Production Guidelines for Book Longevity
of the Council on Library Resources

Printed in the United States of America

3   5   7   9   10   8   6   4   2

CONTENTS

PREFACE

THE COMING AGE will be known and remembered, I believe, as the age in which the human mind was discovered. I can think of no equal intellectual achievement. The purpose of this book is to propose a reframing of the study of English so that it comes to be seen as inseparable from the discovery of mind, participating and even leading the way in that discovery, gaining new analytic instruments for its traditional work and developing new concepts of its role.

I speak from a known frame about a new frame, or more accurately about a new activity of framing. I offer a provisional version of that new frame. I conduct illustrative case studies within it. Of course, I am invested in the intricacies of these particular case studies, having lived with them. But my final investment is not in the details of these particular studies or even in their chosen themes and problems; it is rather in the activity of reconsidering and reframing the study of language, literature, and mind.

This book is offered as a means to that activity. I present a series of incitements. I do not map the borders and divisions of future inquiry but ask the reader to begin a revision that will affect the path of our research in ways we cannot know. The crucial result of this book is to be found not within this book but rather within the reader who has been persuaded to begin that reconsideration.

The human mind is linguistic and literary; language and literature are products of the everyday human mind. The future for which this book is written is one in which traditional humanistic studies will be centered once again upon the study of the human mind, and the study of the human mind will be centered upon human acts that are the subject matter of the humanities. To give an adequate suggestion of this future, I am forced to work in greater detail than the current state of research permits. This book is something like a detailed report about a future that cannot be known in such detail.

I begin with a Pretext—"Professing English in the Age of Cognitive Science"—offered primarily to future members of the profession of English. I survey the fragmented, isolated, and inconsequential state of literary studies and explore the causes of their decline to peripheral status. I argue that while contemporary critical theory is unanchored, its objects—the acts of language and literature—are permanently anchored in the full human world by being anchored in how the human mind works. I propose a new common ground for the profession of English: the analysis of acts of language, including literature, as acts of a human brain in a human body in a human environment which that brain must make intelligible if it is to survive.

The constructive project of the book—to shape an inquiry into language, literature, and mind as inseparable objects of analysis—begins in chapter 1, the "User's Manual." Readers who feel by temperament or prior interest attracted to this project but who see nothing at stake in a discussion of the profession of English can begin without loss at chapter 1. It is a guide to the use of this book as an instrument for revisiting and revising basic concepts so automatic and powerful in our thought as to constitute a kind of floor plan of our thinking. I discuss the entrenched nature of these concepts, their ubiquitous unconscious use, and the sources of our resistance to their loss. In "Floor Plan," I examine particular basic concepts that we must change if we are to reconstitute the profession along the lines I propose. I consider concepts of the human person, the body, the brain, thinking, consciousness, concepts, language, literature, and the humanities. My purpose in these chapters is finally not to survey the existing floor plan of our thought but rather to offer a replacement.

These chapters are the opening frame. Collectively, they offer a design for research that might be called "cognitive rhetoric." The second part of the book offers topical introductions to that design through four case studies. Each provides a specific point of access to the kind of research that would be necessary at the project's start. I think of them as early laboratory experiments in the mode of investigation I propose.

The third part of the book—titled "The Poetry of Connections"—presents an overview of larger issues in cognitive rhetoric. I close the book with a practical application and a brief envoi. The practical application brings the instruments of cognitive rhetoric to bear upon questions of cultural literacy, to indicate how cognitive rhetoric might serve as a basis for our pedagogy. The envoi sketches possible lines of research and instruction under a new frame of inquiry whose purpose would be to rejoin the study of language with the study of literature, in concert with the study of the mind and the brain.

What follows is therefore not a humble book, but as it is my attempt to reconstitute the profession, I hope the arrogance needed to write it at all will be excused. It is a proposal to change our conception of the humanities—or at least that branch of the humanities that concerns language and literature—by grounding it in the study of human cognition. It is my attempt to do what I can to restore the profession of English to its once-central position. I hope especially that my colleagues in the profession of English will take it as the offering of someone dedicated to our profession and to its future at the center of humanistic and scientific activity.

ACKNOWLEDGMENTS

THIS BOOK was written during 1989–1990, my fellowship year at the National Humanities Center. My debt to the center and to the members of my class is absolute. I would like to thank W. Robert Connor, the center's effervescent new director, for his many humanistic virtues—his goodwill, his good humor, his wisdom on the uses of classical texts today, and his insight into the possible futures of the humanities.

My thanks go also to associate director Kent Mullikin and to the rest of the staff for every conceivable assistance; to Duke University, the University of North Carolina at Chapel Hill, and North Carolina State University for their support of the center; and to the Educational Computing Service of Research Triangle Park. I am additionally grateful to the National Endowment for the Humanities for its support of the National Humanities Center and, in a trickle-down fashion, of me.

I am grateful to colleagues who have invited me to present parts of this work at Duke University, the University of California at Berkeley, the University of California at San Diego, the University of Chicago, Mount Union College, George Washington University, the University of Waterloo, Pennsylvania State University, the Georgia Institute of Technology, North Carolina State University, the University of North Carolina at Greensboro, the University of Maryland, the University of Oklahoma, and Temple University.

What I owe intellectually rivals the national debt. The section called "Pretext" is based on an institutional document I wrote with the assistance of Francis-Noël Thomas. I would like to thank him for his expert and invaluable editorial assistance in that section and in my thinking about the rhetorical design of the book. His own interest in iconography stimulated me to think about the iconography of thinking and the iconography of the person. An earlier version of chapter 3 appeared in *Poetics Today* as "Poetry: Metaphor and the Conceptual Context of Invention." That chapter and the book as a whole owe an obvious debt to Mark Johnson's work on the theory of image-schemas. I am grateful to Gilles Fauconnier, Ronald Langacker, Cathy Harris, Jeff Elman, David McNeill, John Goldsmith, Jim McCawley, Nancy Dray, Peter Dembowski, and David Palermo for conversations about the contents of chapter 3. I thank Nancy Dray for examples, and James Arnold and Philippe Bernard for checking my translation from Georges Perec's *l'infraordinaire*. Chapter 4 draws on my earlier article in *Language and Style* 19 (1986). Part of chapter 6 incorporates and revises material that I published in an anthology titled *Analogical Reasoning*.

I am grateful for readings to John Bienz, Claudia Brugman, Gregory Colomb, Donald Freeman, Norman Holland, Mark Johnson, Michael Murrin, Neil Randall, Philip Stadter, Eve Sweetser, Joseph Williams, and Steven Winter, whose attentions have helped me to make many fewer errors than I would have made on my own. Aside from details or specific ideas on individual problems, Claudia Brugman, Mark Johnson, George Lakoff, Eve Sweetser, Francis-Noël Thomas, William Wimsatt, and Steven Winter have in different ways deeply shaped many of my views in this work. Parts of chapter 7 draw on work I did with George Lakoff in *More than Cool Reason: A Field Guide to Poetic Metaphor*. The cliché that all errors—conceptual to rhetorical—are the author's deserves the fullest acknowledgment of all, especially in a work as necessarily tentative and speculative as this one.

Permission to reprint the following is gratefully acknowledged: "At North Farm" from *A Wave* by John Ashbery. Copyright © by John Ashbery. Reprinted by permission of Viking Penguin, a division of Penguin Books USA Inc.; Carcanet Press Limited; and Georges Borchardt, Inc., for the author. Material from Mark Turner, "Categories and Analogies," *Analogical Reasoning*, ed. David Helman (Dordrecht: Kluwer, 1988), pages 3–24. Copyright © 1988 Kluwer Academic Publishers. Reprinted by permission of Kluwer Academic Publishers. "Approches de quoi?" from *l'infraordinaire* by Georges Perec. Copyright © Editions du Seuil, 1989. Reprinted by permission of Editions du Seuil.

Reading Minds

PROFESSING ENGLISH
IN THE AGE OF COGNITIVE SCIENCE

THE WORLD of contemporary literary criticism, as represented by the professors and dissertation students in our research universities, as advertised in the pages of the *New York Review of Books,* and as sampled in the articles on our shelf of academic journals, has no equal as an uncanny marvel of self-sustaining institutional and human ingenuity. It is to the humanities what the self-sustaining fission reaction in a critical mass of mutually exciting unstable heavy molecules is to the natural sciences. It generates ever more subtle and masterful readings of ever more texts for an ever more specialized group of readers. Fuel is found not only in writing—new writing, old writing, texts resurrected from pit graves of discard—but also in nontextual representations, mute artifacts, and ultimately human behavior itself, treated as if they were texts to be read. Finally criticism has become its own fuel, susceptible of a higher-order critical analysis that is not merely self-sustaining but, beyond fission, self-feeding, its output continuous with its input, a perpetual breeder reactor, unrestrained by laws of entropy. There is no obvious limit to the levels of self-awareness and inward illumination through which the bootstrapping critic can ascend. It is like chess about chess, a game about the concept of games, a mandarin activity beyond any naive ordering, beyond any positivist ranking of types. Modern literary critics are among the most ingenious minds our culture has spawned. Certainly they deserve recognition as such, despite the fact that it is uniformly denied them outside their own ranks. With an eerie consistency, they are discounted in both popular and intellectual culture as self-absorbed but mostly harmless irrelevancies, modern successors to the sophists of Aristophanes' thinkery, a queer and bloated island species that survives by reproducing itself in a niche institutionally secured.[1]

This special world of contemporary critical theory—however heady or marvelous in its gists and piths—is ungrounded and fragmented. By contrast, its objects—language and literature—are deeply grounded. Language and literature are suffused by the full human world of the everyday. That is their basis. This full human world, the world that comprehends language and literature, exists for us independently of any academic theory. Whether the academic theory is invented or not, whether it attains an ascendency or vanishes, the full human world, its language and literature, abide, exactly because our grasp of this world and our operation within it depend not upon academic theories but upon a commonplace conceptual apparatus that is textured and powerful. Literature is the highest expression of our commonplace conceptual and linguistic capacities. Literary criticism touches home base, the full human world, to the extent that it sees literature as the expression of everyday capacities and helps us to understand them. Contemporary critical theory fails to connect with the full human world to the extent that it treats objects in literature that can be seen only by means of the theory: in that case, if the theory vanishes, its objects vanish.[2]

The neglect of contemporary critical theory to analyze literature as the expression of everyday capacities and to help us understand those capacities cuts it off from the full human world, making it a special world, simpler than the human world, smaller and marginal, exhilarating as a magic kingdom contained within its own walls, often viewed derisively as an exclusive Disney World for literary critics.

Literature lives within language and language within everyday life. The study of literature must live within the study of language, and the study of language within the study of the everyday mind. When embedded in this way, the study of literature is automatically connected to whatever is basic to human beings. The wisdom in giving English departments names like "The Department of English Language and Literature" lay in the emphasis on the inseparability of literature and language. Historically, the problem with such names was that they implied sequence: first one studies language, and then, if there is a balance of time remaining, one studies literature, rather than studying them simultaneously, and rather than studying literature as a *mode* of language.

The principal substitute for grounding the study of literature in the study of language and hence in the study of the everyday mind is to ground it in a canon, a list. The canon has come to form the character of the profession and to define its research activity. To be sure, some canonized authors are so vital that a research university will profitably include professors whose acquaintance with those works is intimate. It is equally certain that a considerable amount of useful curatorial research remains to be done upon certain works. But acquaintance is not research and curatorial research is not infinite. Belief in the canon as defining the profession—as exemplified by belief in the inherent importance of the works of a particular author—has become the justification for publications treating those works. The security of those works in the canon ensures the security of the professor who specializes in them on the faculty of a department of English in a research university. Such a faculty member produces, through graduate students, new professors of those works, who turn dissertations on those works into books on those works, and who in their own turn create new professors of those works, in a repetitive process that stabilizes the employment profile of departments of English at the cost of embracing the view that there will always be an indefinite amount of curatorial labor remaining to be done on those works.

There is a scene about the canon in the movie *Animal House*. A professor of English is lecturing to a class about Milton. His students perform obediently what they take to be their role: they are to pretend to be attentive; they are to hide meaningful activities like doodling; when he fixes his gaze and says something pointedly, they are to move their heads and hands in a way that approximates the activity of note-taking. They are to do this for one hour. Of course it is clear that they have been given no reason for their presence aside from institutional coercion. The professor informs them that Milton is great and wrote long works a long time ago. The students betray no effect of this information because it has not been made clear to them what the approved effect might be. The professor lets them in on the secret that Milton's most interesting character is Satan. He writes "SATAN" on the chalkboard, finishing this pedagogical achievement with a gesture of emphasis, and adding a subtle dramatic citation by taking a bite from an apple. They have no idea what they are supposed to do with this confidence, and so smile wanly or avert their gaze as an all-purpose response, one that cannot clearly count as wrong. As the class hour ends and the students rise on cue to file out, oblivious of him, he admits that Milton does not translate well into our generation, but, he says, "that does not relieve you of your responsibility for this material." The room is nearly empty. "I'm not kidding," he says. "This is my job."

This scene strikes a few recognizable chords. The first is that all first-year college students know it is bizarre to read and write essays about books on a list, in the absence of any demonstration of why these activities are important. Undergraduates who decide to become English majors frequently suppress their knowledge that this is odd. They come to believe in the importance of these lists, and in giving readings of texts on the lists, and consequently they come to believe in the importance of what they are doing, and this belief sustains the profession. Belief, with its power to admit the believer to our elite Disney World for literary critics, substitutes for touching home base.

The second chord it strikes is not for students so much as for teachers. What is criminal about this scene is that the professor has taken something that is crucially important, but not obviously so, and, by neglecting to demonstrate its importance, led the students to see the work as irrelevant and the profession as silly.

Speaking within the professional family, we might admit that although we can continue to produce ever more specialized treatments of our favorite works for an ever more specialized audience, we lack any common and commonly respected conception of the activity of the profession. Part of the definition of a profession is that practitioners not too far removed from each other in time must be able to recognize each other's activities. The differences in a profession that occur over a reasonable amount of time should never obscure the profession's identity to insiders. We do not meet this description of a profession. It is not just that, if a scholar from the recent past were brought back and given the program of the Modern Language Association's annual convention, he would not be able to recognize most of the topics listed there as part of his profession, would not know what most of the papers count as, and would not know what he was supposed to do with them, but that members of the profession alive today do not in the main know what they are meant to do with each other's papers.

We do not in the profession acknowledge a common activity that makes us one profession, and do not have one place where we touch home base and ground our work in the full human world.

This chapter is written to encourage a reconstitution of the profession of English. It asks us to reconsider what our home base should be. I propose that what the profession lacks is a concept of language and literature as acts of the everyday human mind. If we had such a concept, our grounding activity would be the study of language and of literature as expressions of our conceptual apparatus. We would focus on how the embodied human mind uses its ordinary conceptual capacities to perform those acts of language and literature. This would provide a global continuity and a global unity to the profession: a synchronic unity making us one profession, and a diachronic continuity making the work of the profession recognizable over time.

To be sure, there are many legitimate local concerns in our profession. For example, we may be concerned with the change of a society from nomadic to agrarian, and the effect on its literature, or the development of the urban model, and its effect on literature, and so on. Certain local issues will be urgent at certain moments. What is urgent at all moments in our profession is the relationship among language, literature, and the human mind.

The grounding activity that I propose is not an organizing hypothesis and is not imperial. I do not propose to organize the profession according to a set of hypotheses or a set of subjects. Rather, I propose that we organize the profession on the basis of what the profession does, a common *activity* that we all recognize, and where we all touch home base.

I propose, roughly, that what is missing from the profession of English is *English*, but I do not mean by this that the curriculum should be richer in language courses, or that lucid prose style should be the anthem of our profession, or that we all should teach composition, or any of the other familiar proposals for changing the profession. Instead, I will argue that what the profession lacks is a grounding, integrated approach to language and literature as acts of the human mind. My argument constitutes a critique of the present state of the profession, based upon a vision of what the profession of English could be. I will begin this critique by looking at the profession's past, problems, and prospects.

Presumably, behind all the professions of the humanities that deal with the study of texts lies the cultural desire to know more about those texts that are indisputably fundamental within a culture—such as the *Iliad* or the Bible—and also to know more about the past, which often speaks to us through damaged documents ripped from their historical contexts, written in lost or only partially understood languages, thus evidently in need of scholarly attention if they are ever to become intelligible. The scholar's warrant, in these cases, is exactly the precritical interest in the text or in the epoch it represents.

For example, in our culture, the Fourth Gospel is taken precritically to be of virtually infinite merit and importance, interesting for what it can tell us about early Christianity, interesting for what it has to say about truth and values, and interesting as a text that has had maximal cultural and literary resonance. It is this precritical interest that makes the Fourth Gospel "sacred" in a secular sense, the same sense in which *Hamlet* is sacred, and that warrants indefinitely many critical treatments of it. This is our implicit model of all the texts we treat. We have taken every text, and indeed everything else that can be "read"—such as pornographic movies, game shows, and cereal boxes—to be sacred literature, automatically warranting and legitimating extensive critical treatment. The result in our profession has been a flood of specific readings of texts.

The great age when precritical interest in texts was general for all texts and thus warranted the scholar's efforts was of course the Renaissance, when there was a pervasive precritical interest in all the texts of classical antiquity. As Charles Martindale has written, "Classicists still frequently act as though they were living in the Renaissance, when the promulgation of the new learning meant that the editing of ancient texts was a central cultural activity. Now, when such work is marginal, they need to find for themselves new roles, which should include more attention to the classical heritage and a greater concern with the intellectual life of our age."[3] The scholarly and critical traditions of the editor, the philologist, the exegete, and the interpreter arose under a precritical warrant and were in place before the inception of our profession. Currently the profession has laid claim to this original warrant by assuming that all literature is sacred or infinitely valuable. We have additionally adopted a second warrant, namely, the implied promise of excitement or ingenuity in the reading, where these qualities can be independent of the value of the text. Indeed, ingenuity of reading has come to confer value on texts.

The profession of English began with a quite different range of interests. The specific graduate study of English in America as it arose in the nineteenth century was altogether unlike the professional world we now inhabit. It began as the study of language and quickly moved on to the study of literature treated by the methods of philology.[4] Before the major revision of the field that was largely accomplished by 1935, literary history, intellectual history, the history of ideas, and historical linguistics had each achieved a recognized role in the "profession of English," and each was at least superficially coordinated with the others. The coordination of these disciplines, however, depended on the view that philology provided a superstructure and valid methodology for the profession and that other disciplines were legitimate to the extent that they produced similar knowledge reached by similar methods.

Literary criticism held a status virtually as commentary or conversation without method. In all the other disciplines in the profession of English besides criticism, conclusions could be regarded as knowledge because each of these disciplines was defined by a method whose validity was widely accepted. Commentary, on the other hand, however impressively learned it might be, did not count as learning, precisely because there existed no commonly accepted method for testing its validity as knowledge. Two commentators, equally learned, could disagree in their commentary, with no method to serve as judge between them. Two philologists could not disagree in the same way, without one of them generally being regarded as wrong.

In the 1930s, there were attempts to reform this situation. One group of reformers consisted of self-described progressive conservatives such as R. S. Crane, who viewed the marginal status of criticism as evidence of the narrowness of the profession. Crane wanted to supplement the existing disciplines with criticism, but did not want to change the prevailing definition of knowledge or the goals of the profession as a whole. He sought to promote criticism to legitimate status within the profession by giving it a common method sufficiently rigorous to allow it a place alongside the other disciplines of the profession.

Another group of reformers consisted of revolutionaries such as René Wellek and Austin Warren who wanted literary criticism to become the center of the profession rather than a peer of the other disciplines. In time, it became clear that they were willing to see the disciplines other than criticism become vestigial.

Crane himself characterized this contrast:

> it was possible to react against the narrowness of the prevailing philological and historical disciplines in either of two ways—a progressive-conservative

way or a root-and-branch way; and what I failed to predict was that the immediate future at least belonged to those radical reformers of literary study—soon to be called, loosely, "new critics"—who were in revolt not merely against the limitations of the older learning but, as it turned out, against the very conception of intellectual method that gave it its status as learning.[5]

It was more than the immediate future, however, that belonged to Crane's radical reformers. They dominated the profession for most of the following thirty-five years. By the end of that time, the study of language as such had become a conceptual backwater to the extent that what had once been clearly central to the graduate study of English moved almost entirely into departments of linguistics. The Lovejovian history of ideas almost disappeared from the field, and as intellectual history became less important in departments of English, it assumed a more important role in departments of history and art history, and found settings in divinity schools and in newly established committees and departments such as those in the history of science.[6] Literary history, of course, did not disappear from the field, but many influential members of the profession came to regard it as practically an antiquarian subject. Literary criticism presented itself as something that replaced the concepts of the past, not as something that built on previous knowledge. It began almost at once to expand in the direction of commentary on contemporary culture. From this point on, every new activity in the profession felt obliged to include some component of criticism; none at its inception felt obliged to respect the criteria of philology.[7]

At present the profession is in the middle of another major revision. Criticism has turned inward upon itself to such an extent that if there were a clearly dominant discipline today that discipline would be theory. The situation is complicated by the fact that the profession is divided first into a contest between competing theories, and then into a group of apparently unrelated fields, some of them traditional, some of them novel. Some of these fields ignore theory in all of its forms while one form or another of theory helps to define some of the other fields. The fields typically have no relationship with one another. Theory itself is divided not into fragments of a field, even an ideal one, but into incommensurate and rival worlds of discourse.

When philology was central, the profession was small and stable. Currently, the profession is large and unstable. Consider, as an illustration of this instability, the condition of the current doctoral student, who, by way of training in the profession, apprentices himself or herself in one of the unrelated fields or one of the rival theories, and acquires through that apprenticeship a specialized competence that may share no common component with the competences acquired by students apprenticed to other fields or other theories. As these doctoral students obtain their degrees and fill the ranks of the professoriate, the fragmentation in the profession and its lack of shared discourse will grow increasingly manifest and painful.

If we imagine R. S. Crane brought back now to observe and assess the situation, we should have to imagine him as surprised by the extent to which one profession has become a collection of partitioned fields. Crane proceeded from the ideal that in his time scholars in different fields read different texts but did not do incommensurately different things with them. Trained as a medievalist, he became a distinguished eighteenth-century scholar. During his early teaching years at Northwestern University, the member of his department who specialized in the eighteenth century died during the term. His department viewed it as plausible that Crane could take over teaching the eighteenth-century classes. The possibility of a medieval scholar's moving to the eighteenth century depended in their view largely on energy. The fields as they existed then shared a common mode of discourse and a common model of method. It was normal then to expect the various disciplines to be intelligible to one another, and taken for granted that they were relevant to one another.

The most serious cause of the profession's instability today is that these expectations and assumptions no longer apply. The profession did well to widen its scope in the past, but failed sufficiently to notice that the parts of this wider profession were no longer defined by a common base. The profession is currently constituted not intellectually but administratively, to meet the temporary and local exigencies of institutions. It is like a library catalogued by the names of the donors. Film, for example, entered English departments because some professors of English became interested in film. There is nothing except administrative convenience that for the moment holds together these accidents of origin, and it is likely that in a few years, current arrangements will seem to be inefficient anomalies. Film, for example, finds its place at various institutions not in English departments but in departments of art or in separate departments of film studies. Foundation professors of novel subjects are always educated in traditional fields; some of the foundation professors of film studies were educated in English departments; hence film is part of English at those institutions where the appropriate historical accidents happened. But there is no reason for the students of such foundation professors to be educated in English departments once their field becomes itself large enough to constitute a department. There is nothing special about film as an example. Language, once central to English departments, is now often treated in the same way.

If the profession of English is not defined by a subject matter, neither is it defined by even a partly agreed upon list of the major unsolved prob-

lems facing us. In many other professions, graduate students and researchers typically expect to work on problems recognized throughout
the profession as important. The outstanding recognized problems constitute a spotty but reasonably accurate map of those professions. The
profession of English is not susceptible of this description. Beginning dissertation students typically spend months "coming up with a problem,"
as they phrase it (and this is different from "choosing a problem"), and
spend the major part of their dissertation's introduction attempting to
convince the reader that the chosen topic both is a problem and is important. The outside world will not respect a profession whose individual
members appear to be inventing individual problems rather than address-
ing problems recognized throughout the profession. The appearance our
profession gives of doing just that accounts, I believe, for the consistent
caricaturing of our profession in both intellectual culture and popular
culture as self-absorbed and unimportant.[8]

The unhappy view I have sketched seems unhappy to me because it is
one in which the profession no longer retains its place at the center of
human culture, no longer shares a place with science, engineering, and
the shaping of social institutions in the vital human work of conducting
human life. It has lost this place since, viewed from without, it has
stopped speaking to that human culture; viewed from within, its disciplines have stopped speaking to one another. This state of things is a
charter for a profession whose future is a postmodern version of Aristophanes' thinkery.

The future I would like to see resembles Crane's description of an
imaginary golden age:

> The great importance of the eighteenth century in the history of the human-
> ities lies in the fact that, for the first and last time in this history, for all the
> differences of method and emphasis, something like a balance was achieved,
> by most of the writers of the period, between the various rival interests of
> the earlier periods. We have seen how earlier periods set humanists, as advo-
> cates of useful knowledge, against dialecticians; natural scientists, as advo-
> cates of useful knowledge, against humanists; partisans of the moderns
> against admirers of the ancients; and rhetoricians and scholars against phi-
> losophers. Resolution of these oppositions, however partial, produced a
> great humanistic age—an age in which the utility of literary studies was sel-
> dom seriously questioned even by educators interested in diffusing natural
> knowledge; in which the central problems of philosophers were the powers
> and achievements of man; in which at the same time that grammarians, crit-
> ics, and historians attempted to be philosophical, philosophers concerned
> themselves in a humanistic rather than merely scientific spirit with language,
> criticism, and history; in which, in short, whether on the side of the literary

men or on that of philosophers, the characteristic effort, in all fields of discussion, aimed at the establishment of some kind of union or harmony—rather than separation—between words and things, the arts of speech and the arts of reason, the determination of facts and the formulation of principles and values, the permanently excellent and the immediately useful, the classics of the past and the new knowledge and problems of the present.[9]

If we ever hope for anyone to look back at our future in the way Crane looked at the eighteenth century, we must discover something in our current activities that can serve as the ground upon which the profession constitutes itself. Crane, given his temperament, would almost certainly call to our attention that the one thing we all do is read, and that we are still expected by others to have a special competence in language and the arts of language. We retain a trace of this popular assumption in the formal names of our departments, such as "The Department of English Language and Literature" or simply "The Department of English." On the most elementary level, it is still the English teacher who is expected to teach students to read. To the extent that this teaching fails, the entire educational system is thought to fail. English teachers therefore have an unarguably central position in the curricula of elementary schools and high schools. It is only at the highest levels of the profession that doubt can be raised about the central importance of English language and literature. It is a commonplace that the members of the profession of English who are not actively engaged in research or scholarship feel themselves to be utterly and scandalously abandoned by their colleagues in the universities. University researchers and scholars have created sophisticated worlds of discourse in the most specialized areas of the profession and have added a number of novel fields, and this is all to the good, but we have devoted less and less of our work to anything with consequences at the foundation points of our understanding of reading and writing—the most permanent and permanently valuable arts for which we have assumed a formal directing responsibility. This, I think, is probably not to the good, at least not for those who would like to see the profession as a central cultural activity.

At the point when we start talking to the entire profession, which as a whole teaches everyone the fundamental arts of language, we will necessarily be talking to everyone. University researchers and scholars have developed a parochial view of themselves as *the* profession of English rather than as *the flower* of the profession. The profession as a whole daily engages and influences fundamental cultural activities. The flower of the profession is sustained by that daily engagement, and in its season, justifies its existence by innovation and leadership.

University researchers and scholars have become sophisticated in every fashionable new field in our profession as currently constituted, but a harsh critic might say that we have regressed in our knowledge of what will always be the logical core of this profession: the elementary arts of language. At present, the Ph.D. in English does not mean that its holder has any special knowledge of the English language. It no longer means that its holder necessarily knows much about English or American literature. It would surely surprise a great American scholar of any earlier era to discover that one can receive a Ph.D. from a department of English language and literature without demonstrating a special knowledge of either the English language or English literature. And it would surprise any great humanist of an earlier era—Aristotle, Dante, Milton, Johnson, Emerson—that a rift has developed between the teaching of literature and the teaching of the arts of language. Fifty years hence, much of what now lives within the profession will be departed, either into other departments, or into the historical record of intellectual fashion. But language and the arts of language will remain.

The acts of literature are able to exist and to have meaning because language and the conventional thought of linguistic communities already exist. What a reader brings to a text is predominantly what a member of the linguistic community brings to the language in which the text is written. To attempt to treat literature independently of everyday language and conventional thought is a brand of solipsism, one that, on days when the view looks dim, seems to have afflicted the profession of English almost throughout its entire existence. Someone who believes that his existence is independent of the world, could be *possible* independent of the world, and can be treated as such, is a solipsist. A member of the profession of English who believes that the concepts in a great literary work can be analyzed without analyzing the concepts that are conventional to the language in which it is embedded, and the way those concepts are disclosed in the shape and structure of the language, is another kind of solipsist, a literary solipsist. It is like thinking that great baseball players can exist and be great baseball players in a world without baseball.

The difference between Shakespeare and his contemporary speakers is not that he speaks a different language, or that he thinks with different conceptual resources, but rather that he is a master of clarity and nuance. The language of great writers does not differ in kind from the language of ordinary speakers. Shakespeare's contemporaries can appreciate his mastery exactly because he is using conceptual resources they use, and speaking a language they know. Essentially, we still speak that language and can share those conceptual resources. Like Shakespeare's contemporaries, we call upon our concepts and our knowledge of language to make

sense of his works, and we augment these capacities not only by understanding aspects of his work that are special to literary expression, but also
by investigating what we share in language and thought with his contemporaries. All literature exploits the resources of its contemporary ordinary
language and conceptual structures. It is a task of our profession to develop analytic instruments for investigating the resources of ordinary language and conventional thought: we do not expect the writer and the
reader to be able to articulate consciously and systematically the linguistic
or conceptual resources they use in reading and writing, but we should
expect our profession to seek to do so. Language and concepts receive
their highest expression in literature, and the analysis of that expression
has always been our central activity. It is our profession's avenue into the
central questions of what it is to be human, the cultural and conceptual
counterpart to the biological and social inquiries that help us understand
our human possibilities.

This sort of analysis would mediate between what might be called
common understanding and special understanding. By "common understanding" I mean to indicate the linguistic skills and conceptual resources
shared by the members of a natural linguistic community; by "special understanding" I mean to indicate those linguistic skills and conceptual
structures shared by special language communities such as novelists,
dramatists, poets, and their most sophisticated readers. The work of a
writer may contain special features, some of them clearly worthy of study,
but almost all of that work and our understanding of that work will derive
from common understanding, and even the special features will consist of
exploitations of what is common. There is an easy assumption in the profession that common language expressing common understanding is simple in itself and too simple for analysis. Mere children can master it, and
we all deploy that mastery unconsciously. Its workings are instinctively
taken to be obvious. There is a tandem assumption that special language
expressing special thought stands apart from the common and is to be
analyzed on its own. These two tacit assumptions—that the common is
simple and obvious and that the special is to be analyzed independent of
it—rob us of any chance to worry that as analysts of the special we have
skipped over the analysis of the common. These assumptions are deadly.
Common language expressing common thought is anything but simple,
and its workings are not obvious. Special language expressing special
thought is an exploitation of the common and to be analyzed only with
respect to it.

Our profession has a more sophisticated appreciation of what is special
than it does of what is common, even though what is special cannot be
analyzed without a prior understanding of its common foundations. Our
studies are consequently unnaturally limited and out of alignment. In

these circumstances, we need instruments for analyzing our common understanding that are as sophisticated as those we already have for analyzing our special understanding. For example, the relationships between a sonnet's three quatrains and its final couplet do not belong to the common understanding of language, but we know more about such special literary expression than we do about the language whose existence makes the sonnet possible, and of which the sonnet is a function.

A metaphor, for example, is not a sonnet. It is less specialized than a sonnet because it deals with something that could—and usually does—have a life in language and not just in a literary structure. We cannot know a language without knowing its everyday metaphors, but we can know a language without even being able to recognize a sonnet. We have educated ourselves to have an analytical understanding of the sonnet that is superior to our analytical understanding of language, superior to our understanding of structures—such as everyday metaphors—that live in both language and literature. We know a great deal about conventions of the literary texts but have only very crude tools for analyzing the language itself. This is backwards, even if it is the powers of literature that we care to explain, since those powers depend upon the reader's ability to use linguistic skills and conceptual resources to construct meaning in response to the linguistic prompts in the text. When we read a text, especially an old text, what makes it puzzling is our ignorance of its literary conventions. It is understandable to the extent that we share its linguistic conventions and the concepts expressed through those linguistic conventions. Language and concepts are longer-lasting and more widely shared than literary conventions.

When our profession does analyze the ways in which special ideas in writers' texts are embedded in understanding common to members of a community, it turns not to language but to fields not intrinsically concerned with language. It would not be unusual, for example, to see an analysis of psychosocial relationships among characters in a given play as examples of supposedly general psychoanalytic characteristics that we all share. It would not be unusual to see an analysis of an author's ethics as a symptom of the general economic conditions of his time. It would not be unusual to see an analysis of an author's gender distinctions as expressions of popular culture. Our profession has a more sophisticated appreciation of nonlanguage fields than it does of the field of language itself. There is nothing intrinsically wrong with such appreciation, but it creates an odd disjunction between the field of criticism and the study of language. This disjunction leaves us without a common base. It has the queer consequence that the profession has dealt with special ideas in writers' texts but has not dealt in a sufficiently sophisticated way with the common thought disclosed in the shape of their language. Doctoral students in English now frequently study Freud and Marx, but almost never English.

I find myself in the odd position of trying to remind the profession that its logical core is the study of language and the arts of language. I do not recall this traditional view—a view that might preserve the profession of English from intellectual isolation and make it important to its sister professions—out of sentiment or piety. My motive is more urgent and less parochial: the desire to participate in the signal intellectual work of our own epoch. The Renaissance integrated the study of language and the arts of language into a powerful intellectual synthesis whose achievement was a landmark in human culture. After the Renaissance, people brought a new concept of the past to their concept of themselves. The study of language and the arts of language was central to that signal intellectual and human change. One might say that the Renaissance *invented* the past, thereby changing the present. The Renaissance invention of the past changed the late fifteenth-century present enough to warrant its self-conferred designation as a new epoch, the "modern." The study of language and the arts of language was indispensable to that invention and that transformation. Just so, our age stands at the threshold of discovering the mind. After this threshold is crossed, people will bring a new concept of the mind to their concept of themselves. Our contribution to that discovery is inquiry into language and the arts of language, the most dramatic and textured expressions of the human mind. The discovery of the mind will require the study of language and the arts of language; those engaged in this signal humanistic and intellectual work will find a way to conduct those studies without us if we choose not to participate.[10] At that point, our solipsism will have been lethal.[11]

Regaining our place in the signal intellectual and humanistic work of our epoch requires the reintegration of the study of language and the study of literature. This reintegration consists in coming to a concept of literature as the most dramatic and textured expression of the human mind, and analyzing it as such. The triumph of literary criticism has given us a concept of literature as the product of circumstances—biographical, psychological, political, economic, and social—not as a product of the capacities of the human mind. We do not ask, what is the human mind that it can create and understand a text? What is a text that it can be created and understood by the human mind? These questions are not at the center or even the periphery of our critical inquiries. From the perspective adopted here, a concept of literature must be simultaneously a concept of the human mind. The triumph of literary criticism has left us with critical concepts and critical theories, but has left behind the study of language and consequently the study of mind. It has therefore left us isolated, out on a limb. We have ceased to treat language as anything but an instrument, so that, in the main, language is no longer a direct object of study in our profession. Part of the reason that current critical approaches so easily can be extended to other humanistic subject matter—painting, music, film, and so on—is that they have left behind what is distinctive to the profession of English—its fundamental connection to a natural language rather than a system analogous to language, such as the "language" of painting or the "language" of music.

What I mean by the study of language is not the vigilant prescriptive approach to language that usefully characterizes most of our training of undergraduates. Those who study language analytically have of course dismissed the prescriptive approach as theoretically unsound and as interfering with their research,[12] and they are correct in this respect, but even they rigorously adhere to and enforce adherence to the equivalent of a style sheet within their professional writing. As a practical matter, such provisional conventional style sheets are inevitable within linguistic communities, and there is everything defensible about courses in the profession of English that apprise students of prevailing conventions, ignorance of which will harm them. But this is not the approach to language that I encourage, since it tells us little about conventional patterns of thought and their automatic and unconscious disclosure in the shape of everyday language.

Nor am I encouraging the study of language as conceived by the most prominent schools in modern linguistics. I propose for the ground of the profession of English neither traditional prescriptive nor modern formal linguistics. Language, having been pushed out as a central component of the profession of English, has migrated mainly into departments of linguistics, so that the prevailing concept of language is no longer closely connected to the concept of literature. In the dominant current paradigms of linguistics, language is treated neither humanistically nor as an aspect of what it means to be human. But human language is an expression of uniquely human forms of thought, forms not available, for example, to a contemporary digital computer.[13] Language is inseparable from conceptual thought; conceptual thought in turn is inseparable from what it means to have a human body and lead a human life.

The sort of study to which I look forward is one that approaches language humanistically, as an aspect of what it means to be human. A human being has a human brain in a human body in a physical environment that it must make intelligible if it is to survive. This is the ground, I think, of human cognition, and the source of the everyday conceptual apparatus we bring to bear in making what is usually automatic and unconscious sense of our worlds. This conceptual apparatus seems to be everywhere expressed in the substance and shape of our language, and to constitute the basis of our literature. The study of language to which I look forward would analyze the nature and processes of this conceptual apparatus, its expression in language, and its exploitation in literature. It would see literary language as continuous with common language, and meaning as tied to conventional conceptual structures that inform both common and literary language in a continuous and systematic manner. Our profession touches home base when it contributes to the systematic inquiry into these linguistic and literary acts as acts of the human mind.[14]

This approach would put nuance back into context. Typically in our profession we note some nuances of meaning available to us consciously as we read a specific work, and we then assume that reporting such nuances constitutes a complete effort, a "reading." But nuance has as its context a vast space of systematic unconscious understanding, and we typically skip over the analysis of that space. We typically ignore the unconscious cognitive component of understanding that informs everyday language, exactly because it is unconscious and therefore seems to us absent, or at least transparent, simple, and obvious. Nuance engages our attention, and has become in our profession the subject of our critical analysis. In making nuance the subject of our work, we focus on a small contingent aspect of the whole, and in focusing further on nuance within a given work, we ignore the systematicity across language, thought, and works that makes idiosyncratic nuance within a given work possible.

We are obliged, as members of our species, to interpret what confronts us. We notice our acts of interpretation to just the extent that they are not entirely unconscious and automatic. Is that rock that hangs above the path stable? Is this beast a threat to us? Is the purpose of that pain to signal tissue damage? Do these shapes make up the letters of a given word? Such questions can surface in consciousness. There may be consequences of these interpretive acts: we might misinterpret the word. Naturally, such interpretation can become automatic and unconscious: we are no longer even aware as we read that we are doing any interpreting of the visual marks at all. Still, some sliver of the interpretive act can be brought into consciousness.

This general need to interpret provides the impulse for "giving a reading" of a text. The text is what we confront and the reading is some sliver of the conscious part of interpretation. "Giving a reading" of a text and "arguing for" that reading "against" other readings has been promoted to principal place among our profession's activities. The justification for such "reading" seems to be that interpretations have consequences. If we "interpret" the rock as stable and it is not, there may be consequences. If we "interpret" what someone says to us in a way he or she did not intend, we might be corrected or we might be killed. When we attribute authority to a text, such as a sacred text, a law, or a prophecy, we see important consequences of how we "read" it, and so are motivated to "get the reading right" and "argue for" it "against" other "readings." When the subject of the text interests us, whether it be an author's opinions or the history of an epoch, we want to know about that subject, and so are spurred to get the reading right and to argue against alternatives.

I offer explorations in this book that do not consist of "giving" and "arguing for" "readings." In my view, our profession takes as given exactly what we should be trying to explain. We take for granted our capacities to invent and interpret, and devote ourselves to exercising those capacities and publishing the results. It is the capacities themselves that need explaining. Reading is not giving a reading; and it is reading, not giving a reading, that I am concerned with. Giving readings is important and could be done better if we understood reading. I do not slight this activity of giving and arguing for readings, which testifies to the ingenuity of critics. But I ask a different and evidently prior set of questions. Given a bit of language, a discourse, or a text, how does a reader understand it? Given alternative readings, what were the different processes that led to those alternative understandings? The most amazing phenomenon our profession confronts, and the one for which we have the least explanation, is that a reader can make sense of a text, and that there are certain regularities across the individual senses made of a given text. How do readers do that? That is a question that leads us to touch home base.

True, these readers could in many cases be led to different understandings of a given text if they were coached in the specific circumstances surrounding the creation, transmission, and reception of that text, but that is not the issue here. I suggest that we investigate the common conceptual and linguistic apparatus readers bring to texts, whether or not they also bring such special factual knowledge.

The activity proposed here differs in another, corollary way from the canonical activity of "giving a reading" as practiced in the profession. Cognitive research into literary acts naturally focuses on common readings exactly because they are more widely shared and thus more likely to show us common conceptual capacities at work. When cognitive rhetoric takes up an uncommon, specialized reading, it predictably focuses on how that specialized reading derives from common conceptual and linguistic capacities. I make an effort to avoid all novel "readings." By contrast, "doing a reading" in our profession usually means striving for novelty. A new reading seems to be more prized the less it shares with previous readings, no doubt because such novelty of interpretation attests to the ingenuity of the critic.

The activity I offer is not principally concerned with originality of reading. It moreover views the originality of an author as an exploitation of the dominant unoriginal apparatus at his disposal. Invention is not originality. The structure of invention, and of particular classic and successful literary inventions, may be wholly unoriginal. Any original achievement in invention exists as an exploitation of a dominant, active, unoriginal, and largely unconscious matrix of conventional conceptual thought. Originality, far from being autonomous, is contingent at every point upon the unoriginal structures that inform it. I offer an approach that focuses on the complex structure of the unoriginal that suffuses, defines, and creates the original.

It is often assumed in our profession that poetic thought employs tools different from those of everyday thought and of reason, and that poetic language is a different kind of language from everyday language. The approach I offer embraces a contrary set of basic hypotheses. Most of the tools of poetic thought not only exist in everyday thought but are indispensable and irreducible there. Reason and poetic thought are not mutually exclusive; they are rather hypertrophies of a common nucleus of human imaginative capabilities. Structures of language supposedly poetic are ubiquitous and irreducible in everyday language.

To investigate the unoriginal aspect of invention, the unoriginal ground of originality, and the connections among poetic thought, everyday thought, and reason is not to homogenize nonliterary and literary activity, but rather to establish a set of coordinates that will allow us precisely to identify what belongs to the poet, against the background of what belongs to poetry, against the dominant background of what belongs to language and conventional conceptual thought.

The approach I offer as a ground for the reintegrated profession of English is foreign at the moment to both mainstream literary criticism and linguistics, but signs of its emergence can be found. Recently, a few researchers called "cognitive linguists" have begun to develop an approach to language that might serve as an example of a kind of linguistics potentially compatible with literary studies. I cite this exploratory program of cognitive linguistics not as a system to be adopted—it is speculative, embryonic, and certain to undergo rapid wholesale transformations in the near future—but rather as evidence that it is possible to have a technical concept of language and a technical approach to the study of language that share with the humanities a concern for the humanness of language.

Cognitive linguistics is concerned with human concepts as the basis of meaning, rather than with truth-conditions as the basis of meaning; with the role of conventional imagery in cognition and language; with figuration in thought and speech; and with grammar as symbolic phenomenon. Much of the empirical research in cognitive linguistics has led to a rejection of those dichotomies that have in practice separated the study of language from the study of literature, namely, the putative autonomy of syntax from meaning, the putative autonomy of the language system from other cognitive systems, the putative separation of the grammar and the lexicon, the putative separation between linguistic (semantic) meaning and extralinguistic (pragmatic) meaning, and the putative separation between literal language and figurative language.

There is an underlying tradition in cognitive linguistics of analyzing conceptual schemas and their role in language.[15] Much of this analysis concerns how we understand linguistic expressions, fixed or otherwise, by reference to conceptual schemas and conceptual cultural models.[16] In such analysis, the cognitive and the cultural go hand-in-hand. Cognitive linguists have produced detailed analyses of basic instruments of understanding—such as our knowledge of force dynamics—and the ways those instruments underlie various patterns in fixed and novel expression.[17] Gilles Fauconnier has produced an elegant theory of the ways in which language prompts us to construct mental spaces and correspondences between mental spaces, a theory that seems to offer tools and methods for the literary critic concerned with the reader's mental construction of fictive realities.[18] Other projects in cognitive linguistics include the analysis of categorization,[19] of metaphor and metonymy,[20] and of images[21] as they occur in conceptual thought, in everyday language, and in novel expression. Ronald Langacker, a founder of the field of cognitive linguistics, offers a useful summary of the field in his 1987 article "The Cognitive Perspective."[22] Mouton de Gruyter has launched the journal *Cognitive Linguistics* to make the field more accessible.[23]

It is an index of its character as a research paradigm that cognitive linguistics allots the key role to semantics. Semantics has a primacy in the cognitive paradigm that is absent from the generative paradigm. Meaning, in the cognitive paradigm, is tied to conventional cultural and conceptual structures—the same structures that presumably then inform both the common stuff of language that every member of the community shares and the special stuff shared by special linguistic subcommunities, such as readers of the *New Yorker* or writers of computer manuals. In the generative paradigm, these conventional cultural and conceptual structures are defined as lying outside the study of language. The theoretical ground of the generative paradigm automatically excludes from its study not only most of the concerns of the literary critic but also most of what we would call literary phenomena; but the theoretical perspective that has evolved from empirical studies in cognitive linguistics is one that the student of literature can embrace. It acknowledges the concerns of the critic as appropriate for the student of language and offers tools that potentially run across the range of linguistic and literary phenomena. Perhaps the most encouraging signs of cognitive linguistics as a potential companion in a reintegrated profession of English are its eagerness to explore all language, including literary language, and its commitment to linguistic research as part of general inquiry into the capacities of the human mind.

I propose inquiry into thought and language as a ground for the profession not in order to create a matrix of disciplines that seeks to define the profession in the way philology once did, but rather in order to locate a common ground. Structuralism, as a theory of literature that precluded other such theories, proposed to organize the profession as an imperial matrix of disciplines and failed, partly because any such imperialism must, in our widened profession, fail. But a cognitive approach to linguistic and literary acts is not a theory of literature that precludes other theories. Language is not superstructural, it is fundamental. A cognitive approach to linguistic and literary acts could potentially serve as common ground for many different theories of literature, conflicting with none of them, however incompatible they might be with each other.

The proposal that the study of language serve as the common ground of our profession does not exclude any of the subject matters our profession now treats. To study common language and conceptual thought as the basis of literary acts does not prevent us from borrowing from disciplines not intrinsically concerned with language or inhibit us from looking at a range of specialized phenomena. The cognitive approach to language would be conducive to those who study the cultural, sociological, and psychological aspects of literature, since it includes the analysis of cultural models and mental processes that inform language.

The study of language links fields in the profession through analogies between language and the subjects of these fields. Film, for example, has both an exact and an analogical connection to language. Insofar as film study belongs to the profession of English, it does so in the way that the study of drama belongs to the profession of English. Film and drama contain natural language and include something specific to themselves that is an analogue of natural language. Each is related to literary studies in a similar way. We can move with integrity from the study of language to the study of analogues of language, such as gesture and cinematography. Language can supply a common ground that can connect the film scholar to the specialist in the lyric; the eighteenth-century scholar to the rhetorician or the Renaissance scholar; and the specialist in drama to the specialist in writing. Other fields cannot do this. The New Critic, the New Historian, the Marxist, the eighteenth-century scholar, and the feminist will all point our attention to something important in literature, and the profession will always contain some trace of these fields. But none of them provides a ground that is common to the whole profession, and each provides a method only for its own field. A Marxist critic may have an influence on what the teacher of Shakespeare talks about, but will provide a method only to other Marxist critics. It is only something that is not itself a critical school—such as the analysis of the nature of language—that can provide techniques that have a chance to contribute to all of them.

Since such an analysis belongs neither to a critical school nor to one of the current rival theories, it differs from them, broadly, in some useful ways. It allows us, in a wonderful phrase of Lord Bolingbroke's, to "creep up, *a posteriori*, to a little general knowledge."[24] This general knowledge is a posteriori in the sense that it begins from and rests upon a great wealth of data, far more than is usual in critical theory. The linguistic data serve as the body from which generalizations are drawn and to which the claims must strictly submit. This allows us to be committed to data rather than to a critical theory. No a priori commitment to a theory that would determine generalizations is needed in the attempt to make sense of data in a way that is consistent with what is known about human cognition. We may instead let the chips fall where they may as we explore language and the arts of language. One refreshing consequence of this commitment to the data would be that our claims would be open to falsification in a way most criticism is not: anyone anywhere—the student, the amateur, the institutionally powerless—could challenge our analysis by producing conflicting data. The status of the challenge, and the challenger's right to an answer, would then depend not, as it usually does now within our profession, upon the status of the challenger and the challenger's critical school, but only upon the existence of the data. Such an approach is also a posteriori when compared to the dominant paradigms in formal linguistics, the most dominant of which, for example, holds an a priori commitment to viewing the structure of language as a branch of recursive function theory.[25]

The approach I offer differs from the approach found in current critical schools in being routinely accretive. In literary theory, when one theory supplants another, the replacement is wholesale. Deconstruction and New Historicism each in its own view swallowed New Criticism without leaving a trace. Neither in its own view began where New Criticism left off. But work on the cognitive basis of language and literature always begins where others have left off, and provides a suitable beginning point for later work. The study of language and the arts of language should, if properly done, be able to contribute to every literary field and every theory, but no one of them has a similar extension. No matter what one's field or critical theory, whatever helps us to read better in a technical sense and to know more about what we do when we read can be welcomed.

In my view, the profession is at a critical fragmentary point, calling upon us to contemplate our concept of what we profess, our idea of the humanities, our place alongside other researchers, and our contribution to the future. The profession can flourish as the marvel of ingenuity it has built itself into, but that flourishing alone will, I think, take it ever further from the dominant humanistic study of our age, namely, the study of the human mind, and further also from the study of human language, which is both the necessary first ground of a study of literature and the field from which the study of mind borrows many of its working insights. As in the Renaissance, humanistic study is intellectually inseparable from the study of what makes us human. In the age of cognitive science, that means inseparable from the study of human cognition. Literary acts are constituted upon the ground of shared human conceptual patterns and conventional language. An attempt to reintegrate the study of language and literature as grounded in human cognition is, I suggest, the most likely path to restoring our profession to its natural place as a central cultural and intellectual activity.

The studies that follow are guided tours exploring the possibility of that reintegration. The general topic of this book and the specific topics of the individual studies are patently beyond my competence; but I have not conceived of another way of launching this program than to take them up with such tools as seem available or helpful, in a spirit of exploration, and with a willingness to see these first forays laid aside in a future time when the state of our knowledge is better. Perhaps these probes can only be addressed to those who have some sympathy with the perspective of this program, and who are willing to see through many local moments, many of which must prove ultimately to have been mistaken, to a conception of a larger purpose. These studies will at best serve as a sort of initial survey from which the reader will depart. They are sightings over a terrain. It is my hope that they will be useful to those who contemplate what form the reintegrated study of language and literature might take.

Chapter 1

USER'S MANUAL

I OFFER this book as a means to an activity. It is an instrument intended to assist us in reconsidering fundamental concepts that form the floor plan of our thinking. We use these concepts without noticing them. If we did notice them, we would probably believe them to be so natural and objective as to be plainly above suspicion. We would be wrong about that.

To reframe the study of language, literature, and mind as inseparable objects of analysis, we must begin by changing some basic concepts. To change them, we must notice them, which is surprisingly difficult to do.

In computing, a start-up program gets us going. This book is like a start-up program, designed to get us going in the activity of reconsidering an extremely influential group of default concepts, which is to say, a group of concepts we fall back on automatically when we do not engage in the arduous work of considering the fundamental ground of our thought and action. This chapter is the user's manual to the start-up program: it explains the uses, purpose, and operation of this book.

This book, if it performs according to design, will encourage us to start revisiting and revising our concepts of the human person, the body, the brain, thinking, consciousness, concepts, language, literature, and the humanities. Doing so will lead us to revisit and revise our concept of the study of English.

To advance in our thinking about these matters, we must move backward. That is the apparent paradox behind this book. Most books want to build upon a level we have already attained. This book wants to move us back to a basic level we moved beyond long ago. Of course, my purpose is ultimately to move us forward, but forward from a point we probably long ago stopped considering. The studies in this book are meant to interfere with some aspects of unconscious and automatic thought enough to make them available to conscious consideration. These studies will take things that we do automatically and unconsciously, slow us way down, and ask us to investigate how we do them. We will consider some of the possible consequences of beginning to look at what we almost never look at and almost never feel a need to look at. One of the consequences of beginning to do this might be the recasting of our concept of literature and our concept of language, with the result that these concepts will seem to be related more intimately and in more complex ways: our concept of literature will in fact become part of our concept of language.

The reach of our thought is limited by the reach of our concepts. The purpose of engaging in the project of this book is to improve our critical thought by improving its underlying concepts. Whether on auto-pilot or fully concentrated, our thinking employs basic concepts in an unconscious manner. Since these concepts do not rise to the surface in conventional introspection, they are usually not the object of our thinking, although they are always the dominant components of our thinking. This book prompts us in a series of ways to reconsider them. It gives some guided tours of what happens when we do. It puts us in a position to begin making appropriate revisions.

Typically, we do not open a user's manual unless we are eager to interact with the program or the appliance that is the subject of the user's manual. In that case, we are pliant, prepared to go along with the user's manual, pleased to become involved. But there may be resistance to this user's manual, and to the project it presents. There are several sources of this resistance.

The studies in this book lead us to reconsider default concepts, but perhaps we do not want to. Default concepts work just fine left to themselves, and we can get away with ignoring them. Everything depends upon them—our understanding, belief, persuasion, opinion, judgment, ethics, policy, language, literature, and social and political action. But we do not have to worry about them. We can and do use them unconsciously, automatically, effortlessly, below the level of reflection. These basic concepts are entrenched and powerful. They seem indispensable and natural. If we do not have to reconsider them, why do it? If it isn't broken, why fix it? We see no reason to engage the project.

In fact, we see reason to shut it down. We are biologically designed to shut it down. As a species, we are designed to perform. Attending to what is automatic and successful would, in general, ruin our performance. If we tried to call into consciousness the details of our thinking and doing, we would be incapacitated. Successful default concepts are more useful to us if they can escape being noticed, or at least escape being scrutinized and reconsidered.

These are cognitive sources of resistance. There is an equally strong psychological source of resistance. Anything that is automatic to us is bound up with our sense of self. We fear that if we alter that which is automatic, we will lose our selves. We do not wish to reopen these parts of our minds.

This complex fear—that changing what we take for granted will make scrap out of our selves—takes many shapes. Some of us are afraid to change where we live, on the feeling that if we move from Broadway to

Main, we will not be who we are anymore. Others are afraid to change how they dress: children and adults can both be made extremely uncomfortable about their selves by changing them into unaccustomed clothes. This notion that we are different if we change into different clothes is a notion acquired in childhood, one rarely reopened for inspection after that stage. It is an example of how we can have extremely sophisticated concepts in some areas and quite unexamined concepts in other areas.

Some of us are afraid of changing the language we speak, which is to say, of learning a foreign language. Accurately or not, some of us feel that to learn it in childlike ways would require us to open up a realm of competence we are afraid to open. There is a sense that language is a scary thing, and that we were lucky to have gotten through learning it the first time. This fear leads to that prevalent style of trying to learn a foreign language without changing or disturbing anything that is already in place—to learn it in adult ways by controlling the learning, regulating the methods of instruction, insisting on seeing every phrase written down, and constantly translating everything into the mother tongue. The result, almost always weak, is nonetheless a level of competence that is acceptable to us because it causes nothing to be reopened or changed; the self, we feel, stays intact.

At the deepest level, we feel that we will lose ourselves if we change our default concepts. We feel that we were lucky to become competent once. We do not want to be faced with it again. Professionally and personally, we feel that a change in our default concepts will suddenly make us incompetent. As a defense, we tell ourselves that we do not have to pay attention to whatever would make us revise our default concepts. We call these things irrelevant.

Our fear that reconsidering fundamental concepts will make us incompetent and rob us of our selves is strong but irrational, since it is a fear of what happens all the time. On a personal level, we have revised these concepts many times since early childhood, although more rarely and less radically after we reached adulthood. On a cultural level, the humanities, like the sciences, have historically gone through many changes in their view of themselves, and these changes have typically occurred when something humanists took to be irrelevant to their activity suddenly became relevant. Even the greatest European painters of the fourteenth and early fifteenth centuries, for example, considered human anatomy to be largely irrelevant to what they did. For most of them, painting was the representation of ideas, generally theological ideas. It involved a drastic change in the concept of painting when Leonardo and Dürer began to consider painting as the representation of visual experience. Anatomy and even dissection, irrelevant to Fra Angelico and Jan van Eyck, became essential to them, and they achieved a level of anatomical knowledge be-

yond not only the previous generation of painters but also beyond all but
a few physicians contemporary with them. That is an analogue for what
this book hopes to bring about. This book focuses on unconscious cognitive operations. There are many professionals who view themselves as interested in these matters—researchers who study language, learning, perception, imagination, vision, hearing, motor control, decision-making,
the forming of judgments, biological responses (such as feeding, fighting,
fleeing, and reproduction), and so on—but their work is usually taken to
be largely irrelevant to literary critics and art historians, musicologists and
philosophers. We have been wrong about that. It is relevant. This book
hopes to lead us to to revise our concept of the humanities by leading us
to reconsider basic concepts that most of us view as having been settled
long ago. But this is nothing that has not happened to the humanities
many times.

Our irrational fear of concept revision may lessen when we observe that
we are constantly engaged in it. That is what it means to be alive. Consider, for example, the concept of tennis. On current television program-
ming there is an advertisement that cuts back and forth between a black-
and-white instructional videotape—in which a bland tennis instructor
lays out routine advice—and a color presentation of two tennis masters
fully engaged in play. The disparity between the instructional concept of
tennis and the master concept of tennis is manifest. The concept in the
black-and-white instructional tape is the one those masters started with,
but they have reconceived their concept of tennis many times to get to
where they are. Similarly, anyone who speaks natively a natural language,
no matter how inarticulately, went through numerous revisions of the
concept of language in order to acquire that competence. At the earliest
stages, these so-called revisions may have been so substantive as to constitute radical transformations. We revise concepts constantly, unaware we
are doing so, on the way to mastering any skill.

But there are certain fundamental concepts we do not ordinarily revise
after early adolescence. We do not get back to them. They are automatic,
and we feel that we do not need to get back to them. We do not want to
get back to them. Consider our concept of sex, by which I mean our
concept of sex acts. We begin with a child's concept of sex. It becomes an
automatic default concept, and therefore strongly bound up with our
concept of self. Left to ourselves, we might never revise it. Some people
manage to encounter adult experience and yet successfully resist reconsidering their child's concept of sex. Others, through simply having to
deal with aspects of the world of sex not accommodated by their child's
concept, do manage to reconsider it, often with some pain, and with a
sense that a change in the concept of sex is a change in self. For many of
our automatic default concepts, there is nothing to force us to reconsider

them in the way we may be forced to reconsider our child's concept of sex. These default concepts work well enough without revision. We simply do not have to get back to them, and certainly we do not want to have to go through what it might mean to get back to them.

This book wants to get us back to them. In doing so, it leads us to do something we do all the time, but now directed consciously at automatic concepts that seem not to need revision and whose revision we strongly resist. This book will offer, provisionally, some rudimentary revisions of these concepts, to give a sample of what they might be. Once we turn our conscious attention to this revision as a project, we might change any of the particular start-up revisions offered here. This book, then, does not seek to offer a fully articulated revision of the humanities—something clearly beyond my competence. It seeks rather to engage us in active reconsideration of fundamental concepts that will lead us to a revision of the humanities—one that will preserve what is valuable from past conceptions, reject what is clearly irrelevant to present problems, and create a space for unpredictable innovation, the activity that makes any discipline a vital one. My own biggest investment is what will be for most of my readers a novel concept of language and literature, their relationship and their identity. It is my concept, in the sense that I rely on it, so naturally I value it, but in the end, it is offered as an example of what sort of change the deep revision of basic or default concepts might lead to. It is not meant to be the last word, more nearly the first word of what I fully expect will be a major revision of the humanities as important and as fundamental as the revision of the humanities that separates the thirteenth century from the sixteenth century. This new revision seems inevitable. The humanities will not disappear in the age of cognitive science, they will not be unrecognizable, they will not lose their identity, but they will add to themselves an unmistakable new dimension precisely because they are vital and must inevitably participate in the great new venture of the present and immediate future: the deep mapping of the mind. It is nothing less than the discovery of a new world, the discovery of our human selves.

Paradoxically, this new concept is a very old one. It is so old that we have forgotten it. Classical rhetoricians sought to discover the basic conceptual apparatus active in the minds of citizens, and upon which nearly every aspect of their thinking, their language, their literature, and their society is based. Over subsequent centuries, classical rhetoric degenerated into tabulating taxonomies of mannered wordplay and memorizing categories of argument. Our present concept of rhetoric is equally degenerate, which is unfortunate. This book includes many things unknown to classical rhetoric, but in essence it offers a conception of the humanities that is a direct continuation of the classical paradigm, however differently that paradigm may play out in the age of cognitive science.

Chapter 2

FLOOR PLAN

AN IMAGE materializes on the screen in front of us. It is a simple image, with a familiar shape. It rotates. We relax when we recognize the image as our everyday concept of who we are.

We zoom closer to the surface of the image. Unconsciously, we expect the zoom to stop in a conventional fashion when we obtain a close-up view of the surface. Surfaces, after all, are what we can see. But the zoom does not stop. It penetrates the surface and moves through levels of detail, gradually stopping only when we reach a deep level of textured granularity and great dynamic activity. We are looking inside a human brain.

THE HUMAN PERSON

A human person is patterns of activity in a human brain, but it sounds odd to say so. Usually, when we think of the human person, we do not think of the brain. When we try to picture the human person, we do not picture the brain or the dynamism of brain activity.

To begin to reconsider our concept of the human person, let us begin with the suggestion that a person is an aspect of a central nervous system. But this seems to leave out obvious and important components of the human person. What about the body, culture, society, language, sex, table manners? Why are we not looking at these things?

We are looking at these things when we look at brain activity. The mind is patterns of brain activity. The brain is part of the body, not something separate from the body. Culture, society, and language do not lie outside of the brain. Culture, society, and language are patterns in brains. Meaning is patterns in the human brain. Meaning is something that the human brain attributes to its world. Things outside the brain do not have meaning in themselves. An arrowhead or a clay pot or a text or any artifact, whether dug out of old ground or sold in shops, may seem to be part of culture or society or language independent of the human mind, but artifacts have no meaning as anything except as that meaning is attributed to them by human brains. The meaning of an artifact is a pattern in a human brain.

The human person is patterns of activity in the brain. If it sounds odd to say so, it is because we have a rival concept of the human person as the centerfold in *Penthouse* or Leonardo's drawing of the Vitruvian man or a

Greek statue or a picture of Grace Kelly on the big screen—in other words: a sack of stuff as seen from the outside, preferably full-length and with its clothes off. When God becomes incarnate, what is the cultural evidence? We get pictures of a baby with genitals showing, pictures of the outside of a person, pictures of a person dying, and then dead as seen from the outside. We do not get any representation of the even more fragile-looking pattern of activity inside a human brain. No theologian has ever said, as a gloss on "the word was made flesh," that God became some brain patterns.

We receive a tacit cultural education in how to think about the human person, the body, the brain, the mind, thinking, language, literature, and the humanities. Much of this tacit cultural education comes to us visually, in representations of the human person, of the body, and of thinking. For example, if we are asked to imagine a *person*, what do we imagine? We imagine a view of someone's body as seen from the outside. If we are asked to imagine the *body*, what do we imagine? Again, we imagine a view of someone's body as seen from the outside. If we are asked to imagine someone *thinking*, what do we imagine? Probably a view of someone's motionless body as seen from the outside. Through this iconography of the person, the body, and thinking, we are trained to think of the person, the body, and thinking by looking at the outside. I suggest instead that we look at the inside, and in particular at the inside of the brain. We have been looking in the wrong places.

THE MIND

Our everyday concept of who we are—displayed on the screen for us—fades away, and a new image appears on the screen. It seems spherical, whole, and solid. It is our everyday concept of the mind. It is not a concept we expound or even claim to believe, but it is one that we constantly use.

In this concept, the conscious mind is the whole mind and thought consists of the processing of concepts in consciousness. On this view, it makes no sense to talk about how concepts absent from consciousness inform our thinking, much less to talk about how our thinking is based upon and suffused by concepts so automatic and fundamental that we almost never notice them in consciousness.

But that is exactly what this book wants to talk about. The conscious mind, far from being the whole mind, is the smallest sliver of mind, the most fragile, the least well equipped, the least powerful. Conscious thought is a slice of thought, usually a reduced slice. To be sure, the mind in its operation allows minimal aspects of thinking into consciousness. We can arrive at a minimal conscious awareness of what is involved in our moving and deciding, our speaking and judging. But conscious thought, far from spherical, whole, and solid, depends upon the full mind's use of concepts so automatic and complicated as rarely to be called, even in superficial aspect, into consciousness.

THE FLOOR PLAN

The image of the mind on the screen now moves away from us, or rather, our perspective telescopes backward: the default concept of mind grows smaller, as it should. It appears to be only part of a larger image whose boundaries swing into view. This larger image looks like a floor plan of some sort. It has named regions, each with doorways into other regions.

This is the floor plan of our mind—not just the conscious mind, but the whole mind. We almost never look at this floor plan in consciousness, both because we do not need to and because our interest is trained on structures above and beyond it, structures that we reach up to build. These higher structures, built upon that floor plan, are informed entirely by the floor plan now on the screen.

The floor plan is made up of what we rely upon unconsciously and pervasively, in systematic ways, when we conduct our thinking. It contains default and automatic concepts. We may know when we consider these concepts consciously that they are inadequate—in the sense that we have experience that is not accommodated by them—but we nonetheless use them unconsciously. As a result, something that runs counter to these concepts sounds bizarre to us, even though it is instead our antiquated notions that are actually bizarre.

One of these default concepts is our concept of the human person, of who we are—the first image we saw on the screen. Another is our concept of the mind—the second image we saw on the screen.

Both concepts reappear now, in reduced form, situated in the floor plan: "the human person" is in the center of the floor plan. Adjacent is "the mind." On the opposite side, adjacent, is "the body," as if the body and the mind are opposed. There are many other default concepts here, each with its named region. They appear to be connected in various ways.

We use these default and automatic concepts as a floor plan exempt from assessment or even notice. We build upon this floor plan in specific ways and according to specific purposes but we do not look down at it. We look up, at cornices, mantles, window frames, where the closet door will swing, the hook for suspending the lamp, the weathervane atop the gable. Let us direct our gaze downward at this floor plan. It appears to be larger than we might have imagined, less inevitable and more complex.

On the screen we see the rapid construction of three-dimensional structures, each rising from one part of the floor plan or another. These

three-dimensional superstructures follow the lines of the floor plan, in-
heriting its structure. They rise and disappear, a different superstructure
each time, each commensurate with the floor plan—an infinity of possibilities, all fundamentally similar because of their similar base.

The screen presents us with a visual analogy. It places next to the floor
plan of the mind the floor plan of a cathedral—it is a cruciform floor plan,
with the transept perpendicular to the greatest length, with the top of the
cross pointing east, toward the dawn, and with the foot of the cross toward the west, where the sun sets. We see, rising in succession from the
floor plan of the cathedral, a series of many different specific cathedrals,
of all sorts and styles, each with different period architecture, ornamenta-
tion, and surfaces. Whatever their differences, they are all similar by virtue
of the floor plan they share. Superstructures based on the floor plan of the
mind similarly share a structure, however different they may appear.

The cathedrals and their floor plan disappear. The superstructures atop
the floor plan of the mind vanish. We are left looking at just the floor plan
of our thinking. We see other regions of the floor plan named "language," "the humanities," and so on. One by one, we begin to open and
view these regions, these concepts, with frequent cross-views of other regions that suggest interconnections.

These are only preliminary and provisional views. This book, after all,
cannot do for us what we can do for ourselves. When the demonstration
of this book ceases, we are invited to use what it has offered to drive the
investigation further, not to some appointed end, but continually, as a
humanistic activity that has been initiated here but that has no end once
we take it over.

THE BODY

The image before us on the screen surveys the floor plan and focuses on
the region labeled "the human person." It then moves over to the region
labeled "the body." That seems appropriate, because the body seems to
be the most important thing left out by the suggestion that we are patterns in brains. We relax, looking forward to seeing how the show in front
of us will contradict itself as it tries to take account of our identities as
human bodies.

Contrary to expectation, we are now asked to conduct a review of our
concept of the body, by looking from the inside out, rather than the outside in. The concept of the human person as patterns of brain activity not
only includes the body, but does so more fully than our old rival concept
does.

The image on the screen zips right through the skin and into the brain.
Let us follow the sequence we have been asked to observe: First, the mind

is the brain and the human person is patterns within the brain. Second, the mind is not just the conscious mind, but includes all the unconscious cognitive operation of the brain, and there is a great deal of it, much more than ever appears in consciousness. Third, the body is mapped in this unconscious apparatus in the brain. The image before us begins to introduce these maps of the body in the brain. There seem to be very many of them, of many different sorts.

We see that although a very few and very simple responses are controlled way down in the spinal cord, anything that has bodily meaning for us happens not in the torso or the appendages or on our skin, but in the mappings of the body that exist in the brain. Itches and twitches and sensations and wigglings and skilled performances of the body happen in the brain—not the toe or the finger or anywhere else—because the brain has mappings of the body and it is these mappings that count with the unconscious part of the brain, the part that does all the work. The other picture we have of the body—Saint Sebastian in a loincloth tied to a post as painted by Antonello da Messina, Grace Kelly in a swim suit, and so on—is just a toy the unconscious mind gives to the conscious mind in order to keep it pacified and away from the real action.

The image before us is focusing on our default concept of the body, asking us to make a comparison. It looks like a very weird comparison, but that is as it should be, since many things here will sound initially weird, given our default concepts. Here is the illustration: A desk looks to us as if it has meaning and structure. It appears to have part-whole functional structure. It appears to have abilities to interact with whoever sits at the desk. But—here the oddity enters—does the desk know that it has these things? Does it know that it has legs, and drawers, and a writing surface? Does it know what it means to have any of these things? Of course not. For all the desk knows, it might as well be a lump of dirt, or a cloud. It might as well not be. To us human beings, to the patterns in our brains, it has meaning. But to itself it has and is nothing. There is a great deal happening in the world, but nobody is in the audience, except brains. Things without brains are not watching anything; certainly they are not watching themselves.

Now consider the body. The body looks as if it has meaning and structure. It appears to have part-whole functional structure, mechanical and dynamic processes, bilateral symmetry, and many other things. But without the brain, the body is just like the desk. To itself, without the brain, the body has and is nothing, and might as well be a lump of dirt, or a cloud. It might as well be nothing at all. To the brain that is in the body, the body has all sorts of meaning and structure. Its meaning and structure consist in brain patterns that constitute its meaning and structure. Its perceptions consist in brain patterns that constitute those perceptions.

Our default concept of the body is unexamined. We think our concept of the body applies to actual limbs and joints and fingernails. The body does not understand that it has matching hands that can clap together; the brain does. The hands do not clap; the brain does. The body does not suffer pain; the brain does. The body does not understand heat or hunger or orgasm; the brain does. Our actual muscles and organs do not respond to sexual images; our brain does.

The human person does not reside anywhere in the body except in the brain. Medical technology is sufficiently advanced that now a brain-dead body can have blood pumping through it. Its lungs can breath. Its limbs can be made to move. Wired up correctly to external machines, the corpse can have various bodily functions. Feedback from the corpse can be fed to machines, which can adjust their manipulation of the body. With a little ingenuity, we could make the corpse do many normal bodily things. But there is no human person there, regardless of what is physically happening to muscle, skin, flesh, bone, or organs. The only difference between this hot-wired corpse and a human being is that a human being has a brain in the place of these external machines. The brain is what knows about the body. The brain manipulates the body. Brain patterns are the body's meaning and the body's understanding. To say that a human being is a mind that is a brain is not to leave out the body. On the contrary, the human body, as something meaningful as opposed to some meaningless physical entity in the galaxy, is in mappings in the brain. The body, as we know and experience it, is in the brain. A physicist who is weighing a body and checking it for wind resistance may actually be using a concept of a body as a physical object that has nothing to do with minds, at least minds other than his own. But when we talk about a body, what we really mean is a certain aspect of the brain.

This sounds bizarre. But upon reflection, we can see that it is only our unexamined concept of a human being that makes it sound bizarre. What is actually bizarre is our default concept of the body, and it results in some truly bizarre, indeed comical commonplace ways of talking. "My knee hurts" is a silly thing to say, when we consider it. "My body wants you" is nonsense, until we see that what we mean by body is a certain aspect of the brain. "My body wants one thing and my mind wants another" is confused, until we see that what we mean is that the aspect of our brain that corresponds to our rational choice is somehow at variance with that aspect of our brain that is our current sense of our bodily state. A bleeding knee does not want to be soothed or healed; the brain that knows about it wants it soothed or healed. The torso does not care what happens to it, or how it is used or abused. The brain cares.

When something that is part of something else becomes singularly important, it gets its own name. One consequence may be that we think of it as separate. Another may be that we think of it as subsuming what is associated with it. The body, as something meaningful, is in the mind, but it is so noticeable that it gets its own name, and we come to think of it as separate from the rest of the mind. Indeed, we begin to attribute to the body things that actually belong to the mind.

Of course, our knees and toes and hips and noses are not the same thing as our central nervous system, although in their live state they are inseparable in their functioning from the central nervous system. But let us assume that it is possible to remove the central nervous system surgically from the body. Let us label the deprived shell without its brain a "corpse-body." Our default concept of the body contains much that belongs not to the corpse-body but rather to the central nervous system removed from it, or more accurately to the functioning of the central nervous system when properly embodied. By attributing to the corpse-body many things that do not belong to it, we can maintain a split between our concept of the mind and our concept of the body. In this way, we conceive of the body as estranged from the mind.

Brain, Mind, Consciousness, and Unconsciousness

Conversely, we conceive of the mind as estranged from the body. Let us observe the nature of this estrangement. It is easy for us to think of a brain and its mind as surgically separated from the body and put into the mad scientist's vat while it hums along in perfect functionality, if a little bit lonely. We enjoy movies and novels about one person's brain in another person's body. Our default concepts, which permit us to think of this as an easy split, are fundamentally untrue to what a human being is. A brain is part of a body and in operation is inseparable from it. Evolutionarily, the brain exists only in order to serve the reproductive and metabolic body of which it is a part, and it is deeply and ineradicably invested with the nature of its body. It is in just this brain, so invested with the nature of its body, that the humanities occur, that language and literature exist. To investigate what belongs to human beings requires us to investigate the nature of this investment.

Just as the body, which seems so important, takes over in our conception many things, in fact its most important things, that are only associated with it, so the conscious mind, which seems so very important because it is the only part of mind that we can routinely notice, takes over in our conception many things that do not belong to it at all. This is why the conscious mind is easily taken to be the entire mind. The image on the screen before us now moves back to this default concept of the conscious mind. It is weird, insupportable, and lethal to the activity of the humanities.

When we think about it, we know that many things belong to the unconscious aspect of the brain. But we tend to think of them as lower-order, bestial sorts of things, involving blood and guts and the raw power of the id. We think of them as brute and blunt powers, not refined, and definitely not the sorts of things involved in the ethereal and sublime faculties of godlike reason or poetic invention. "What a piece of work is man! How noble in reason! how infinite in faculties! in form, in moving, how express and admirable! in action how like an angel! in apprehension how like a god!"

True, the unconscious is dark, in the metaphoric sense that our conscious mind cannot with its standard illumination look into it. But it is definitely not lower-order, brute, or unrefined. The image on the screen now displays successively a series of things that are not only unconscious but absolutely unavailable to consciousness.

The unconscious aspect of the brain knows how to stand erect. It knows how to see the visual field, which isn't easy. The unconscious aspect of a woman's brain knows how to gestate and how to give birth. It is no overstatement to say that this knowledge is fabulously complicated, intricate, and refined. The conscious aspect of the brain cannot see that knowledge. Indeed, that knowledge is too difficult for the powers of consciousness, and too indispensable to be made available to the unreliable conscious mind. Imagine having to go consciously through a process as complicated as giving birth, or calculating the many muscle adjustments needed to stand erect. Imagine having to integrate consciously all the information in our perception of the visual field. Even if we could do it accurately, it would be so slow that it would be like having to read a book every time we wanted to look at something.

The sensation of sound waves, the sensation of tickling, the many intricate sensations of pain, the orienting of the body in space or to stimuli, all of these belong to the knowledge of the unconscious aspect of the brain, a knowledge that cannot be called into consciousness.

We have been looking at knowledge that is entirely unconscious, knowledge unavailable to consciousness. That is one extreme. The other extreme is knowledge that is learned and that never seems to become completely automatic. Doing our income taxes or making a gourmet dessert like a blanc manger or a Charlotte Russe seems always to require conscious attention if we are not to screw it up.

Between these two extremes lies a gradient whose middle forms of knowledge are just those we want especially to look at, not only here, but in the rest of this book. These are things that seem to take conscious attention when we learn them, and that seem to us to be available to consciousness after we learn them, but which become principally automatic and unconscious, and whose learning may have been dominantly a matter of the unconscious mind to begin with. Riding a bicycle, learning to ski or skateboard or throw a frisbee, speaking a language—these are things in the middle, neither absolutely unavailable to consciousness nor requiring the constant attention of consciousness.

Suppose you teach someone to ride a bicycle. What does it consist of? It consists of holding the seat. You hold the seat, and ultimately your pupil can ride, and this counts as teaching someone to ride a bicycle. What have you taught your pupil? Could you write it down? Now suppose you are the person learning to ride the bicycle. Certainly it seems to take conscious attention. You are certainly aware that you are trying to learn to ride a bicycle. But when you have learned it, what have you learned? Could you write it down? Could you learn it from a book? Could you read a book about riding a bicycle, and then get on the bicycle for the first time, and ride it?

Even when we are consciously aware that we are trying to learn to ride a bicycle, or consciously aware that we are trying to teach someone to ride a bicycle, by far the largest component of the learning is unconscious, and unavailable to consciousness. The unconscious aspect of this learning dominantly and ineradicably informs that thin and relatively minor aspect of the knowledge that we can consider in consciousness.

Language is like this. Consider learning to read. In childhood, we try to learn our letters. We are aware that we are trying to learn. We even seem to ourselves to be trying very hard, to be bringing the full concentrated powers of consciousness to bear on learning our letters. But there are two points to be made here. First, by far the largest and most dominant aspect of the learning is unconscious and is not available to consciousness. Second, once we have learned our letters and gone on to learn how to read, the process becomes so automatic that it is almost impossible when we encounter a text for us to notice the individual letters or even individual words. It is in the unconscious that the interesting and powerful stuff is really happening. The smallish aspect that can be considered in consciousness depends utterly upon the unconscious aspect that makes it possible. This is true of cycling, language, and literature.

This unconscious aspect depends in turn upon the brain's ineradicable embodiment. To use this book as an instrument, we must remember that we have a body, and that the unconscious aspect of our thought is suffused with knowledge of our body. Although we often forget it when we talk about language and literature, a human being has a human brain in a human body in a physical environment that it must make intelligible if it is to survive. This is the ground, I suggest, of human cognition, and the source of our basic concepts of up and down, forward and back, right and left, continuity and discreteness, linearity, circularity, paths, progress, boundaries, contact, interiors and exteriors, centers, penetration, covering, occlusion, discovery, pain, and the great rest of the basic conceptual apparatus we bring to bear in making what is usually automatic and unconscious sense of our worlds. This conceptual apparatus is everywhere disclosed in the shape of our language, and serves as the basis of our literature. The study of these basic concepts is therefore the ground of literary criticism. I admit that this proposition sounds unusual, but that is only because our default concepts, the floor plan of our thinking, cannot accommodate it.

All but the smallest fraction of our thought and our labor in performing acts of language and literature is unconscious and automatic. When we reflect or introspect, we might be able to bring slightly more of it into consciousness. But the unconscious and automatic components of thought are too complex and indispensable to be trusted to the meagre resources of consciousness.

The conscious aspect of any thought is always embedded in a much larger and dominant unconscious aspect, upon which it depends for its existence and its meaning. Conscious aspects of thought are simple, relative to the complexity and intricacy of unconscious aspects.

THE ICONOGRAPHY OF THE PERSON AND THE ICONOGRAPHY OF THINKING

We get a rest here. The display we have been watching has a slide show in store for us, of familiar pictures that we like, and some of which we saw a moment ago when the display first got rolling.

The display is flashing a series of pictures of people on the screen.

One of the reasons that we have the default concepts we have and not those this book wants to suggest is that we receive a whole tacit cultural education in how to imagine the human person, the body, and thought. We do not easily separate this education from ourselves. We may think that if we give up the default concepts we have received from this tacit cultural education, we will disappear. We will not be who we are anymore. We will lose ourselves. The screen now displays a picture of ourselves disappearing.

The concepts offered here sound weird because humanists have received a formal education founded on the tacit cultural education that includes default concepts in conflict with the concepts offered here. If we reconsider some of these default concepts, the current activities of humanists, far from being bent out of shape or denatured, might become more comfortable and less strained.

What is this tacit cultural education? It has to do with the iconography of the person, the images that have just flashed before us on the screen. For a second time, let us imagine the body. What do we imagine? There it is: some examples flash up on the screen. They are visual images of someone else's body, or of a sketch of the body, as viewed from the outside. There is a sketch of a naked woman. There is Leonardo da Vinci's Vitruvian man again. Now imagine again someone thinking. What do we imagine? The display flashes up a series of images. There is Saint Jerome in his study, motionless, pondering. Next we see someone standing alone on a bluff, gazing out to sea. Then we see Rodin's familiar statue of someone sitting, chin resting on hand, transfixed in thought. It is through such images that the person, the body, and thought are presented to us.

I give the name "iconography" to the visual component of our tacit cultural education. The iconography of the human person is the conventional system of representing the human person visually.

The pictures in the slide show and the images we have imagined demonstrate that the iconography of the body presents the body by giving us the visual image of the outside of the body. The iconography of the human person also presents the human person by giving us the visual image of the outside of the body. This is what we can see. It is what we can principally notice in consciousness. We will always think that what we can remark in consciousness is the important part, and the interesting part. What we cannot see is the inside of the body. Certainly we cannot see the body in the mind, which is to say, the central nervous system's knowledge and understanding of the body. Nor can we see the human person in the mind, which is to say, the patterns of brain activity that constitute the human person. We receive, through the iconography of the body and of the human person, a tacit cultural education in how to imagine them. That education reinforces our default concept of them. It blocks us from thinking of the body or the person in the way I suggest, namely, from the inside, as things whose meaning resides in the brain. In suggesting that we think of the body and the human person by looking at the inside, at activity in brain patterns, I am struggling against the entire tacit cultural education we receive, which asks us to think of the body and the person as these images of the outside.

The display runs a second time through the slides of people thinking. Here is something curious: the iconography of thinking, just like the iconography of the person, presents us with an image of the outside of the body. Why should our image of someone thinking be an image of the outside of the body?

Significantly, the iconography of thinking presents us with a still image of the outside of the body, thereby implying that the mind, in order to work, must shut down the body, still the body, transcend the body, ignore the body. This aspect of the iconography of thinking makes it easy to imagine thought as disembodied. We routinely talk of being distracted from our thought by bodily sensations. A noise makes us lose thought, for instance. The iconography of thinking shows us the outside of a body. This body is still and insensitive to its environment. This suggests that the body must be suppressed if the mind is to think.

Let us make a distinction: the stasis of the corpse-body during thought does not imply that the mind in thought is separate from the knowledge of the body with which it is informed. The outside of the body may sometimes be still while we are trying to engage in conscious thought, but the body in the mind is extremely active and dynamic as it suffuses all our thought. Events that happen to the corpse-body can distract our thought. Sometimes, we wish to eliminate sensory distraction while we are thinking. But this does not mean that the mind is separate from the body, only that the mind sometimes prefers not to notice present sensations in consciousness.

The mind, at all moments, is suffused in its thinking with its knowledge of the body. To imagine it as such, we must distance ourselves from the concept of the body as a sack of stuff viewed from the outside, and think in terms of the body as the brain's knowledge of the body, which resides of course in the brain, and not on our skin. When the mind is at its most concentrated, it may have attempted to eliminate present distractions, but it is fully engaged with the body as mapped in the mind. The body as mapped in the mind is the basis of many sorts of knowledge, including abstract knowledge, and routinely suffuses thought, of all varieties. That we do not usually engage in calisthenics while trying to solve a logical puzzle has nothing to do with the relationship between the body and thought.

The display flashes back and forth between two sorts of slides: the first sort consists of still, placid images of motionless people thinking; the second consists of dynamic images of brain activity in a thinking brain. The cover of this book is an attempt to give a sense of the disparity between these two kinds of images, but unfortunately the cover is static, and so we will have to use our imagination to see the dynamism and activity of the brain.

These two sorts of images look very different. It is the first one—the still image of the motionless person thinking—that is misleading. By preferring dynamic images of brain activity, I am proposing a new iconography of thinking, one opposed to the standard iconography of the human person and of thought. I propose that we become comfortable with these dynamic images of an extremely active network of concepts competing with each other, reinforcing each other, inhibiting each other, becoming partially active, inhering within each other, and so on.

In the standard iconography of thinking, the dramatic dynamism of the unconscious aspect of the brain is absent, and we see only a placid outside. The display before us now presents an image of someone thinking. We observe this person. The facial features are perfectly still. The body is still. Suddenly, there is a movement. What is the moment at which that placid outside changes? What does it signify, in the standard iconography? At what moment does the iconography of thinking show us a raised eyebrow, a snap of the fingers, a clenched fist, a gesture of accomplishment, a light bulb over the head? *When something has finally emerged into the arena of consciousness.* When Rodin's thinker breaks his posture to look up, what has just happened? *Something has finally surfaced into consciousness.* This reinforces our default concept that what is really happening is happening in consciousness. It leads us to think, without reflection, that the real action is in consciousness, because when something emerges into consciousness, the body acts, the image changes. This suggests that it is consciousness that is powerful and active and important. This is a weak concept to have, but it is one that comes naturally to us, given the ways we have been tutored to imagine thinking.

We imagine things as visible, as static pictures. This is just a primary way that we have of imagining things. In ordinary discussion, people do not distinguish between a picture of a man and a man. They say, "Look at this man," when they are pointing to a picture of a man. This makes it seem as if the thing we can see, the image of the outside of the body, is much more important than it is. It makes it seem as if a person is the image of the outside of the body. In ordinary discussion, people say, "He is lost in thought" to convey an image of a relatively placid outside of a body. This makes it seem as if the person is the image, and as if thinking is something that is separate from the body, indeed opposed to the body. To talk about the body and the human person as inside the brain; to talk about thoughts and concepts as competitive and dynamic; to talk about thought as suffused by the body is to cut against our default concepts of the body, the mind, and the human person. All of our iconography asks us to imagine these things by looking at the outside. This book—do we really want to listen to it?—suggests that we try to imagine the body, the mind, and the human person by imagining not the outside, but the inside.

The Special versus the Common

The display moves back to the floor plan. When it first began to cycle through regions of the floor plan, the order of its presentation appeared to be comfortably fixed and linear. But now it seems to be moving around more freely and quickly. It appears that the display is prepared to move from any one part of the floor plan to any other, at our request. Indeed, it would prefer to move from each part to every other part simultaneously, but as a courtesy will not because we could not follow it. The order of its movements is a suggestion of ways we might move once we begin to take the project over.

The display moves now to our default concepts of the special and the common, which are sketched, in the floor plan of our thinking, as mutually exclusive regions, with the special as worthy and important and complicated, and the common as base and unimportant and simple. The display wants to turn this sketch on its head. It wants to do with the distinction between the special and the common just what it did with the distinction between the conscious and the unconscious. In the floor plan of our thinking, the conscious and the special are big and elaborate and interesting places, while the unconscious and the common are boring and dull little waiting rooms, so simple and obvious as to need no analysis. The display is asking us to reverse the descriptions: it is the common and the unconscious that are large and complicated; these are the areas where the significant action happens. The special and the conscious are merely anterooms.

There is a reason our floor plan favors the special and slights the common. We are designed as a species to notice in consciousness not the obvious and unoriginal but rather the novel and nuanced. We are vigilant for the new and the variable. Our consciousness is attuned to fresh and special aspects of our world. When we talk about thought, when we talk about literature, we typically talk about nuance, and take everything else as background. But the unconscious, automatic, unoriginal aspects of thought are anything but background, in the sense usually conveyed by that description. The unconscious, automatic, unoriginal aspects of thought are where the action really is. We simply do not attend to these aspects in consciousness because doing so would foul and slow our thought disastrously. Relative to the rest of the mind, consciousness is a small trick. The marvels of the human mind are not to be found contained within it. Acts of language and literature, like acts of thought, are acts of the human mind, the whole human mind. For the most part, and in the most interesting ways, they are acts of the unconscious mind. The original aspect of any thought is always embedded in a much larger and dominant unoriginal aspect, and exists only as a very slight exploitation of the unoriginal conceptual structures that inform it. Original aspects of thought are simple, relative to the complexity and intricacy of unoriginal aspects.

The one reliable universal truth about acts of language and literature is that they are products of the human brain in the human body. Thought is not an out-of-body experience. Thought hardly belongs to consciousness. Literature is not an out-of-body experience. Literature hardly belongs to consciousness. Literature is not essentially to be analyzed as something that happens in the diminutive anterooms of the conscious and the special, but rather as something that happens in the full forum of the unconscious and the common, some aspects of which spill over into the anterooms of the conscious and the special.

To investigate the special against the background of the common is like investigating differences in human bodies against the background of their common genetic endowment. We are all different, but from another perspective we are all nearly the same. Genetically, we are extremely close to one another. This genetic closeness is what it means to belong to the same species. Members of a species can mate within that species and produce offspring. Organisms that are not close in their genetic endowment may attempt to mate, but their offspring will be sterile, or no offspring will result at all. The evolutionary reason for denying offspring to organisms far apart in their genetic endowment is clear: the genotype of the offspring is a combinatory selection out of the genotypes of its parents; if the genotypes of the parents are not quite close, then the chance that the combinatory selection made from them will express itself in a phenotype fit for dealing with the world is negligible. There is virtually no evolutionary pay-off in conceiving the offspring since it will almost certainly fail in every way, indeed fail even to come to term; and there is strong evolutionary disincentive to conceiving such an offspring since it will tie up progenerative resources with negligible chance of reproductive success. It is true that we are different, and this is important: if we all had the same genotype, then a virus that could kill one of us would kill all of us, and farewell to humankind; if we all had the same genotype, then our only chance for variation in our genetic disposition would lie in rare and probably lethal mutations. We differ, and it shows: some of us are men and some women; some of us have blue eyes and some brown; some of us have blonde hair and some black. But we all have reproductive organs, all see, all have hair. We notice the blue color or brown color of eyes, because eye color is a nuance, and we are designed to attend in consciousness to nuance. But how much more important is the eye than the color, what we take for granted against what we notice? Our conscious mind lives in nuance. But these nuances are the very slightest variations against a great background of commonality, which we do not notice at all. These nuances are only slight exploitations of a much larger and dominant system. It is this system that makes the contingent and special nuances possible. It is only with respect to this system that those contingent and special nuances can be intelligible.

A Concept

One part of the floor plan—in the northeast corner—appears to be a partial sketch that fits many of the other parts: it is our default concept of a concept itself.

We employ concepts in thought. We often speak as if concepts are something different from thought, as if we have a mental file cabinet of concepts that we trot out to organize thought.

On the contrary, concepts are not different from thought, but rather inhere in thought. Thought is an activated pattern in the brain, and a concept is an activated pattern inhering in thought. We do not have a given concept except when its pattern is active in thought. What we have instead is a latent capacity for the pattern to be activated. Concepts are active, dynamic devices in the brain that compete with each other to become active in the attempt to make sense of things. Concepts are themselves thoughts. They do not structure thoughts the way a mold structures clay or concrete or wax. They are rather a feature of thought.

A concept does not have hard edges. If we think of a concept as an activated set of links in a pattern, then different links in the pattern will have different degrees of strength, and there will be no clear boundary to how strong any link must be to qualify as belonging to the pattern. Concepts fade out at their boundaries, as opposed to stopping abruptly.

A concept has no fixed degree of texture. A concept is a schematic feature of thought, consisting of an activated pattern of strong links. Whether the concept is full or skeletal depends purely on where we draw the line on "strong." A concept can be extremely skeletal or extremely full.

Concepts are not monolithic; they have aspects. Our concept of a house, for example, has many different aspects: the home-base aspect, the shelter aspect, the compartmentalized interior aspect, the architectural style aspect, the financial investment aspect, and so on. An aspect of a concept is just a concept, a pattern of activated links. Accordingly, it does not have hard edges and is not monolithic.

This characterization of concepts can be translated into speculative neurophysiology, along the following lines: Neurons are free agents. Neuronal group patterns compete for the participation of individual neurons. The result is a plastic, dynamic system in which links and patterns of links, both excitatory and inhibitory, can grow stronger or weaker. There are maps in the brain that correspond to sensory modalities, and there are cross-modal connections across those maps. Thought is the activity across such neuronal group patterns. Concepts are not objects but rather processes of activity that exist only when they are active. Concepts do not have essences but rather functions; they are competing recognition devices. They can reinforce or suppress other patterns. Concepts at one level can inhere within concepts at another level because patterns of links can inhere within larger patterns. The mind is not a machine that works on objects, but rather a process that involves activating many linked subprocesses that are themselves composed internally of the activation of links.

Some patterns in the brain are inherently meaningful to human beings with human bodies because those patterns correspond to human bodily situations and are linked to episodic memories in which they inhere. Patterns in the brain not inherently meaningful derive their meaning through links to patterns that are inherently meaningful. In other words, patterns that are inherently meaningful can be present in other concepts, such as abstract concepts, whose meaningfulness is given to them by the inherently meaningful concepts inhering within them. Our default concept of a concept sketches concepts as independent of the body in which they exist. Our revised concept of a concept sees concepts as ineradicably embodied.

The display is doing some tieing-up now. It is dynamically projecting bundles of fibers from one thing to another, from one concept to another. The fiber bundles represent kinds of connections possible between concepts. One sort of connection, for example, reinforces what it connects to; another suppresses what it connects to. Activating a given concept can increase the likelihood that certain other concepts will be activated, and decrease the likelihood that yet a different set of concepts will be activated. Concepts can thereby reinforce and suppress each other. There is no sharp distinction between what a concept "contains" and what it only "reinforces."

Concepts are not given to us by the world, but are the product of our attempts, as a species and as individuals, to make sense of our worlds. They are ineradicably imaginative, and exist only in the brain. Usually, concepts are discussed as if they are bedrock, hard-edged, general bits of common sense that stand apart from our messy, richly textured thought. We talk about them as if they were prior to imagination. We are prone to think that although imagination can combine these commonsense concepts in imaginative ways, each concept is internally free of imagination. We see imagination as something that comes after these basic tools of common sense, as something to the side of these solid concepts. But on the contrary, this book, with its very odd ideas, is asking us to see our most basic concepts as inherently imaginative. Our most stable concepts are stable not because they are internally free of the imagination but because they have become entrenched in our conceptual faculties.

THE HUMANITIES

The display telescopes backward again. Our default concept of a concept falls into its place in the northeast corner of the floor plan. Right in the middle of the floor plan is our concept of who we are, the human person. Inexplicably, the region of the floor plan labeled "the humanities" is way down the hall from our concept of the human person, as if these two concepts had very little to do with one another.

The display begins by opening and unfolding our default concept of the academic pursuit of the humanities. What we see is not very attractive. This default concept of the humanities, especially as it is developed in college textbooks, does not contain a sense of discovery, and only grudgingly allows a small place to the sense of creation. It consists instead of the codification of certain subject matters, like literature and painting. The aims, objects, and methods of the humanities in this codification are taken to be separate from and opposed to those of the sciences.

This concept of the humanities is inexplicable. It is hard to imagine how it ever got started. I would mock it as an old curiosity, except that the concept I prefer is even more antique. In the fourteenth, fifteenth, and sixteenth centuries, the humanities were founded upon creation and discovery. Humanistic subject matters such as music and literature seemed to be at the center of inquiry into what constitutes a human being. The activity of codifying subject matters was undertaken in the service of this inquiry. Efforts to recover and develop philological skills—as well as skills associated with logic and rhetoric—were undertaken not simply so classical texts could be codified, but rather so they might be studied and contemplated as aids in the inquiry into what belongs to human beings.

Historically, the humanities arose by contrast with the study of divinity. Divinity studies what belongs to divine beings. The humanities study what belongs to human beings. Since human thought depends upon human brains in human bodies, and is inherently human exactly because of that dependence, the investigation of human thought belongs to the humanities, as does the investigation of human language and literature. There are no humanities among the angels, because angels do not have human bodies, and therefore do not have human thought, human language, or human literature.

In our age, the inquiry into what constitutes a human being has been taken over by exotic disciplines like cognitive science, but in a way that, unfortunately, separates it from exactly those subject matters we now think of as constituting the humanities—literature, music, painting, and so on.

This book asks us to arrive at a new dispensation. It asks us to revive a concept of the humanities as concerned with discovering what belongs to human beings. In this dispensation, the historical rise of scientific methods after the separation of the humanities from divinity means not that the humanities now have a smaller scope, but rather that they have a larger array of conceptual instruments.

I propose a revised concept of the humanities as the inquiry into what constitutes human beings and human acts. I take language and thought as constitutive of what is human. On this view, the fundamental activity of the humanities is the discovery of the nature of human language and human thought.

This new concept of the humanities looks strange, relative to our default concept. Many things in this book will look strange, at least until we become familiar with them. Perhaps, once that happens, it is our default concepts that will look strange.

The central fact of the humanities is the central nervous system. But our default concepts are not founded upon that fact, and so we have skewed concepts of both the human person and the humanities.

The display before us returns to the view of our floor plan. In that view, the humanities are way down the hall from the human person. We should bring these two areas together. As long as we keep the default concept of the humanities as codification of various discrete subject matters like literature and painting, the humanities and the human person will seem to have very little to do with each other, and it will be easy to think of "the human person" as an object appropriately to be studied by any range of researchers except those in the humanities. Under the new dispensation of the humanities as the study of what belongs to human beings, these two concepts should become inseparable.

LITERATURE, LANGUAGE, AND THE HUMANITIES

The display returns to its opening theme. The human person is patterns of activity in the mind and its brain. Culture, society, subjectivity, language, art, dance, and all the subjects of the humanities are patterns of activity in the mind and its brain. The study of the humanities is thus fundamentally, criterially, constitutively the study of the mind and the brain.

In this book, I am interested in the study of language and literature as acts of the human mind. I propose to conduct some investigations into the ways we think and how those ways make language and literature possible. To speak and to make sense of speech, to write and to make sense of writing, are linguistic acts. They are the basis of literary acts. These acts are acts of the human mind.

Language is an expression of stable conceptual patterns. This is why the shape of language discloses the structure of cognition. It is not just that some thoughts get put into some words. More fundamentally, our conceptual apparatus is disclosed in the system of language itself, in its structure and operations. In everyday thought, we use these conventional conceptual structures. Our everyday speech reflects them.

The display before us on the screen places our default concept of thought next to our default concept of language, and opens each to reveal three separate compartments inside. On the left are everyday thought, poetic thought, and reason. On the right, corresponding, are everyday language, poetic language, and the language of reason.

We want to redraw this situation entirely. In the new sketch, poetic thought and reason become overlapping spaces, contained within the larger space of everyday thought. In the new sketch, poetic language and the language of reason become overlapping spaces, contained within the larger space of everyday language. Particularly important for our purposes in this book, the forms of thought and language we thought were poetic appear now to be ubiquitous in the everyday. Poetic thought is part of everyday thought; poetic language is part of everyday language. What is poetic derives from what is everyday. To understand what is poetic, we must understand what is everyday.

What is the relationship between the everyday and the poetic, between language and literature? Let us consider an analogy. When a master chef makes an audacious and delicious special dish of his own design, such as saint-pierre aux deux olives, he begins by knowing about his materials— that is, the physical characteristics of the saint-pierre, which is a particular kind of fish. He knows this very, very well and he also has, let us suppose, the greatest gastronomic imagination of the twentieth century, so he can see constraints—the saint-pierre will not go well with drain cleaner—and possibilities—it will go very well with the sauce aux deux olives.

When it comes to literature, however, we cannot think of words— mere squiggles on the page—in the way the maître cuisinier thinks of saint-pierre, because words—mere squiggles on the page—have no characteristics analogous to those possessed by the saint-pierre, hence no constraints and no possibilities. But language as a mental system has many constraints and many possibilities. Language is an act of the human mind, which is a human brain in a human body in a human environment. This situation imposes on the human mind many constraints and possibilities, which are inherited and disclosed in language. If we wish to understand literature, we must consider the mind of the human being who has (by inheritance from Adam) invented language. The human mind has constraints and affinities; language has them by virtue of being an act of the human mind that is constrained by the human body; literature has them by being part of language. If, therefore, we want to be as sophisticated in literary criticism as the maître cuisinier is in gastronomy, we must understand language as he understands saint-pierre. Would anyone imagine that knowing the characteristics of saint-pierre is not the central and indispensable part of knowing the nature of the saint-pierre dish? Would anyone imagine that knowing the nature of language is not the central and indispensable part of knowing about the nature of a work of literature? Since the constraints and possibilities of language come from the nature of human thought, why should anyone think that knowing the nature of thought is not the central and indispensable part of knowing the nature of literature?

The scope of our research in the humanities is limited by the adequacy of our concepts. The reach of our literary studies is limited by the reach of one particular concept, our concept of language. But our concept of language has very little reach at all, being essentially a rudimentary concept of language that we have not in the main reconsidered because we do not have to and do not want to. I suggest provisionally that our conceptual apparatus is everywhere disclosed in the shape of our language, and is the basis of our literature. The study of these basic concepts is therefore the ground of literary criticism. This book invites us to reconsider, with prompts, some of our basic concepts. The result will be a view of the humanities and its research agenda that will look bizarre at first, because of our conditioning, but that after reflection may look much more natural than the bizarre view of the humanities and its research that now holds sway within our disciplines.

The display is telescoping backward again. It appears now, in historical context, that this new view of the humanities and the agenda of the humanities is actually very old, and fundamentally conservative. It derives its outlook from classical rhetoric, as updated by cognitive scientific discoveries over the last two millennia. From this view, the present profession of English has ceased to consider the relationships among the body, thought, language, and literature because it has lost touch with the intellectual agenda of classical rhetoric. In the next four chapters of this book, we will take guided tours of what our research might look like if we were to return to that intellectual agenda.

In order to see the path the modern humanities might follow if they were informed by a classical intellectual agenda, this book has focused on the clearly central topic of poetic thought. But its perspective is not to isolate poetic thought from other kinds of thought in the fragmented modern fashion. Its perspective is instead a modern revision of a classic one: poetic thought *is* thought.

The essential suggestion of the Pretext was that the contemporary profession of English has introduced fragmentation in place of classical integration and has not been able to see poetic thought as thought. The four chapters that follow are four case studies, searches toward a form of inquiry that might help us correct this situation.

Chapter 3

POETRY AND INVENTION

POETIC INVENTION is an amorphous subject, not much discussed in contemporary criticism. Invention seems to be either precritical or beyond analysis, yet our practice of making critical distinctions about invention—as when we judge one poet to be more inventive than another—implies that poetic invention should be susceptible of analysis. Classical rhetoric viewed invention as susceptible of analysis, and indeed took this analysis as one of its defining professional tasks. What do classic and successful inventions tell us about particular formal and public acts of literary representation and the tacit and private preliterary way we understand our selves and our experience?

Invention is not originality. Only since the Romantics have these two cognitive phenomena been typically confused with each other. The structure of invention, and of particular classic and successful literary inventions, may be wholly unoriginal, or may have a dominant unoriginal aspect that serves as the floor upon which its contingent originality plays. We are vigilant for the new and the variable and concentrate upon it. Consequently, our consciousness is habitually blind to the unoriginal, which we take to be merely background.

Of course, the unoriginal is not background, at least not in the sense usually conveyed by that description. The unoriginal is normally the dominant active matrix in any original achievement. Originality is no more than the exploitation of what is unoriginal. Originality, far from being autonomous, is contingent at every point upon the unoriginal structures that inform it. When we step into a room, or into a poem, we do not have to think consciously "this is a room" or "this is a poem." The automatic nature of our interactions with the unoriginal leads us to think of the unoriginal as simple in itself and too simple for analysis, but this apparent simplicity is false. Relative to the complexity of the unoriginal conceptual context of invention, it is the original in invention that is simple. The concept of a "room" or a "poem" is immeasurably more complex than the original aspects of any one room or any one poem. Explaining the structure of an original moment is relatively easy, once we can explain the underbrush of unoriginal structures it exploits, but that is hard. In this study, for example, I will consider one small automatic constraint on invention. This constraint is a profoundly unoriginal component of invention, and is routinely exploited to achieve originality. But far from being obvious, this constraint seems to have gone unnoticed in poetic theory. Far from being simple, it shows a complexity that I can do no more than indicate.

The purpose of calling attention to an unoriginal aspect of invention in poetic expression is not to homogenize nonliterary and literary practice. It is rather to tease out what belongs to the poet, against the much larger background of what belongs to poetry, against the vastly larger background of what belongs to language, against the all-inclusive background of what belongs to the mind. The imagination must operate in a known space; it must work with unoriginal structures of invention. These are the conditions that the imagination must meet in order to be intelligible. Originality is just a step away from pedestrian thought, which accounts for most of the invention in any poem. A room is more pedestrian than the Sistine Chapel, but the invention of the "room,"[1] which belongs to no individual, is beyond the original inventive range of any individual architect, even Brunelleschi or Michelangelo. This unoriginal concept informs every exceptional room, as it does every pedestrian room.

Let us begin a demonstration of these propositions by turning to John Bunyan's *The Pilgrim's Progress*. In one component of its literary invention, *Pilgrim's Progress* is unswervingly unoriginal: it is structured by a conventional metaphoric understanding of life as a journey. That conventional and wholly unoriginal metaphoric understanding is constrained in certain ways that are derived from a general constraint, one that I will soon claim applies to all metaphor, original and unoriginal. *Pilgrim's Progress* never requires of itself or its readers any work to meet those constraints. The conventional metaphoric understanding of life as a journey already conforms to those constraints, and *Pilgrim's Progress* simply inherits those prefabricated and quite unoriginal satisfactions.[2]

Let us walk through a sequence of inquiries into these unoriginal satisfactions. First, we will need some terminology having to do with metaphor: A metaphor is a mapping of a source conceptual schema[3] (such as our conceptual schema for journey) onto a target[4] conceptual schema (such as our conceptual schema for life). For example, in the conceptual metaphoric understanding of life as a journey, various components of the schema for journey are mapped onto corresponding components of the schema for life: the person leading the life is a traveler; his purposes are destinations; the means for achieving purposes are routes; difficulties in life are impediments to travel; counselors are guides; progress is the distance traveled; and so on. The target schema, life, is understood in terms of the source schema, journey.

In any such conceptual metaphor, the mapping is one-to-one: two distinct elements in the source are not mapped onto one element in the target, for that would destroy the identity of that one element in the target. In the conventional metaphoric understanding of life as a journey, this constraint against violating identity in the target is automatically satisfied by a fixed mapping. For example, in the source schema, the traveler is distinct from the destination; in the target schema, the person leading the life is distinct from one of his or her goals; and the conventional metaphor maps those two distinct elements in the source respectively onto those two distinct elements in the target. The fixed ontological mapping in the conventional metaphoric understanding of life as a journey carries distinct elements in the source onto distinct elements in the target. *Pilgrim's Progress* simply inherits this prefabricated and quite unoriginal satisfaction of the constraint against violating identity in the target.

If we look at an extension of the conventional metaphoric understanding of life as a journey, we find that the constraint against violating identity in the target applies even in cases that are beyond the conventional metaphor. For example, if we say, "I am a traveler in life and I am the destination," then we find ourselves constrained to take the first and second "I" as pointing to two different elements (such as the knowing self and the self to be known) so that two different elements in the source (traveler and destination) do not map onto one element in the target.

We move now from the identity of elements in the target to relations of order in the target. Here, too, we will find our metaphoric invention constrained. First, let us consider some order relations in the target and in the source. We conventionally conceive of the moments of life as being temporally ordered.[5] For any two moments of life, one must precede the other; no moment precedes itself; and precedence is transitive. We also conventionally conceive of the points on a path, such as the path of a journey, as spatially ordered. For any two spatial points on the path, one must precede the other; no point precedes itself; and precedence is transitive. And we conventionally conceive of a traveler on a journey as encountering the spatial points on the path in a temporal order corresponding to the order of their physical succession. Now let us consider what happens when we try to map ordered components of the source onto ordered components of the target.

When we understand life metaphorically as a journey, we are constrained not to violate the order of moments in our concept of life. We cannot without provoking remark say, for example, "First I was getting somewhere in life and then I got off to a good start," because we take this as asking us to violate the original temporal order of two moments in the target: the prior moment in the target ("First I was") is forced to correspond to the later moment in the source ("getting somewhere") and the later moment in the target ("and then I") is forced to correspond to the prior moment in the source ("got off to a good start"). This reverses the order of moments in our schema of life—which is the target—and disturbs us badly.

The conventional metaphoric understanding of life as a journey automatically and fixedly satisfies this constraint by mapping spatial priority in the source onto temporal priority in the target, and *Pilgrim's Progress* inherits and deploys this prefabricated and unoriginal satisfaction of the constraint against violating order in the target.

But there are texts that ask for originality in satisfying these unoriginal constraints. The Farewell Discourse (chapters 13–17) in the Fourth Gospel is a locus classicus whose exceptionally rich history of commentary wrestles with many of these demands. Before we turn to this text, it will be helpful to pause to make some framing and theoretical remarks.

First, we must remark that it is worthy of wonder that any such constraints exist upon metaphoric invention, original or unoriginal. These constraints, once stated, may seem obvious, but that is only because their automatic transmission fools us into thinking that they are inevitable and require no explanation. There is nothing inevitable about them, or rather, we have no explanation as yet of how they could be inevitable. They are constraints concerned with preventing the violation of the target, but notice that they apply only to particular parts of the target; other parts of the target can be violated with impunity. Why are some parts of the target protected while others are not? That requires an explanation, and the shape of the explanation is neither obvious nor simple. Metaphoric thought is notoriously cavalier, and metaphoric language is notoriously slippery: when we understand some target concept metaphorically, we frequently violate or discard indispensable parts of it. Through metaphor, inanimate objects can become people ("My car refused to start this morning"), moods can become colors ("I'm feeling blue"), thoughts can become physical objects while minds become bodies ("I cannot grasp this notion"). The wide latitude of metaphor in thought and language often makes it seem unconstrained in its operation, a species of pure free play. Consider, for example, "Trees climb the hills toward the Golan and descend to test their resolve near the desert." Here, a static configuration appears to be understood metaphorically as a dynamic movement, and the agentless event of dynamic movement appears to be understood metaphorically as an action by an intentional agent. We are not bothered that dynamism is mapped onto stasis, that an action is mapped onto an event, or that intentional animate agents are mapped onto plants. Why then are we bothered when, as in the case we just considered, the ordering of a sequence is violated?

Aristotle originally noticed that a metaphor is constrained not to violate various things about the target. He expressed this by saying that the source must fit the target in certain ways, including what appear to be conceptual ways.[6] Considering that the problem of fitness was raised by Aristotle, and that metaphor theory has in many ways been a series of responses to and developments of Aristotle's few comments on metaphor, it is odd how little inquiry has been made into the actual details of what makes a metaphor conceptually fit. This topic has been overshadowed by other topics in the theory of metaphor. There has been voluminous work on what constitutes metaphor and how metaphoric language is demarked from other forms of language, on how it is that a metaphor can mean, and on whether or not metaphor can have truth-value, but relatively little work on the conceptual details of metaphor.[7]

To be sure, there have been blanket general characterizations of the conceptual process of metaphor, such as Aristotle's apparent characterization of the invention of metaphor as the perception of similarity in dissimilar things (*Poetics*, 1459a), Max Black's characterization of metaphor as the interaction of two different entire systems of implications,[8] Nelson Goodman's characterization of metaphor as "a transfer of a schema,"[9] or as concerned with "withdrawing a term or rather a schema of terms from an initial literal application and applying it in a new way to effect a new sorting either of the same or of a different realm,"[10] and Paul Ricoeur's elaborate characterization of metaphor, quite difficult to summarize, as novel attribution that creates semantic tension (because of its deviance from the literal) that results in new meaning (all at various levels, from the word to the sentence to the text).[11]

At the opposite pole, there have been multitudinous specific analyses of how specific linguistic metaphors can be read.[12] Literary criticism, particularly criticism of poetry, frequently presents thick descriptions of the workings of a specific poetic metaphor in a specific poem. New Critical approaches promoted this activity to central place in the criticism of poems. Deconstructive approaches have done the same thing, although with the ambition of finding incoherence and instability, rather than coherence and stability, in texts.

But there has been very little work at a level between these blanket characterizations and these self-contained case studies. There has been little mid-level work that would tell us about the general constraints on conceptual fit between source domain and target domain in a conceptual metaphor.[13]

Let us turn now to a famous passage in the Fourth Gospel to demonstrate how an original aspect of invention can be constituted as an exploitation of an unoriginal constraint in metaphoric invention. Jesus speaks to the Apostles (John 13.36–14.6):

"Set your troubled hearts at rest. Trust in God always; trust also in me. There are many dwelling-places in my Father's house; if it were not so I should have told you; for I am going on purpose to prepare a place for you. And if I go and prepare a place for you, I shall come again and receive you to myself, so that where I am you may be also; and my way there is known to you." Thomas said, "Lord, we do not know where you are going, so how can we know the way?" Jesus replied, "I am the way; I am the truth and I am the life; no one comes to the Father except by me."[14]

The subject of this passage is trust. In the first part of the passage, Jesus says he will take a journey and implies that he will return to take the Apostles on the same journey to the same destination. This may be read literally or metaphorically or both. The metaphoric reading calls upon the conventional metaphoric understanding of life as a journey and upon its conventional extension to the metaphoric understanding of death as a departure.[15] In the first part of the passage, there is no felt violation of the target. The metaphoric reading simply inherits prefabricated satisfactions of constraints from conventionalized metaphoric understandings, as we have seen before in the case of *Pilgrim's Progress*.

At that point Thomas asks a perfectly sensible question that makes sense either literally or metaphorically. It concerns the state of the Apostles' knowledge. The first reading of his question is literal: How can we know the physical path to a destination whose location is unknown to us? The second reading is metaphoric: How can we know the "way" that will "lead" us to a goal when the goal is unknown to us? This is a question about conceptual structure, and applies equally to the literal and the metaphoric readings.[16]

When Jesus answers that he is the way, both the literal and the metaphoric readings fall apart. Literally, his statement violates our schema of a journey because a person cannot be a way, much less both a traveler and a way. Metaphorically, his statement asks us to map two elements in the source, namely, both the traveler and the way, onto one element in the target, Jesus. We feel this construal to be a flagrant violation of protected structure in the target.

It is this dissonance that signals to us that we must perform some original work to arrive at a different construal that satisfies constraints. One strategy is to attribute to the passage a double reading: Jesus is taking one journey, whether literal or metaphoric, in which he is the literal or metaphoric traveler; and we, or the Apostles, are to take another journey, a metaphoric journey, in which we, or the Apostles, are the metaphoric travelers and Jesus is the metaphoric way or conduit to a state of being that is metaphorically both a location and the destination of this particular metaphoric journey.

There are other ways to attempt to satisfy constraints. We might observe, for example, that divinity in the Fourth Gospel is marked not by iconographic attributes or miracle stories but rather by discourse that violates what we take to be reliable conceptions. In this text, divinity talks like this. The divine, unlike the mortal or the everyday, can be a traveler and a way, an agent and a path. The divine can violate identity, as when, in trinitarian doctrine, we are told that three are one.[17]

It is not just that the divine can violate constraints, but that the divine frequently is signaled exactly through such violation. The constraint on preserving identity is violated, and its violation is a carrier not just of some significance, but of a particular significance. We would not recognize the attribution of divinity in this passage if we did not know constraints.

We have seen a few specific manifestations of what may be a general constraint on metaphor, and demonstrations of the unoriginal and original exploitations of that general constraint in literary invention. Now we turn to the general constraint.

This constraint has to do with the forms of our experience, and with how these forms structure our thoughts. We experience images in various modalities: a visual image of a road, an auditory image of a scream, a kinesthetic image of a pinch, an olfactory image of the smell of pine, and so on. No rich image is wholly unique; rather, it shares skeletal structure with other, related images. We have a skeletal image of a scream that inheres within our rich images of particular screams. It is an abstract image that cannot be identified absolutely with any particular scream, yet we know a member of the category *scream* when we hear one, based on our image-schema of *scream*. The same is true of a phoneme: a phoneme is an abstract category of sounds that cannot be identified absolutely with any one of its members. Yet we know a member of the category when we hear one, based on our image-schema of the phoneme. We have a skeletal image of a flat bounded planar space that inheres within our rich images of individual tables, individual floors, individual plateaus. We have a skeletal image of verticality that inheres within our rich images of individual trees, individual buildings, individual people. Following Mark Johnson, I will use the technical term "image-schema" for such skeletal forms that structure our images.[18]

As I conceive of them, image-schemas are extremely skeletal images that we use in cognitive operations. Many of our most important and pervasive image-schemas are those underlying our bodily sense of spatiality. They include our image-schema of verticality, of a path leading from a source to a goal, of forward motion, of a container (or more accurately of a bounded space with an interior and exterior), of contact, and of such orientations as up-down, front-back, and center-periphery. We have many image-schemas of part-whole relational structure. We also have dynamic image-schemas, such as the image-schema for a rising motion, or a dip, or an expansion, and so on. When we understand a scene, we naturally structure it in terms of such elementary image-schemas.

We are headed toward a first approximation of the general constraint on metaphor. This first approximation will concern exclusively how the constraint applies to images. It appears to be the case that when we map one image metaphorically onto another, we are constrained not to violate the schematic structure of the target image. For example, a verticality schema in the target cannot have mapped onto it its inverse; a bounded interior in the target cannot have mapped onto it both bits of an interior and bits of an exterior; and so on.

Consider, for example, Auden's lines from "1929":

> But thinking so I came at once
> Where solitary man sat weeping on a bench,
> Hanging his head down, with his mouth distorted
> Helpless and ugly as an embryo chicken.[19]

The hanging head of the solitary man is a bounded interior, with an exterior; it has an internal up-down structure (for example, the top of the head and the bottom of the head); its direction is roughly downward (looking down); its open mouth is a concavity in the boundary; its parts (mouth, eyes, top of head, and so on) have relational structure such as adjacency. Although our rich image of the hanging head may include all sorts of detail, that detail is structured by these image-schemas. I refer to this structure as the "image-schematic structure" of the target image. We are constrained not to violate it when we map the image of the embryo chicken onto it: the interior of the chicken head maps to the interior of the human head, the boundary to the boundary, the verticality to the verticality, and so on.

The next consideration to bring to bear in formulating this constraint is that many things other than images appear to be structured by image-schemas. Our concepts of time, of events in time, and of causal relations seem to be structured by these image-schemas. We like to think of time, which has no shape, as having a shape, such as linear or circular, and of that shape as having skeletal structure. We like to think of events in time, which have no shape, as having shape, such as continuity, extension, discreteness, completion, open-endedness, circularity, part-whole relations, and so on. We like to think of causal relations as having such skeletal shapes as links and paths. These shapes, these image-schemas, need not be static. We have a dynamic image-schema of one thing coming out of another, and we use it to structure one of our concepts of causation.

With this addition, we can reformulate the general unoriginal constraint on metaphoric invention:

In metaphor, we are constrained not to violate the image-schematic structure of the target; this entails that we are constrained not to violate whatever
image-schematic structure may be possessed by nonimage components of
the target.

The formulation of this constraint requires many clarifications and
comments. First, the constraint says nothing about what can or cannot,
or should or should not, be mapped from the source to the target, nothing about which components of the target can or should be involved in
the metaphoric invention, and nothing whatever about strategies of mapping or of reconception that might be used in the service of satisfying the
constraint.

Second, the constraint is not inviolable; however, if it is violated, the
violation is to be taken as a carrier of significance. Usually, we assume that
violations are to be avoided as we construct a meaning for an utterance.
The constraint guides our understanding by blocking certain possibilities.
But when we conclude that the utterance is to be taken as violating the
constraint, then we must look for some significance in the violation. For
example, we might take the violation as an aggressive and intentional request that we change our conception of the target in exactly the way indi-
cated by the violation. We then take the violation as urging us to form
some different conception of the target, that is, one not violated by the
utterance. To put the same point differently, one drastic way to satisfy the
constraint is to build a new conception of the target. But we assume that
a violation of the constraint is never insignificant or to be ignored. If ultimately we find no significance in the violation, we will find the metaphoric invention either faulty or beyond our powers.

Third, this formulation is summary, and does no more than hint at the
complexity of the subject. I am not offering a definition or taxonomy of
image-schemas, a theory of how they arise and work, or an explanation of
their role in structuring concepts. My formulation of this constraint does
offer a challenge to anyone who thinks that what is automatic and unoriginal in invention is simple in itself and too simple to need analysis. It
is manifest that our unoriginal understanding is informed by something
like image-schemas, that metaphoric invention is constrained in ways having to do with image-schemas, and that originality in metaphoric invention can be constituted as exploitations of these constraints. Yet finding
a fair characterization of these phenomena would require a theory of
image-schemas, of their relation to images, of their origin, of their synes-
thetic relation across modalities[20] (as when we talk of a "screaming red"
or a "sharp tartness"), of their use in structuring concepts, and, beyond
all this, a larger theory that could account for why they seem to have
privilege in metaphoric invention.[21]

Fourth, the constraint does not concern cases where an indeterminate part of a target is imbued with new structure. If, for example, we have an indeterminate sense or no sense at all of the causal relationship between two languages called Alpha and Beta, and someone says, "Beta is the off-spring of Alpha," then the constraint is not violated because there is no determinate structure to be violated. But if we hear that "Latin is the daughter of Italian," we sense a violation because we have a determinate sense that Latin did not derive from Italian.

The fifth and last comment on this constraint is elaborate. It concerns the status of the target. When we map onto a target, what are we mapping onto? What does the target consist of? Where does the target come from? So far, we have been talking about "violating" a target. This is a meta-phor and it carries its own connotations, some of them wrong. "Viola-tion" connotes an improper act perpetrated upon something that already exists. To think of disturbing a target as "violating" it may lead us to the erroneous views that a target exists in some supposedly objective, mind-free reality and that violating a target is an improper falsification of that reality. This is a standard objectivist conception of metaphor as an expres-sion that falsifies reality. A target is a concept. As we discussed in "Floor Plan," concepts exist only in the brain, not in the world outside the brain. Concepts are constructed biologically and culturally, in the history of the individual, its species, and its culture, under the constraints of fitness. This biological and cultural construction of concepts is often difficult to recognize. Let us consider an illustrative example, taken from Gerald Edelman's *The Remembered Present: A Biological Theory of Conscious-ness.*[22] The world appears to us to contain objects and events. This way of looking at the world is so basic as to seem to be a consequence of the way the individual human central nervous system develops in its very early stages. Yet our stimulus world is not partitioned in this way, and certainly not uniquely partitioned in this way. In our stimulus world, there are no necessary boundaries separating object from object, event from event, or object from event. Object and event assuredly exist, in just the way we imagine, but the site of their existence is in the brain. As Edelman writes,

> While the real stimulus world obviously obeys the laws of physics, it is not uniquely partitioned into "objects" and "events." An organism must con-tain or create adaptive criteria to develop information allowing such a parti-tion. Until a particular individual in a particular species categorizes it in an adaptive fashion, the world is an unlabeled place in which novelty is fre-quently encountered.

When we "violate" a target concept, we are not violating the world. We are not falsifying reality. We are rather altering something that is a mental construction in the brain. "Violating" a target consists not in misrepre-senting an objective mind-free reality but rather in disturbing protected

parts of a concept. There is nothing evil or even insensitive about doing
so. Where the target is full of such protected parts—but of course constructed—that fullness can constrain a metaphoric mapping onto the target. Where the target is indeterminate, no violation can take place because there is nothing there to violate. In cases of indeterminate target
structure, the metaphor has exceptionally wide power to *impart* meaning
to the target. Indeed, this may be the source of much of our abstract
conceptual knowledge. Much of the structure of an abstract concept may
have been created by imparting to it through metaphor the image-
schematic structure of a source. Much of our abstract reasoning may be
a metaphoric version of image-schematic reasoning.

Let us return for just a moment to the lines we inspected briefly earlier,
"Trees climb the hills toward the Golan and descend to test their resolve
near the desert." We asked earlier why we are not bothered by the violations in this poetic metaphor, and now we can answer. We will look first
at the mapping of images, then at the mapping of event structure, and
then at the mapping of causal structure. We begin with images. We can
understand the form of the image of the line of trees[23] as the trace of a
movement (or "summary scanning," to use Langacker's term[24]): the trace
of a climb that crests and then descends has the same image-schematic
structure as the line of the trees. Consequently, when one is mapped onto
the other, there is no violation of the image-schematic structure of the
target. So much for the images. Now consider the events and actions in
this passage. The target is an event that involves the trees and the desert:
the trees occupy a position (a literal position) and are opposed in their
occupation of that position by desert forces that may dislodge them from
that position. The source for understanding this target event metaphorically is an action: testing one's resolve. Such testing has an event-shape:
we occupy a position (metaphoric or literal) and are opposed in that occupation by some force that would (metaphorically or literally) dislodge
us; if we abandon that position, we say our resolve failed. The event-
shape of the source corresponds to the event-shape of the target. Both are
structured as a positioned entity that has been moved to that position by
one force exerted upon it, and that encounters in that position a countervailing force. The outcome is either the stasis or movement of that entity,
and this outcome is determined by the size of the vector forces. Again,
the image-schematic structure of the target (here, the image-schematic
structure of the event-shape) is not violated. So much for the events and
actions. Finally, consider the causal structure of the target: there is a
causal link between the desert and the stasis or recession of the endpoint
of the line of trees in the target. In the source, there is a causal link between the desert and the intentional holding or abandoning of the occu-

pied literal or metaphoric position. Mapping one onto the other does not violate the causal structure of the target: a link is mapped onto a link.[25]

Let us introduce now, as a last example, a poem that draws upon the same conventional metaphoric understanding of life as a journey that we saw in *Pilgrim's Progress* and the Fourth Gospel, but one that is more difficult than either of them. *Pilgrim's Progress* simply inherited the conventional and unoriginal satisfaction of the image-schematic constraint from the conventional metaphoric understanding of life as a journey. The passage from the Fourth Gospel asked us to do some original work in order to satisfy that unoriginal constraint. "At North Farm" by John Ashbery moves further out along that gradient:[26]

> Somewhere someone is traveling furiously toward you,
> At incredible speed, traveling day and night,
> Through blizzards and desert heat, across torrents,
>   through narrow passes.
> But will he know where to find you,
> Recognize you when he sees you,
> Give you the thing he has for you?
>
> Hardly anything grows here,
> Yet the granaries are bursting with meal,
> The sacks of meal piled to the rafters.
> The streams run with sweetness, fattening fish;
> Birds darken the sky. Is it enough
> That the dish of milk is set out at night,
> That we think of him sometimes,
> Sometimes and always, with mixed feelings?

Pilgrim's Progress virtually compels the reader with multiple linguistic cues to understand it as structured by the conventional metaphoric understanding of life as a journey, and inherits from that conventional metaphoric understanding a prefabricated and unoriginal satisfaction of the image-schematic constraint. The passage from the Fourth Gospel virtually compels the reader to understand it as structured by the conventional metaphoric understanding of life as a journey, but requires of the reader (and apparently of the Apostle Thomas) some original conceptual work in order to satisfy that constraint. The violation of the constraint is indeed the spur to perform that work, which we take to have been accomplished exactly when the constraint has been respected.

"At North Farm," by contrast, only suggests that we take parts of it as structured by the metaphor of life as a journey, and leaves quite widely open to us the range of possible metaphoric construals if we choose to do so. Yet as we go about those construals, we are guided by the expectation that they are to respect that unoriginal image-schematic constraint.

In "At North Farm," there are no or few overt indications that the expressions must be understood metaphorically. The entire second stanza, for example, can be taken as a literal description. The questions of the first stanza can be equally literal. Only the first sentence—with its description of incredible speeds and travel without rest through extreme conditions—offers extravagances that seem unlikely to be literal. If we do bring our capacities for metaphoric construal to bear on this first sentence, and, in the interests of consistency and richness, extend them to the rest of the poem, we find ample warrant to take the schema of travel and journeying as the source: in the expressions "somewhere someone is traveling," "toward," "speed," "traveling day and night," "Through blizzards and desert heat," and so on, we can find unproblematic expression of our conventional metaphoric understanding of life experiences as journeys—especially of progress toward goals as journeys toward destinations, where impediments and hardships in the journey correspond metaphorically to difficulties in reaching the goal.

Beyond that, the possibilities for metaphoric construal open in many directions. Some of the possible metaphoric correspondences might be the correspondence of apparent physical capacities of the traveler to personal capacities of the person with the goal (specifically, physical stamina may correspond to psychological stamina); the correspondence of physical relentlessness of the traveler to the psychological or social relentlessness of the person with the goal; and the correspondence of reaching the physical location of the person addressed ("you") to beginning a psychological and social interaction with that person.

To take a complex example, one reminiscent of the passage from the Fourth Gospel, consider that there appears to be doubt about whether the traveler knows the location of the person addressed ("you"). This location constitutes the traveler's destination, but how can the traveler who does not know the location of that destination know the path to it? As the Apostle Thomas said, "Lord, we do not know where you are going, so how can we know the way?" There is additionally doubt about whether the traveler can even recognize the sought person. We can take this entire situation first as just talking about the source domain of travel: we may construe these doubts as indicating that the traveler knows or hopes that the sought person exists, but is not certain where, and consequently does not know the path, but is exploring possible avenues. The traveler may not even recognize the sought person. Alternatively, given the ambiguity of "will he . . . recognize [and] give," we may construe that even if the traveler finds the sought person, the traveler may decline to recognize that person socially and give whatever he has to give. What might be the metaphoric reading of these construals? One strong possibility is that being ignorant of the physical path to the location may correspond metaphorically to being ignorant of how to engage "you."

These are only some of the possible metaphoric construals, and I will not pursue others, but observe that as we go about these construals, we are guided and empowered by the unoriginal constraint that we not violate the image-schematic structure of the target. For example, we are not to destroy the image-schematic "one-ness" of an element in the target by mapping onto it two different elements in the source. Nor are we to destroy the order of moments in the target. Nor can we map a potentially dead-end path (in the source) onto a successful interaction (in the target), for that would violate the image-schematic relation of "leading to": if in the target the interaction certainly leads to the goal, but in the source the path does *not* certainly lead to the destination, then mapping that destination in the source onto that goal in the target and mapping that path in the source onto that interaction in the target would violate the image-schema of "leading to" in the target, and we are constrained against doing that. Conversely, if in the target the interaction does *not* certainly lead to the goal, but in the source the path certainly leads to the destination, then mapping the destination onto the goal and the path onto the interaction would equivalently violate the image-schema of "not leading to" in the target. In all cases, we are guided by an image-schematic constraint that applies, I claim, to the myriad complex, inventive, and original possible metaphoric construals that we can consider.

There is a system to imagination. Although infinitely variable and unpredictable, imagination is grounded in structures of invention either wholly unoriginal or with an originality that consists of exploitations within a known and unoriginal space. Were imagination free, we would take its products as unintelligible, meritless caprices rather than as significant, valuable achievements. Metaphoric imagination, including metaphoric imagination in those poems we regard as most original, suggestive, and demanding, appears to be guided and made meaningful by an utterly unoriginal constraint so unrecognized in criticism and so daunting in its complexity that it cannot even be formulated, but must be gestured toward, with a heavy reliance upon the reader's intuitive sense of what it means: the image-schematic structure of the target is not to be violated.

It is predictable and unobjectionable that literary criticism would attend in the main to those aspects of imagination that might be expected to vary from age to age, or country to country, or author to author, or even passage to passage. We are vigilant for the new and the variable. But attending to what varies and not to what abides means that we see only a contingent aspect, when we believe ourselves to be seeing the whole. In one respect, to understand the sophisticated ways in which the Ashbery poem can work we must understand the unoriginal structure of invention it shares with both *Pilgrim's Progress* and the Farewell Discourse from the

Fourth Gospel. To understand its originality is in one respect to understand its movement to satisfy an abiding unoriginal constraint on metaphor that *Pilgrim's Progress* satisfies in a prefabricated way and the Farewell Discourse satisfies in its own original way: a constraint that governs, guides, and empowers all these poems. It is not possible to analyze an arresting and novel poem such as "At North Farm" without considering those unoriginal structures of invention that are the known space in which imagination moves, and whose constrained exploitation *is* poetic originality.

Elite contemporary critical theory looks away from what I am here trying to demonstrate. But there are elite contemporary authors who not only look at this demonstration but who offer, in brief, their own version of it. Foremost among them, Georges Perec has challenged his readers to observe that it is the everyday, the common, and the unoriginal where the real and complicated action occurs. The daily news—and the critical journals—focus exclusively on special and local observables. This focus, according to Perec, excludes us and our meaning. It leads to analysis that is hollow since it treats the special as autonomous from the common, rather than as a thin dependent aspect of it. Perec's commentary begins with a characterization of what we notice in consciousness:

> What attracts our attention, it seems to me, is always the eventful, the unusual, the extraordinary: five-column banner headlines. Trains do not exist until they derail, and the more fatalities, the more the trains exist; planes decline to exist until they have been hijacked; automobiles have as their unique destiny crashing into trees: fifty-two weekends a year, fifty-two body counts: so many dead, and so much the better for the news if the numbers never stop rising. We demand a scandal, a fissure, a danger behind events, as if life must not reveal itself except through the spectacular, as if what speaks or signifies to us were always abnormal: natural cataclysms or historic upheavals, social conflicts, political scandals . . .[27]

But this focus on the noticeable leaves out exactly that which is important and essential:

> In our great haste to measure the historic, the significant, the revelatory, let us not leave aside the essential, the truly intolerable, the truly inadmissible: the scandal isn't the coalmine gas explosion, it is the work in the mines. The "social ills" are not "preoccupying" during labor strikes; they are intolerable twenty-four hours a day, three hundred and sixty-five days a year.
> Tidal waves, volcanic eruptions, collapsing towers, forest fires, tunnels that cave in, the Publicis drugstore suspiciously ablaze and Aranda the oracular investments wizard with connections in high places singing to the au-

thorities! Horrible! Terrible! Monstrous! Scandalous! But where is the scandal? The true scandal? Has the daily news said anything except, "relax, life goes on, with its ups and downs; things happen"?

The daily papers talk about everything except the everyday. They bore me, they teach me nothing; what they report does not speak to me, asks me nothing and moreover certainly does not respond to the questions I ask or would like to ask.

Where is the rest? All the rest? The real events, the ones we live? The everyday things that actually happen every day: the banal, the quotidian, the obvious, the common, the ordinary, the infra-ordinary, the background noise, the habitual—how can we describe these things, how can we question them, how can we account for them?

To investigate the habitual floor plan of our thinking; to probe that which is automatic; to uncover the conceptual apparatus that constitutes the form of our thought is not easy, exactly because that conceptual apparatus is automatic. That which is automatic works better when unattended; it trenchantly resists being investigated:

> To question the habitual. But that's just it—we are habituated to it. We do not question it, it does not question us, it seems not to present a problem, we live it without thinking about it, as if it could convey neither question nor response, as if it could transmit absolutely no information. But this is not even conditioning any more, it is anesthesia. We sleep our lives away in a dreamless sleep. But where precisely is . . . our life? Where is our body? Where is our space?
>
> How to talk of these "common things"? how to flush them out? how to bring them out of hiding, to lift them out of the matrix in which they stay glued? how to give them a sense, a voice: let them speak finally of what is, of what we are.

Perec suggests—as do I—that to investigate what is common and to make it speak, a new profession will be needed, one that will attempt to develop tools for analyzing the common that are as sophisticated as those that have been developed for analyzing the special:

> Perhaps it is finally a matter of founding our own anthropology: one that will speak of us, that will seek within us that which we have so long pillaged from others. No longer the exotic, but the endogenous.
>
> To question that which seems to go so totally without saying that we have forgotten its origin. To recover some of the astonishment that Jules Verne or his readers could experience when confronted with a device capable of reproducing and transporting sounds. Because this astonishment, and thousands like it, existed, and it is these that patterned us.

What we must interrogate is brick, concrete, glass, our table manners, our utensils, our tools, our schedules, our rhythms. To interrogate what seems to have ceased forever to astonish us. We live, certainly; we breathe, certainly; we walk, we open doors, we walk down stairs, we seat ourselves at table to eat, we go to bed to sleep. How? Where? When? Why?

Describe your street. Describe another one. Compare them.

Make an inventory of the contents of your pockets, your purse. Ask yourself about the provenance, the usage, the future of each of the objects you have pulled out.

Question your little teaspoons.

What is beneath your wallpaper?

How many motions does it take to dial a phone number? Why?

Why don't they sell cigarettes in grocery stores? Why not?

It matters little to me that these questions may be, here, fragmentary, barely indicative of a method, much less a project. It matters greatly to me that they may seem trivial or futile: that is exactly what makes them at least as essential, if not more so, than all the others through which we have vainly tried to capture our truth.

It matters little to me that the guided tours I offer are only topical, barely indicative of a method, or that my project must finally be carried out by the users of this book rather than by the book itself. It matters greatly that the objects of my investigation may seem—because we live them, speak them, use them effortlessly—obvious or trivial, simple in themselves and too simple for analysis, as if they go without saying. Nothing goes without saying—least of all what seems to us to go without saying. This book asks us to consider the possibility that it is precisely the things we take for granted that are both more essential and more complicated than their dependents—the things conventional criticism and commentary address.

Chapter 4

THE BODY OF OUR THOUGHT
(AND THE THOUGHT OF OUR BODY)

IF WE STRETCH out our arms and look at our two hands, we see something that no longer seems remarkable to us: they are symmetric.

If we inspect the title of I. A. Richards' poem "Harvard Yard in April: April in Harvard Yard," we notice that it is also symmetric.

Symmetry seems obvious to us. We recognize it unconsciously. But this unconscious act of understanding is an object of wonder, intricately complex, surprisingly wide in application, grounded in the most basic and universal common understanding available to us, namely, our sense of our body's situation in our world.

Symmetry seems obvious to us, but that makes it suspect. In this book, we are suspicious on principle of what is obvious, and suspicious most of all of the assumption that what seems obvious to us will prove to be simple once we begin to analyze it. Unconscious, automatic, obvious acts of mind and language seem simple only because we do not conduct them consciously. These unconscious acts constitute virtually the entire body of our thought, and provide the dominant component of conscious thought. They are too complex and indispensable to be managed by the meagre and unreliable resources of consciousness.

It will always seem to us that what we remark in consciousness is inherently that which will be interesting under analysis. How we understand the obvious is not something that we consciously remark. But, as a phenomenon under analysis, how we understand the obvious is more interesting than how we understand the remarkable. Understanding the obvious is complex and basic. Understanding the unusual is simple—a slight extension of understanding the obvious.

It should be remarkable, for example, that we can see a connection between the visual image of our hands and the linguistic construction "Harvard Yard in April: April in Harvard Yard." It should be even more remarkable that such a mysterious recognition is conducted unconsciously, automatically, and effortlessly.

We will explore this obvious connection here. This exploration will lead us to a unified account of a range of poetic constructions that might at first blush have seemed altogether independent of one another.

Let us look again at our hands. As Hermann Weyl observed in his classic work, *Symmetry*,[1] a body in the world innately incorporates its environment. Consider a small organism that is not self-propelled and that floats in the ocean at a depth where the upward pressure of the water balances the downward force of gravity on the organism. To such an organism, all directions are the same. The world impinges upon it indifferently from all directions. Its environmental interactions are in general the same in all directions. The body of such an organism tends therefore to be the same in all directions, which is to say, spherical.

Now consider an organism fixed to the ground. It must interact with gravity. For such an organism, up is not the same as down. Its body incorporates this difference. A tree, for example, has a top and a bottom that differ. But yet there are directions for such an organism that are the same. In general, all directions perpendicular to the vertical gravity vector are the same (not counting, for example, local differences in light, wind, water, and so on). The body of such an organism tends therefore on average to be the same in all directions perpendicular to its vertical axis from any given point on that axis.

Now consider an organism that is subject to gravity and that is self-propelled. Its interactions forward differ from those behind. Such an organism may sense that the world before it is the same in general as the world behind it, but its interactions ahead will not be the same as its interactions behind: it runs into what is ahead of it, not what is behind. As a consequence of this difference in interactions, such an organism will have, in addition to an up-down differentiation, a front-back differentiation.

We are such an organism. We are subject to gravity and we are self-propelled. Our bodies therefore differ up to down and forward to back. But in general, the world on our left is the same as the world on our right. What can happen from the left can happen from the right, and conversely. What we can do on the right can be done on the left, and conversely. This is a fundamental fact of having a human body in a human environment. Our bodies incorporate innately this aspect of our interaction with our environment: our right hand is the same as our left hand. Technically, if we bisect the human body with a plane containing the up-down axis and the front-back axis, and we pick a point on that plane, and we draw vectors from that point left and right, we find that the human body is morphologically the same along those two vectors. We say of such a body that it is bilaterally symmetric. In art criticism, we say of such a body or such a form that it has heraldic symmetry.

The merest constraints of fitness require us to have an unconscious, automatic, and powerful capability to connect the right and the left. Sensing something at a point to the right had better not be fundamentally different from sensing the same thing at a corresponding point to the left. Performing a movement to the left had better be very tightly connected to performing the mirror movement to the right. We would be fatally inefficient if we had to learn everything twice, once to the left and once to the right, where the learning was fundamentally different in the two directions.

We have a felt, schematic, embodied understanding of bilateral symmetry, and we employ this schematic understanding constantly, moment to moment, in every aspect of our existence, to make sense of our world and to interact with it. The nature and details of this employment are the principal topic of this study. This schematic understanding operates across modes of perception, activity, and imagination. We grasp this schema of bilateral symmetry when we touch our toes, when we balance the volume of stereo headphones, when we do jumping jacks, when we grasp the handlebars of a bike, when we look both ways before crossing the road, when we look through binoculars, when we feel the ocean on our legs, when we pry or push two things apart, when we form the mental image of a tree, and when we hug someone.

Our embodied and indispensable schema of bilateral symmetry overlaps with our schema of balance. As Mark Johnson has demonstrated, symmetry and balance are not identical.[2] For example, physical balance can occur in cases where bilateral symmetry is absent. Nonetheless, our prototype of the balance schema is the schema of bilateral symmetry. Something bilaterally symmetric is balanced, although not conversely. To achieve balance, we typically resort to bilateral symmetry. We use this basic schema of right-left symmetry constantly, and grasp it ubiquitously in our perceptions, actions, and imaginings. We use it to cast order upon the world.

The Generic Concept of Symmetry

Our understanding of the right-left symmetry of our body and its interactions with the world is a specific understanding. It involves a great deal of detail that belongs only to physical bodies, indeed only to human physical bodies, indeed only to particular human physical bodies—our own. But it also contains a core of skeletal information that is not specific to any one body, or even to bodies at all. We have a generic concept of symmetry that applies to a great many things. Where does it come from?

Our specific understanding of right-left symmetry has, through the conceptual metaphor GENERIC IS SPECIFIC, a generic projection.[3] To explain this will take several steps.

The first step is to examine the nature of the GENERIC IS SPECIFIC conceptual metaphor, which underlies expressions such as "When the cat's away, the mice will play." We recall that a metaphor has a source domain and a target domain: the target domain is understood in terms of the source domain. The proverb "When the cat's away, the mice will play" refers only to the source domain of cats and mice, but through the GE-NERIC IS SPECIFIC conceptual metaphor, we can understand it more generally as a potential comment on a wide range of targets. The context of its expression may direct us to a specific target: if workers are shirking while the boss is absent and someone explains, "When the cat's away, the mice will play," we know to map from the specific source domain of the cats and mice to the specific target domain of the boss and workers.

We do this by using GENERIC IS SPECIFIC, which selects from the source domain of the cats and mice its generic-level information. That generic-level information is: there is an agent whose powers permit it to govern a lower rank of agents and who typically does so; the exercise of that governance depends upon attention; the governing agent is absent and thus cannot attend; so the ungoverned agents do things usually prevented by the governing agent. This extracted generic-level information constitutes a generic-level schema, which can be instantiated by many other specific-level schemas, such as the schema of the workers who shirk duties when the boss is absent. In this specific-level understanding, the cat corresponds to the boss; the cat's physical and instinctual domination corresponds to the boss's supervisory control; the mice correspond to the workers; the hierarchy of the animal world—cats above mice—corresponds to the hierarchy of labor—bosses above workers; play corresponds to shirking; and so on.

Suppose, however, we encounter the proverbial expression "When the cat's away, the mice will play" in some context—like a list of proverbs—that directs us to no specific-level target domain. We can still understand it metaphorically through GENERIC IS SPECIFIC because the generic-level schema consisting of the generic-level information in the specific-level source schema can itself count as an acceptable target. When we read such a proverb in isolation, we can use GENERIC IS SPECIFIC to arrive at a generic metaphoric projection of the proverb. We can muse over the range of different specific-level situations to which it might apply. It might apply, for example, to students cheating when the professor is out of the room, or to a spouse's infidelity when the mate is out of town.

Suppose the source domain is our felt, schematic, embodied understanding of bilateral symmetry in ourselves and our environment. When we apply the GENERIC IS SPECIFIC conceptual metaphor to this specific-level source domain, what is the result? What is the generic-level information in our understanding of right-left symmetry in our present environment? Roughly, the generic-level information is that there is *interchangeability* in the source domain. We can interchange left and right and still have the same environment. The world is the same, in general, to the left as it is to the right. In general, if we interchange left and right in the natural world, we have not changed anything except local facts. If we look at a picture of the natural world and a picture made from the reversed negative, we cannot tell which is correct; both are possible. Indeed, after a fashion, we can interchange left and right by doing an about-face. Doing an about-face certainly changes our interactions with what was before and behind. (Prior to the about-face, our eyes, ears, and nose were attuned to a part of the world they are not attuned to after the about-face. Prior to the about-face, our voice was directed toward that part of the world, our hands could reach out to it, and our natural progress took us toward it. The about-face radically changes all that when it interchanges what is before us with what is behind us.) But the about-face also interchanges the right and the left with no such changes in our interactions with the environment or in our disposition toward it. What before would have transpired on the right now merely transpires on the left, and we have the same capacities for dealing with it as we had before the about-face.

We can make this notion of interchangeability more precise. If we bisect our body with a plane defined by the up-down and front-back axes, and then interchange each point to the right with the corresponding point to the left, we get back the same gross external anatomy. Such an interchange is a mapping of our body onto itself. Each point on the body is mapped onto its mirror-image point on the other side of the plane, and the result is that we get the same body back.

The generic-level information here is:

—There is something with parts.
—The parts are related in ways that concern us (for example, the points of the body are related by relations of adjacency, of boundary and interior, of up-down, forward-back, and so on).
—There is a mapping of that thing onto itself. This mapping takes each part of the thing onto exactly one other part.
—The mapping preserves those relations that concern us.

Our sense that the mapping gives us back the "same" thing comes from the fact that the mapping loses none of what concerns us. It preserves both the uniqueness of the parts and the relations among them.

This generic-level information constitutes a generic-level schema. It is a metaphoric projection by means of the GENERIC IS SPECIFIC metaphor, which selects from our schema of bilateral symmetry in our body and its environment just the generic-level information. We can apply this generic-level schema to many specific-level schemas to understand them metaphorically in terms of our embodied symmetry. Some of these specific-level schemas are linguistic, and some of them are literary.

Consider the poem title "Harvard Yard in April: April in Harvard Yard." This is a set with seven lexemes or parts—"Harvard Yard," "in," "April," ":," "April," "in," and "Harvard Yard"—and there are many, many relations defined upon those parts. If we map this title onto itself by interchanging each lexeme on the left with its mirror-image lexeme on the right, we get back the identical poem title, "Harvard Yard in April: April in Harvard Yard." The set has been preserved, and all the relations we care about have been preserved.

When something fits the generic-level schema that is the generic-level metaphoric projection of our bodily understanding of right-left symmetry, we can grasp it through that generic-level schema, and we call it symmetric. The target schema (such as a poem title) does not have to share any of its specific-level information with the source schema of bodily and environmental symmetry. As a consequence, the word "symmetric" is highly polysemous: we apply it to wide ranges of things that share no specific-level information. We apply it to visual phenomena, auditory phenomena, sketches, natural organisms, tactile perceptions, and a host of other things, not because they share some specific-level feature but because they can all be grasped through the generic metaphoric projection of our understanding of embodied symmetry.

That generic-level metaphoric projection contains a crucial subtlety: if there is a mapping of something onto itself that preserves certain relations, then we understand that thing to be symmetric under that mapping *with respect to those relations.* Accordingly, we may feel that something is symmetric with respect to some relations but not others. Suppose we paint the right half of a human body black and the left half white, and then perform the same mapping. Do we get back the "same" thing? We feel that the answer is yes and no. Yes, because all the gross anatomical relations have been preserved, and yes because the chromatic opposition of the two halves of the body has been preserved, but no because now the right half is white and the left half is black, where before the reverse was true. The relation of right-left directionality to color is not preserved. With respect to some relations, this mapping fits the generic-level metaphoric projection. With respect to others, it does not. Consequently, we feel that the painted body is symmetric under this mapping with respect to those relations that are preserved and not symmetric with respect to those relations that are not preserved. It seems to us to be partially symmetric.

Consider, as another example of partial symmetry, a Pythagorean table of opposites. It contains pairs such as:

Light	Dark
True	False
Straight	Curved
One	Many
Good	Evil
Right	Left
Male	Female

This is a set with relations defined upon it. One such relation is the opposition between terms in a pair. Another such relation is the conceptual correlation between elements of a column, according to the Pythagorean outlook. Let us map this set onto itself by transposing each term with its opposite:

Dark	Light
False	True
Curved	Straight
Many	One
Evil	Good
Left	Right
Female	Male

This mapping preserves the distinctness of parts in the set, and it preserves the relations we mentioned: each pair is composed of contraries, and the terms in each column are conceptually correlated, at least according to the Pythagorean outlook. But there is a relation that is not preserved, namely, the correlation of the left side of the table with the concept *right* and its related concepts, and the correlation of the right side of the table with the concept *left* and its related concepts. Before the mapping, "left" is on the right and "right" is on the left. After the mapping, "left" is on the left and "right" is on the right. Consequently, we feel this table to be asymmetric under this mapping with respect to this one relation. It is partially symmetric, and we can say precisely just wherein its symmetry lies, and just what that means.

Specific Projection, Generic Projection, and the Gradient between Them

Our concept of symmetry runs from the detailed specific-level understanding of the symmetry of our body and of its interactions all the way up to the skeletal generic-level projection of that understanding. When we understand something by projecting onto it specific information from our specific understanding of a static human body, we can thereby project onto it stasis, spatiality, or bilaterality. At the opposite pole, when we understand something by projecting onto it just the generic-level structure contained in our specific understanding, we do not project stasis, spatiality, or bilaterality, because the generic-level projection of symmetry does not by itself involve stasis, spatiality, or bilaterality. Let us review this generic metaphoric projection:

—There is something with parts.
—The parts are related in ways that concern us.
—There is a mapping of that thing onto itself. This mapping takes each part of the thing onto exactly one other part.
—The mapping preserves those relations that concern us.

This generic metaphoric projection of symmetry contains nothing having to do with stasis, spatiality, or bilaterality. It can apply to spoken words that have no spatial component. It can apply to events in time that have no static or spatial component. It can apply to cyclic events that have no bilaterality or stasis. It can apply to recursive arguments that have no stasis, spatiality, or bilaterality.

To understand something as symmetric is to grasp it necessarily as conforming to the generic-level projection of symmetry. That is a minimal requirement for the perception of symmetry. But any level of our specific understanding of symmetry below the generic level includes that generic structure, and we can understand something as symmetric by projecting onto it any level of our specific understanding. When we understand something as symmetric by projecting onto it some level of our concept of symmetry below the generic level, we may thereby involve stasis, spatiality, or bilaterality in the understanding.

The projection of bilateral symmetry includes both generic symmetry and specific information below the generic level; it thereby restricts the generic symmetry in a special way. This projection of bilateral symmetry has as a special consequence the projection of equilibrium. When a physical, spatial object in our world is bilateral about the gravity vector, it is typically in physical equilibrium, and its axis of equilibrium typically runs vertically through its spatial center. Projecting bilateral symmetry onto a target imparts to that target a metaphoric equilibrium and a metaphoric axis of equilibrium that is the vertical midline between its opposites.

Such balanced bilateral "heraldic" symmetry seems to have been useful from the earliest days of Western and ancient Near Eastern art as an instrument for representing power and importance, as in Minoan seal rings that position a central, bilaterally symmetric goddess between bilaterally symmetric flanking beasts, or as in the Lion Gate at Mycenae, where a central bilaterally symmetric column is flanked by bilaterally symmetric lions with their front paws on the pedestal of the column.

If we consider as visual spatial marks on the page the phrase

able was I ere I saw elba,
we see a spatial midline through the mark "r" and a bilaterality about that midline. This bilaterality is moreover symmetric, since the two sides can be mapped onto one another in the way we have discussed, provided we preserve the spatial orientation of each letter when it is mapped. Consider as visual spatial marks on the page the parallel phrase

Harvard Yard in April: April in Harvard Yard

If we partition this phrase into parts ("Harvard Yard," "in," "April," and ":") and apply our mapping just to those parts, preserving their spatial orientation, then this phrase too has a spatial midline, through the colon, and it is bilateral about that midline. It is symmetric, since its bilateral halves map onto each other in a way that satisfies the generic metaphoric projection of symmetry.

THE GENERIC PROJECTION OF SYMMETRY IN CONCERT WITH OTHER CONCEPTUAL TOOLS

We have seen cases where we understand something by projecting onto it some specific level of our embodied sense of right-left symmetry. Often the specific level we project is spatial and bilateral symmetry, which contains inhering within it generic symmetry. In many cases we project only that generic concept, which applies to a great range of phenomena, from the spherical symmetry of a sphere to the cyclic symmetry of an argument.

This generic projection of symmetry can operate in concert with other conceptual tools. For example, the generic projection itself does not impart metaphoric spatiality or bilaterality to a target, but it may work in concert with a separate conceptual metaphor that does. In these cases, the target is understood as metaphorically spatial and bilateral through some metaphor other than the generic projection, and is understood as symmetric through the generic projection. The target is thus metaphorically spatial and metaphorically bilateral through one conceptual metaphor, and metaphorically symmetric through a different conceptual metaphor. Let us look at some examples.

We often conceive of time metaphorically as something that moves forward along a path. The present is metaphorically a spot on the path where we are located; the past is metaphorically the part of the path that lies "behind" us; and the future is metaphorically the part of the path "ahead" of us, which is to say, the part of the path that we are metaphorically "facing." The spot corresponding to the present moves linearly "forward." Time is thus imbued with a metaphoric linearity. A period of time is thus a metaphoric line segment. As such, it has a metaphoric midpoint. It is therefore metaphorically bilateral.

Because we read in time, text inherits this metaphoric linear structure, so that a word at the end of the first "line" comes "before" the word at the beginning of the second "line." We think of the entire text in a book as lying along a continuous line, from the first word to the last, regardless of how the print exists physically on pages.

Since text inherits from our interaction with it in time this metaphoric linearity, we can understand a text as metaphorically linear, and consequently as metaphorically bilateral about its interactional midpoint, regardless of whether it lies on an actual physical line. It can then be further understood as symmetric if it accepts the generic metaphoric projection of symmetry. We consider "Harvard Yard in April: April in Harvard Yard" spatial and bilateral regardless of whether all the words fall on one line of text or lap over from one line to the next. It may have *visual* and *spatial* bilaterality only if all the words lie along one line. But it has a metaphoric linear spatiality and a metaphoric bilaterality even when they do not lie on one line. It also has, by virtue of the generic metaphoric projection of symmetry, a metaphoric symmetry. It is thus metaphorically spatial and metaphorically bilateral through one metaphoric projection and metaphorically symmetric through another. Speech, which has no visual component, may nonetheless be understood as having metaphoric bilateral symmetry with respect to its metaphoric linearity in time.

The combination of generic symmetry with the metaphoric spatial linearity and bilaterality that text inherits from the metaphoric conception of linear time produces a literary equivalent of heraldic symmetry. It can be noted not only in "Harvard Yard in April: April in Harvard Yard," but also in what John Wilson has noted as the Egyptian "strong sense of balance, symmetry, and geometry" that "comes out in [Egyptian] literature, where the best products show a deliberate and sonorous parallelism of members, which achieve dignity and cadence."[4] He illustrates with a text whose speaker is an Egyptian king:

> Give heed to my utterances / hearken unto them.
> I speak to you / I make you aware
> That I am the son of Re / who issued from his body.

Narration occurs in metaphorically linear speech or writing, and inherits that metaphoric linearity. This narrative "line" can therefore be metaphorically bilateral. It can in addition be symmetric, through the generic projection of symmetry. Homer, for example, routinely frames the presentation of an incident by beginning it with an oral formula and closing it with the same or nearly the same formula. He will often open and close a speech with the same phrase. Cedric Whitman refers to this as a "framing device, whereby the episode or digression is rounded off by the repetition at the end of the formula with which it began."[5] Homer frequently mentions a string of things that are to be picked up in reverse order, as when Odysseus in the underworld asks the shade of his mother, Anticlea, five questions, which she answers in reverse order.[6] It is important to see that in no sense is the speech of this presentation spatial. In order to grasp it as spatially symmetric, we must first grasp it as metaphorically spatial. This occurs through a conceptual metaphor in which moments in time are structured according to the image-schema of a directed path. Our experience with a text in time inherits that metaphoric spatiality. Once we conceive of the narrative as metaphorically spatial and bilateral, we may project upon it metaphoric symmetry.

Whitman has in fact demonstrated that the entire *Iliad* is structured according to a truly elaborate symmetry of just this type:

> In the *Iliad*, the old device of hysteron proteron has been expanded into a vast scheme far transcending any mere mnemonic purpose, a scheme purely and even abstractly architectonic. Not only are certain whole books of the poem arranged in self-reversing, or balancing, designs, but the poem as a whole is, in a way, an enormous hysteron proteron, in which books balance books and scenes balance scenes by similarity or antithesis, with the most amazing virtuosity.[7]

The metaphoric "line" of presentations in the *Iliad* is metaphorically balanced about a metaphoric midpoint, the Great Battle, and individual "line segments" in the line have a similar microcosmic metaphoric bilateral symmetry, as when an important scene is heavily framed by matched pairs of scenes. In this way, the larger metaphoric bilateral symmetry is composed of smaller parts that are metaphorically bilaterally symmetric. As Calvert Watkins, among others, has written, "ring composition" of this sort served as

> an extraordinarily widespread organizing device in the archaic Indo-European-speaking world. . . . [It] is of enormous importance in oral literature for isolating unities within a larger discourse, as in the case of Greek epic. Like most poetic features, it is by no means confined to verse; in Vedic prose, for example, it may function virtually as punctuation, as an index of topical paragraph boundaries.[8]

We automatically feel a connection between the one-dimensional bilateral symmetry of a line segment about its midpoint, or the two-dimensional bilateral symmetry of concentric circles about a vertical axis, or the three-dimensional bilateral symmetry of the body about a vertical midplane, and this narrative structure in the *Iliad*. It seems obvious, and it is. But the nature of the connection is marvelous. The first sorts of symmetry are spatial; the symmetry of the narrative structure in the *Iliad* is not spatial. Indeed, the *spatial* bilateral symmetry and the *narrative* bilateral symmetry share, in reality, nothing at the specific level. One is static and the other dynamic. One is physical and the other is not. The seemingly obvious connection between them comes through the coherent operation of two conceptual tools, one a metaphor in which the present moves metaphorically along a directed spatial path that—in the nature of paths—is composed of segments with midpoints, and the other a generic projection of symmetry that we can apply to the structure of such segments. The first metaphor lets us think of the narration as spatially linear and bilateral. The second lets us think of its metaphoric spatial linearity and bilaterality as symmetric. Through their coherence, the narration in the *Iliad* becomes "bilaterally symmetric."[9]

Let us take up another case in which the generic metaphoric projection of symmetry operates in concert with an independent metaphor. There is an elaborate conceptual metaphor in which concepts and propositions are understood as having metaphoric locations on a metaphoric surface. To believe such a proposition is metaphorically to stand upon its metaphoric location on the metaphoric surface. We say, "Where do you stand?" to mean "What is your opinion?" We say, "This is my position" to mean "This is what I believe." We say, "You've shifted your position" to mean "You have changed the proposition you proposed." These are all expressions of a basic metaphor in which PROPOSITIONS ARE LOCATIONS and ASSERTING A PROPOSITION IS STANDING ON ITS LOCATION. It is a subset of the basic metaphor THE MIND IS A BODY MOVING IN SPACE, in which the space over which the mind moves is a surface of concepts and propositions that the mind can "come to" and "stand upon." This metaphor can be fleshed out productively: contrary concepts and propositions not only have metaphoric locations on this metaphoric surface, they have *contrary* locations. What does it mean for them to have contrary locations? It means that they are endpoints of a line segment that has a midpoint. This metaphoric line segment can be understood as symmetric about its midpoint: mapping the line segment onto itself about the midpoint produces a line segment with the same endpoints. The contrary concepts are thus polar opposites. Conceptual contraries are understood metaphorically as endpoints of a line segment bilateral about its midpoint, but not conversely: not just any two metaphoric points on the metaphoric surface are contraries, even though a line segment connects them. Once we conceive of conceptual contraries as endpoints of a line segment, they become spatial opposites. That is why conceptual contraries like good and evil are called "polar" opposites, because we conceive of them metaphorically as endpoints (or "poles") of a *spatial* line segment that has a metaphoric equilibrium point equidistant from each pole. Polar expressions in Greek (and consequently in English) like "mortals and immortals," "land and sea," and "openly and secretly" use the pair of poles as metonymic for the metaphoric gradient lying between them. From Homer on, G. E. R. Lloyd observes, "Greek writers seem to have had a special fondness for coupling terms in this way, using opposites as points of reference by which to indicate a class as a whole or to make distinctions within one."[10] Lloyd indicates that such polar couplets are used sometimes to express alternatives and sometimes in place of a single inclusive term to express a general notion. To say "by word and by deed" is to say "by all signifying actions." To say "by guile and by force" is to say "in all manners"; to say "by land and by sea" is to say "everywhere."

Projecting metaphorically onto conceptual contraries a linear bilateral symmetry creates for us our way of classifying things with respect to those conceptual contraries. It creates a "linear" "scale." We classify things by locating them at a metaphoric point along that scale. This classifies them not only with respect to the contraries, but with respect to everything else so classified. Change can be understood metaphorically as movement along this scale. Control can be understood metaphorically as the achievement of equilibrium on this scale. These metaphoric operations greatly reduce the complexity of our conceptual system. Still greater simplicity and power can be achieved by correlating pairs of polar opposites as in the Pythagorean table of opposites, or as when we connect experiences such as bright, sharp, hard, light (in weight), quick, high-pitched, and narrow, and set them against their correlated polar opposites dark, blunt, soft, heavy, slow, low-pitched, and wide, as Roman Jakobson, quoting Whorf, noted.[11] We often use such metaphoric polar opposition as a basis for axiology, when we attribute opposed values to the poles. We think of *up, forward*, and *right* as good, and *down, back*, and *left* as bad.[12] "Grey areas" in value are called "grey" because we understand both Good-Bad and White-Black as polar opposites with gradients between them, and correlate the White-Black gradient with the Good-Bad gradient, so that the grey areas lying between white and black correspond to the value areas lying between good and bad.

The metaphoric projection onto contraries of a linear bilaterally symmetric scale is an extremely basic tool of human understanding and invention, and it is ineradicably metaphoric. It has a tremendous general scope, but is not a mere formal abstraction. Instead, it is grounded in our embodied understanding of the symmetry of our bodies and our environments.

We experience physical forces. When they are bilaterally symmetric, they are in bilateral equilibrium. This is knowledge we have about the world of forces by virtue of our ability to recognize symmetry in our world. We project this knowledge of symmetry and equilibrium onto a great variety of conceptual situations involving proposals or assertions. This projection is the basis of our intuitive, unconscious knowledge of moments that require a decision. We know of our environments that when something is still, when there is stasis, it is because the opposing forces impinging upon it are symmetric. We know of our environments that change results from breaking that symmetry. This schema for stasis and change can be mapped metaphorically onto situations like the following, where Odysseus speaks to himself in the *Iliad*:

> Odysseus now, the good spear, stood alone;
> no Argive held that ground with him, as fear
> had gripped them all. And grimly vexed,
> he spoke to his own valor: "Here is trouble.
> What will become of me? A black day, this,
> if I show fear and run before this crowd;
> but worse if I am captured, being alone.
> Zeus routed all the rest of the Danaans.
> But why this bandying inward words, my friend?
> Cowards are men who leave the front in war.
> The man who will be worth respect in battle
> holds on, whether he's hit or hits another."[13]

Odysseus, and we, understand his situation metaphorically. His alternatives, to fight and to run, are conceived of metaphorically as forces in bilateral equilibrium. More colloquial examples expressing this metaphor are "I am being pushed in two different directions at once" and "I am torn between the alternatives." These contrary forces impinge upon his activity, resulting in stasis, a moment of decision between countervailing forces. The stasis is broken when one set of arguments, conceived of as a force, grows greater than the other, breaking the symmetry, and metaphorically impelling Odysseus along with it. Odysseus assesses the first choice as stronger with respect to safety and the second choice as stronger with respect to honor, and of course sees greater force in honor.

Just this sort of metaphoric construal of alternatives provides the general structure of forensic rhetoric. Formal rhetoric conceives of the issue to be debated (its *status causae* or *constitutio causae*) as the mean between two opposing powers. It is the equilibrium meeting point between two opposite forces, each of which is driving toward one of the contraries. The purpose of argument is metaphorically to break that symmetry. The rhetorical tradition has given us general taxonomies of kinds of rhetorical equilibria. They include accusation of a crime versus denial of the act constituting the crime; accusation of a crime versus admission of the act but denial that the act fits the definition of the crime; and accusation of a crime versus denial that the concept of criminality applies. The first metaphoric equilibrium is called factual, the second definitional, and the third qualitative. The job of the rhetor in debate is metaphorically to break a symmetry so that one force can overbalance its opposite and drive to a predetermined spot. That spot is the position upon which the rhetor wishes to stand.

Important events in our lives often occur exactly when an actual physical or biological equilibrium is broken. Metaphorically, a situation or event, such as Odysseus's decision, can be understood as important exactly because it is the breaking of oppositional symmetry. Change occurs when equilibrium is broken. Consider Hamlet's soliloquy:

> To be, or not to be, that is the question:
> Whether 'tis nobler in the mind to suffer
> The slings and arrows of outrageous fortune,
> Or to take arms against a sea of troubles
> And by opposing end them. To die: to sleep.
> No more; and by a sleep to say we end
> the heart-ache and the thousand natural shocks
> That flesh is heir to: 'tis a consummation
> Devoutly to be wish'd. To die: to sleep.
> To sleep? perchance to dream. Ay, there's the rub;
> For in that sleep of death what dreams may come,
> When we have shuffled off this mortal coil,
> Must give us pause.
>
> (Act 3, scene 1)

Hamlet suffers here, as generally in the play, from an unbreakable symmetry, a stasis. The soliloquy begins with a bare opposition, "to be or not to be," which we understand metaphorically as symmetrically opposed forces. This defines a stasis of action and decision. The question is repeated and refined. The first "To die: to sleep" introduces one force, the argument for one side. The second "To die: to sleep," occurring at exactly that point in the line where its predecessor occurred, introduces the symmetrically opposed force, namely, the argument for the opposing side. But Hamlet never decides. Instead, he remains at the point of equilibrium. The question abides unresolved while the remainder of the speech elaborates the case for acrasia and indecision. Revenge heroes typically state the case, resolve the point, and act, but Hamlet perpetually oscillates about stasis.

Similar rhetorical moments can be seen in any number of those speeches so frequent in Thucydides or Josephus, in which one side speaks and the other side refutes, or in the *Iliad* when one man (such as Achilles) speaks and another man (such as Odysseus) refutes, whether in council or on the battlefield. Action and decision are understood in these cases by projecting metaphorically onto the world of human thought and behavior our embodied sense of bilateral oppositional symmetry and its breaking.

Hamlet's stasis in equilibrium is, from another point of view, imbalance: he is declining to restore equilibrium to a disequilibrated situation.

Revenge tragedy usually takes as its subject the search for recompense and requital, balancing act for act, conforming to the Aristotelian concept of compensatory justice or the "eye for an eye" of the *lex talionis*. In *Gorboduc*, for example, Gorboduc has divided his kingdom between his sons Ferrex and Porrex. The first metaphoric vector of metaphoric disequilibration is the murder of Ferrex by Porrex. Videna, their mother, attempts to reestablish equilibrium by killing her son Porrex. The people, moved with the cruelty of the act, rise in compensatory rebellion and slay both father and mother. The nobility slays the rebels. The land lies desolate after civil war, the equilibrium lost. This is the method of disastrous revenge tragedy in general: After an initial vector of wrong or evil, any new balance inexorably results in an imbalance of a different kind: the solution to the problem recreates the problem, under a new relation, in a different incarnation. The compensatory revenge violates other equilibria (such as kinship respect) and calls for yet another compensatory revenge. Repetition of the problem and attempted solutions engender general slaughter, and new order can be created at the end not by some participant in the existing order who manipulates the existing order, but rather only by someone outside the existing order who imports a new order.

Vladimir Propp has argued that the structure of the folktale depends upon an initial equilibrium and a force that breaks it. The opening movement of the folktale is created when the villain disturbs a balance by causing harm or injury to a member of a family. The hero—whether seeker or victim—sets about to restore the balance. Those tales not beginning their movement with an act of villainy begin it with the disturbance of balance by some insufficiency or lack. In either case, the response is that "the seeker agrees to or decides upon counteraction."[14]

At least one literary critic has been so extravagant as to argue that symmetry of just this oppositional sort is the basis of aesthetics in literature. Justus George Lawler argues, in my words, not his, that the perception of beauty requires a special symmetry. He claims "that the beautiful object is congruent with what is commonly called 'human nature'; otherwise, man would not find such an object beautiful at all,"[15] and that there is a myth, which he sees as the theme of M. H. Abrams' *Natural Supernaturalism*, meant to explain our nature: "Put most conventionally, the myth affirms that man has a sense of having come forth from unity, or dwelling halfway between unity and disunity, and of therefore wanting to return to unity, but to a unity which, precisely because it is attained by journeying through disunity, must somehow be a higher state than that originally remembered."[16]

Lawler sees man as a finite localized agent lying at the midpoint between two metaphorically balancing infinitudes, and he argues that we find poetry beautiful when it expresses this balance, whether that expression occurs at the level of phonology, syntax, semantics, or discourse structure. He gives elaborate analyses of many such expressions, such as the opening of Yeats's "Prayer for My Daughter":

> Once more the storm is howling, and half hid
> Under this cradle-hood and coverlid
> My child sleeps on. There is no obstacle
> But Gregory's wood and one bare hill
> Whereby the haystack and roof-levelling wind,
> Bred on the Atlantic, can be stayed;
> And for an hour I have walked and prayed
> Because of the great gloom that is in my mind.
>
> I have walked and prayed for this young child an hour
> And heard the sea-wind scream upon the tower,
> And under the arches of the bridge, and scream
> In the elms above the flooded stream;
> Imagining in excited reverie
> That the future years had come,
> Dancing to a frenzied drum,
> Out of the murderous innocence of the sea.

The setting here moves from the vastness of nature, to the focus of a man walking and praying over a cradle, and back to the vastness of nature. The setting is metaphorically bilaterally symmetric around the metaphoric midpoint of the stanza break. George Herbert, Lawler notes, attempts to duplicate this thematic symmetry in the visual symmetry of each stanza of the poem "Easter Wings":

> Lord, who createdst man in wealth and store,
>   Though foolishly he lost the same
>   Decaying more and more
>   Till he became
>   Most poore:
>   With thee O let me rise
>   As larks, harmoniously
>   And sing this day thy victories:
> Then shall the fall further the flight in me.

In Herbert's presentation, man is first close to God, then far from God, and then again close to God. This stanza (like its twin) is metaphorically bilaterally symmetric about its metaphoric midpoint with respect to man's closeness to God. It is also visually symmetric about a horizontal midline. (The poem is occasionally printed sideways, so that this midline becomes vertical.) What is not preserved by this symmetric mapping of the stanza onto itself about its midline is the nature of the closeness to

God. At the beginning of the stanza, that closeness is prelapsarian. At the end, it is postlapsarian. The stanza is symmetric with respect to degree of closeness but asymmetric with respect to the status of that closeness.

As a last example from Lawler, consider this passage from Tennyson's "Morte d'Arthur":

> So all day long the noise of battle rolled
> Among the mountains by the winter sea,
> Until King Arthur's table, man by man,
> Had fallen in Lyonnesse about their lord
> King Arthur; then, because his wound was deep,
> The bold Sir Bedivere uplifted him,
> Sir Bedivere, the last of all his knights,
> And bore him to a chapel nigh the field,
> A broken chancel with a broken cross,
> That stood on a dark strait of barren land.
> On one side lay the ocean, and on one
> Lay a great water, and the moon was full.

Lawler writes of this passage, "The basic pattern is figured forth in the great expansive opening and closing images (rolled among the mountains by the winter sea; the ocean, the great water, the full moon)"[17] with man, the limned finitude, lying wounded between. The structure of this passage can be grasped by means of the generic metaphoric projection of symmetry. That same metaphoric projection structures what Lawler considers to be the basic myth about human nature. What makes the poem beautiful, Lawler seems to argue, is that the same metaphoric symmetry structures both the myth and the poem; we see the myth expressed in the poem because we see the metaphoric symmetry of the myth in the metaphoric symmetry of the poem. Perhaps. My concern is rather to emphasize that neither the structure of the poem nor the structure of the myth is basic, and that one is not directly a mirror of the other. What unites them instead is their metaphoric grounding in our embodied understanding of symmetry.

GENERIC SYMMETRY

We have noted that the generic metaphoric projection of symmetry includes nothing about spatiality or linearity or the kind of relation preserved. Certainly it stipulates nothing about bilaterality. What it does include is: there is a set with parts; there is a mapping of that set onto itself that preserves the distinctness of the parts and the relations defined upon them that are of interest to us. We say of such a set that it is symmetric with respect to that mapping under those relations.

This generic metaphoric projection of symmetry is so useful in mathematics and physics as to have been given a technical name. Such a mapping is called an *automorphism*. When something has an automorphism, it is said in mathematics and the natural sciences to "have a symmetry." The symmetries of something are completely given by its set of automorphisms. The concept of the automorphism has been applied with great fruitfulness to number systems, crystals, space-filling wall decorations, and elementary particles. Indeed, the set of automorphisms possessed by something has interesting properties in itself, properties that qualify any such set of automorphisms as a mathematical structure called a *group*. These properties are: any set of automorphisms contains the identity mapping, which consists of mapping each element to itself—so that everything has at least one symmetry, called the identity automorphism; for every automorphism there is an inverse automorphism; and the composition of two automorphisms is also an automorphism. This seems very rarefied and abstract, like something that does not impinge upon our lives, something invented by specialists concerned with special concepts. But the definition of an automorphism is instead exactly the generic metaphoric projection of our embodied and interactional understanding of symmetry in ourselves and our world. We use it automatically, unconsciously, and effortlessly in a manner that is inherent and indispensable to what it means to have a human life. The rarefied mathematical concept of an automorphism is a metaphoric invention that we know unconsciously and use automatically. If we did not, we would not be able to survive.

To illustrate the generality of this metaphoric invention that mathematicians call an automorphism, consider a sphere. Pick any axis, including the horizontal, and rotate the sphere about that axis by any angle. The rotation is a mapping that carries the points of the sphere onto themselves in a one-to-one manner that preserves relations. It is therefore a symmetry. In fact, any rotation of the sphere about its center is a symmetry. It is not a *bilateral* or *heraldic* symmetry, but it conforms to the generic metaphoric projection of symmetry nonetheless, and we understand its structure through that generic metaphoric projection.

Poetic thought and expression are often metaphorically symmetric in ways that are not bilateral or metaphorically bilateral. In those cases, they are structured by the generic metaphoric projection, since that projection does not involve relations of spatiality or bilaterality. In such poetic cases, we see the generic projection of symmetry working on its own. Consider, for example, the following text:[18]

> Swiftly the year, beyond recall.
> Solemn the stillness of this spring morning.

To be sure, there is a metaphoric bilateral symmetry between the first and second lines: the first line concerns speed and loss, the second stillness and stasis. This is oppositional and bilateral. We are presented with conceptual polar opposites. There is a balance between the first and the second sequences in the lines.

But that bilateral and oppositional symmetry is not the only sort of symmetry we can recognize here. Consider "swiftly" and "beyond recall." They evoke dynamism. "Year" conforms to this imposed structure easily, so that it also evokes dynamism, as an indication of the passage of time. "Swiftly," "year," and "beyond recall" are *interchangeable* with respect to dynamism. Any permutation of them preserves that relation. They are therefore symmetric with respect to that relation. They are not bilateral or spatial, but they are symmetric: the generic projection of symmetry is working on its own in this mapping. Similarly, consider "solemn" and "stillness." They involve stasis. "Spring morning" conforms easily to this imposed structure, indicating a single point in time. "Solemn," "stillness," and "this spring morning" are interchangeable, or symmetric, with respect to that relation.

Thus, each *line* is metaphorically symmetric in certain ways with respect to certain relations that are *not* metaphorically bilateral. The *text* as a unit is metaphorically symmetric in certain ways that *are* metaphorically bilateral.

We do not conventionally call this sort of nonbilateral structure "symmetric." We nonetheless grasp it through the generic metaphoric projection of symmetry just as we grasp the structure of the sphere through the generic metaphoric projection of symmetry. There are other sorts of structure that we do not colloquially call "symmetric" but that are structured by the generic metaphoric projection of symmetry.

Let us begin to examine some phenomena in poetry that we grasp as metaphorically symmetric even though we do not colloquially describe them as symmetric. Samuel Levin, building on insights by Saussure, Jakobson, and Hjelmslev, has analyzed at some length symmetry of linguistic structures as a technique of poetry.[19] Consider the expression "good food and soft music." If we map this expression onto itself by interchanging "good" with "soft" and "food" with "music," which is to say by transposing the noun phrases, we get "soft music and good food." What does this mapping preserve? First, it preserves the grammatical form of the expression. The formal structure of the expression remains unchanged. So the expression has this metaphoric symmetry under this mapping with respect to form. But the same would be true if we permuted "good food and legal argument" into "legal argument and good food." There is something beyond form that is preserved in the first case but not the second. The phrase "good food and soft music" evokes the context of creature comforts, and in that context there is conceptual overlap between *good* and *soft*. (The case would be different if the context were ethics, as we can see from the opposition between *good* and *soft* in "good virtues and soft morals.") *Food* and *music* also overlap conceptually in the context of creature comforts. By virtue of the overlap, transposing "good food" and "soft music" leaves some conceptual relations undisturbed. So "good food and soft music" is symmetric with respect to two different kinds of relation, one formal and one semantic, under the mapping that consists of transposing the two noun phrases. This event, Levin claims, is characteristic of poetry. He calls it "coupling." In its simplest form, as in the example "good food and soft music," it consists of the use of equivalent syntactic structures to present related semantic forms—the kind of parallelism one finds in "Monday's child is fair of face / Tuesday's child is full of grace," or in longer structures like Pope's

> A Soul as full of Worth as void of Pride,
> Which nothing seeks to show, or needs to hide,
> Which nor to guilt nor fear its Caution owes,
> And boasts a Warmth that from no passion flows.

Consider the following variety of mappings of Pope's passage onto itself: the interchange of "full of Worth" and "void of Pride"; the interchange of "seeks to show" and "needs to hide"; the interchange of "guilt" and "fear"; the interchange of the second and the third line; the interchange of "nor to guilt nor fear its Caution owes" and "boasts a Warmth that from no passion flows"; and so on. Each of these mappings preserves both some positional and some semantic relations. For example, interchanging "full of Worth" with "void of Pride" preserves some *positional* relations by preserving the grammatical function of each word-position and each phrase-position. It also preserves certain *conceptual* relations: before the mapping, both phrases modify the concept of the soul referred to; both present that soul as a metaphoric container metaphorically filled to some degree with a quality that is understood metaphorically as a substance; the third word in each phrase concerns the metaphoric substance filling the soul; the first word in each phrase concerns the degree to which that quality fills the soul; the first word in each phrase is conceptually opposed to the first word in the other phrase; and the third word in each phrase is conceptually opposed to the third word in the other phrase. After the mapping, all of this remains true. Therefore, under this mapping, the passage is symmetric not just with respect to some positional relations but also with respect to some conceptual relations. It is this double symmetry that is Levin's concern: "Now, any two forms occurring in equivalent positions represent a pairing of convergences; only if the forms are naturally equivalent, however, do we have COUPLING, the structure that is important for poetry."[20] As Levin explains, this formulation owes much to Jakobson's earlier enigmatic assertion that "The poetic function projects the principle of equivalence from the axis of selection into the axis of combination."[21]

Levin acknowledges that a natural paradigm may be made up of forms connected by phonetic affinities rather than semantic connections, but his analysis focuses on natural semantic paradigms. He does analyze how meter and rhyme scheme create a conventional matrix so that (in my words, not his) we can have positions that are equivalent with respect to meter or rhyme scheme even though they are not necessarily equivalent grammatically. A given mapping of a passage onto itself can then have symmetries not just with respect to grammatical and semantic relations, but also with respect to metrical and rhythmical relations. For example, in the passage from Pope above, if we interchange "Which nothing seeks to show, or needs to hide" and "Which nor to guilt nor fear its Caution owes," we preserve certain grammatical relations (for example, both lines remain relative clauses attached to "Soul"); we preserve certain semantic relations (for example, both clauses describe that soul as honorable and secure, and its behavior as springing from proper motivations); we preserve the principal features of the metrical scheme (iambic pentameter); but we do not preserve the terminal word rhyme scheme. This passage therefore has symmetries under this mapping with respect to form, semantics, and meter, but not with respect to terminal rhyme. On the other hand, interchanging "nor to guilt nor fear its Caution owes" with "boasts a Warmth that from no passion flows" does preserve terminal rhyme scheme, in addition to preserving certain grammatical relations, certain semantic relations, and the principal metrical relations. As Levin explains, "when phonically or semantically equivalent forms occur in positions that are equivalent with respect to the meter or rhyme axis, that is, in equivalent genre positions, we have another structure that is important for the unity of the poem."[22] Levin brings this machinery, much elaborated, to the analysis of many poems, chiefly Shakespeare's Sonnet 30.

We back up now, to see where our analysis has led us before we move into less familiar territory. Two things are basic to this analysis. First, we have an unconscious, automatic, effortless, and extremely powerful understanding of right-left symmetry in our bodies, our worlds, and our interactional activity in our world. It is so obvious to us as to seem simple and unremarkable when pointed out. Second, we have a conceptual metaphor, GENERIC IS SPECIFIC, that extracts the generic-level information from that specific understanding and constitutes out of that generic-level information a generic-level understanding that we can use to understand a range of specific situations. The GENERIC IS SPECIFIC metaphor locks together with our embodied understanding of right-left symmetry to produce a generic metaphoric projection of symmetry that we can apply widely and powerfully in our perception and thought. This generic metaphoric understanding of symmetry lets us structure not only metaphoric bilateral symmetry but also many things that we would not have described colloquially as being symmetric. This generic metaphoric projection might in isolation seem abstract and unanchored, a matter of elements and relations, but it is firmly and constantly grounded in our daily bodily experience. It is indispensable to what it means to have a human life, in any culture, in any place, at any time.

Whenever we can map something onto itself in such a way as to preserve a relation, then we can understand it as having a symmetry with respect to that relation. In poetry, these relations can be phonological, metrical, semantic, syntactic, orthographic, visual, and so on. Sometimes, a poem can be symmetric under a mapping with respect to more than one kind of relation. When that happens in such a way that one of those relations is conceptual, we feel that the poem has the kind of structure that both Jakobson and Levin consider to be peculiarly poetic.

It is important to see that grasping the symmetries of a poem is understanding its structure. For example, we can "know" the meter of a poem in one sense by just flat out memorizing the meter line-by-line for every line, without recognizing the relationship between the metrical weights in one line and those in any other line. But we mean something different when we say that we "know" the meter of a poem. We mean that we know the symmetries to which the meter of the poem conforms. We know what is interchangeable with respect to meter, and what is not, and how.

This kind of knowledge gives us an extremely efficient way of remembering poetry without having memorized it. Suppose that we are trying to think of what comes next in a poem whose first few lines we have memorized. Suppose further that we have not memorized the meter per se of the next line, but that we do know the metrical symmetries of the poem as a whole, and so know what meter the next line must fit. We thus have knowledge about the meter of that next line without in fact having flat out memorized that next line or its meter. We may also know symmetries of rhyme, of grammatical position, and of conceptual relations in the poem as a whole. We thus have knowledge about the rhyme, grammatical position, and conceptual relations of that next line without in fact having flat out memorized that next line. Knowing these symmetries is knowing information about the line when we do not know the line itself. This information constrains what can come next. Enough constraints of this sort will give us so much knowledge of what comes next that we will be channeled to the right memory even when we have not actually memorized the poem. A poem is memorable not because we have memorized it (the phone book can be memorized), but because we grasp its metaphoric symmetries when we understand it, and our knowledge of those symmetries guides us to a memory of what we may not in fact have memorized. Levin quotes Valéry, who seems to have anticipated this point: "The poem, on the other hand, does not die for having lived: it is expressly designed to be born again from its ashes and to become endlessly what it has just been. Poetry can be recognized by this property, that it tends to get itself reproduced in its own form: it stimulates us to reconstruct it identically."[23]

Poetry is remarkably fit at replicating itself in the niches of the mind. Our bodily knowledge of symmetry and our capacity to project it metaphorically dispose us to structure things according to symmetries when we can. Poetry feeds that disposition. In encountering poetry, we recognize its multiple symmetries. Our knowledge of those symmetries leads us to recreate it identically even when we have not memorized it.

Let us turn to yet other poetic phenomena that we structure through the metaphoric projection of symmetry. To begin, we observe that although Levin recognizes the poetic phenomenon of coupling, he does not connect it with our understanding of symmetry. Levin thus isolates coupling as a peculiarity of poetry that could be of interest only to the specialist. In fact, coupling is a special case of the incomparably wider common use of the generic metaphoric projection of symmetry, and, far from esoteric, it is grounded in our most basic daily lives.

The range of phenomena Levin considers is subsumed in the much larger range of poetic phenomena we understand through the metaphoric projection of our embodied understanding of symmetry. Levin is primarily concerned with grammatical position, and considers only couplings that involve grammatical relations. But poetry can be symmetric independent of grammatical relations. We perceive relations of rhyme, meter, phonology, syntax, orthography, semantics, concepts, and so on, and can grasp the symmetries of a poem with respect to any of these relations. We can add relations of intonation, of accompanying gesture, or of accompanying music—such as the music to which a lyric poem is set. We can consider how the symmetries of the poem under any one of these relations relate to symmetries of the poem under other relations. Jakobson in fact seems to suggest this observation in his earlier essay, "Linguistics and Poetics," on which Levin has drawn.

Levin considers only conventional meters or rhyme-schemes. But finding the symmetries of a poem with respect to stress (or quantity) defines its full metrical structure, including small local variations. Knowing the poem's symmetries with respect to rhyme includes knowing internal and multiple rhyme.

I find it remarkable that we can grasp symmetric structures in poetry quickly, intuitively, and completely, and I hope the reader joins me in this wonder. Our ease in recognizing symmetries, of all sorts, may lead us into thinking that we are dealing with something simple, but that would be a mistake: what we can do easily and unconsciously is typically more intricate and complicated than anything we can do through conscious struggle. Obviousness is inherently suspicious. Our understanding of the obvious is complicated.

ASYMMETRY AND BREAKAGE

Our ability to grasp metaphoric symmetry gives us the ability to grasp asymmetries and breakages. When we attempt to project symmetry metaphorically onto a text and meet with considerable success, we are thereby alerted strongly to just those locations and aspects in the text where the attempt breaks down. These are the cases where the generic projection of symmetry cannot be imposed completely upon a specific target schema because something in that specific schema stands out as resisting the imposition.

This ability to recognize the breaking of symmetry is indispensable to us as organisms in the world. To the extent that some aspect of our world conforms to a background symmetry, we can know it without memorizing its details. The local details of its symmetry can be inferred from our higher-order knowledge of the symmetry in which it is embedded. Given just the smallest amount of knowledge about something, coupled with knowledge of the ways in which it is symmetric, we can complete the pattern without having memorized the details of the pattern. But we cannot tell from this where the symmetry will break. We must attend to breakage specifically, for itself.

We try to understand why a prevalent symmetry breaks down: when we have accounted for information by understanding it as generally symmetric, we need a special account for those places where the prevalent symmetry breaks. It is part of our routine bodily and interactional experience to attend to and ponder just those moments or locations that break symmetry.

This grounded interaction with the breakage of symmetry is used by artists and poets to alert us to certain aspects of their work, and to lead us to think about those aspects. A poet or artist who sets up a symmetry also sets up an expectation of its continuation and completeness. We become habituated to it. When he then breaks the symmetry, he both alerts us and gives us something that cannot be accounted for as constant background. He emphasizes that aspect and challenges us to account for it. Consider, as an example, an image in which a central fallen soldier is flanked by a line of mourners left and right, all facing him, symmetrically balancing each other, with the exception that the first mourner to the left has fallen to her knees and is reaching out to him. We grasp the symmetry as background, and automatically understand that whatever lies in the middle is made important by its location, since the equilibrium point is always crucial. But recognizing this symmetry entails recognizing where the symmetry breaks—in the mourner on her knees. Our attention is thereby drawn to this figure, and we are challenged to account for it.

This is a visual example of the breaking of symmetry. Let us consider a poetic example, Shakespeare's Sonnet 138:

When my love swears that she is made of truth
I do believe her, though I know she lies,
That she might think me some untutored youth,
Unlearned in the world's false subtilties.
Thus vainly thinking that she thinks me young,
Although she knows my days are past the best,
Simply I credit her false-speaking tongue;
On both sides thus is simple truth suppressed.
But wherefore says she not she is unjust?
And wherefore say not I that I am old?
O, love's best habit is in seeming trust,
And age in love loves not to have years told.
Therefore I lie with her and she with me,
And in our faults by lies we flattered be.

We understand this poem, on one level, as structured by an elaborate metaphoric symmetry. There is a symmetric opposition and reciprocity between the man and the woman and between their respective acts. Perpetually, word by word, the male opposes the female, in balance, and this opposition is mirrored in the heavy use of lexical and phonological chiasmus. Each lies with the other, each is flattered as a result, and each credits falsity. Their superficial motives for lying are the same, that is, to lead the other to love better: he desires to make her think he is young, not old, and she desires to make him think she is just, not false. Each knows the other knows ("though I know" in line 2 versus "Although she knows" in line 6). And both have as a true motive to act better at love and to have better habits in false subtleties: lines 9 and 10 ask in tandem, with symmetric reciprocity,

> But wherefore says she not she is unjust?
> And wherefore say not I that I am old?

Lines 11 and 12 answer, but with a twist: line 11 can be read as answering why *he* does not say *she* is unjust ("O love's best habit is in seeming trust"), and line 12 why *she* does not say *he* is old ("And age in love loves not to have years told"). These are not answers to the questions asked. The questions have a mirror symmetry but the answers, read this way, have a chiastic symmetry. Each lover refrains from speaking the truth about the other because the other does not want to hear it; but this does not explain why neither lover says the truth about himself.

To this point, the poem can be understood, on one level, as the construction of an exhaustive symmetry. Reciprocity, a particular kind of symmetry, is the expectation established by the poem, the major background of the poem. Stephen Booth's commentary emphasizes this: "every quality or identity the poem has or presents is fused with its opposite"; "the emphasis in line 8 is on mutuality"; "both deceive, both are deceived; both recognize all lies as lies, and believe all the lies they hear and all they tell." Booth writes of "the complementary actions announced in line 13, their presentation in urgently parallel constructions."[24]

It is just this grasping of the ways in which the poem fits the generic metaphoric projection that can lead us to notice, and in fact to emphasize, what appears to be an asymmetry in the poem: her falsity is volitional but his age is not. This key asymmetry, which we can take as being highlighted by its very embedding in an otherwise relentless balance, challenges us to account for it. One such account might be that despite his admission and analysis of deception and self-deception, despite his subtlety of mind, and despite his incisive probe into the intricacy of dissembling and bad faith, the speaker is deceiving himself, using a relentless symmetry to force himself to see the situation as balanced. He tries to achieve stasis by justifying her volitional fault with some corresponding fault in himself, to make her fault tolerable by opposing his own flaw.

Of course, our disposition to impose symmetry might lead us to a different construal. We might come to the view that although his aging is not volitional, nonetheless his engagement with her despite his age is, and that this completes the symmetry. Both of these interpretations are based upon our attempt to attribute structure to the poem through the metaphoric projection of our embodied understanding of symmetry.

Symmetry, in the wider sense used in this analysis, is ubiquitous throughout histories and cultures, and we might have taken up such symmetry in the parallelism of Hebraic writing, the symmetric arrangement of ancient Near Eastern, Presocratic, and Classical representations of the cosmos, or Anaximander's understanding of equilibrium as a consequence of symmetric arrangement, and his metaphoric conception of justice in the universe as compensatory repayment according to the assessment of time. Symmetry is the basis of the Pythagorean conception of world harmony as a balance of music made of numerical relations. Oppositional symmetry is the basis of the classical adversary system of jurisprudence, of Aristotle's conception in the *Physics* that between two opposing rectilinear movements exists a conceptual point of stasis, and of his conception in the *Ethics* that goodness of soul is equilibrium of soul and moral virtue is the tendency to choose golden means between opposing qualities.

Monuments to symmetry include the harmony of Heraclitus, the *concordia discors* of Pliny, the Platonic and Ciceronian music of the spheres, Plutarch's parallel lives, the pervasive rhetorical approach to all matters *in utramque partem*, and Leonardo da Vinci's Vitruvian man, a frontal, bilaterally symmetric figure in two positions superimposed and symmetrically balanced within a square and circle circumscribing.

But this poetic and artistic use of symmetry hardly belongs to special understanding; it belongs instead to the very core of common understanding. It is not marginal, but central. It is not a decoration, but an indispensable conceptual instrument. This common understanding, which is an unconscious, automatic, and immensely powerful component of what it means to have even the most ordinary human life, arises from two things. First, we have an embodied understanding of the symmetry of our world and our interactions within that world. This bodily experience is reflected in our gross anatomy and even in the structure of our central nervous system. Second, we share a common conceptual metaphor of wide scope, the GENERIC IS SPECIFIC conceptual metaphor. We apply the GENERIC IS SPECIFIC metaphor to our specific embodied understanding of symmetry to arrive at a generic metaphoric projection. We use that generic metaphoric projection to grasp structure in a vast range of phenomena, including poetic phenomena, many of which we would not have described colloquially as symmetric, and which often do not seem to us consciously to share any common feature.

SYMMETRY AND THE BRAIN

Here I would like to offer a speculation about the relationship between our understanding of symmetry and our brain processes. I do so in the spirit of the following passage, written by Michael Gazzaniga and Joseph LeDoux as an introduction to *The Integrated Mind*:

> In this book we are trying to illuminate the persistent and nagging questions of how mind, life, and the essence of being relate to brain mechanisms. We do that not because we have a commitment to bear witness to the boring issue of reductionism but because we want to know more about what it's all about. How, indeed, does the brain work? How does it allow us to love, hate, see, cry, suffer, and ultimately understand Kepler's laws?[25]

Although my conjecture is motivated by evidence from the neurosciences, the data needed to test it are not yet available. I have not seen the conjecture made elsewhere. It is offered, then, just as a conjecture. It is based on the fact that the right and left cerebral hemispheres can be thought of as crumpled-up rectangular sheets composed of layers of neurons, and that these two sheets are connected by commisures, the dominant one being the corpus callosum, a massive tract of nerve fibers. As Gazzinaga and LeDoux and many others report, these interhemispheric fibers largely connect homologous areas in the two half-brains, which is to say, they largely connect areas in one of the two sheets to their mirror image areas in the other sheet. Additionally, an interhemispheric nerve fiber that begins in a given layer usually terminates in the same layer on the other side, putting the layers into register.

The nature of interhemispheric transfer has been considered previously in the cognitive sciences, as in Patricia Churchland's excellent introduction, *Neurophilosophy*,[26] but the theme in these considerations has been the nature of the self and consciousness: when the corpus callosum is severed (as it is during a surgical procedure performed experimentally upon severely epileptic patients) and thereafter the two hemispheres appear to be able to operate to some extent independently and even in conflict, questions arise about our notions of a unified self with a unified consciousness.

My theme is not the self but rather the phenomenon of grasping symmetry. Let us consider how interhemispheric commisures transfer information from one half-brain to the other. As Gazzinaga and LeDoux write:

> A paleoniscid swims in its prehistoric aquarium in search of food. A suitable prey is detected in the right visual field, moving rapidly to the left. Before the primitive vertebrate can change its course, the prey crosses the visual midline and enters the left visual field. Because the optic projections of the fish are crossed, the right visual field is seen by the right eye and the left half-brain, and vice versa. Does this mean that when the prey moves out of one visual field and into the other, the neural control over the chase switches from an informed to a naive half-brain? Hardly!
>
> The commisural system (which is more accurately called a system of decussations in nonmammals) provides each half-brain with a copy of the sensory world directly observed by the other hemisphere. It is by way of this incredible feat of neural engineering that the integrated organism responds to sensory stimulation selectively channeled to one half of the brain.[27]

We now have two of the three components underlying my conjecture. The first component is the apparent symmetric projection from an array of neurons in one half-brain onto its mirror area in the other half-brain through the nerve fibers of the corpus callosum. The second is the evidence that each half-brain projects to the other a copy of the sensory world it observes. The third is that there are topographic maps in the nervous system, as Patricia Churchland explains:

> One of the most promising and puzzling discoveries about the organization of nervous systems is that many structures abide by a principle of topographic mapping, whereby neighborhood relations of cells at one periphery are preserved in the arrangement of cells at other locations in the projection system. If we think of the neurons at the sensory periphery as forming a receptor sheet, then deformed versions of that sheet are represented in a

large number of CNS [Central Nervous System] regions. Whatever the functional principle served, it must be served successfully, since wide areas of the cerebral cortex as well as other structures abound in such maps, and new research is turning up more all the time.[28]

There are topological relations (such as adjacency) in sensory sheets, and those relations are often preserved when those neurons project to a higher set of neurons. This is referred to as "topographic mapping." There are additionally topographic maps in kinesthetic and motor sheets, and there is some speculation about brain patterns that would put these topographic maps of various kinds into registration with one another.[29]

The conjecture is this. When we sense something, one half-brain projects a mirror-image copy of a pattern upon a topographic map to the other half-brain. When we focus on the midline of that image, then a half-brain has at its disposal both one-half of the image and the mirror image of the other half, and can check, through some as yet unknown mechanism, to see whether they are the same. If so, we recognize symmetry. To give a nonvisual example, suppose we feel a weight on our right palm and a weight on our left. Mirror-image symmetric copies of arrays on topographic maps are sent across the commisures, and checked for a match, to determine whether the situation is symmetric.

I conjecture further that patterns for recognizing bilateral symmetry in neural maps corresponding to one modality are connected to the correlated patterns in neural maps for the other modalities (sensory, kinesthetic, and motor), through reinforcing and excitatory connections between them. Gerald Edelman has only recently proposed a process, called reentrant mapping, by which such networked mappings from modality to modality can develop and persist.[30] The cross-modal core of this neuronal network would be, when activated (and it would almost constantly be activated, at least in part), our cross-modal sense of bilateral symmetry.

I do not know what in the brain might correspond to a generic-level metaphoric projection of this multimodal and embodied understanding of symmetry, but a guess is not out of order: the networked activity of neuronal group patterns that corresponds to our specific sense of embodied bilateral symmetry contains, inhering within it, a skeletal pattern that corresponds to the generic-level projection of symmetry. This pattern is the pattern that inheres within our understandings of other things as symmetric. An alternative, functionally equivalent hypothesis would be that the skeletal pattern corresponding to the generic-level projection of symmetry is connected in reinforcing and excitatory ways to patterns that inhere within our understandings of other things as symmetric. Generic symmetry, in this model, is not a static concept but rather an active process that we use to impart structure to aspects of our world and to invent abstract concepts. It is not something we have stored away in memory but rather something that exists only in use.

If such a generic-level projection exists at the level of neuronal group activity, then the range of phenomena discussed in this study would be explained: the projection gives us a generic concept of symmetry, which, like all concepts, is a recognition device; we use this concept to recognize and hence make intelligible a wide variety of things. To be sure, there is much in this conjecture that is fantastic, but nothing, as far as I know, that runs counter to what is known about the brain.

Symmetry seems obvious to us. We recognize it unconsciously. But the nature of that unconscious understanding is complex, complicated, and much more systematic than we might have expected. It is also firmly grounded in the most basic and universal common understanding available to human beings everywhere, at all times, in all cultures, namely, our felt, schematic, embodied understanding of bilateral symmetry in ourselves and our environment. The many moments of poetic invention that depend upon our embodied understanding of symmetry and its generic metaphoric projection might seem to us original and compelling. But they consist of small exploitations of a basic conceptual instrument so unoriginal as to belong to the unexamined floor plan of our thinking. We are struck by remarkable poetic moments, and feel the strong desire to explain them. To do so, we must discover the conceptual system that makes them possible.

Chapter 5

THE POETRY OF ARGUMENT

WE HOLD a default concept of reason. At rare moments, we may sense that this concept is inadequate to some particular bit of our experience, but that sense does not significantly interfere with the concept. Only exceptionally do we recognize that we have this concept of reason, or recognize the extent to which it grounds our mental space.

We may freely profess doubts about reason, but that is a different thing from scrutinizing our concept of reason, and altogether different from effectively changing our reliance on that concept. Our moments of doubt are unusual singularities in our otherwise comfortable dealings with this concept. Cases that stimulate this doubt seem to us special cases, singularities for which the reliable concept is less than fully adequate. Neither the unusual moment nor the unusual case threatens the substance of the concept. Neither diminishes the scope of its suffusion throughout our thinking. Neither prompts us to overhaul our effective relation to that default concept. As we discussed in the user's manual, we have needs that lead us to combat against reconsidering any such powerful and fundamental default concept. We have the cognitive need of automatic competence and the psychological need of a sense of continuity of self.

In our default concept of reason, reason has certain characteristics: it is a conscious activity; it is both a universal human activity and the highest human activity and hence defines what it means to be human; it is a disembodied activity, in the sense that our rational ability depends upon our capacity to transcend and ignore the body; it is concerned with truth; and, being concerned with truth, it is opposed to the imagination, and certainly to poetic imagination or poetic tools like metaphor; it is peculiar to human beings and a source of pride; its exercise is the definitive ingredient of law, legislation, science, and policy-making. Until recently, this view underlay the discipline of the history of ideas: to trace the products of conscious, rational thought was to trace what was distinctive about our species.[1]

The concept of rational argument is at the heart of our concept of reason. When we engage in rational argument, we say that we "reason" with each other. We argue with ourselves, internally, in this manner. Even solitary formal deduction seems to partake of the concept of argument: in formal deduction, when we ask ourselves whether a particular formal transformation is legitimate, and deliberate over that question, we argue with ourselves. We ask the question, "Is this transformation legitimate?" and try to resolve it. That questioning and those attempts to resolve the question are argument.

Let us begin to reconsider our concept of argument. The result of this reconsideration might be that our concept of rational argument would appear to be a product of poetic thought. The details of this reconsideration might imply that without metaphor, we could not have the concept of argument we have; that without a body, we could not have the concept of argument we have; and that, in particular, without a symmetric body, we could not have the concept of argument we have. This study, then, is an instrument for leading ourselves away from the default concept of reason and argument.

We are familiar with claims that rational argument can degenerate into "mere" metaphors, and we caution ourselves against weakening our arguments by basing them on metaphors and other poetic figures. Locke and Hobbes both warned against the seductions of metaphor in reasoning.[2] We all know that particular arguments use particular metaphors. Deconstructive approaches have made an industry out of locating particular metaphors in particular arguments, with the intent of showing how the metaphor undercuts the argument. But the use of particular metaphors in particular arguments is not the concern of my study.

We are also familiar with claims that there are metaphoric aspects of inference patterns in argument. Stephen Toulmin, in *The Uses of Argument*,[3] for example, noticed that certain kinds of deduction—such as the syllogistic "all A are B, all B are C, therefore all A are C"—are based metaphorically on geometric, or what I would call image-schematic, thinking: C, B, and A are concentric circles, with A contained in B and B contained in C, and therefore with A contained in C. This form of deduction arises through metaphor; its source is our knowledge of containers. Much in the spirit of Toulmin, Mark Johnson, in *The Body in the Mind*, has analyzed the metaphoric basis of various forms of deduction, such as the law of the excluded middle.[4] But the metaphoric origins of inference patterns are not the concern of my study either.

What I do wish to look at is how our very concept of argument itself, in its fundamental constitution, is metaphoric. This has consequences at many stages. The metaphoric understanding of argument guides our notion of what qualifies as a well-formed argument. It guides our notion of the stages of argument. It guides our notion of what tools of argument are available to the rhetor. It guides our notion of the circumstances surrounding argument. It guides our behavior not only in forensic but also in deliberative activity.

I begin by introducing a path-breaking essay by Otto Alvin Loeb Dieter, "Stasis," published in 1950.[5] Although a landmark, this essay is not as widely known as it deserves to be. The 1987 *Handbook of Argumenta-*

tion Theory, for example, acknowledges neither the essay nor, inexplicably, its concerns.[6] In many ways, what I wish to do here is to push further the seminal analyses Dieter offered in 1950.

The core component of our concept of argument is that an argument is constituted by a conflict of claims. Not just any two claims conflict, and given two conflicting claims it is not clear just where the argument lies. What is a claim? When do two claims conflict? What does it mean for claims to conflict? What sort of argument results from conflict? Here, I distinguish two questions. The first, prior question is, what constitutes an argument? The second, subsequent question is, how does one argue once an argument has been constituted? We will see that these two questions are related.

The study of the first question, what constitutes an argument, is, in classical and modern rhetoric, the study of στάσις, *stasis*. In classical rhetoric, an argument is said to exist when *stasis* has been shown to exist. Dieter notes that "[t]here would seem to be a sort of a tacit belief, a kind of an unexpressed understanding among those who know, that the rhetorical *stasis* is wholly unique, separate, and distinct, not related to any other thing, that it sprang full bloom from one man's mind, and that his reason for designating it *stasis* was wholly esoteric and past all finding out."[7]

Dieter points out that, on the contrary, *stasis* is a metaphoric concept, very much related to another idea, specifically to Aristotle's idea of forces. "[T]he *status* described in pseudo-Augustine's *Vorlage* is the *stasis* of Aristotelian physics and is, therefore, to be understood as a metaphoric use of a clear and precise term of physical science."[8] Dieter's article is principally a demonstration of this claim.

But there is a crucial and revealing fact about Dieter's analysis. As we will see in this study, he confuses two different things. Stasis, whether physical or metaphorical, is presented and talked about by Dieter in two different ways, and he never recognizes that he is conflating the two. Dieter sees these two characterizations as forms of the same thing. That is very revealing. It implies that these two forms are based on something prior.

That prior basis is our everyday understanding of forces. We use image-schemas to structure our understanding of forces. These everyday force-dynamic image-schemas are to be found not only in Aristotle's *Physics*, but wherever there is a human brain in a human body. As we will see, the concept of rhetorical stasis is metaphoric, and its source domain is not Aristotle's *Physics* but rather that which underlies Aristotle's *Physics*, our everyday understanding of force-dynamic image-schemas.

I begin with Dieter's analysis. Consider a physical point that begins at location A, moves rectilinearly to a point C, and then reverses its motion to return to A. This is a movement in time, and we can reproduce it for ourselves by moving our left hand in front of us from left to right and then moving our right hand back along the same line from right to left. The ending point (C) of the first movement is the starting point of the second movement, which is a counter-movement; and the ending point (A) of that counter-movement is the starting point of the initial movement. Since these are consecutive movements over time along the same line, it is difficult to represent them in a sketch, but I make an attempt:

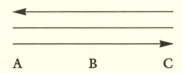

The point moves all the way from A to C. But then a contrary motion takes the point from C back to A. C, in Aristotelian physics, is called *stasis*. Let us explore what is involved in this statement. First, C is a middle. It is the middle on the total path traveled. Second, it is a point between two contraries, in a consecutive sense. The initial motion and the counter-motion are contraries, and C is the point that is obtained in between these consecutive contrary motions. Third, C is a point of singularity in the nature of the movement. Before it, the movement is to the right, but at it, the rightward movement stops and becomes a leftward movement. Fourth, and relatedly, C is a point of rest.

The concept of stasis depends upon the concept of bilateral symmetry. Stasis can only be understood by someone who already possesses the concept of bilaterally symmetric opposition along an axis. As Dieter points out, had the first movement been along a horizontal axis and the second along a vertical axis, there would have been no stasis, because horizontal and vertical are not bilaterally opposed. If the second motion had formed with the first an acute angle, then there would have been a horizontal component to the second motion, contrary to the first horizontal motion. There thus would have been bilateral opposition, allowing a point of stasis to be constituted. The concept of stasis, whether physical or metaphorical, thus depends upon the prior concept of physical bilateral symmetry.

We can see this concept of stasis in some of Dieter's language. He describes the point of stasis as resembling the point at which a piston is at "top-dead center": the point has gone all the way in one direction, and then will go back in the opposite direction.[9] Expressing stasis in terms of consecutive vertical motions instead of horizontal motions, Dieter writes,

In terms of vertical dimensions, the middle *stasis* is the point of reversal, that in which both the end of the prior upward motion and the beginning of the subsequent [downward] motion co-exist, consist, or stand still together. Between all opposite, or contrary, motions, movements, functions, or actions, there must needs always be stasis.[10]

Here, "between" is temporal: stasis occurs temporally between two *consecutive* motions in time.

Dieter quotes a passage from Cicero in which stasis is expressed metaphorically in terms of motions *consecutive* in time: "stasis . . . in quo primum insistit quasi ad repugnandum congressa defensio." Dieter comments on this passage:

> i.e., stasis is where (the place at which) the defense, set to meet the attack, first steps into the affray, so to speak, for the purpose of fighting back (or making a "retort," or staging a "come-back"). The lines of action, as here presented by Cicero, are orientated as they are in Aristotle's *Physics*: it is at [the symbol for stasis] that the prior motion comes to rest; the first speaker, i.e., the plaintiff, evidently intends his statement to be a final one, but his "rest" is immediately disturbed, for the defendant, set, as it were, to meet the attack, steps in, puts his foot down, as it were, on the same ground, and insists on using the plaintiff's resting-place as the starting place of his contrary motion.[11]

This succession of events in time actually occurs in debate: first one speaker "carries" the argument all the way to the place he seeks; then the second speaker "drives" the point all the way back to the contrary place, the one sought by the second speaker. The physical locations, A and C, are understood as contrary locations, or places, and those contrary places stand, metaphorically, for the contrary claims. C is where the first speaker wishes "to rest his case." To be at physical location C is metaphorically to have made the claim whose metaphorical location is C. But A is where the counter-speaker wishes the point "to rest." To be back at physical location A is metaphorically to have made the counter-claim, and to have driven the point all the way back to its beginning. It is important to see that in this model the place where the rhetor wishes to stand—the point he wishes to make—is not the place where he starts but is rather the place he is driving toward.

This model sees stasis in terms of consecutive contrary motions. I label it the *consecutive* model. It is one that we all possess, and it is expressed conventionally when we talk about "coming back with a counter-claim," "rebutting the charge," making a "retort," or "hurling the opposition back."

But there is a second model that Dieter uses to express the metaphoric nature of stasis, without recognizing a distinction between the two. In this model, the two contrary motions occur not *consecutively* but *simultaneously*. They run into each other, and immobilize each other, as in this sketch:

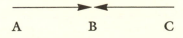

A   B   C

I label this the *simultaneous* model. In it, stasis corresponds to the point where the two contrary forces meet. Dieter expresses this simultaneous model in certain phrases, as we will see in the following passage. This passage is technical, and requires some introduction. Dieter first quotes Cicero from the *De inventione,* in a passage where Cicero is concerned with the process that gives rise to stasis. This process is called *constitutio* or *systasis.* Dieter then considers how *systasis* and *stasis* both depend upon the simultaneous model:

> "We," wrote Cicero, "call this *quaestio ex qua causa nascitur*," a "*constitutio.*" The term is clearly a Latin equivalent for the Greek *systasis* and admirably meets the requirements of the specific context in which he uses it. That a configuration of forces which might be represented graphically thus, or so, ──►◄──, should be called a *systasis*, or a *constitutio*, would seem intelligible to any educated Greek or Roman without argument. For the vectors obviously represent opposite, or contrary movements, or motions, on one and the same straight line, in head-on collision, meeting and stopping one another. Between such opposite, or contrary, *kinesis* [κίνησις], or *motus*, there must needs be stasis, or status, single in number, but dual in function, a two-in-one, or a one-in-two. The two forces involved are clearly "*hama* [ἅμα]," or "standing together" in the sense of 226b18 [of Aristotle's *Physics*]; *haptesthai* [ἅπτεσθαι], or "touching" in the sense of 226b25, i.e., "standing in contact with one another" in that their extremes are "together."[12]

Behind this thicket of technical terms and references is the simultaneous model. The characteristics of head-on collision, and of each force stopping the other, belong to the simultaneous model but not to the consecutive model. In the *consecutive* model, the first motion has exhausted its potential energy by the time it reaches the point of stasis; it has "come to rest" on its own at that point of stasis; the first motion does not stop the counter-motion; the counter-motion drives the point back after the first motion has stopped pushing it. But in the *simultaneous* model, the first motion is full of potential energy at the point of stasis, as is the second motion; they have a head-on collision and they stop each other. This is the simultaneous model, not the consecutive model.

The simultaneous model is also evident in a passage in which Dieter comments on Cicero's use of the word *constitutio* in the *De inventione.* Again, once we get past the technical terms and allusions, we can see the simultaneous model at work in certain parts:

> Here in his introduction to rhetorical analysis Cicero has incidentally also proposed a new term for general use in Latin rhetoric, i.e., *constitutio* should be used for *quaestio* in certain contexts. That this change in terminology,

however, did not imply any deviation in his theory, or basic thinking, becomes very clear from his subsequent remarks. "A constitution," he explains immediately, "is the original clash, or primary conflict of causes." Causes, according to 1013b25 [of Aristotle's *Physics*], are the origin, source, or beginning of every change and every stasis. Two causes of the same species, contrary in dynamis, are the origin, or beginning, of every natural stasis, or constitution: a cause of action and a cause of reaction, or reciprocation. The initial conflict of the causes is the constitution of the controversy. The superficial and observable moving apart or going asunder (◄——►) is the secondary phenomenon; the primary conflict with which the rhetor must concern himself first of all is the originative antagonistic standing ——►◄—— or the genetic contrariness, in the immediate, or proximate causes of the whole development: no other understanding or analysis of a controversy is adequate for rhetorical purposes; no one can argue a controversy intelligently who does not thoroughly comprehend the conflict out of which it developed. This interpretation of a *constitutio* is reiterated in I, xiii, 18: "The Question is the individual controversy which develops from the conflict in the causes, that is to say, e.g., the controversy: 'You were not justified in doing it' 'I was justified in doing it.' The conflict of the causes is that in which the *constitutio* (or the 'standing together') consists, (i.e., not the *amphisbetesis* [ἀμφισβήτησις], or the 'going apart')."[13]

The graphics Dieter uses here (——►◄——) and the phrases "originative antagonistic standing" and "standing together" express the simultaneous model.

The simultaneous model is the more common metaphoric model of stasis. In 1966, Lee S. Hultzén published a paper that not only cites Dieter, but, according to the footnotes, was read by Dieter in manuscript. Hultzén offers the simultaneous model:

> STATUS—The condition of opposition where the movement of a rhetorical procedure is brought to a stand by the confrontation of assertion with denial. The category of opposition in such a situation. As a corollary, the rhetorical procedure can resume movement toward ultimate decision only when the static impasse ceases to be, in that the efficient audience efficiently agrees with the assertion or denial, i.e., puts aside the contradictory and so resolves the opposition.[14]

Of course, we all possess the simultaneous model of argumentative conflict, and we express it conventionally when we talk of "having reached an impasse," "blunting the force of the charge," "being at a stand-off," or "having a head-on collision" with someone in an argument.

The simultaneous model has components that are absent from the consecutive model. In the simultaneous model, the opposed forces are in equilibrium, but have potential energy. If one of the two forces disappears, the other moves. If one of the forces grows weaker, it must fall back under the stronger force, which advances upon it. In the metaphoric understanding of argument, it is a metaphoric entailment that if one opponent "gives way," the other will advance. It is a metaphoric entailment that if one opponent "grows weak," he may have to "fall back" because the other opponent "puts pressure" on him.

When we talk of argument in everyday language, we mix the simultaneous and the consecutive models. Dieter does this too, using the consecutive and simultaneous models not only in different passages but even in the same passage. Earlier, we saw a passage in which Dieter used a graphic (——▶◀——) expressing the simultaneous model, and used the words "originative antagonistic standing" and "standing together," which probably express the simultaneous model. But in the same passage, Dieter uses phrases expressing the consecutive model, when he speaks of "a cause of action and a cause of reaction, or reciprocation." He thus blends the two models.

We also saw earlier a passage from Cicero in which stasis was conceived of as the point at which a prior motion comes to rest and from which it is then driven back: "the first speaker, i.e., the plaintiff, evidently intends his statement to be a final one, but his 'rest' is immediately disturbed, for the defendant, set, as it were, to meet the attack, steps in, puts his foot down, as it were, on the same ground, and insists on using the plaintiff's resting-place as the starting place of his contrary motion." This is the consecutive model of stasis. In the immediately subsequent sentence, Dieter, again with a wealth of allusions, uses the simultaneous model of stasis:

> Like the two brothers mentioned by Aristotle (1167a22, cf. Euripides, *Phoenissae*, 588), plaintiff and defendant both insist on having one and the same thing, each for his own purpose, both desire "to have things their own way," to rule, to dominate, to be supreme, and consequently, they *stasiazein*, or make stasis with one another, i.e., block one another.[15]

Here, Dieter has switched to the simultaneous model. The characteristic of "blocking one another" belongs not to the consecutive model, but to the simultaneous model. We can see this as follows. In the consecutive model, the stasis point is C. The first speaker does not want to go any further than C. He has reached his point. He is not blocked. "Blocked" implies that he has not yet reached his point. It is only in the simultaneous model that the first speaker, or the first motion, has not reached his point, C, and can be said therefore to be blocked.

Dieter reveals his confusion of the two models when he presents a diagram of Cicero's concept of stasis. The diagram works from bottom to top, beginning at 1 and ending at 6:[16]

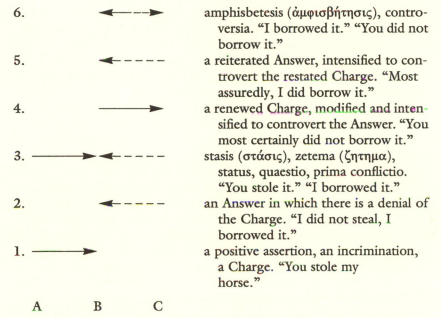

6.   amphisbetesis (ἀμφισβήτησις), controversia. "I borrowed it." "You did not borrow it."

5.   a reiterated Answer, intensified to controvert the restated Charge. "Most assuredly, I did borrow it."

4.   a renewed Charge, modified and intensified to controvert the Answer. "You most certainly did not borrow it."

3.   stasis (στάσις), zetema (ζήτημα), status, quaestio, prima conflictio. "You stole it." "I borrowed it."

2.   an Answer in which there is a denial of the Charge. "I did not steal, I borrowed it."

1.   a positive assertion, an incrimination, a Charge. "You stole my horse."

A   B   C

I have added to this diagram only the markers for points "A," "B," and "C." Let us now look carefully at stages 1, 2, and 3. Under the consecutive model, the point where the first movement ends should be the point where the second movement begins, and the point where the second movement ends should be the point where the first movement began. But if 3 is the combination of 1 and 2, then the points do not fall where they should fall according to the consecutive model. 1 should end at C, but ends at B. 2 should end at A, but ends at B. The picture in 3 is a representation of the consecutive model as equivalent to the simultaneous model.

It is easy to see why Dieter conflates the consecutive physical event with the simultaneous physical event. Earlier, we moved our left hand to the right and then moved our right hand to the left along the same line. That was a consecutive model. If we make those two motions simultaneously, the two hands run into each other in the middle, and immobilize each other. They put pressure on each other. If one force grows weak, it falls back, and gives way as the other advances. This is the simultaneous model.

Each of the two models of stasis contains a concept of a stasis point, and these two concepts of the stasis point, although not identical, cohere in crucial ways, making it easy to think of these two concepts as equivalent. Both points are middles: stasis in the consecutive model is the middle of the entire out-and-back reciprocating movement of the initial point; stasis in the simultaneous model is the middle of the line segment between the two extremes. Both are between contraries: the consecutive stasis lies temporally between two consecutive contrary motions in time; the simultaneous stasis lies spatially between the contrary polar opposites of the line segment. Both are points of singularity in the nature of the movement: in the consecutive model, stasis is where the first motion to the right stops and becomes a leftward movement; in the simultaneous model, stasis is where the character of both forces changes from advance to arrest. Finally, both are points of rest: in the consecutive model, stasis is the location where the moving point would stand at rest if not impinged upon by the second force; in the simultaneous model, stasis is where both forces are arrested, stopped.

These two models share a prior basis. They are coherently structured by our prior understanding of force dynamics, and in particular the force dynamics of a bilaterally symmetric human body. Mapping the domain of force dynamics metaphorically onto the domain of propositions creates this concept of rhetorical stasis, and hence our concept of argument.

There is in fact a third way in which force dynamics structures our concept of argument. It is not discussed by Dieter, but fits deliberative rhetoric, coheres with both the simultaneous and consecutive models, and is conventionally expressed in our language. To introduce this third way, I must return to the observation that in the metaphor of stasis, propositions correspond metaphorically to places. Propositions are located metaphorically on a surface like the earth's surface. Contrary propositions are located in contrary places on this surface. Someone who tries to move an opponent to the proposition he prefers can be viewed, as in the first two models, as trying to push the opponent to that place. But equivalently—and this gives us the third way—he can be seen as trying to pull the opponent to that place. In this model, the rhetor is already at his preferred place, pulling toward it, rather than distant from the place, pushing toward it. Rhetoric does not favor this model, since it wishes to see the rhetor standing firmly on his proposition only once he has won his case, not before. Still, there are moments when rhetoricians use this third model. Arne Naess, for example, characterizes the pro-aut-contra survey of arguments for and against the opinion as a "tug of war," which uses the model of pulling rather than the model of pushing.[17]

So far, we have seen ways in which the central component of our concept of argument, *stasis*, is metaphoric. The source of the metaphor is the domain of forces. The target of the metaphor is the concept of argument. Physical locations on the surface in the source correspond to intellectual propositions in the target. Being at a location on the surface corresponds to establishing the proposition. Spatially contrary locations correspond to intellectually contrary propositions. Contrary physical forces correspond to attempts to establish contrary intellectual propositions. The success of one contrary force over another, which drives the "point of contention" to a certain location, corresponds to establishing one of two contrary intellectual propositions and defeating the other.

Now let us consider how this metaphoric model provides us not only with the central concept of stasis, but also with other associated components in our larger model of argument.

The condition achieved in the two models of opposition is stasis. The process of achieving this condition is called by classical rhetoricians *systasis*, a word we have already encountered in a passage from Cicero. The consecutive model of stasis and the simultaneous model of stasis are models not only of a condition achieved, but also of the process of achieving that condition, namely, *systasis*. Dieter recognizes that the model of stasis is also a model of *systasis*. He draws the point very clearly, immediately subsequent to the passage we saw earlier, in which he discusses Cicero's concept of *constitutio*:

> [T]he vectors obviously represent opposite, or contrary movements. . . . Clearly, then, this is not only a *stasis*, or a *status*, but also a *systasis* and a *constitutio*, i.e., a constitution in the sense of the formative, or generative action or process of constituting, as well as in the sense of the composite substance, or corporate being, concrete of matter and form, thereby constituted, made to consist, or brought into existence. That this terminology was well suited for use in context with generation and genesis may likewise easily be demonstrated.[18]

The force-dynamic metaphor gives us our conception of both stasis and *systasis*. But that is just the beginning of what it gives to our default concept of argument. It is part of the source domain of conflicting forces that they occur upon a surface like the surface of the earth. This surface is the source of another part of our concept of argument, namely, the concept of *common ground*. An argument can be constituted only if there is some common ground that contains the two contrary propositions. If there is no ground for physical forces to meet upon, then they cannot meet, and therefore cannot achieve stasis. Metaphorically, if there is no common intellectual ground, then the two contrary assertions cannot meet; they therefore cannot achieve stasis; they therefore by definition cannot constitute an argument. In the absence of common ground, there may be plenty of squabbling and accusation, but there will be no constitution of a legitimate argument.

Arguments come in different kinds, and with different sorts of circumstances. These kinds and circumstances are understood in the classical metaphor in terms of the kind of ground upon which stasis is constituted, and upon the nature of the environment. As Dieter writes,

> Just as every kinesis is a motion of a specific thing so every stasis is an individual event, a real occurrence involving specific things, surrounded and sup-

ported by specific things which collectively are referred to as its *peristasis* and individually are designated as its *peristaseis*, or circumstances. The things which surround, envelop, or are involved in the opposite, or contrary movements are the things likewise which are involved in the intervening stasis. Any doctrine, theory, or system of rhetorical *amphisbeteseis* or *staseis* must therefore take its beginning from and be founded in the *peristaseis*.[19]

Every individual argument will have its own individual set of circumstances. There are, however, four major types of circumstances in classical rhetoric. They are the four major grounds upon which stasis can be constituted. One sort of ground concerns Fact or Being or Existence or Conjecture (*an sit*), as in the opposed claims, "You injured me!" versus "I didn't do anything!" The second ground concerns Definition (*quid sit*), as in the opposed claims, "You injured me!" versus "What I did does not count as an injury!" This is the ground of interpretation, including legal interpretation of a statute and literary interpretation of a text. It is sometimes called the "legal" ground. The third ground concerns Quality (*quale sit*), as in the opposed claims, "You injured me!" versus "And a good thing too, since I did it to stop you from committing treason!" This is a ground of right versus wrong, and is sometimes called the "juridical" ground. The fourth and last ground concerns Objection, as in the opposing claims, "You injured me!" versus "This court is not the appropriate place to consider such a charge!" This ground is sometimes omitted in classical treatments of grounds.[20]

Let us turn now to another part of our concept of argument that derives from this force-dynamic metaphor. Two forces can achieve stasis, but they can also also fail to achieve stasis. Just as the metaphor gives us a way to understand how stasis can be achieved, so it gives us a way to understand how stasis can fail to be achieved. Two forces that achieve stasis are called *stasiastic*. Two forces that fail to achieve stasis are called *astasiastic* or *astatic*, and are of two kinds. The first kind of *astasiastic* forces are the *synestotic*. Synestotic claims are those that reinforce, complement, or continue each other. They are understood metaphorically as two parallel forces. Parallel forces do not achieve stasis. The second kind of astasiastic forces are the *asystatic*. Asystatic claims are those that do not constitute an argument because there is some deficiency in the claims or the context. Metaphorically, they are understood in terms of deficient motions. For example, an environment can be inadequate as a medium for motion because it is nonexistent or partly nonexistent. Metaphorically, a ground can be inadequate to permit the constituting of an argument because it is partly unknown or in some way intellectually deficient. Adequate motion cannot exist in inadequate circumstances or in an inadequate medium; metaphorically, claims adequate to constitute an argument cannot exist in an inadequate topography of knowledge or in other inadequate circumstances.

There are other ways in which two claims can be asystatic, and all are understood through the same metaphor. Suppose two opponents direct the same charge at each other, in such a way that anything said by one may be equally said by the other. Then these two "movements" are too "like" to constitute stasis: it is said that there are only ostensibly two movements, that they can be seen under analysis to be one movement; consequently, they do not constitute stasis. Or suppose that the peristasis is such that all the possible arguments belong to one side. Then only one movement exists; the second, counter-movement cannot happen. Therefore, no stasis. Lastly, a conflict may be asystatic because it is internally conflicted; such an internal conflict is also understood in terms of the force-dynamic metaphor: "Critical analysis of a matter of this kind reveals an *aporon*, i.e., an aporia. The movements in a matter such as this are so indistinct, unstable, fluctuating, and confusing that it is impossible for any one to find a logical way through it."[21] Aporia is the unexpected failure of the usually successful projection of force-dynamic knowledge onto argument. As such, individual aporias and the general rhetorical concept of aporia are grounded in stable patterns that give them, by contrast, their existence.

It is important to see that in these situations the force-dynamic metaphor provides the rhetor with the principal mental instrument he is to use in trying to understand any sort of rational encounter. The metaphor gives the strategy for *Noesis*, which is cogitation or how to think about the encounter. In trying to understand the nature and category of the rational encounter, the rhetor is to try to locate metaphorical forces, to determine whether they are "contrary," to determine whether the forces are "in the same direction," to determine whether they are "stable," and so on. The rhetor is to map from the domain of force dynamics onto the domain of rational proposition. A particular image-schematic structure of forces will be mapped onto the rational propositions that the rhetor is considering. Knowing which particular image-schematic structure can be mapped metaphorically just is knowing the nature of the argument; in particular, it is knowing whether one is dealing with a constituted argument, what sort of argument has been constituted if one has been constituted, and how the argument fails to be constituted if it fails.

As a corollary, this metaphor gives the rhetor a strategy for constituting the argument to his best advantage. If the rhetor wishes to constitute the argument upon a particular ground, he must find a way to map onto the conflicting propositions an appropriate force-dynamic conflict of the preferred sort. If the rhetor fails to do this, he will not be allowed to conduct his argument upon that preferred ground. If his opponent succeeds in mapping onto the propositions a force-dynamic conflict of the sort the opponent prefers, then the opponent will be allowed to conduct the argument upon the opponent's preferred ground.

So far, we have put into place two parts of the metaphoric concept of argument. The first part is that propositions are places in an intellectual topography. This first part contains the further detail that contrary propositions are contrary places and that the common ground of two contrary propositions is the ground that contains both. The second part is that an assertion of a proposition is a force directed toward the place of that proposition. This second part contains the further detail that contrary assertions are contrary rectilinear forces; that an argument is constituted by the impasse created when these two forces meet head-on; and that the midpoint between the two contrary extremes corresponds to the question of the argument. For example, when one proposition, "You committed an immoral act!" is met with the contrary proposition, "I did not commit that act!" then the stasiastic midpoint corresponds to the question of the argument, "Did the defendant commit this act?" This is a stasis of conjecture. Similarly, when the proposition "You committed an immoral act!" is met with the contrary proposition "It was not immoral!" then the stasiastic midpoint corresponds to the question of the argument, "Was this act immoral?" This is a different stasis, one of definition.

A little more metaphoric work gives us some other parts of our extended concept of argument in addition to the two parts just summarized. In our common experience, force is often exerted by agents, and in particular, by human beings. If we add to the metaphor already in place the additional information that these forces in argument are exerted by intentional agents, then the conflict is not merely between forces, but between agents who intend to exert force, who do so, who understand the nature of forces, and who have an interest in succeeding. This gives us the common metaphor that RATIONAL ARGUMENT IS COMBAT BETWEEN INTENTIONAL AGENTS.[22] In actual combat, much depends upon the ground chosen, and actual combatants jockey for ground, trying to gain advantage by determining the ground upon which the conflict will occur. In metaphorical combat, which is to say argument, combatants try to pick the metaphorical ground upon which the metaphorical stasis will be constituted, because particular grounds give them particular sorts of advantage and disadvantage. Classical rhetorical theory lays this metaphor out explicitly and in conscious detail, as David Goodwin notes:

> The place where [the combatants] meet provides the terrain, and consequently, many of the argumentative options open to the disputants. The terrain dictates, for instance, who has the high ground (namely, presumption), and what manoeuvers are most likely to work against the opponent. Obviously, from the defender's position, establishing that no crime oc-

curred or that he was elsewhere at the time provides a better defense than conceding everything and then arguing from mitigating circumstances. If possible, then, stopping the attacker on the beaches—in this case, on the issue of Conjecture—opens up strategic possibilities not available once the argument shifts to other grounds.[23]

So far, we have considered how metaphor provides us with our concept of the topography of propositions, the constitution of argument upon that topography, the processes by which an argument comes to be constituted or fails to be constituted, the nature or ground of the argument, the opportunities available to human beings engaged in argument, and the strategies available to human beings engaged in argument.

Now let us consider how the metaphor provides us with our concept of how an argument proceeds. Constituting an argument is different from conducting an argument. Dieter is quite clear in saying that the metaphor provides us not merely with an understanding of the concept of argument or an understanding of the structure of a particular stasis, but also with a concept of how in performance to conduct an argument:

> Hermagoras represented stasis as that which in rhetoric performs a most important function, i.e., as that which serves as the guiding principle of both rhetorical Noesis and Poiesis. In rhetorical analysis [Noesis], the subject matter is intellectually laid hold upon, or "grasped" and investigated logically with reference to its stasis, i.e., to determine whether it be asystatic, synestotic, or stasiastic, and if stastic, what type of stasis it exhibits. In Speechmaking [Poiesis], the stasis is rhetorically "handled," "managed," or treated in two speeches: opposing rhetors present to a third party as the judge both a *synechon* and an *aition*, i.e., an argument why the stasis should be maintained and established permanently as well as a reason why it ought to be resolved in a contrary motion. Both speakers strengthen their causes with proofs drawn from the special *topoi* which rhetoric has devised for their use. The judge considers the stasis in the light of both the *synechon* and the *aition*, i.e., he weighs the *krinomenon*, or the thing to be judged, and in accordance with his verdict, reached with the cooperation of the rhetors, will be the final disposition, conclusion, end, or settlement of the stasis (Cf. *diatithesthai*, Sextus Empiricus, *Against the Rhetoricians* II, 62). Hence, it was from actual rhetorical practice that Hermagoras derived his functional description of stasis (Quintilian, III, vi, 21, and *Rhetores Graeci*, vii, 173 and v. 78, 10) as that (1) with reference to which a subject matter is investigated and analyzed in Noesis, and (2) that with reference to which (in Poiesis) both speakers must present arguments in their speeches.[24]

The first part of an argument is to constitute it; the second part is to conduct it successfully to an end. To succeed in conducting an argument is metaphorically to move from stasis to the place corresponding to the proposition one prefers. In the source domain, such movement is accomplished either through strengthening the force on one side, or weakening the force on the other, or both. We project this metaphorically onto the domain of argument: we understand evidence for one side as "strengthening" its vector according to the persuasiveness of the evidence, and evidence against the other side as "weakening" the other side according to the persuasiveness of the negative evidence. We try to make opposing evidence look "weaker" and make our own evidence look "stronger."

During combat on a certain ground, when one side is losing, the losing side may redirect the opponent in an attempt to shift to different ground, so as to gain advantage. Metaphorically, the losing side may attempt to move to another ground so as to reconstitute the argument and thereby to gain advantage.

These are the limits of the classical analysis of the concept of argument in terms of the force-dynamic metaphor. But modern theorists who have considered the theory of stasis and argument have added to it. Here we will see that what they have done, rather than offering a different concept of argument, extends the metaphoric concept of argument.

In considering the utility of stasis theory for modern rhetoric, various theorists have commented upon the inadequacy of the classical taxonomy of grounds. Jeanne Fahnestock and Marie Secor, for example, have proposed that a modern theory of stasis would have—in addition to the classical grounds of Conjecture, Definition, Quality, and Objection—a major stasis for questions of Causal Agency. "We suggest elevating to the level of stasis a question that classical rhetoricians did not ignore, though they did not single it out for the overwhelming importance it has acquired since the age of Newton: the question 'What caused it?' "[25] Fahnestock and Secor's proposal preserves and depends upon the metaphoric understanding of stasis as an impasse between contrary forces, and suggests that when such an impasse occurs upon the ground of causal agency, the impasse should qualify as a stasis of the same rank as stasis on the classical grounds of Conjecture or Existence, Definition, Quality, and Objection. Certainly Hart and Honoré's work on *Causation in the Law* would support Fahnestock and Secor's claim.[26] Fahnestock and Secor further show some complicated ways in which stasis can be recursive—so that one stasis can give rise to another stasis—and show the ways in which one stasis can entail, by virtue of hierarchy, another stasis.[27]

Lee Hultzén has offered another proposal for adding new grounds to the theory of stasis provided by this metaphor.[28] Forensic rhetoric concerns adjudication. Deliberative rhetoric concerns what we might call the setting of policy, the making of choices between alternatives. Hultzén argues that the classical grounds of Conjecture, Definition, Quality, and Objection are complete for forensic but not for deliberative, and offers four new grounds for deliberative: Malum or Ill ("Is there this ill in the present state of affairs?"), Sanabilitas or Reformability ("Is this ill curable, caused by a reformable condition?"), Remedium or Remedy ("Will the proposed remedy actually cure us of this ill?"), and Pretium or Cost ("Will the cure cost too much?"). Hultzén argues that the classical questions of Conjecture, Definition, and Quality apply to each of these four new grounds, thereby producing twelve types of stasis for deliberative.

In 1958, Chaim Perelman and Lucie Olbrechts-Tyteca, in their landmark work *La Nouvelle Rhétorique*, observed that in some cases, the ground of the stasis virtually determines the future of the argument. They give a demonstration in which a Romanticist confronts a Classicist in an effort to determine upon whose ground the argument will be constituted.[29] David Goodwin has built upon this work to argue that modern rhetoric must reconsider the classical geography of stasiastic places:

> [W]hile we might retain the concept of argument as motion, we could not, at the same time, transpose the classical geography of stasiastic places or grounds on to the map of contemporary rhetorical theory. . . . When Classicist argues with Romanticist, or Hegelian with Marxist, the issue to be resolved is, on whose grounds will the conflict rest? The decision in such a case is all: establishing whose set of categories, arranged in which order, will in turn determine the nature and resolution of the conflict at hand. Contemporary argumentation, then, makes stasis itself the object of debate. . . . The first, most important, and comprehensive grounds on which modern argument rests is not Conjecture, as in classical theory, but on whether the debate can be relocated or transferred (*translatio* is another classical term for *metalepsis*) to a different jurisdiction, system of rules and values, or procedural context, one more favourable to the case or more unfavourable to the claims of the opponent.[30]

Goodwin considers the strategies available to a rhetor for reconfiguring his opponent's argument to his own advantage by shifting the ground. Both Chaim Perelman and Kenneth Burke, he notes, have offered models of argument suitable for analyzing meta-stasis.

These models are extensions of the same metaphor with which we have been dealing. Perelman points out that conflict arises not only between points contained in a common ground, but also between different grounds, different general places, different *loci*. "[T]o the classical *locus* of the superiority of the lasting, one may oppose the romantic *locus* of the superiority of that which is precarious and fleeting."[31] For example, there is a stasis between the propositions "X is superior to Y!" and "No, it is not!" but this conflict can occur in either the classical locus of the superiority of the lasting or the romantic locus of the superiority of that which is precarious and fleeting. Opponents in this argument try to drive each other first to the preferred ground, and then to the preferred place within the preferred ground.

Burke's model is subtle but similar. For Burke, there are twenty different types of ground. In any issue, there are five elements: scene, act, agent, purpose, and agency. Choosing all possible pairs of these terms produces twenty dyadic ratios (such as agent-purpose), each with its own priorities.[32] Any conflict can be considered according to the characteristic orientation or bias of any of these twenty ratios. Applying the ratio to any conflict reconfigures it upon a different ground. Just as opponents in Perelman's different loci cannot constitute an argument, so opponents inhabiting different dyadic ratios cannot constitute an argument. They can, however, be belligerent in ways that do not technically constitute argument. Goodwin writes, "As Burke points out, much philosophic warfare, if not actual war, occurs because one ratio remakes the whole world in its image, blind to the existence and claims of other ratios."

Let us step back for a moment for a panoramic view. We began with a metaphor in which argument is understood as the conflict of bilaterally opposed forces, and showed that if we add to this metaphor the information that the forces are exerted by intentional agents, the result is the basic metaphor RATIONAL ARGUMENT IS COMBAT BETWEEN INTENTIONAL AGENTS.

That is the bottom-up view. Now consider the top-down view. There is a very large, very general, and very productive metaphor, THE MIND IS A BODY MOVING IN SPACE, studied by Eve Sweetser.[33] This metaphor shares much with the force-dynamic metaphor for argument: there is a space that contains a surface; the surface corresponds metaphorically to an intellectual topography; locations on the surface correspond to propositions; movement occurs in this space.

THE MIND IS A BODY MOVING IN SPACE contains yet further information. The mind and its thinking are understood metaphorically as a sentient human being moving within this space, over this intellectual topography. It is quite possible for there to be only one agent in this metaphor, as in "My mind is wandering."

THE MIND IS A BODY MOVING IN SPACE gives us a general metaphorical understanding of thinking and the thinker: the thinker is an agent moving over an intellectual topography, from point to point, taking in the view, considering different locations, trying to see how to get from one location to another. This metaphor does not require the presence of an adversary.

Consider the proverb, "Vanity is the quicksand of reason." Our understanding of this proverb relies upon our knowledge that THE MIND IS A BODY MOVING IN SPACE. Here, reason is personified as an agent moving over a terrain. Progress in thought is understood metaphorically as distance traveled over that terrain. Lack of progress in thought corresponds metaphorically to "getting stuck." In the source domain, one of the things that can immobilize the traveler is quicksand. In the target domain, vanity is understood metaphorically as quicksand, as something that can immobilize reason. This understanding does not require a personified adversary. It requires the concept of a journey, but not the concept of combat.

When Stephen Toulmin considers argument in *The Uses of Argument*, he is principally concerned with the process of conducting an argument, which is to say, with how a rhetor argues toward his proposition after stasis has been achieved. The model he offers of making arguments is an extension of the metaphor THE MIND IS A BODY MOVING IN SPACE. Toulmin describes an argument as a *movement from* accepted data *through* a warrant *to* a claim. Data, according to Toulmin, are what you have *to go on*. The claim is *where you are going*. The warrant provides *how to get there*. Indeed, the warrant is that part of an argument that authorizes the mental *leap* involved in *advancing from* data *to* claim. The job of the warrant is to *carry* the data *to* the claim.

If we now add to the metaphor that THE MIND IS A BODY MOVING IN SPACE certain special information, we get a special case. Let us add that there are two human beings in this space, not just one, and that each wishes to drive the other to a contrary location. Then the result is RATIONAL ARGUMENT IS COMBAT.

RATIONAL ARGUMENT IS COMBAT is not the only instantiation of THE MIND IS A BODY MOVING IN SPACE, and thus not the only concept of argument available under THE MIND IS A BODY MOVING IN SPACE. There are many things that can happen when two agents moving contrarily in space encounter one another and bring each other to a stop. One of the things that can happen is combat. But persuasion is also a possibility. Instead of killing one's opponent, one might persuade one's opponent. Instead of viewing one's opponent as an enemy, one might view one's opponent as a potential ally. There is yet another choice that declines combat in favor of courtship. Here, we move away from the concept of argument used in classical rhetoric. We retain all of the metaphoric understanding of argument as a force-dynamic event, but we decline to understand the two opposed forces as combatants. As Goodwin notes, it is this alternative understanding of argument that Burke seems to have offered: "Ideally, the rhetorical understanding offered by a new stasis theory will court us with the promise of profound co-operation, persuading us by example to abandon negative for positive closure and the rituals of killing for the rituals of courtship."[34]

We began this study with Dieter's observation that theoreticians considered stasis as if it were an autonomous concept, born from one man's mind, and related to nothing else. We followed Dieter to see that stasis is a metaphoric concept, a case where argument is understood in terms of motion, or at least in terms of a model of motion in Aristotle's *Physics*. We then noted that Dieter, and others, conflated two different models of stasis without recognizing the conflation. We found the reason for Dieter's conflation: there is something much more fundamental upon which the concept of stasis is based, namely, our everyday understanding of force dynamics. We then explored the way force dynamics structures our concept of argument in many of its components, including stasis, the process of achieving or failing to achieve stasis, and the process of conducting an argument. We then saw that this force-dynamic understanding of argument was part of the metaphor RATIONAL ARGUMENT IS COMBAT, which is a special case of the larger, much more flexible, and much more productive metaphor THE MIND IS A BODY MOVING IN SPACE. So we have gone from viewing our concept of argument as autonomous to viewing it as coherent with our most common metaphoric view of the mind in all its operation. Our embodied knowledge of force dynamics and stasis is the basis for both the concept of stasis in physics and the concept of stasis in argument.

The systematicity of these connections is larger still. I will only mention very briefly the smallest bit of this systematicity. Len Talmy has shown that force dynamics underlies our understanding of certain causal constructions in language; of grammatical classes such as conjunctions, prepositions, and the modal system; and of lexical systems relating to physical, psychological, and social events.[35] Susan Kline has argued that the same model that gives us classical staseis in argument gives us our concept of conditions on speech-acts.[36] George Lakoff and Mark Turner, among others, have considered the understanding of social and psychological situations in terms of force dynamics.[37] Mark Johnson has considered extensively the force-dynamic basis of logic.[38] Eve Sweetser, in her book-length examination of the role of THE MIND IS A BODY in semantic structure and semantic change, has argued that this metaphor underlies our understanding of conjunctions, modals, speech-acts, logical necessity, conditionals, and reasoning. As Sweetser writes, the reasoning process is understood metaphorically "as following *a spatially linear trajectory sequentially moving from one point to another.*"[39]

I will not consider these demonstrations of the conceptual systematicity in which our metaphoric concept of argument participates. Instead, I will look at a connection that is much more speculative and tenuous than any of those I pass over. I want to consider this connection because of its relation to the concept of stasis in the history of rhetorical thought and in legal practice. Borrowing from Steven Winter, I will consider the concept of *standing* in the law. To have *standing* means, very roughly, that one has the right to invoke the authority of a court in judging a case. If you do not have standing, you cannot get a hearing. As Winter has shown in "The Metaphor of Standing and the Problem of Self-Governance" in the 1988 *Stanford Law Review*, the concept of standing is amorphous. He has also shown that it is metaphoric.

Stasis is not standing, of course. Stasis can be constituted in all sorts of arguments that will never be heard by a court ("You don't love me!" versus "Yes I do!"). But there appears to be a force-dynamic structure that is shared by both the concept of stasis and the concept of the events surrounding standing. This force-dynamic structure is exactly the one noted by Dieter, which will bring us back to the starting point of this study.

Winter observes that "It is generally accepted black letter law that the 'case or controversy' requirement of article III means that a party who invokes the court's authority must show personal injury or 'injury-in-fact.'"[40] But what is the legal concept of an injury? Once an injury has been established, what is the legal concept of legal redress? Winter observes that, in the private rights model of injury and redress, both the injury and the redress involve paths in a space. The injury consists of the injured party's having been *moved* from *his original position* to a *new position*, one of injury. Redress consists of the court's attempting "to put the plaintiff *back in the position he occupied*" (or as *near* as possible) before the occurrence of the legal wrong.[41] This is strongly coherent with the model of stasis. In stasis, the metaphorical ground over which movement occurs is the intellectual topography of propositions. In the private rights model of injury, the metaphorical ground is different: it is the topography of conditions in the private individual's life. But in both concepts, there is a motion and a counter-motion. In stasis, the first motion is the charge and the second motion is the rejection of the charge. In the private rights model of injury, the first motion is the injury and the second motion is the legal redress that attempts to "restore" the injured party to the previous condition or to a condition metaphorically "near" it.

Let us consider in more detail the relationship between the *injury* that creates standing and the *charge* that is the first force involved in the consecutive model of stasis. A charge is often understood as a burden, and there are many uses of the word "charge" that indicate metaphorical burdens. But a charge is also, in combat, a force that displaces its object. A charge laid against us in law or in argument can be thought of as a displacing force, against which we must fight to regain ground. And an injury can be thought of as a displacing force. There is a coherence here between three things: the military charge that drives us away from a preferred location, the argumentative charge that moves us off our preferred proposition, and the injury that moves us from an original position to a worse position.

The responses to these charges are also coherent. Militarily, we attempt to move the opponent back. Rhetorically, we attempt to drive the opponent back so that we can stand upon the point we prefer. Legally, we ask the court to redress the injury by moving us back to our original condition. In all these cases, the understanding is structured by the same force-dynamic image-schema. That force-dynamic image-schema is symmetric in consisting of action and symmetric reaction.[42] In the military domain, the force-dynamic image-schema is not metaphoric. In the rhetorical and legal situation, the force-dynamic image-schema is projected metaphorically.

We began this investigation with Dieter's observation that prior theorists had viewed our concept of argument as founded on exactly nothing. Stasis, in the view of these theorists, was an autonomous module, a windowless monad, an idiosyncratic notion that gained some currency in the dry and academic world of rhetorical studies. By now, we have seen that our concept of argument is so deeply grounded in poetic thought and the body, and that its many possible exfoliations are so thoroughly motivated and supported by the rest of our conceptual apparatus, that it may indeed, as many have thought, stand as a marker of that which is human, although not in the positivist way it has usually been presented.

By virtue of the body, the brain has an understanding of force-dynamic image-schemas. Our bilaterally symmetric body makes it particularly easy for us to understand oppositional forces, equilibrium between them, and the consequences of strengthening or weakening a force. We can project this knowledge metaphorically onto the domain of propositions, giving us a metaphoric default concept of rational argument as the conflict of two bilaterally opposed forces situated in certain ways in the space of propositions. A common extension of this force-dynamic metaphor is RATIONAL ARGUMENT IS COMBAT, which is an instantiation, but only one, of the much more flexible and productive metaphor THE MIND IS A BODY MOVING IN SPACE.

Our default concept of rational argument, which is at the heart of our default concept of reason, is thus not isolated. It is not disembodied, or principally conscious. Rather than opposed to the body and poetic thought, it is their product, and shares this derivation with many of the strongest and most universal parts of our thinking. Far from belonging to any specialized endeavor or academic discipline, it is an inherent part of the rhetoric of everyday life.

Chapter 6

CONCEPTUAL CONNECTIONS

SOME CONNECTIONS seem real: the sun is a star. They are called true and are taken to constitute categories.

Some connections seem fanciful: the sun is a jewel. They are called poetic, imaginative, or heuristic, and are taken to have nothing to do with real categories.

We tend to think of categories as fixed. Whether we imagine our mental categories as mirror copies of categories supposedly existing in a real objective world or as mental constructs that help us make sense of our world, we tend to think of them as inviolable, and of a connection as true when it is part of the structure of these immutable categories. Fanciful, poetic, imaginative, heuristic connections, so the logic goes, have nothing to do with true categories: they lie outside this fixed structure of categories, opposed to it, false.

I would like to propose that we reexamine these notions. It may seem perverse to ask for such a reassessment. What is there to reconsider? What could be wrong? The answer is almost everything. In this study, I will argue that there is a continuum between category connections and imaginative connections, not a distinction in kind. Our view of category connections as primary and imaginative connections as parasitic is backward: it is the imaginative mappings that are primary; these imaginative mappings create category structures; such structures can become entrenched so that the imaginative mappings are no longer perceptible to consciousness. Our seemingly fixed category structures are actually highly entrenched structures of an imaginative sort. Our conceptual system is structured by links that may be more or less fluid or more or less entrenched but that are not distinguished as real versus fanciful.

To start this reexamination, I need a blanket term to cover all cases in which we understand one concept in terms of another concept, to any degree or by any process. I will adopt the term "analogy" to refer to such cases generally. Analogy thus includes metaphor. We tend to think of analogical connections as being opposed to categorical connections: for example, the analogical connections between electricity and water or between a journey and a life seem to us conjured or even whimsical, without legitimate claim on our category structures. I will argue that, on the contrary, categorical and analogical connections are not orthogonal to each other, but are more like flip sides of a coin, interdependent upon each other.

Why do we categorize? If we responded to each thing in the world as being unique, we would be swamped by the variety in our world. Perceiving difference takes conceptual work: evolutionarily, there is no genetic pay-off in perceiving difference except where it increases fitness. To operate efficiently, we categorize. Our categories cut up our worlds into clusters, so we can deal with clusters instead of elements. The fitness of our cognition depends upon the fitness of these conceptual cuts. Accordingly, evolutionary forces and cultural forces cooperate to develop fit mental systems of categories.[1]

A culture's category structures highlight certain connections between concepts and mask possible alternative connections. Analogies exist to unmask, capture, or invent connections absent from or upstaged by our category structures. For example, the expression "Language is a virus" asks us to entertain a range of conceptual connections that are not part of our category structures. To recognize a statement as an analogy is to recognize that it is in some way putting pressure on our category structures. Therefore, the act of recognizing analogy depends upon the details of our category structures. Principles of recognizing a statement as an analogy are influenced by and reflect principles of categorization.

When we attempt to interpret a statement like "Beauty is Truth," we do so by taking it as a request that we seek and find, or even create, a conceptual connection between the equated concepts. How do we recognize which of these equations are analogies? Technically, how do we decide unconsciously and automatically to try to take a particular equation as expressing analogical connection rather than category connection ("John is a man") or some other variety of conceptual connection? I will argue that how we approach the equation depends on where the two equated concepts are located within our category structures. It is in general false that we recognize analogy by first recognizing categorization, then rejecting the categorization as false, and then doing secondary reconstructive work. On the contrary, under certain conditions we prefer to recognize analogy first, as in "A child is a mirror" or "Language is a virus."

The (mistaken) notion that categorical connections differ in kind from analogical connections seems to derive from the notion that the members of a category (like *tree*) all possess criterial features that define the category. For example, trees all have branches, all flower in the spring, all have vertical trunks, and so on. The common possession of such criterial features just is, so the logic goes, the connection between any one kind of tree (oak, pine, magnolia) and its supercategory *tree*, between any two kinds of tree, between any one particular tree and its kind, between any two particular trees (the one in my back yard and the one in yours), and so on. Analogical connections do not seem to be the same sort of thing as these category connections, because the analogical links between two concepts (like *sun* and *jewel*) are not a matter of sharing criterial features the possession of which places them into a category defined by those features.

Certain connections are so deeply entrenched in our conceptual systems that we cannot imagine what it would be like to operate without them. To imagine this, we would require a fundamentally different mind. These deeply entrenched connections seem inevitable, fixed, true, actual. We take some of them to be uncreative category connections. For example, recognizing a connection between one physical object and another or between one zebra and another might conceivably have been, at one time in the history of the species or the infant individual brain, highly creative, but no longer. Very many things "downstream" in our conceptual systems depend upon these connections. Yanking them from our conceptual systems would rip out massive dependent domains. They have a high degree of generative entrenchment, as I will discuss later; they have a high degree of cognitive indispensability.[2]

Other connections are less deeply generatively entrenched. For example, we routinely understand events not caused by animate agents in terms of actions performed by animate agents, as in "Death took him" or "Trees climb the hills toward the Golan and descend to test their resolve near the desert" or "That wall finally gave up and collapsed." Such mental connections between the concept of an event and the concept of an action are less generatively entrenched than our mental connections between one physical object and another or between one zebra and another.

Still further up the gradient from deep to shallow entrenchment, our fanciful connection between food and craved things (as in "I hunger for your love"—where desire is understood in terms of hunger) is slightly less generatively entrenched again. Yet less generatively entrenched is the analogy that life is drama (we all take roles, have masks, experience changes in settings, and so on). The connections suggested by the analogy "Time is an isosceles triangle" have no generative entrenchment at all.

Deeply entrenched analogical connections do not seem inventive to us. We regard them as straightforward category connections. At the other end of the gradient, a surprising and arresting analogical connection may be missing from our conceptual apparatus altogether. "Time is an apple," for example, seems to express no conventional conceptual connection.

The gradient between extremely entrenched category connections on one hand and surprising analogical connections on the other is a wide middle ground. Many conceptual connections belong to this middle ground, differing not in kind but in degree of entrenchment.

For example, the conventional sexist analogies that a man is a rock and a woman is a flower belong to our conceptual system—we are familiar with them—but they do not belong to our entrenched category structures. If we ask someone to list rocks and flowers, and he or she produces two lists,

agate	daisy
turquoise	petunia
granite	peony
quartz	rose
man	woman,

we will not find the lists very inventive, but we will surely sense a jump at the last term in each list: we know the conventional analogical connections between *men* and *rocks* and between *women* and *flowers*, but these connections are not entrenched in our category structures.

An equivalent way to characterize this relation between analogical and categorical connection would be to say that any analogy bids to establish or influence category structures. If we understand the analogy, it succeeds partially in its bid, because it becomes less surprising as an analogy, and from that position can bid further to encroach upon our category connections. The connections a conventional analogy proposes as candidates for category connections can become shallowly entrenched in our conceptual systems, relative to our more deeply entrenched category structures.

As a mundane example, consider the way a taxpayer might argue with the Internal Revenue Service over his legitimate tax category and his consequent schedule of taxes. Imagine the taxpayer's lawyer arguing as follows: "Your honor, the Internal Revenue Service is trying to tax my client as a resident. But he is just like a nonresident taxpayer, such as a migratory worker who has come up from Mexico. The migratory worker crosses the Rio Grande, and my client crosses the Atlantic Ocean. True, he has a house and family here, but he pays taxes to the United Kingdom, comes in and out of the United States on a temporary and irregular basis, and so on. We tax migratory workers only on income arising in the United States and we should tax my client only on that income because, like the migratory worker, he is a bona fide resident of a foreign country subject to its tax laws." In effect, the lawyer is drawing an analogy between his client and the migrant worker and inviting the judge to extend his own category of nonresident taxpayers to include, in this case, a jet-setting American citizen with flats and jobs in London. I am summarizing here an actual case as reported to me. I am told that the argument offended the judge's middle-class soul, but that he ultimately felt obliged to go along with it. What started out as a rather suspect-looking analogy became a shaky category connection.[3]

That there is a gradient—not a dichotomous opposition—between analogical and categorical connection means that our category structures are dynamic and subject to transformation under the pressure of analogy. Analogies deal with our categories by side-stepping them. Analogies can inventively induce us to construct new connections, and recast or tune others. A powerful analogy can restructure, disturb, influence, and change our category structures, and successful analogical connections (light is a wave) can ultimately become part of our category structures. Some of the connections that analogies propose might mesh with our category connections and thus be easily assimilated. Others might be deeply disruptive, with the consequence that their assimilation will be resisted by the conceptual apparatus we already have in place. A deep, surprising analogy that leads us to form weird but powerful connections that challenge our category structures will not settle readily into our conventional knowledge. It will remain suggestive, never achieving a location in our conceptual apparatus. It will not be used up—assimilated and naturalized—as we go through it repeatedly: we will be able to return to it again and again, and find it fresh, because the connections it suggests cannot be established in our category structures (or maybe even in our conventional conceptual apparatus) with impunity.

To begin to analyze the relationship between categorical and analogical connection, let us take up some current research in the theory of categorization.

THEORIES OF CATEGORIZATION

Classical theories of categorization assume that members fall into a category because they share the criterial attributes that define the category.[4] This principle applies all the way up the taxonomic tree: categories (at any level) belong to a supercategory when they possess its criterial attributes. If we keep going all the way to the top, we come to the highest category and its criterial attributes, usually a small set of general features. If we descend back down a step, we find that the subcategories of the highest category inherit its criterial attributes. Each sub-subcategory inherits the criterial attributes of its governing subcategory. This principle of inclusion applies all the way down the tree, until we arrive at particulars. Its product is the familiar model of a category as a hierarchical inverted tree: the top node is the most general; branches descend from it to subnodes that are subcategories, and so on recursively until the branching ends at particular instances. Each node in the tree is defined by features that are possessed by every node below it.

These classical theories have influenced semantics, where concepts are often represented as tree categorizations of semantic markers. Sometimes the trees are explicit, sometimes implicit.[5]

These classical theories of categorization have been challenged by the tradition of research associated with Eleanor Rosch.[6] George Lakoff has extended Rosch's suggestions to a theory of categorization.[7] In this study, I will use the following points from this tradition:

The first point concerns the *vertical dimension* of categories in a hierarchy of category inclusion (for example, Everything–Physical Objects–Organisms–Animals–Dogs–Setters–Irish Setters–my Irish Setter Muffy). In classical theories of categorization, no vertical level has special status other than the top and bottom levels, which are distinguished only as endpoints of the chain. Rosch showed that this model of categories is wrong. In research on the categorization of concrete objects, Rosch showed that there is one level of abstraction (for example, *dog*) around which most information is organized. Categories at this level make the most powerful conceptual cuts in knowledge; they give the most information for the least cognitive work. Levels of category above and below this special level depend upon it. Rosch calls this the "basic" level, and shows that it is the level where category members are recognized fastest, the level used in neutral contexts, the highest level at which category members share perceived shapes, the highest level at which an image can stand for the category, the highest level at which members call for similar interactional motor patterns, the level most codable and most coded and earliest coded in language, and the level learned first. It is the most inclusive level at which there are attributes common to all or most members of the category. Greater knowledge about a conceptual domain can lower its basic level (a lawyer's operational basic level for illegal acts is doubtless lower than mine), but a particular linguistic community or unit of discourse marks out what it takes to be the default basic-level categories shared by its speakers.[8]

The second point that I will borrow from this tradition of research concerns the *horizontal dimension* of categories. If we scan horizontally across a category structure, then we get a string of contrasting categories, like *animal* versus *vegetable*, or like *dog* versus *cat* versus *giraffe* versus *horse*, and so on. The basic level, Rosch found, is the level of maximal differentiation between contrasting categories. At lower levels, there is less differentiation between contrasting categories. For example, the basic-level categories *chair* and *table* seem quite different. But one level lower, most kinds of chairs seem to us to be quite similar, as do most kinds of tables. Contrasting categories above the basic level are less strongly differentiated than contrasting basic-level categories, but any individual attribute (for example, animate) associated with a category above the basic level (for example, animal) is generally a strong indicator of difference between members of that category and members of contrasting categories.[9]

In sum, in the next sections of this study, I will make use of the following points from this tradition:

—In mental categories, there is generally very little overlap between contrasting categories at or above the basic level.
—In mental categories, there is generally high overlap between contrasting categories below the basic level.

I will use these points to discuss how we recognize equations as analogies. I will discuss equations between categories at, above, and below the basic level; equations that are instantiations; equations that assert class containment; equations between two instances of one supercategory; and equations that involve a radically changed concept, as we see in "A leopard is *a tiger with spots instead of stripes.*"

Beforehand, I observe that an equation between different noun phrases need not be an analogy. There are identities (Two is four halves), definitions (A cygnet is a young swan), true assertions of class membership (Peter is a man), inferences (Flattery is fear—on the reading that from an act of flattery we should infer a cause of fear), causal statements (Ignorance is bliss—on the reading that ignorance causes bliss), legal status (Delivery is sale—on the reading that a customer's taking delivery legally constitutes a sale), and so on. In fact, the range of connections that we can express through the copula *to be* is so staggering as to constitute complete evidence that sentences do not have meanings so much as we impose upon them meanings suggested by hints they contain.[10] Consider, as an example, the commercial for a breakfast cereal that boasts "An open box is an empty box," where we can read "is" as expressing something like "must necessarily and quickly become, given normal circumstances." Consider, as a second example, the proverb "Catching a falling leaf is good luck for a whole month in the coming year," where we can read "is" as expressing something like "confers." There is additionally the vast range of cases, so astutely analyzed by Gilles Fauconnier in *Mental Spaces*, where we take "is" as indicating a link between members of different mental spaces, as we see from expressions like "In the movie *Some Like It Hot*, the singer is Marilyn Monroe." Here, the mental space of the film contains the character of the singer; the mental space of the speaker's reality contains the actress Marilyn Monroe; there is a conceptual connection between the actress Marilyn Monroe in the mental space corresponding to the speaker's reality and the character of the singer in the mental space corresponding to the film. Such connections are called "mental space connections," and can be expressed in English as equations of the sort "The singer is Marilyn Monroe."[11] Context will often predispose us to recognize an equation as one of these nonanalogical forms. Alternatively, context can predispose us to recognize an equation as an analogy. For example, the expectation that theological discourse is dominantly analogical, and that it often presents analogies as identities, may predispose us to take "God is light" or "God is love" as an analogy, an identity, or, what is unusual, both simultaneously.[12]

EQUATIONS BETWEEN CONTRASTING MENTAL MODELS AT THE BASIC LEVEL

When we say we know what a dog is, we mean, I take it, that we have a mental model that we apply to many different things, all of which we call "dog."

The way we recognize analogies shows that we organize knowledge around mental models at basic levels. Consider the observation, later to be refined:

—An equation between different mental models at the basic level is a candidate for analogy.

"A man is a rock" or "A woman is a window" or "A child is a light bulb" can all be recognized as analogies. "A fortress is a prison" can be recognized as an analogy. "A chicken is a fence" can be recognized as an analogy, but will then probably be rejected because in all likelihood we will fail to understand it as an analogy. In these cases, we can recognize analogy because we can recognize maximal distinction. To remain within our category structure would be to maintain that distinction. To transcend the distinction, we transcend the category structure by recognizing analogy.

Here are some examples in which a mental model is equated with a contrasting mental model at (what would appear to be) the basic level:

> Men are wolves.
> Insanity is often the logic of an accurate mind overtaxed.
> The body is the socket of the soul.

Consider "A rope is a key." We can recognize this as an analogy because we can recognize maximal distinction. We know that *rope* and *key* are maximally distinct because we know they are contrasting basic-level mental models. But consider "A rope is a golden key." We can recognize this as an analogy in the same way we recognize "A rope is a key" as an analogy. We need not compare *rope* with *golden key*. We need not even bother to understand *golden key*. We need only recognize that *golden key*, like *silver key*, or *brass key*, is an instance of the mental model *key*. In general

> —An equation between (an instance of) a basic-level model and (an instance of) a contrasting basic-level model is a candidate for analogy.

The particular instance of the model may be important for understanding the analogy, but we do not need it for recognizing the analogy.

The case is similar for "A strong rope is the necessary key." Recognizing this as an analogy requires only noticing that a basic mental model (*rope*) is equated with a contrasting mental model (*key*).

CONFLICT OF ATTRIBUTES ABOVE THE BASIC LEVEL

Rosch showed that above the basic level, contrasting categories of concrete objects overlap little. If this phenomenon generalizes to categories of things other than concrete objects, it explains how we can recognize analogy merely by recognizing contrast of attributes at levels *above* the basic category. Because these higher contrasting categories overlap very little, we assume that two mental models belonging to one structure of categories are very different if some category in that structure that is higher than the basic level contains one of them but not the other. This gives us a very quick way to recognize analogy. Typically, some simple, general, higher category distinction suffices to signal an analogy. This is a case where we can provisionally enlist simple grammars we know that schematize complicated aspects of meaning. For instance, one sort of simplistic grammar associates features with categories, and we can use those features as a quick indication of conflict. It is important to realize that, as I will discuss in a moment, this recognition of feature contrast does *not* work in the same way below the basic level to signal analogy.

Feature contrast is not significant except as situated in our elaborate knowledge of how the two equated mental models reside within our category structures. Let us consider a range of examples where we can recognize analogy because higher-order feature contrast indicates that there is some category above the basic level that contains one of two concepts in the equation but not the other:

PHYSICAL OBJECT = NOT-PHYSICAL-OBJECT: "Moderation is the silken string running through the pearl chain of all virtues." "A man's action is only a picture-book of his creed." "Conceit is the finest armor a man can wear." "Cunning is a short blanket—if you pull it over your face, you expose your feet." "Sweet mercy is nobility's true badge." "The adjective is the banana peel of the parts of speech." "Beauty is truth's smile when she beholds her own face in a perfect mirror."

PERSON = NOT-PERSON: "A proverb is the child of experience." "Admiration is the daughter of ignorance." "The will is the strong blind man who carries on his shoulders the lame man who can see." "Think then, my soul, that death is but a groom, which brings a taper to the outward room." "Man is a sun; and the senses are his planets." "Shall I compare thee to a summer's day?" "Old men are only walking hospitals." "Everyone is a moon, and has a dark side which he never shows to anybody." "And what are kings when regiment is gone / But perfect shadows in a sunshine day?" "I am a parcel of vain strivings tied by a chance bond together." "The best mirror is an old friend." "A faithful friend is the medicine of life." "You are what you eat." "A baby is God's opinion that the world should go on." "What I am is the way home." "He is / a wilderness looking out / at the wild." "His ancestor is the hill / that rises in the winter wind / beyond the blind wall / at his back."

NOT-EVENT = EVENT: "Every extreme attitude is a flight from the self."

PERIOD OF TIME = NOT-PERIOD-OF-TIME: "Women's hell is old age." "Beauty is eternity gazing at itself in a mirror." "Antiquity is the aristocracy of history." "Youth is a blunder; manhood a struggle; old age a regret."

FOOD = NOT-FOOD: "The sky is the daily bread of the eyes."

LEGAL AGREEMENT = NOT-LEGAL-AGREEMENT: "Convictions are mortgages on the mind."

LINGUISTIC STRUCTURE = NOT-LINGUISTIC-STRUCTURE: "A happy marriage is a long conversation that seems all too short" (Andre Maurois). "Art is a lie that enables us to realize the truth" (Pablo Picasso). "Life is an unanswered question" (Tennessee Williams). "The adjective is the banana peel of the parts of speech." "Poetry is the dream through which man aspires to a superior life" (René Sully Prudhomme). "Poetry is the lava of imagination whose eruption prevents the earthquake" (Byron).

"Poetry is the devil's wine" (St. Augustine). "Poetry—all of it—is a trip to the unknown" (Vladimir Mayakovsky).

BELIEF = NOT-BELIEF: "Religion is a disease, but it is a noble disease."

There is a large class of analogies beginning "Life is . . . " Examples are "Life is playing the violin solo in public and learning the instrument as one goes along," "Life's a beach," "Life's a jest with a bad punch-line," "To misconstrue the point-of-view Socratic, / Life is a painful, stammered-out emphatic / Pronunciation of the word Goodbye" (Gjertrude Schnackenberg), and "Life is first boredom, then fear" (Philip Larkin). It may seem that *life*—like some other concepts—has such varied meanings that finding a feature conflict above the basic level between it and an analogous concept would be hard. I think this is not so. "Life" is not a physical action, not a linguistic structure, and so on. Its principal meanings concern "the class of living things," "that which makes us animate," and "a period of time." But in none of its major alternative meanings is it a linguistic statement or act, for example. I have found no "Life is . . . " analogy whose recognition as an analogy cannot be produced by some conflict such as those listed above.

INSTANCES OF A MODEL

The topic of instantiation yields our next principle for recognizing analogy:

—An instantiation believed to be false signals analogy.

Legitimate instantiations belong to our category-structural representation of knowledge. Analogy—which transcends this representation of knowledge—can announce itself by violating legitimate instantiation, as in "The president is a pig."

A second principle for recognizing analogy is closely tied to the first:

—An assertion of category containment believed to be false signals analogy.

Statements such as "Man is an actor" assert that *man* is a subcategory of *actor*. Although a given man may be an actor, we do not believe that the entire category *man* is a subcategory of *actor*: we do not believe that every member of *man* is a member of *actor*. Other examples are:

—The human being is a blind man who dreams that he can see.
—A metaphysician is a blind man in a dark room, looking for a black hat which isn't there.
—Every book is a quotation.

These structures assert false category containment, and so signal analogy.

Equations (and Similarities)
between Two Instances of
One Supercategory

Analogies exist to make connections between mental models, but not just any connections. They exist to make connections that are not already captured by our category structures.

Consider two mental models that share a supercategory: *rocking chair* and *steno chair* share the supercategory *chair*. The following seems true:

> —Equations (and similarities) between two mental models that are instances of a supercategory at or below the basic level are never preferentially recognized as analogies.

For example, we resist taking "A steno chair is a rocking chair" as an analogy. If two mental models share a supercategory, then some connections between them are already captured in our category structure. As Rosch showed for concrete objects, contrasting categories below the basic level overlap; we think of them as relatively close. We feel that the connections between them are simply too well captured by our category structures for analogy to play much of a role. But contrasting categories at or above the basic level overlap little: analogy thereby has its warrant. For example, *truth* and *beauty* are both instances of *abstract quality*, but that is a very weak connection since so little knowledge is organized around *abstract quality*. *Man* and *rock* (or *woman* and *window*) are both instances of *physical object*, which is some connection, but still not very impressive, because *physical object* is still above the basic level at which most knowledge is organized. *Peter* and *James* are both instances of *man*, and now the connections are robust and detailed, because so much knowledge is organized around the mental model *man*. Consequently, analogy has less warrant at this level. There are many ways to understand "Peter is James"—as an identity, as a false identity, or as a mental space connection on the reading "The actor Peter plays the character James." But we resist taking it as an analogy.

Consider:

> —A man is a rock.
> —A child is a light bulb.
> —A daisy is a petunia.

Man and *rock* are differentiated but share the supercategory *physical object*. *Child* and *light bulb* are differentiated but share that same supercategory. *Daisy* and *petunia* are differentiated but share the supercategory *flower*. In all these cases, the differentiation can be abbreviated in the simplistic form of feature contrasts. For example, *man* and *rock* are *animate* versus *inanimate*, as are *child* and *light bulb*. *Daisy* and *petunia* are *perennial* versus *annual*. *Daisy* and *petunia* in fact have a range of feature conflicts in color, texture, shape, morphology (petals versus no petals, for example), habitat, and so on. These three cases look similar, but the third case stands apart from the first two. We can recognize "A man is a rock" and "A child is a light bulb" as analogies, but we will strongly resist recognizing "A daisy is a petunia" as an analogy. *Man* and *rock* share the supercategory *physical object*, but *physical object* is a relatively thin mental model: it is above the basic level. So we are unimpressed by these thin connections, and do not view *man* and *rock* as overlapping much, and we can recognize analogy. Similarly for "A child is a light-bulb." But now, although there are many distinctions between *daisy* and *petunia*, we are relatively unimpressed by these distinctions because we view *daisy* and *petunia* as very close and overlapping: they share a supercategory, *flower*, which we regard as a richly detailed basic-level category. We therefore strongly resist taking "A daisy is a petunia" as an analogy.

To clarify, let me recapitulate what I take to be the differences between four exemplary cases:

—A man is a rock.
—A child is a light bulb.
—A chicken is a fence.
—A steno chair is a rocking chair.

The first three examples prompt us to recognize analogy because they equate mental models that are at the basic level. The first is conventional and easily understood. The second is less conventional and perhaps less easily understood. The third is bizarre and resists my attempts to understand it. But the fourth example has a different status entirely: it resists being recognized as an analogy because it equates concepts that share a supercategory at the basic level. This does not mean that it cannot be easily understood as an analogy if its recognition is forced, as follows: We could take *rocking chair* as metonymic for the long, slow, boring, repetitive, inconsequential act of rocking in a rocking chair, and further take that act as either an instance of or a metaphor for *wasting life through meaningless routine* ("He just sits there, rocking back and forth"). We could then take *steno chair* as a metonymy for *clerical work*. Combining these interpretations, we could view the analogy as asserting that clerical work is wasting one's life through meaningless routine, that the job is like the empty retirement to which it leads. Forcing the reading in this fashion, we can *understand* this analogy, but we are prevented from doing so because we resist recognizing it as an analogy in the first instance: the two equated concepts, although contrasting on many features, share a basic-level supercategory. The case is similar for

—A 2-by-4 is a 4-by-4.
—Parsley is cumin.
—A mug is a tumbler.
—A daisy is a petunia.

We simply resist recognizing any of these as an analogy in the first place. To recognize such a statement as an analogy would be to acknowledge its bid to establish a category, but we believe that there already exists a wealthy and powerful category capturing the useful connections, so we resist believing that the bid is being made.

We can override this rubric that an equation between mental models sharing a supercategory at or below the basic level does not signal analogy by using strong pragmatic cues and highly conventional symbols and metaphors. For example, "A Pekinese is a Doberman" will be resisted as an analogy, even though "Doberman" is already for us a conventional symbol of aggression. But if, when I arrive at your house for afternoon tea, your Pekinese snarls, lunges, clenches its teeth in my pant leg, and attempts to yank me left and right over the Afshar rug, then I might say, "This Pekinese is a *Do*berman!" in such a way that you will recognize an analogy. There are many cues here that combine to override the rubric. (1) Relevance prompts you to take my remark as an appropriate comment on the dog's behavior. (2) The deictic "*this* Pekinese" clarifies that I am not talking about the category *Pekinese*, and thus I am not endeavoring to transcend category structures. We all know that a category can have some unusual particular members, and that to comment on one particular member is not to disturb the category. (3) We already know symbolic meanings of "Doberman," and so are primed to take "Doberman" not as a category name but rather as a symbol. Labrador Retrievers can be rather fierce on occasion, but if I had said, "This Pekinese is a Labrador Retriever," it would have been much less clearly an analogy. (4) There are intonational cues of emphasis in my pronunciation of "*Do*berman," and in the rising pitch of my voice as I say the words before it, that may form a pattern signaling judgment—and hence controversy, and hence analogy—as opposed to uncontroversial categorization. Compare the steep rise-fall intonation of "This man is an *id*iot," "Your idea is *gar*bage," and "This joker is a *fo*ol," all of which imply judgment, although the last sentence, in a different pronunciation and in a context such as a court scene in a Shakespearean play, could be a straightforward categorization. It seems possible to say "Sam is a *butch*er" with a judgmental intonation, which would prevent it from being understood as uncontroversial categorization.

There are other, similar cues that might have been used to the same effect. I might have said "This Pekinese is a real Doberman," where "real" suggests "not actually," as part of the systematic inversion we find in phrases like "The phone was literally ringing off the hook," "I was virtually dead on my feet," "He was absolutely starved," and "The hunter is truly an eagle."

The claim that analogies do not exist between "very like" or "overlapping" concepts requires argument. If there are no analogies between very like concepts, then what are we to say about equations between very like, indeed identical concepts, such as "Business is business"? If the two concepts in the equation are given identical readings, then the equation cannot be an analogy. We might have other reasons for not taking it as a vacuous tautology, but that is another matter. Analogies are not constructed between very like concepts.

Here is a tougher example of the same general point that analogies do not exist between very like concepts. Suppose, in some doldrums of pious, unimaginative sentimentality, the following sentences are said in succession in group conversation:

"Children are treasure."
"Peace is treasure."
"Silence is treasure."
"Love is treasure."

and then some cynical wag, arching one brow, retorts, "Treasure is treasure." Suppose more that the drop in pitch between the first and second syllables in his first pronunciation of "treasure" is greater than usual, and that there is a pause between the first "treasure" and "is." Then an analogy may be recognized. Is this then an analogy between very like concepts? Not at all. Context predisposes us to recognize an analogy, but to do so, we must contrive for the two "treasures" to be rather unlike: the first is a physical object, like coins or diamonds, or, by extension, something with commercial exchange value, like stocks, oil wells, or a certain bank balance, while the second involves a psychological, ethical, or aesthetic valuation. It is not merely that an equation of rather unlike concepts suggests analogy, but, conversely, that a predisposition to recognize an analogy requires construing the two equated nouns as evoking rather unlike concepts.

Because mental models that share a supercategory at or below the basic level overlap, equations between them can be used for definitional purposes, including emphasizing components of mental models. Suppose an astrophysicist says he wants to prove something about Titan, and starts giving us equations for the moon, and we say, "Hey! I thought you were talking about Titan!" and he replies blandly, "Titan is just the same as the moon, for the purposes of the investigation I am pursuing." This is no analogy. Rather, he is *emphasizing* the overlap between two mental models that share a supercategory at or below the basic level, and explicitly removing the conflict as a carrier of significance.

One reason we do not have to recognize as analogies equations between "very like" concepts is that we assume nobody makes them. But what if someone were perverse enough to try? Consider "A leopard is a tiger" or "Recursion is iteration." The probable response—"No, it isn't"—takes the phrase as an identity or definition or instantiation, but as false and mistaken. But suppose we know that the speaker doubtless knows the falsity. Still, we can guess that his intent is to emphasize part of a mental model or to dismiss differences. For example, consider a senior accountant for a zoo, transmitting his knowledge to a junior accountant as they inspect the records. Senior accountant: "Expenses for tigers go here." Junior accountant: "And for leopards?" Senior accountant (screwing up one side of his face and flicking his hand away in dismissal): "Leopards are tigers." This means, "For these purposes of accounting, forget those differences important in other discussions and treat leopards as the same as tigers." This is closely linked with definition, in the sense that it asks us to acquire a notion of leopard-as-an-object-of-accounting by ignoring certain parts of what we know about *leopard* and emphasizing the overlap between *leopard* and *tiger*. If your sand-blind father says he liked the tiger at the zoo, and your beaming helpful child says, "You mean leopard, grampa," you might say to the child, collusively, "A leopard is a tiger," meaning "To a sand-blind grampa, a leopard looks like a tiger." We can take such statements as asking us to emphasize an overlap in mental models and dismiss their important differences.

But suppose none of these or similar dodges seems warranted to us. Then we might as well try to take the equation as an analogy, in which case our first tactic may be to assume that the speaker is using mental models other than those we have selected, or is delving deeper into the concepts for more detail, because whatever concepts the speaker is using must be further apart than the ones we are using—otherwise he would not be making this analogy.

Dedre Gentner has written about similes between concepts that are very close versus very far apart.[13] Gentner claims that analogy maps object-relations but not object-attributes from source domain onto target domain, and that "literal similarity" maps object-attributes as well as object-relations. She offers as examples "The atom is like our solar system" (analogy) versus "The K5 solar system is like our solar system" (literal similarity).

This view, while successful for many cases, apparently runs into a problem with a certain kind of evidence. There are many kinds of statement that we feel to be analogies, and not literal similarities, that call for mapping of object-attributes. Examples would be "He's a brief but blazing star," "She's a fragile and delicate flower," and "A neuron, like a person, is excitable." Gentner takes as her examples cases where the source domain is *solar system*—a concept with a highly articulated structure of object-relations—and so she is less likely to encounter the mapping of object-attributes. Gentner's analysis also usually concentrates on similarities rather than equations. We resist recognizing as an analogy "The K5 solar system is our solar system" not because the map involves so many object-attributes that we consider it to be a literal similarity, but rather because the two concepts share a basic-level supercategory.

RADICAL CHANGES TO A MENTAL MODEL

I have said that we resist recognizing as analogies equations between two mental models that share a supercategory at or below the basic level. But there are cases where one of the mental models has been radically changed. For example, "A leopard is a tiger with spots instead of stripes" radically denies to *tiger* something we feel to be a feature of *tiger* and radically adds something we feel not to be a feature of *tiger*. In such cases, the supposed conflict between the two concepts expressed in the equation is thrown into doubt, and it becomes a subtler matter to recognize analogies and definitions. A radical change to a mental model is a passport through the gates of categorization. It creates diplomatic immunity. We recognize it as a technique of transcending and manipulating local constraints in our representation of knowledge.

Consider:

—A rhombus is a square pushed over.
—A leopard is a tiger with spots instead of stripes.
—Ambition is but avarice on stilts and masked.
—A historian is a prophet in reverse.

In such cases of radical change, we must perform a fair amount of the work of understanding parts of the statement before we can decide what sort of statement it is. The radical change invalidates various easy rubrics for recognition. Instead, we must:

—Change the affected mental model. The mental model with which it is equated will furnish some of the details of how to conduct the change.
—Match it against what we know of the other mental model.
—Decide whether the match is grossly wrong.

For example, if I am trying to remember what a rhombus is, and you say "A rhombus is a square pushed over," then I search for something I can do to my mental model of *square* that could plausibly be called "pushing it over" such that the result matches well one of the polygons I know. If I can manage that, then I have a fair match, and I take the statement as definitional in the sense of emphasizing or imparting the greater part of a mental model, indeed, sometimes imparting *all* of it. If, on the other hand, I do not know at all what a rhombus is, you will probably have to say something more than "pushed over." To be successful, you might have to say something like "A rhombus is a square with its top pushed off-center, so the sides lean." You might even add "like an old barn," or show me the angle with your hands. Since I have no mental model for *rhombus*, this radically changed *square* will not conflict with my mental model for *rhombus*, and I will again take it as some species of definition.

Similarly, if I am trying to remember what a leopard is, then "A leopard is a tiger with spots instead of stripes" will help. It will also help define *leopard* if I do not know what a leopard is.

Such phrases are used to communicate sketches of mental models; we recognize this as a form of definition. This accounts for the fact that examples of this genre typically spell out the differences perceived to be important, rather than leaving the understander to search for them. A definition meant to help us construct a concept must include the important parts of that concept. If I have no idea what Titan might be, and you know or assume that, and I ask you, "What is Titan?" and you say, "It is just the same as the moon," and you do not mean that it revolves around Earth, and I know you do not because I know we both know Earth has only one moon and that "Titan" is not one of its names, then I can accuse you of not fully answering the question, because you have left out the one thing you must not leave out when defining moons in our solar system: what they revolve around. No such conditions or strictures operate with clear cases of analogy: we may say "Time is money" or "Beauty is Truth," and leave out worlds of meaning for our understander to fumble through.

GENERATIVE ENTRENCHMENT AND THE LITERAL
VERSUS FIGURATIVE DICHOTOMY

Our inquiries are often limited by the analytic instruments we possess for framing them. Our most common instrument for framing and discussing the matters treated in this study is the distinction between the literal and the figurative. The vast literature employing this distinction has been surveyed elsewhere.[14] The reader might turn to John Searle's "Metaphor," H. P. Grice's "Logic and Conversation," or Jerrold Sadock's "Figurative Speech and Linguistics" for a taste of the ways in which this distinction is used.[15]

The most important aspect of this distinction of literal versus figurative is that it is a dichotomy easily aligned with a range of other dichotomies: true versus false, real versus imaginary, conventional versus novel, dead versus live, stable versus unstable, categorical versus analogical, denotative versus connotative, fixed versus dynamic, primary versus secondary, and so on.

Before now, the analysis of the recognition of metaphor and (equations expressing) analogy has been founded upon this distinction between the literal and the figurative; indeed, the analysis has consisted of a restatement of this distinction between the literal and the figurative. This analysis occurs in H. P. Grice's "Logic and Conversation." According to Grice, we can recognize a statement as expressing fanciful resemblance because we assume that communication is governed by the conversational maxim of quality, "Do not say what you believe to be false." A statement that is literally false can be taken either as a violation of the maxim of quality or as an attempt to communicate something other than the literal falsity. For the sake of preserving the maxim, we choose the second alternative, and try to rehabilitate the literal falsity by taking it as a gesture toward a fanciful resemblance. Loosely, when a speaker says something everybody knows to be false, we try to transform the meaning of the statement to remove the falsity. Strictly, recognizing metaphor or (equations expressing) analogy is recognizing that a speaker intends us to recognize that he intends to make a statement that he believes to be false and that he believes we will believe to be false. Here is Grice's example:

> Examples like *You are the cream in my coffee* characteristically involve categorial falsity, so the contradictory . . . will be a truism; so it cannot be THAT that such a speaker is trying to get across. The most likely supposition is that the speaker is attributing to his audience some feature or features in respect of which the audience resembles (more or less fancifully) the mentioned substance.[16]

Stephen Levinson points out that Grice's account does not purport to offer insight into the conceptual workings of metaphor and analogy, and gives only partial explanation of how we recognize a statement as metaphoric or analogical.[17] The explanation is partial first because it is often wrong. Levinson notes that sentential metaphors are not necessarily false and are not categorical falsehoods. (An example of a sentential metaphor is the statement "The lion roared" as an answer to the question, "What did your boss say?") Many theorists have noted that a statement can be true both literally and figuratively, as when one expresses the character of one's brother the Marine by saying "He's a Marine." Grice's explanation is partial second because the flouting of a maxim can lead to recognizing a variety of figures, and because the flouting of this very maxim of quality can lead us to recognize figures other than analogy, such as irony.

Grice's analysis makes it sound as if first we recognize that the literal (in this case, categorical) meaning of a sentence ("You are the cream in my coffee") is not true, and then we try to rehabilitate the sentence by assuming that the speaker means its contradictory (that is, he is being ironic, and means "You are not the rich dairy product that I put into the liquid that I brew from coffee beans"), and then we reject this assumption as mistaken, because the contradictory of a categorical falsity is automatically true, and so finally we are driven to recognize the statement as metaphoric or analogical.

This analysis faces many difficulties. We have seen many statements—like "Parsley is cumin"—that seem false exactly because they assert something in violation of our category structures, but whose categorical falsity does not lead us to take them as figurative or fanciful; and we have seen other cases where we prefer to recognize analogy first without going through any process of considering a "literal" meaning or an "ironic" meaning—as in "Language is a virus" or "A child is a window." Grice's analysis aligns the dichotomy of literal versus figurative with another dichotomy, the dichotomy of primary versus secondary. For Grice, our primary construal of any expression is its "literal" meaning; we may construe it figuratively only after rejecting its literal meaning, as when we recognize that the speaker intends to make a statement that he believes to be false and that he believes we will believe to be false.

I am struck by the way in which the dichotomy of literal versus figurative drives our discussion of these matters. William C. Wimsatt was struck in 1985 by the way the dichotomy of *innate* versus *acquired* appeared to be driving the discussion of the ontogenetic expression of traits or features. He proposed to replace the dichotomy of innate versus acquired with a gradient of what he called "generative entrenchment." In Wimsatt's account, evolution should be increasingly conservative at earlier stages of development because features that are expressed earlier in development have a higher probability of being required for features that will appear later, and will on the average have a larger number of "downstream" features dependent upon them. Wimsatt writes,

> Of course, a feature may occur very early in development and still have little or nothing which depends on it. For this reason it is better to distinguish features not in terms of when they appear in development, but in terms of whether they are needed for other traits. I will, therefore, speak of features as being "generatively entrenched" in proportion to the degree that they have a number of later developing traits depending on them.[18]

A feature is generatively entrenched to the extent that downstream features depend upon it.

Let us take a cue from Wimsatt and speak of concepts and their connections as having degrees of "generative entrenchment," where degree of generative entrenchment is the extent to which the rest of the conceptual system depends upon or is invested in that connection. This would allow us to keep our sense that certain concepts and certain connections are so indispensable as to be fixed, literal, and true, and that other connections are so dispensable as to be fanciful and false. It would leave open the middle ground for connections of intermediate generative entrenchment. It would also allow us to characterize the axes along which our conceptual apparatus is open to change, and would introduce into our models of conceptual structure an essence of dynamism running throughout conceptual structure. The uniform constraint on change that it be limited in proportion to the generative entrenchment of its object would have differential strength across components of the conceptual apparatus because different components of the conceptual apparatus have different degrees of generative entrenchment. Profoundly generatively entrenched components would be virtually fixed, while less generatively entrenched components would be more susceptible to pressure and change. The full range of these differential phenomena, from fixity to fancy, would derive from the same systematic principles. Phenomena that look so different as to seem different kinds of phenomena would be accounted for by the same model, in which variability derives not from varying principles of operation but rather falls out as a consequence of uniform principles operating across the conceptual apparatus. This view would suggest that our dynamic conceptual apparatus results from the same processes that transform it.

As an example of the dynamism in the intermediate range of generative entrenchment, consider that certain researchers in early artificial intelligence, such as Allen Newell and Herbert Simon, worked so continuously under the guidance of the analogical connection between the brain and a contemporary serial digital computer, and the inverse analogical connection between a contemporary serial digital computer and the brain, that they ultimately came to see them as in truth literally the same thing, belonging to the same category.[19] In their research paradigm, the analogical connections acquired a high degree of generative entrenchment.

Under the "generative entrenchment" view of conceptual structure, what matters for a conceptual system is its fitness, its capacity to empower us to operate within forms of life. What does not matter in any respect is the provenance of a conceptual connection. The fitter a conceptual connection, the more generatively entrenched it will, probabilistically, become, simply because it will ultimately have many "downstream" features of our conceptual apparatus dependent upon it. While the conceptual connections we employ in making sense of language may be of any degree of generative entrenchment, we are likely to use those concepts and connections that are more generatively entrenched when we have the choice.

Abandoning the dichotomy of literal versus figurative would dispel many problems in the theory of meaning, by unasking the questions that produced these problems. We would no longer have to investigate how to distinguish sharply between the literal and the nonliteral. We would no longer have to seek the direct relation between language and the world, or make arguments about how literal language refers to the world. There would be, in the generative entrenchment view, no direct relation between language and the world. There would be a relation between language and the mind, in the sense that we would use our conceptual apparatus, with its variety of concepts and connections, to make sense of language, and we would do this by trying to take a bit of language as expressing an instance of some mental model or mental connection we already know.[20]

In this view, when we respond to the freshness or surprise of analogy, we need not be responding to falsity or inappropriateness, but only to low entrenchment and to the way the analogy disrupts entrenched patterns. Novelty would not be the cause of the strangeness of figures, except in so far as novelty overlaps with low generative entrenchment. For example, the basic metaphor that courtship is a game is sufficiently generatively entrenched that many specific *novel* metaphoric expressions derivable from it ("My date said he needed a time-out") are more likely to seem stale than fresh, unless they involve unusual parts of the concept of love or the concept of game. Conversely, an analogy of very low generative entrenchment can be experienced as fresh however often we hear it, unless it begins to become generatively entrenched.

Given the very entrenched status of the dichotomy of literal versus figurative in our discourse, it may seem merely impertinent to call it into question. But my motive here is conservative rather than contrary. We must preserve in our models of thought and language a place for our undeniable felt sense of clear cases of the literal versus clear cases of the figurative. Whatever models we propose must accommodate that clear sense. But to accommodate that felt sense does not require us to incorporate into our models of language and mind our folk notion of a sharp distinction in kind between the literal and the figurative. Many of our most heated discussions over the nature of language and mind appear to derive from our prior premise of this sharp distinction at both the conceptual and linguistic level. I do not see its use in explaining, for example, the recognition of analogy, the task to which I now return.

Pragmatic Effects

Having questioned Grice's account of the use of the maxim of quality, I would now like to give him his due on another maxim, namely, the maxim of quantity, which repeatedly comes into play in the recognition of analogy. Grice claims that we expect communication to be governed by the maxim of quantity, "Be as informative as is required and not more so," and this seems to be correct in general and to account for certain cases of the recognition of analogy. Consider "Man is an animal." As a category statement, this violates the maxim of quantity, so we prefer to take it as an analogy. Of course, there are cases where we expect to be reminded rather than informed: if an introductory biology text includes the assertion "Man is an animal," we would find an excuse for it—perhaps the author wishes to address a less-informed audience, or give a complete exposition, or introduce a new analysis by starting from old information. The maxim of quantity can even be suspended by certain locutions such as "to be sure," "needless to say," "as everyone knows," "of course," and even, sometimes, "now."

The maxim of quantity also guides us in recognizing certain equations that include superfluous true information. Consider "A yellow canary is a bird." This is a bit odd all by itself—of course a yellow canary is a bird, because all canaries are birds, so why would anyone add the specification "yellow"? It is more informative than is required. Making it appropriately informative would require a naturalizing context. For example, suppose that a detective has found evidence of the presence of a bird, and believes without thinking about it much that he should seek out a large undomesticated bird, and so overlooks the little yellow canary, and his helpful sidekick says, as he points at the yellow canary, "Well, what's the difficulty: a yellow canary is a bird." Or suppose we are trying to emphasize the diversity of kinds in a given biological category, and we say, "A bald eagle is a bird, a California Condor is a bird, an African emu is a bird, and a yellow canary is a bird." Either of these situations gives us a way to account for the superfluous information. Information that is superfluous with respect to category membership is not superfluous with respect to other considerations in these cases, and so we are content.

But there is another way to legitimate the information: view the class membership as *analogical* as opposed to *taxonomically categorical*, and the information as significant with respect to that analogical class membership. Consider "Man, when impassioned, is an animal" or "Impassioned man is an animal," or "Man, when deprived of sleep, is an animal." The qualifiers are superfluous information for taxonomic categorization, but not superfluous for the *analogical* connection between man and animal, because they suggest that unimpassioned or well-rested man is not analogically an animal.

A special case of superfluous information occurs when a (usually extreme) instance of a category is asserted to belong to the category, as in "A broken man is a man," or "The president is a human being." The maxim of quantity guides us to take this as asserting that the category obtains (and often that we should therefore behave, judge, or consider accordingly) even though the instance is singular. Often a cue like "still" or "yet" suggests this understanding. A related special case is the obvious instance of a category, as in "I am a human being" or "Your mother is a woman." Both cases would (in the absence of certain contexts) run afoul of the maxim of quantity if we tried to take them as simple taxonomic categorizations. But we have no reason to take them as analogies, either. Usually, we will take them not as analogies but rather as definitional, in the sense that they emphasize aspects of schemas.

SIMILARITIES

How we respond to a similarity ("Time is *like* money") differs from how we respond to an equation ("Time is money"), but in just the ways we would expect by now. Many theorists, including Aristotle, have viewed metaphor as elliptical simile at the level of language, so that "x is y" is just a way of saying "x is like y." And this seems right for cases like "time is money" and "time is like money." But below the basic level, the situation is more complicated. We do not respond to "A daisy is a petunia" in the same way we respond to "A daisy is like a petunia." We decline to recognize "A daisy is a petunia" as an analogy because *daisy* and *petunia* belong to a basic-level category that captures, we feel, many strong connections between them. We are therefore unwilling to assume that a bid is being made to establish competing connections through analogical mapping. Unless the context directs us to do so, we are also unlikely to take the equation "A daisy is a petunia" as definitional, in the sense of emphasizing the overlap between schemas. By contrast, we are more willing to take the similarity "A daisy is like a petunia" as definitional in exactly the sense of emphasizing the conceptual overlap between their schemas.

THEMATIC EFFECTS

A daisy is a flower but a flower is not always a daisy, which goes to show that in English the instance is mentioned first and the category second in a bare equation meant as a category statement. Statements that ask us to understand some concept as analogically a member of a class ("The sun is a jewel") therefore must mention the proposed instance first. In such cases, the instance is the target and the category is the source. The rubric that the instance comes first and the category second entails for these cases of analogy that the target comes first and the source comes second.

But even in cases where class membership is not at issue, the target typically comes first. For example, consider "This problem is Mount Everest," "Julius Caesar is the North Star," and "My boss is Hitler."

Each equates two particulars, but the target comes first. Observe the difference between "Dreams are keys" and "Keys are dreams," between "Time is money" and "Money is time," and between "Flesh is grass" and "Grass is flesh." We take "Sensations are rapid dreams" as an analogy but "Rapid dreams are sensations" probably as a debatable assertion of membership in a category.

There are many cases where the target does not come first, because intonation, context, or explicit cues can point out the target and so save us from needing the default rubric that the target comes first. One case where the target-first rubric does not come into play occurs when an extremely basic source domain with many analogical connections in our conventional apparatus—such as *root, key,* or *fountain*—is expressed with the determiner "the," as in "the root," "the key," or "the fountain," and used in an equation, such as "Patience is the key" or "The key is patience." In such cases, the source is marked, and we do not need to turn to the rubric of target-first and source-second.

But the rubric of target-first and source-second is so strong as a default rubric that in cases where some common metaphoric source is in the second position of an equation, we may recognize an analogy even when otherwise unprompted to do so: the combination of the rubric of target-first and source-second and the appearance of a common source in the second position is enough in these cases to lead us to recognize analogy. Consider "His property is garbage," "His idea is a joke," "His project is hell," and "His contribution is trash," all of which have clear nonanalogical readings, but all of which we take nonetheless as analogies under the weight of the rubric of target-first, source-second. In these cases, the second term of the equation is an extremely basic concept with many analogical associations in our conceptual apparatus. Our response to these equations is to recognize analogy first before we ever even attempt a "literal" reading.

The rubric of target-first and source-second may be a consequence of a larger and more controversial hypothesis about the relationship of language to thought, specifically the relationship of word order to meaning. This more general hypothesis, which concerns the way we expect sentences to communicate, is called "functional sentence perspective."[21] Functional sentence perspective is described oversimply as a principle of word order: the subject of the communication is presented first, and the comment on the subject is presented second. It is often difficult to show functional sentence perspective at work in English since word order in English is used to indicate grammatical relation: in the sentence "Julio gave Rosie a kiss," the grammatical functions are, in order, the first noun phrase ("Julio"), the verb phrase ("gave"), the second noun phrase ("Rosie"), and the third noun phrase ("a kiss"). The order in which these words occurs tells us their grammatical relations: "Julio" is the subject, "gave" is the verb, "Rosie" is the indirect object, and "a kiss" is the direct object. These grammatical relations in turn correspond to semantic roles: *Julio* is the agent of the action, *gave* is the action, *Rosie* is the recipient of the action, and a *kiss* is what the recipient receives. When we change the word order to "Rosie gave Julio a kiss," we preserve the grammatical functions (for example, "Rosie" is still a noun phrase), but we change the grammatical relations (for example, "Rosie" is no longer the direct object, but is now the subject), and we change the semantic roles (for example, *Rosie* is no longer the recipient of the action, but is now the agent of the action). The use of word order in English to indicate grammatical relations limits the extent to which word order can be influenced by functional sentence perspective. Apparently, in some languages, like Czech, grammatical relations are not so rigidly tied to word order, and therefore functional sentence perspective has much more leeway to control word order. The fact that in English functional sentence perspective has little control over word order has led to a tradition in which researchers have asserted that functional sentence perspective is not solely a matter of word order. These researchers have tried to generalize the notion of functional sentence perspective to show that there are other indicators of functional sentence perspective in English than word order, and that functional sentence perspective is thus stronger in English than one might think.

But "*x* is *y*" analogies might give us a rare insight into functional sentence perspective. We have just seen that "Flesh is grass" cannot be expressed synonymously as "Grass is flesh": we are not free to transpose *x* and *y* in a bare analogy. The source of this constraint cannot be that transposing *x* and *y* changes the grammatical functions of *x* and *y*, or (what have traditionally been viewed as) their grammatical relations (such as subject, verb, object, indirect object, and so on), or their semantic roles: all these things remain the same under transposition of *x* and *y*. Rather, we are constrained against transposing *x* and *y* because doing so violates the rubric of target-first. Target-first is a constraint on the expression of conceptual metaphor. It may be a special consequence of a much larger system of constraints on expression, namely, the constraint that the topic precede the comment. English word order, which is elsewhere constrained by its use to indicate grammatical relation, can here in the case of "*x* is *y*" analogies be constrained instead by functional sentence perspective. The symmetry of the construction leaves functional sentence perspective leeway to operate, and therefore to dictate that the subject of communication, *x*—namely, the target of the analogy—shall be mentioned first, and that the comment upon that target *x*—namely, that the target *x* can be understood analogically by mapping the source *y* onto it—shall come second. If this is true, then the rubric of target-first and the requirement that the instance shall be mentioned before its category both derive from functional sentence perspective.

CONCLUSION

Our practice in our forms of life suggests that we operate according to a certain model: there is a real world; we are in it; there are truths about that world that are reflected in our thought; our language lets us talk about that world and ourselves in it; and there is a direct connection between our language and the real world.

On reflection, we might acknowledge that the connection between language and the real world must go through the mind. But in any case, we are inclined to think that all of this transpires at a literal level: the real world is exhaustively literal; literal language refers to it; literal concepts mirror the literal world; literal language evokes literal concepts. Some of the literality in the real world appears to us to concern category connections: they are true and fixed. Separate from all this, so the folk theory runs, there are mental imaginative connections that are false; they are expressed in nonliteral language or literally false language; we must transform the meaning of this language to arrive at interpretations of it that can be literal and true.

We seem to think of entities in the world as composed of features, like hot and brittle and transparent and red, and of categories as defined by the features possessed by all the members of the category. On this view, literal equations that are true may express many different relations, but none of these relations involves a conflict of features. For example, a true equation between two noun phrases may express identity ("A bachelor is an unmarried male") or may express category membership ("A cygnet is an animal"), but in either case, if the assertion is true, if it fits the real world, then there will be no conflict between the features possessed by the two entities.

From this perspective, the recognition of analogy could be explained easily, and even though that explanation is wrong, it seems natural: when the two entities equated have a conflict in their features, as in "Money is bread," where money is inedible but bread is edible, then we recognize that the statement is false; we may then try to rehabilitate it by interpreting it figuratively. On this view, figuration is always secondary and parasitic. Figurative connections are always of a different kind from literal connections.

We have now seen that this view is inaccurate in some respects. Conflict of features between two concepts is not a reliable indicator of figuration. To recognize an analogy requires us to bring to bear our detailed knowledge of category structure. To recognize analogy, we must know in detail where the equated concepts stand within our entrenched category structures, and how they are related to each other in those category structures, and at what level of categorization those relationships hold. In short, analogies exist by virtue of category structures; categories and analogies inhabit the same conceptual space. A statement is an analogy not with respect to the world but with respect to the category structure that is brought to bear upon it.

The view of categories as trees with a uniform constitution of nodes and links isomorphic to a structure of categories in objective reality is just a folk theory. Our conceptual categories are of course constructed, along with the rest of our conceptual apparatus, under the sole constraint of fitness, which is to say, under the constraint that they empower us in our lives.

We recognize that poetic forms of thought, such as the analogic, help us to make sense of our experience. We may even recognize that we often prefer to turn to such connections when we attempt to make sense of language. But yet it is a strongly held and strongly felt part of our folk model of language and the world that there is a difference in kind between the true, literal connections and the false, poetic connections. This feeling can be accounted for by the extremes of generative entrenchment. It cannot be assumed as a premise of our models of thought and language.

This guided tour now comes to a close. This study has attempted to engage us in reconsidering the nature of certain conceptual connections and the way those connections are disclosed in language. This engagement is part of the general defining enterprise of this book, an enterprise that might be referred to as "cognitive rhetoric."

At certain moments—particularly at thickly technical moments such as those we have witnessed in this guided tour—the themes and the methods of cognitive rhetoric may seem foreign to garden-variety literary criticism. Our conditioned reaction to this surface strangeness might be to conclude—without thinking about it much—that cognitive rhetoric must be extrinsic to literary criticism, safely to be ignored by the literary critic as irrelevant to his practice. Unaccustomed to cognitive rhetorical issues, and understandably eager to find a way to make training in cognitive studies seem inessential, the literary critic may seize upon the unfamiliarity of these themes and methods as a defense against engaging the program of this book. To do so would be to take the current state of literary criticism as an assured ground whose necessary foundations are known to the literary critic.

But my intentions are radical upon this point: I would like to lead us to revise our default concept of literary criticism itself. One result of such a revision would be that the concerns of cognitive rhetoric would come to seem properly indispensable to literary criticism.

The guided tour we have just taken analyzes the nature of our conceptual connections and the way those conceptual connections are disclosed in our patterns of reading and writing. This project has immediate consequences for literary criticism, once we agree to think about it. To draw those consequences in detail would produce another book, or perhaps several books, which would be works of applied criticism, not start-up programs for cognitive rhetoric. Nonetheless, some of those consequences might be briefly sketched here.

There are three levels at which this particular project in cognitive rhetoric impinges upon literary criticism. The most obvious level is the level of individual phrases. Perhaps half of the phrases used in this study are taken from literary sources, often from authors whose works are placed in the most elite echelon of the literary canon. Examples would be Donne's "Think then, my soul, that death is but a groom / which brings a taper to the outward room," Marlowe's "And what are kings when regiment is gone / But perfect shadows in a sunshine day?" and Thoreau's "I am a parcel of vain strivings tied by a chance bond together." The fundamental problems these statements present are those of conceptual connection. The cognitive rhetorical project of analyzing the nature of conceptual connection is consequently indispensable to the analysis of such literary expressions. The same is true of theological utterances such as "God is love."

This level—the level of the individual expression—will interest critics sensitive to phrasing in language and to other local phenomena of language. But it may seem less immediately interesting to critics who wish to investigate overarching aspects of literary texts. For these critics, I propose two other levels of important connection between literary criticism and the cognitive rhetorical project of this study.

The first overarching level is that at which a literary work is inspired and informed globally by a controlling conceptual connection. Examples would be the connection between a journey and self-discovery in *The Odyssey* or between conversational wit and sex in *Much Ado about Nothing*. For example, shall we take the connection between conversational wit and sex as analogical, or shall we view conversational wit and sex as subcategories of some higher category such as heterosexual friction? Interpreting these works, and indeed any other work of literature, is fundamentally inseparable from coming to a certain view of the nature of the connection between informing concepts.

The second overarching level at which the cognitive rhetorical project of this study underlies literary criticism is the most global level of all: genre study, the project of grouping literary works into kinds and analyzing the nature of the connections between them. How is it that readers, from naive to sophisticated, carve up the literary continuum (or the linguistic continuum that includes that literary continuum)? What are the principles that the genre theorist uses, perhaps unaware? How are those principles based upon everyday principles of conceptual connection? How are genres such as lyric poetry connected to or derived from commonplace concepts such as our powerfully rich and supple commonplace concept of conversation? We have a standard commonplace notion of genre, of course: A genre is defined by criterial features possessed by every member of the genre. But this is exactly the standard commonplace philosophical notion of a category so thoroughly discredited by cognitive studies during the last decade. Given the cognitive scientific study of the nature of categories, we should not be surprised to find effects of the basic level in genre categories, or prototype effects in genre categories, or metaphoric members of a genre category, or radial categories within our conception of a given genre, or a gradient from the categorical to the analogical in the ways literary works are connected, or (perhaps most obviously) family resemblance as a creator of genres, and so on. The analysis of genre theory in the light of the cognitive scientific study of conceptual connections would be a large, intricate, and important work. It is so necessary and obvious that its development as a literary critical project in the age of cognitive science seems inevitable. I leave it to the reader to imagine the forms such a literary critical project might take.

Chapter 7

THE POETRY OF CONNECTIONS, I

WE DRAW BACK at this point in our enterprise for a panoramic view. In the preceding four chapters, we have engaged in four case studies. Any one of these case studies, taken alone, could be of interest only to the specialist. Taken together, they teach us something general. In each case study, we have inspected specific acts of language and literature that seem to us remarkable, special, and inventive. We have looked at arresting poetic uses of metaphor, complicated symmetries in elite texts, fine points in the rhetoric of rational argument, and provocative assertions of imaginative conceptual connection. In each case, we have seen that the remarkable and special phenomenon is the smallest tip of the iceberg. Our attempt to analyze these remarkable and special acts of language and literature has driven us to analyze the incomparably larger and more interesting background conceptual system that makes them possible. The true intricacy and power lie with this background conceptual system. We have seen special moments constituted as exploitations of this conceptual system. We have seen how special moments, embedded within this background conceptual system, are thereby anchored in our everyday embodied knowledge of image-schemas, event-shapes, bodily symmetry, force dynamics, category structures, and the rest of the everyday mind. To count as analysis, a treatment of these special moments must explain what is special about them in terms of the underlying basic forms of knowledge. The analysis of the special must start and end with the analysis of the everyday.

These are the beginnings of the conceptual revision suggested in the floor plan. It is a revision that asks us to think of the human person not as the outside of the body but as patterns of activity in the brain; of the body as mappings in that brain; of knowledge as ineradicably invested with those mappings; of conscious acts as dependent and small relative to unconscious processes; of special thought as dependent and small relative to common thought; of acts of language as anchored in this background conceptual system; of acts of literature as anchored in this background conceptual system; of concepts not as objects to be worked on but rather as competitive, dynamic, and plastic patterns of activity; of conceptual relations as competitive, dynamic, and plastic links between active processes; of imagination and reason as hypertrophies of the same conceptual capacities; of the poetic as part of the everyday; of conceptual and linguistic capacities as the essential human endowment; and of the humanities as criterially the investigation into these capacities.

In the next three chapters, collectively titled "The Poetry of Connections," we will take up the larger cognitive rhetorical program that has emerged from our four case studies. We begin with a review and expansion of our previous discussion of concepts.

A CONCEPT

In chapter 2, when we looked at the floor plan of the mind, we attempted to reconsider concepts, connections between concepts, and relationships between concepts and language. Let us summarize:

—We often speak as if concepts are something different from thought, as if we have a mental file cabinet of concepts that we trot out to organize thought.

—On the contrary, concepts are not different from thought, but rather inhere in thought.

—Thought is activated patterns in the brain, and a concept is an activated pattern inhering in thought. We do not have a given concept except when its pattern is active in thought. What we have instead is a latent capacity for the pattern to be activated.

—Concepts are active, dynamic devices in the brain that compete with each other to become active in the attempt to make sense of things.

—Concepts are themselves thoughts. They do not structure thoughts the way a mold structures clay or concrete or wax. They are rather a feature of thought.

—A concept does not have hard edges.

—A concept has no fixed degree of texture.

—Concepts are not monolithic, but have aspects.

—Our default concept of a concept represents a concept as independent of the body in which it exists. Our revised concept of a concept sees concepts as ineradicably embodied, which is to say, invested with maps of the body in the brain.[1]

—Concepts are not given to us by the world, but are the product of our attempts, as a species (with a phylogenetic past) and as individuals (with a personal past), to make sense of our worlds.

—Our most stable concepts are stable not because they are internally free of the imagination but because they have become entrenched in our conceptual faculties.

—There are many different sorts of conceptual links or structured bundles of conceptual links between concepts.

—Language is a tool for expressing such concepts and connections between them.

—This is why the shape of language discloses the structure of cognition.

Let us begin to look, in this and the next two chapters, at the nature of links between concepts and the ways those links are expressed in constructions in language. Later, we will look at pedagogical implications. In the final chapter, we will look at implications not just for the study of literary language but for the study of entire literary works, entire literary types, and entire general concepts of literature.

Links between Concepts

When we begin to look at the way concepts can be linked, we find that two different conceptual patterns can overlap, and can have connections impinging upon each other. Activating one pattern can influence the potential of the second to be activated. Let us introduce now some of the ways in which two different patterns can be connected. When activating a first pattern increases the potential of a second to be activated, I will label such an influence "reinforcing." In the contrary case, when activating a first pattern decreases the potential of a second to be activated, I will label such an influence "suppressing."

Two patterns of connections can be compatible in the sense that they can be activated fully and simultaneously as a composed unit. We may think of them as being superimposable. For example, in the concept *house*, we can activate both the *shelter* aspect and the *home-base* aspect compositely. The two patterns can be activated fully and simultaneously as a composed unit.

Alternatively, two patterns of connections can be incompatible under composition. Each resists the superimposition of the other. For example, two members of a category, such as *jaguar* and *tiger*, are incompatible under composition. If we are making sense of a story or of a visual field, and have determined that we are dealing with a big cat, but do not know what sort of big cat, we might activate either *jaguar* or *tiger*. Or we might settle for activating the pattern *big cat* that inheres schematically in both. But we cannot activate both *jaguar* and *tiger* fully and simultaneously as a composition, because each full pattern suppresses the other full pattern. We cannot activate *jaguar-tiger* as a single composed pattern. We cannot recognize a single thing that is both a jaguar and a tiger, unless we are willing to change our category structures. Changing our category structure in this case would mean specifically changing the mutual suppression into mutual activation. *Jaguar* and *tiger*, rather than mutually suppressing under composition, would then be mutually activating under composition.

But although *jaguar* and *tiger* are incompatible under composition, these two incompatible patterns are connected. Inhering within each pattern is a schematic pattern corresponding to the category *big cat*. Activating *jaguar* or *tiger* automatically activates *big cat*. Activating *big cat* increases the potential of both *jaguar* and *tiger* to be activated. Activating either *jaguar* or *tiger* may increase the potential of the other to be activated as a distinct pattern. But activating either *jaguar* or *tiger* suppresses the potential of the other to be activated compositely.

Two incompatible patterns not connected through a conventional category connection can be connected through a metaphoric or analogical connection. For example, consider "Hunger is the best sauce." *Hunger* and *sauce* are incompatible under categorical composition: they cannot be activated simultaneously in composition as a single taxonomic unit. They suppress each other under categorical composition. But a metaphoric connection can be drawn between these two patterns. A metaphoric connection is one in which parts of the target pattern are created or modified and imbued with the structure of the source pattern. Through metaphoric connection, the target can be *understood* in terms of the source, without being composable with the source and without sharing a category schema with the source.

PROPERTIES OF CONNECTIONS

Before we consider the nature of metaphoric connections, let us inspect some of the properties of connections between patterns of connections. Here we will take several minitours of the different properties of these kinds of connections.

First, a mental connection between patterns may be more or less *conventional* in our thought and our language. Suppose, for example, someone tells us that "The moon is a monkey wrench." The connection between our concept of the moon and our concept of a monkey wrench is not conventional. We have no routine automatic connection in our thought and language between these two concepts, or in general between types of heavenly bodies and types of tools. To understand this phrase, we must create some connections. One person might reflect that the moon is like a monkey wrench because both can expand and contract, which is to say, the moon's waxing and waning has image-schematic structure shared by the opening and closing of the monkey wrench. Another person might claim after reflection that he can see no connection. But now suppose someone says to us, "My fear is a hole I cannot get out of." The connections suggested by this phrase are already conventional and unconscious—we routinely conceive of mental situations in terms of bodily situations; our language expresses these metaphoric connections: we speak of feeling "trapped by circumstances," "carried away by passion," "crushed by rejection," and "beaten down by anxiety."

A mental connection may be more or less *productive* in our thought and language. The conceptual connection between how the mind operates and how the human body moves through space is highly productive. We say, "I'm making progress toward a solution," "I'm stuck, and I just cannot see where to go next with this problem," "He took an unfortunate position in the argument," "The answer was there all the time, right in front of my nose," "This part of the problem tripped me up," and "He's letting his mind wander."

A mental connection can be more or less *coherent* with other connections. For example, consider the following metaphors:

LIFE IS LIGHT and DEATH IS DARKNESS
LIFE IS HEAT and DEATH IS COLD
LIFE IS DAY and DEATH IS NIGHT
LIFE IS A FLAME and DEATH IS BEING EXTINGUISHED
A LIFETIME IS A YEAR and DEATH IS WINTER
LIFE IS WAKEFULNESS and DEATH IS SLEEP

The connection between life and light is coherent with the connection between life and heat, or life and day, or life and flame, or lifetime and year, or life and wakefulness. All of these connections share a structure. In our conceptual understanding of *day, flame, year,* and *wakefulness,* each has a three-stage scenario, where the middle stage is the most intense: dawn waxes to noon, which wanes to twilight; fuel for the flame catches fire, which wanes to ashes and embers; the beginning of spring waxes to summer, which wanes through fall back to winter; and a waking state waxes to full wakefulness, which wanes to sleepiness. In each case, the stage of greatest intensity is associated with light and heat. The source concepts (*day, flame, year, wakefulness, light,* and *heat*) cohere in sharing this structure. Consequently, the metaphoric connections between the concept *life* and these other concepts cohere accordingly. We can say, for example, that those who are in the springtime of life are most awake to its warmth and brilliance, and feel that the metaphor is coherent, even though it is severely mixed. Consider, by contrast, the mental connections between the concept of life and the concept of a dramatic performance. This metaphoric connection underlies expressions such as "It's curtains for him," "You're on in five minutes," "She's my leading lady," "Take a bow!" "She likes the spotlight," and so on. This connection is highly conventional and highly productive, but it is not particularly coherent with other ways of understanding life. For example, we have no conventional link between the sequence of acts in a play and the sequence of seasons in a year, and so it seems to us less coherent (although comprehensible) to say "The *curtain* went up on the *springtime* of his life" (which mixes only two metaphoric connections) than it does to say "Those in the springtime of life are most awake to its warmth and brilliance" (which mixes at least four, but at points where they cohere).

Lastly, a connection between patterns can be more or less *entrenched* in our conceptual system. There are two ways a connection can be entrenched. First, a connection can be used so frequently that it becomes stable regardless of the degree to which other connections depend upon it. I will call this use-entrenchment. Use-entrenched connections exist everywhere we find arbitrary but indispensable connections imposed by random assignment: we connect a telephone number to somebody, and entrench that connection through conceptual use. Yet nothing else in our conceptual system depends upon that connection, and it will weaken if a new telephone number is assigned. Use-entrenchment pertains not only to positive connections but also to negative connections: if the use of a pattern that is frequently used consistently suppresses another without meeting resistance, then the inhibitory connection from the first to the second becomes use-entrenched.

The second form of entrenchment, which we discussed in chapter 6, occurs when a connection can be entrenched with respect to other connections. This kind of entrenchment is called "generative entrenchment." A pattern is more generatively entrenched according as more connections in our conceptual apparatus depend upon it and according as those "downstream" patterns are more or less important. A connection that is deeply generatively entrenched resists disturbance because to disturb it is to disturb all the conceptual forms that depend upon it.

Let us summarize the relationship between use-entrenchment and generative entrenchment. A pattern that is use-entrenched is entrenched because it is frequently used. A pattern that is generatively entrenched is use-entrenched, but in two ways: it is used frequently in itself; it is also used frequently in the use of anything that depends upon it. A generatively entrenched pattern is always use-entrenched, but not conversely.

The neurophysiological basis for the entrenchment of conceptual connections lies in the plasticity of neuronal connections, which can be strengthened or weakened, as well as formed, over time. Neurons are all free agents. Patterns of connections between them are not fixed but are degenerative. Neuronal patterns compete for the participation of neurons. To use a neuronal connection is to reinforce it. A deeply generatively entrenched pattern of connection is reinforced often, since it is involved in the use of a great range of dependent patterns. A less generatively entrenched pattern of connections is reinforced less often and so is more likely to dissolve as components of the pattern are absorbed more strongly into other patterns. Use-entrenched connections that are not at all generatively entrenched are reinforced only each time they are specifically used, and so are liable to degenerate quickly if the specific utility of that connection disappears. A conceptual system consists of dynamic and plastic patterns that are lost if not used. Concepts themselves are not fixed objects but rather activities; they do not have essences but rather functions. The mind is not a machine that works on objects, it is rather a process, a dynamic process, and it is plastic.

Let us consider an example of generative entrenchment. We begin with the visual system. We routinely use patterns for recognizing a movement in time in a given direction from a source to a goal along a path that is traced by that movement.[2] Inhering within these patterns is a general pattern for recognizing such SOURCE-PATH-GOAL movement: this general visual schema is used any time a specific SOURCE-PATH-GOAL event is recognized. All such specific recognitions are connected for us conceptually exactly because they all use the general visual SOURCE-PATH-GOAL image-schema. This visual image-schema is generatively entrenched because so many specific recognitions use it in dependent fashion. This visual image-schema is moreover connected to the image-schema for recognizing the static trace of such a movement, as when a finger draws a line in the sand and the static line abides to be seen and recognized.

This generatively entrenched pattern for visual understanding is correlated to generatively entrenched patterns in other modalities, such as our motor systems. We use a motor SOURCE-PATH-GOAL image-schema whenever we reach for something. The pattern for vision is connected to the pattern for motion: this is indispensable, for example, to hand-eye coordination. We also have an auditory SOURCE-PATH-GOAL image-schema, used for example when we *hear* but do not see something moving toward us. We have a tactile SOURCE-PATH-GOAL image-schema, used for example when we feel something move along a path on our skin or trace a path with our index finger. All of these generatively entrenched patterns are correlated by generatively entrenched reinforcing patterns of connections between them, creating a cross-modal pattern corresponding to a spatial SOURCE-PATH-GOAL image-schema of extremely deep generative entrenchment.[3] This deeply generatively entrenched image-schema furthermore is used to structure a wide range of abstract concepts, as we saw for example in chapter 5, when we discussed the metaphoric understanding of argument, thought, and reason in terms of movement along paths in space.

The most profound entrenchment possible for connections is to come to constitute a schema that is used as part of our category structures. For example, none of us has ever experienced the morning that will occur tomorrow; it is certain to be different from every other morning. But we feel that all mornings are in some sense the same, because we attribute to all of them an inhering schema that is the category *morning*. All the poems in the world are different; all the rocks in the world are different; all the sisters in the world are different. But we think of all poems as somehow the same, all rocks as somehow the same, and all sisters as somehow the same, because in each case the connections between them are so entrenched as to constitute a category. It is important to see that these categories are not obvious and inevitable, generally speaking, and that the criteria of membership in these categories are not obvious. Consider the category *poem*, for example, and the member *Paradise Lost*. To those who have a certain historical and theoretical training in Western literature, it may seem that *Paradise Lost* is not only a poem, but in fact the highest poem and a paragon of the category *poem*. But to many beginning undergraduates, *Paradise Lost* does not look like poetry at all. The undergraduate concept of poetry applies mainly to short, free-verse, first-person lyrical expressions of a personal state, usually contemplative, perceptual, or affective. In asking these students to consider *Paradise Lost* as a *poem*, we bring pressure to bear on their conception of the category *poem* through what, for them, are at first metaphoric connections.

METAPHORIC CONNECTIONS

When two patterns of connections are not fully composable as a categorical unit and do not share an inhering category schema but are nonetheless connected, we usually take that connection as poetic. The dominant form of such connections between patterns is metaphoric or analogical: we understand one concept in terms of the other. How do we understand one concept metaphorically in terms of another? The answer has many parts.

Basic Metaphors

One very rich part of the answer concerns just those cases where we have to do no new conceptual work whatever to understand one concept metaphorically in terms of another, and no new conceptual work whatever to understand an utterance as an expression of that conceptual metaphor. These are cases where our conceptual apparatus already contains a basic metaphor.[4]

A basic metaphor is a connection through which one conceptual domain is understood in terms of the other. It has certain additional characteristics. A basic metaphor has three parts: first, a fixed conceptual domain that is the source; second, a fixed conceptual domain that is the target; and third, a fixed metaphoric mapping at the conceptual level of entities, relations, knowledge, reasoning patterns, image-schemas, and schematic structure from the source to the target. The target is usually in some degree structured and created by that mapping. To activate the target is automatically to activate both the mapping that structures it and the source domain in terms of which it is structured. For example, in the basic conceptual metaphor LIFE IS A PLAY, the source is our concept of a play; the target is our understanding of life-as-a-play; and the metaphoric mapping connects our concept of a play to our understanding of life-as-a-play. In this conceptual mapping, the person leading the life corresponds to an actor; the people with whom he interacts correspond to fellow actors; his pattern of behavior corresponds to the dramatic role the actor is playing; those who merely attend to his behavior and do not interact with his life correspond to the audience; and so on. The target is a pattern of connections inextricably connected to the source pattern of connections. Activating the target automatically activates the source in terms of which it was created.

Such basic metaphors as LIFE IS A PLAY are conceptual. They are automatically and conventionally available to us, and our use of them is usually unconscious. We need to do no new conceptual work to understand life in terms of a play: all we need to do is activate the understanding of life-as-a-play that is part of our conceptual apparatus.

Such basic metaphors are manifested in our language when we automatically discuss the target in language associated with the source. For example, when we say "It's curtains for him," meaning that someone will die, we are expressing that metaphoric understanding of life-as-a-play. And when we understand "She's my leading lady" to mean "She's my main romantic interest in life," we do so by taking "She's my leading lady" as a linguistic expression of our metaphoric understanding of life in terms of a play. We do no new conceptual work when we understand life in terms of a play; we simply activate a metaphoric understanding of life we already possess. We do no new conceptual work in uttering or understanding such statements; we simply take them as the conventional expression of that metaphoric understanding.

By virtue of activating this basic metaphor, we can understand language about the source domain as referring to the target domain. For example, the phrase "You're on!" could be taken as simply indicating that the moment has arrived for a stage-entrance. But by activating the basic metaphor of life as a play, we can take it as referring to the domain of life, and as indicating that the moment has arrived for someone to commence performing certain actions in life. In such a way, the basic metaphor LIFE IS A PLAY underlies many everyday expressions, such as "She always wants to be in the spotlight," "The kid stole the show," "That's not in the script," "What's your part in this?" "You missed your cue," "He blew his lines," "He saved the show," "She brought the house down," "Clean up your act!" "He always plays the fool," "That attitude is just a mask," "He turned in a great performance," "Take a bow!" "You deserve a standing ovation," "He plays an important role in the process," "He played only a bit part in my life," "He's waiting in the wings," "I'm improvising," and "It's showtime!"

Some basic metaphors are so entrenched that they seem to be cognitively indispensable, and it is hard for us even to notice that any metaphor is involved at all. For example, the basic metaphor DEATH IS DEPARTURE FROM HERE, as in "She's gone" and "He passed away," is so entrenched that it is difficult to notice at first that the "departure" associated with death is a metaphorical "departure," and the "from here" is a metaphorical "from here."

We share many basic metaphors. These basic metaphors, like all connections, vary in degree of conventionalization, productivity, mutual coherence, and entrenchment. They account for a prodigious slice of our thought, reasoning, and language.

But the theory of basic metaphors does not answer the question of how we connect one concept metaphorically to another, because it does not take up the issues we thought we were raising when we asked, "How do we understand one concept in terms of another, and how do we make sense of language expressing these conceptual metaphors?" The theory of basic metaphors responds: "You seem to think that to understand one concept metaphorically in terms of another or to make sense of metaphoric language, we have to do some constructive work at the conceptual level. But we do not. Those metaphoric connections are already captured in patterns in our mind. We do not usually notice them, even though we use them constantly. All we have to do to make metaphoric connections is to activate what we already know. All we have to do to understand metaphoric language is to take it in the conventional way as an expression of a basic metaphor we already know."

This answer, true for a staggering and powerful range of metaphoric connections, is nonetheless incomplete, because we want to know just what conceptual work is involved in conceiving of a metaphoric connection and in making sense of metaphoric language, and, from the theory of basic metaphors, we receive the answer that no work is involved because it has all already been done. What is fascinating about this answer is that it is in part quite true: for a great many cases, and important cases, we do not have to bother to do any constructive work in order to think metaphorically or understand or speak metaphorically; all we have to do is think in utterly automatic and conventional ways, and speak in utterly and automatic and conventional ways, and we will already be thinking metaphorically and making sense of language as expressions of conceptual metaphors. But this observation leaves unanswered questions like the following:

—What about cases like "Gifts are hooks" and "Kingdoms are clay" and "Las Vegas is the American Monte Carlo" and "Life is like a parachute jump: you have to get it right the first time" and "Oaths are the fossils of piety" and "Adams Morgan is the Greenwich Village of Washington, D. C." and the

infinity of other cases where there is no evidence that activating a basic meta-phor delivers the appropriate metaphoric connection? When we must do new conceptual work to connect concepts metaphorically and to make sense of metaphoric language, what is the work that we do, and how do we do it?
—There are many, many basic metaphors, and metaphor researchers discover new basic metaphors constantly. Is there a unity behind these basic meta-phors? Are they all the result of higher-order cognitive work that is in fact constructive?

We will find that the answers to these two questions are connected. The tools we use to forge a metaphoric connection when no basic meta-phor accomplishes the trick are the same higher-order tools that govern the conceptual workings of basic metaphors.

Generic-Level Metaphors

There are levels of schemas. This fact will lead us to add something to our description of a basic metaphor: A basic metaphor connects *specific-level* schemas, such as the schemas for DEATH and DEPARTURE. Specific-level schemas are contrasted with generic-level schemas, but the two are re-lated. Here, we will describe the nature of specific-level and generic-level schemas. For starters, to get a feel for the distinction, consider how DEATH—which we will take as an example of a specific-level schema—is an instance of the schema EVENT—which we will take as an example of a generic-level schema. Similarly, DEPARTURE is a specific-level instance of the generic-level schema ACTION. A generic-level schema is a schema that consists of certain kinds of parameters. Those parameters can be instanti-ated by specific-level information. Some of the generic-level parameters that can be instantiated by specific-level information are basic ontological categories (such as entity, state, event, action, and situation), aspects of beings (such as attributes and behavior), event-shape (such as instantane-ous or extended; single or repeated; completed or open-ended; preserv-ing, creating, or destroying entities; cyclic or not, that is, with or without fixed stages that end where they begin), causal relations (such as en-abling, resulting in, bringing about, creating, and destroying), image-schemas (such as bounded regions, paths, forces, and links), and modali-ties (such as ability, necessity, possibility, and obligation).

Each specific-level schema has such generic-level structure, as well as structure at the lower, specific level. Specific-level detail is, therefore, of two types: First, there is the detail that comes from specifying the generic-level parameters; second, there is lower-level detail. For example, DEATH is a specific-level instance of the generic-level schema EVENT: it fills out the generic-level structure of EVENT further by specifying the values of generic-level parameters. For example, EVENT contains a parameter for event-shape; the DEATH schema specifies the event-shape as one in which an entity, over time, *reaches a final state, after which it no longer exists.* The causal structure of the DEATH schema indicates that the passage of time will eventually *result* in that final state's being reached.

A basic metaphor connects *specific-level* schemas. It exists at the specific level of our conceptual apparatus. It connects a fixed specific-level source schema to a fixed specific-level target schema, by means of a designated ontological mapping of a list of entities in the source domain onto a corresponding list of entities in the target domain. Further, not just any specific-level conceptual metaphor is a basic metaphor. A basic metaphor is a specific-level conceptual metaphor that is conventional in thought and language.

In addition to basic metaphors, there are generic-level metaphors. Generic-level metaphors are vastly more general and flexible than basic metaphors. They operate at the level of generic-level schemas, and as such they need have neither a fixed specific-level source domain nor a fixed specific-level target domain. Nor do they have a designated ontological mapping of a list of entities in the source onto a corresponding list in the target.[5]

Consider an example of a generic-level conceptual metaphor, namely, EVENTS ARE ACTIONS. We commonly understand an event not as just happening but rather as being caused by some agent and thus as being the consequence of an action. An impressive proportion of the events that happen to us are, indeed, caused by agents, as when the vase falls off the table and we note that the cat knocked it over. Additionally, events that need not be thought of as caused by agents are often understood as if they are. For instance, we often make sense of natural events by ascribing some agency to an aspect of nature, as when we speak of the wind knocking over a tree and killing the person in the car underneath it.

We very commonly conceive of agentless events metaphorically as if they were caused by agents, as in:

> The boulder resisted all of our efforts to move it.
> Events conspired to delay the game.
> The computer wiped out my buffer.
> The computer spewed garbage at me.
> My car just refused to start this morning.

Such cases are all instances of EVENTS ARE ACTIONS, which imputes agency to something causally connected to the event. Such metaphorical agents are frequently taken to have human qualities.

EVENTS ARE ACTIONS gives us tremendous creative powers: it allows us to understand virtually any event metaphorically in terms of some action, by attributing agency to something in the specific-level schema of the particular specific-level event that concerns us. But not just any action will do as a source for understanding the target event, and we cannot attribute agency to just anything in the schema of the specific-level event. Unlike a basic metaphor, which contains a fixed ontological mapping, a generic-level metaphor gives only constraints on possible mappings. For example, EVENTS ARE ACTIONS limits the range of actions that can serve as source domains for understanding the event, and limits how the action can be mapped onto the event. It does this guiding through the constraint we saw in chapter 3: We are constrained against violating the image-schematic structure of the event.

For example, consider "The boulder resisted all of our efforts to move it." The image-schematic structure of the generic level of the target event includes:

—Agents intend to change the location of a physical object by exerting physical force upon it.
—They exert such force.
—The nature of the object results in a physical event: physical forces (inertia) oppose and withstand the forces exerted on the object, resulting in another physical event: the object does not move.

To conform to the constraint on generic-level metaphors, this image-schematic structure of the target event must not be violated. This means that if we wish to understand the target event in terms of some source action, that action must have generic-level structure that is compatible with the image-schematic structure of the event in the target.

How can we meet this constraint? To what does this constraint guide us? If we change the target in the way EVENTS ARE ACTIONS always does, we get

—Agents intend to change the location of a physical object by exerting physical force upon it.
—They exert such force.
—The object acts to oppose and withstand physically the forces exerted on it, so that it does not move.

What sort of action fits this bill? The obvious answer is resistance by the object. Is it acceptable to understand the event of stasis by the boulder as the result of an act of resistance? Yes, because doing so does not violate that part of the generic-level structure of the target that must not be violated. It does not violate event-shape: the general shape of the target event is that one thing exerts force on another and is met by an opposing force, with a result of stasis. This event-shape is preserved in understanding the event as the result of an action of resistance. The causal structure of the event is also preserved: there is a causal connection between the boulder and its stasis, namely, the boulder possesses certain properties (mass), and these properties result in the opposing force (inertia), which results in the ineffectuality of the force exerted on the boulder, which results in the stasis of the boulder. Understanding the boulder metaphorically as a resisting agent preserves this causal connection: the boulder is an agent who resists by exerting its capacities to create an opposing force; this results in the ineffectuality of the force exerted on the boulder; this results in the stasis of the boulder.

EVENTS ARE ACTIONS guides us in understanding an event metaphorically as an action by limiting the range of actions that can be sources for the metaphorical understanding, and by limiting just what nonagents in the event can be understood metaphorically as agents of the action.

It is important to see that we are guided very strongly in what can and cannot be personified as the agent of this action. We cannot, for example, think of the *color of the boulder* as the agent. Although we can say naturally "The boulder resisted all our attempts to move it," we cannot say naturally "The color of the boulder resisted all our attempts to move the boulder." The reason for this is that the target event does not allow a causal connection between the color of the boulder and the stasis of the boulder. To personify the color as the agent would be to impose a causal connection that violates the causal structure of the target.

Consider another example of EVENTS ARE ACTIONS. Two people unknown to each other are in an elevator. The elevator goes up. It stops at the next floor, the door opens, no one gets in, the door closes, the elevator begins to ascend. The first person turns to the second person and says, "A cruel lie." There is an event-shape to the elevator event, and an event-shape to a cruel lie. We map the lie onto the elevator event in such a manner as does not violate the event-shape of the elevator event. In the elevator event, there is an initial event that leads those who experience it to expect something; the expectation proves to be false; those who hold the expectation are displeased at having been led to that expectation. EVENTS ARE ACTIONS maps the liar onto the elevator door; the act of lying onto the event of the door's opening; the content of the lie onto the deduction that someone is about to enter the elevator; the realization that the lie is false onto the realization that the deduction is false; and the disappointment at having suffered the lie onto the disappointment at having suffered the useless delay. The target event has the same event-shape as the source action, except that the source is an action with an agent and the target is an agentless event. EVENTS ARE ACTIONS exists to change the agentless event metaphorically into an action by an agent.

EVENTS ARE ACTIONS is a general conceptual metaphor, enabling us to construct metaphorical understandings of events in terms of actions and to understand nonagents metaphorically in terms of agents. It allows us to understand an infinity of utterances as expressions of particular instances of EVENTS ARE ACTIONS. It underlies "My car decided to give out on me," "The wind crept under the door and nipped at Mary's ankles," "The overstuffed armchair embraced John's overstuffed body," "The acid ate through the metal," "The fire burned cheerfully," "The farmer took this field from the desert, and every year, the desert wants it back," "Inscribed on the cover of the book, in large and *friendly* letters, are the words, 'Don't panic,'" and so on.

This generic-level metaphor not only guides our metaphorical understanding of events in terms of actions when no basic metaphor does the trick, it also governs various basic metaphors that are in fact conventional instances of EVENTS ARE ACTIONS.

Consider, for example, the basic metaphor DEATH IS DEPARTURE. It is an instance of the generic-level metaphor EVENTS ARE ACTIONS. Through this metaphor, the event of departure is understood as the result of an action by an agent. We can attribute this agency to a variety of components in the event schema and still meet the constraints on EVENTS ARE ACTIONS. For example, we can view the person who dies as the agent of his own departure, as when we say "He left us" or "He departed this earth" or, in a phrase I have heard in Ireland, "He left the island." But we can also see Death-in-general as the agent, as when we say "Death took him." We can also see a more specific cause as the agent of departure, as in "Leukemia took him."

Consider, as another instance of EVENTS ARE ACTIONS, the basic metaphor TIME IS A CHANGER. We have a conception that, as time passes, certain changes will take place. Through TIME IS A CHANGER, we can view these events of change over time as the results of actions by a personified Time, as when we say "Time eroded the land." This basic metaphor is a special case of the generic-level metaphor EVENTS ARE ACTIONS, and it meets the expected constraints. For example, the particular target event of change will have a general shape, and the source action must not violate that general shape. Suppose the particular target event of change is death understood as ceasing to exist, with no return. What are appropriate source actions for understanding this target event? Eating and theft result in events of change in which something (the food or the possession) goes out of existence and does not return, so eating and theft are acceptable source actions. Time the changer in this case can therefore be further specified as Time the devourer or Time the thief and still meet the constraints on EVENTS ARE ACTIONS. But massaging or whipping is not an acceptable source action because neither has the same event-shape as death. So Time the changer in this case cannot be further specified as Time the masseur or Time the whipper and still meet the constraints on EVENTS ARE ACTIONS.[6]

A single generic-level metaphor, EVENTS ARE ACTIONS, both guides us in our metaphorical understanding of events as actions when no basic metaphor does the trick for us, and governs the multitude of basic metaphors that are instances of EVENTS ARE ACTIONS. In this way, there is a systematicity to basic metaphors, which otherwise would appear to be less organized; and there is a connection between conventional metaphorical understandings we already know and new metaphorical understandings we construct.

Consider, as a further example, a very different generic-level metaphor, CAUSATION IS PROGENERATION.[7] This generic-level metaphor has a wide scope of variable targets: any domain with causal structure is a potential target of this generic-level metaphor, provided it meets the appropriate constraints. CAUSATION IS PROGENERATION, unlike EVENTS ARE ACTIONS, has a specific-level source domain: the domain of human progeneration. CAUSATION IS PROGENERATION operates on the generic level of that specific-level source domain. This generic level source domain on which CAUSATION IS PROGENERATION acts includes the following structure.

—There is a being who has the efficacy to produce from itself another being, and who does so.
—This efficacy is nondeterministic, and neither sufficient nor necessary for the production: there is no requirement that in identical circumstances an identical being would be produced, no requirement that the first being's efficacy is all that is needed for the production, and no requirement that the second being could not have resulted from a different first being.
—The moment in which the second being comes to exist as an entity in the world is brief.
—The second being appears out of nowhere—not exactly nowhere, but out of things or components that are in themselves relatively insignificant or imperceptible. The production is thus of something of one order of significance out of things of an order of much lower significance.
—The first and second being both have cohesion, individuation, and duration of the sort that we associate conceptually with human individuals. For example, a human being abides complete during his lifetime; a human being does not fragment into parts and continue living.
—The single progeneration is a manifestation of general progenerative capacity.
—When the progenitor and progenerated being share properties, it is because the progenitor has passed them on to the progenerated being.

The generic-level metaphor CAUSATION IS PROGENERATION exists explicitly to change cause-effect relationships metaphorically into parent-child relationships; that is, where the target contains a cause-effect relationship, it can be understood in terms of a parent-child relationship.

CAUSATION IS PROGENERATION is constrained in its operation by the usual constraint that, for the parts of the source and target that are to play a role in the mapping, the metaphor must not violate the image-schematic structure of the target.

Thus, although CAUSATION IS PROGENERATION has a sweeping variability in its potential target domains, including all conceptual domains in which there is some causal structure, nonetheless not just any causal relationship can be understood in terms of the generic-level structure of PROGENERATION. In order for the potential target to qualify as an acceptable target, mapping the generic-level structure of PROGENERATION onto the target must not violate the target's image-schematic structure.

The potential target domains that do meet these constraints are very many, and of very many different kinds, as in "Necessity is the mother of invention," "Invention, nature's child," "Elizabeth was a child of the Italian Renascence," "Virtue is the daughter of heaven," "As a child of the modern era, I believe that there are all sorts of physical regularities," "Italian, eldest daughter of ancient Latin," "Night is the mother of fear," "Despair is the mother of madness," "Filth is the mother of stench and disease," "Fear is the mother of superstition," "Solitude is the mother of anxiety," "Violence is the child of fear," "Ignorance is the mother of suspicion," "Hatred is the child of misunderstanding," "Gambling is the child of avarice," and "Death is the mother of beauty."

FORM IS MOTION is a generic-level metaphor operating over all forms as targets. This generic-level metaphor allows us to understand a form in terms of the motion whose trace would be the image-schema of that form. It does this by mapping the trace of the movement onto the static form, where the image-schema of the trace is compatible with the image-schema of the static form. This generic-level metaphor underlies phrases like "The road runs on for a bit and then splits," "The path stretches along the shore of the lake," and "The fence dips and rises in parallel with the terrain."

Let us consider one last generic-level metaphor, THE GREAT CHAIN METAPHOR.[8] This generic-level metaphor has tremendous variability in both its potential source and target domains. THE GREAT CHAIN METAPHOR is based on our commonplace notion of the hierarchical order of beings. I label this commonplace notion "The Great Chain"; hence the name of the metaphor. In the Great Chain, forms of being at any level have certain kinds of attributes. Forms of being at any particular level have all the kinds of attributes of forms of being at all lower levels, plus some kind of attributes not possessed by forms of being at lower levels. For example, physical objects have physical attributes. Physical objects with part-whole structure have not only physical attributes (such as brittle, friable, and black) but also part-whole structure that is not possessed by mere physical objects; plants have not only part-whole structure and physical attributes, but also genetic and biological attributes; lower animals have not only physical attributes, part-whole structure, and biological attributes, but also instinctual attributes; human beings have not only physical attributes, part-whole structure, biological attributes, and instinctual attributes, but also higher cognitive attributes.

Our commonplace notion of the Great Chain combines with our commonplace notion of The Nature of Things. The commonplace notion of The Nature of Things is that being leads to doing—the attributes possessed by a form of being lead to the way that form of being behaves. For example, glass is brittle, and hence it breaks easily. The Great Chain metaphor operates on the conjunction of the Great Chain and The Nature of Things: it maps one level of attribute (and hence behavior) onto another level of attribute (and hence behavior). For example, we use the Great Chain metaphor to understand human emotional behavior in terms of instinctual behavior, as when we say, "He's been burned before" to explain the behavior of an individual who has had a painful romantic experience and is now reluctant to enter any romantic involvement. Here, the instinctual behavior is the bodily avoidance of a natural form of being (fire) that has previously caused bodily pain. The emotions and emotional behavior of the individual who has had an unpleasant romantic experience and now shuns romantic involvement are understood metaphorically in terms of these instincts and instinctual behavior, by means of THE GREAT CHAIN METAPHOR.

Since different forms of being are characterized by their highest level of attribute, THE GREAT CHAIN METAPHOR also maps forms of being at one level onto forms of being at another level, by virtue of mapping attributes (and hence behavior) at one level onto attributes (and hence behavior) at another level. For example, we can describe a certain sort of human social behavior by saying "All bark and no bite," where we are understanding psychological and social behavior of a human being in terms of the instinctual behavior of a dog. The mapping between attributes of different orders thus induces a mapping between two different orders of being, namely, human and animal.

THE GREAT CHAIN METAPHOR, in the absence of any indication to the contrary, operates on the highest level of attribute (and consequent behavior) of a form of being. For example, if we hear someone described as "a spider," we know that it is the spider's instinctual nature and behavior that are to be mapped, not the spider's physical attributes, such as the fact that it has a round body and thin limbs.[9] If the speaker of this metaphor wants us to consider the physical attributes of the spider as part of the mapping, the speaker must give us some extra cue to do so, such as making a gesture or saying that someone "looks like a spider."[10] The fact that

THE GREAT CHAIN METAPHOR operates on the highest level attributes (and hence behavior) of a form of being is not some special part of this metaphor. Instead, it derives from a general Gricean principle at work whenever we understand language, namely, the maxim of quantity, which says that we all share an expectation that speakers will not be more or less informative than necessary.[11] If a speaker described someone as "a spider," and meant to indicate that the person had a round body and thin limbs like a spider, that speaker would have violated the maxim of quantity, because, by mentioning "spider," he would have given us a tremendous amount of superfluous information, namely, all the higher-order attributes and behavior of the spider.

THE GREAT CHAIN METAPHOR does not violate the image-schematic structure of the target. Consider the moment in *King Lear* when Kent interposes himself between Cordelia and her father the king. King Lear, angered at Cordelia, warns Kent, "The bow is bent and drawn, make from the shaft." We use THE GREAT CHAIN METAPHOR to map the physical and part-whole attributes and behavior of the bow and arrow onto the emotional, psychological, and social attributes and behavior of Lear. The bow and arrow are physical objects with a part-whole structure, a nature, and a characteristic structured behavior: the drawn bow has a tensed nature that leads to an event when it is released: the arrow strikes its object. This is the source domain. We map this nature and behavior onto the target domain of Lear's psychological attributes and consequent behavior: Lear's psychological state is metaphorically tensed; when he releases that metaphorically tensed energy, it will metaphorically strike its object, Cordelia. More accurately, it will convey its metaphoric force along a directed metaphoric path from Lear to Cordelia and metaphorically strike anything along that metaphoric path, including Kent, if Kent is rash enough to place himself metaphorically in the metaphoric way. In performing this mapping, we are constrained not to violate the image-schematic structure of the target. For example, the general shape of the event is not to be violated; the image-schemas of tension, directed force, and release of that force in a direction are not to be violated; the causal relationship between the internal tension and the externally directed force is not to be violated.

The theory of generic-level metaphors subsumes the theory of basic metaphors and gives us a more encompassing answer to the questions of how we understand metaphorically and how we make sense of metaphorical language. The theory of generic-level metaphors implies the theory of basic metaphors: (at least many) basic metaphors are entrenched special instantiations of conventional generic-level metaphors. Nonetheless, the theory of generic-level metaphors is a very different theory from the theory of basic metaphors as it was originally proposed.

In the theory of basic metaphors, understanding one thing metaphorically in terms of another requires no new conceptual work, but only the activation of a fixed knowledge structure we supposedly all have. Indeed, in the theory of basic metaphors, new conceptual work is forbidden in the central parts of the metaphorical understanding, although new conceptual work can be allowed in the ways certain optional parts of the metaphor are filled in, and in which specific instantiation the metaphor takes. In the theory of basic metaphors, understanding metaphorical language requires no new conceptual work, but only the taking of the language in the conventional ways as expressions of the fixed knowledge structures called basic metaphors.

But in the theory of generic-level metaphors, knowing a very few generic-level metaphors gives us tremendous constructive powers of mind for understanding metaphorically and making sense of metaphorical language. In the theory of generic-level metaphors, basic metaphors are conventional knowledge structures that ontologically derive from the constructive powers of mind.

Generic-level metaphors are not special-case metaphors, in the ways that basic metaphors are. The scope of a generic-level metaphor is not restricted to just two domains, a fixed source and a fixed target. Instead, a generic-level metaphor is a more powerful and general tool. A generic-level metaphor does not contain a designated ontological mapping. Indeed, a generic-level metaphor can be used to map a source onto a target *in different ways*, as, for example, when EVENTS ARE ACTIONS can be used to map agency from the source ACTION to the target EVENT in a variety of ways, leading to a variety of personifications, but all in accord with very strict constraints against violating image-schematic structure.

The theory of generic-level metaphors indicates how a few patterns of thought give strong guidance in the creation of many specific new metaphorical understandings. It indicates how we can make sense of many new metaphorical expressions by taking them as prompting us to construct new metaphorical understandings, which we construct by applying a generic-level metaphor. The theory of generic-level metaphors also provides a higher-order explanation for the existence of (at least many) basic metaphors. It shows that basic metaphors are not random and unconnected: they come in clusters with a strong systematicity and a shared structure because all the members of the cluster derive from a particular generic-level metaphor, and are thus all constrained to operate according to the constraints on that generic-level metaphor.

Of course, there is still no getting around the fact that the theory of generic-level metaphors, like the theory of basic metaphors, insists that we must have particular knowledge structures if we are to go about metaphorical understanding: we must already have the generic-level metaphor as a knowledge structure. But the theory of generic-level metaphors requires many fewer such structures, and each is much simpler than any basic metaphor that might derive from it. We turn now to a higher-order explanation of why generic-level metaphors should work just as they do.

IMAGE-SCHEMAS AND IMAGE METAPHORS

We have seen this explanation before, in chapter 3, when we encountered the constraint against violating image-schematic structure during metaphoric mapping. Here, I want to consider some of the details of that explanation. In chapter 3, we considered image-schemas and image metaphors briefly. Image-schemas are extremely skeletal images that we use in cognitive operations. We have many such image-schemas: of bounded space, of a path, of contact, and of human orientations such as up-down, front-back, and center-periphery. We also have dynamic image-schemas, such as the image-schema for a rising motion, or a dip, or an expansion, and so on. When we understand a scene, we naturally structure it in terms of such elementary image-schemas. Consider, for example, our image of a table. We naturally structure the image of the tabletop in terms of a broad, flat, planar, bounded region. Consider our image of a plateau. We naturally structure the image of its top in terms of a broad, flat, planar, bounded region. It is because this skeletal image-schema of a broad, flat, planar, bounded region applies to both a table and a plateau that in Spanish one refers to both by the same name, *la mesa*. This image-schema applies to the various things we refer to as "plate glass," "home plate," and "plateau."

Our images are structured by image-schemas. Just as detailed conceptual knowledge can have schematic knowledge inhering in it, so a detailed image can have schematic knowledge inhering in it. A rich image of a particular table will include all sorts of detail, including the grain of the table, the location of certain dents, how the edges were nicked, how the sunlight moved across it as the sun passed outside in the sky, how the shadows of the tree branches outside moved across it, how a certain scratch felt to the touch, and so on. Inhering within such an image will be image-schematic information that structures the image. The image of the top, for example, is structured by the image-schema for a broad, flat, planar, bounded region. Similarly, our rich image of the street leading by our house, which includes colors and sounds and intensity of sunlight and shadow and so on, has inhering within it the very skeletal image-schema of a path.

An image metaphor maps a source image onto a target image. In doing so, it may map some of the very rich imagistic detail of the image. For example, when we hear a certain postmodern painting described as looking like oatmeal and hashed browns spilled on a cafeteria floor, we map over very detailed imagistic knowledge of textures, colors, materials, and so on.[12]

When we map one image onto another, we do so according to the principle introduced in chapter 3: we are constrained not to violate the image-schematic structure of the target image. When we map the image of a pear onto the figure of a certain person, we preserve (in the absence of an indication to do the contrary) the image-schematic orientation of up and down: the upward direction of the pear corresponds to the upward direction of the person's figure. We also preserve the image-schematic information of relation of parts: the middle of the pear maps onto the waist of the person. It is important to see that in no way does the utterance "He has a pear shape" tell us to map in this way. We know to perform the mapping in this way because we observe a constraint against violating image-schematic structure in metaphorical understanding. If we say of a weightlifter that he has a pear-shape, and give a bodily gesture to indicate that his stomach corresponds to the top of the pear and his chest corresponds to the bottom, the inversion will be remarkable and perhaps amusing.

When we hear that someone's teeth are like a keyboard, we know to map each individual key to an individual tooth, not because the utterance tells us to, but because we are constrained not to violate the image-schema of part-whole relationships that structures each image.

INVARIANCE

As we observed in chapter 3, we structure many concepts that are not themselves images in terms of image-schemas. Our concepts of time and of events and of actions and of causality, for example, are structured in terms of image-schemas.[13] Indeed, most of what we have called generic-level structure appears to be image-schematic in nature. When we observe that image-schematic structure is always generic-level structure, and that most generic-level structure (such as event-shape, causal-shape, and so on) is actually image-schematic structure, it becomes clear why the constraint against violating image-schematic structure is so manifest in the case of generic-level metaphors. This constraint was given in chapter 3, in the body of the text, as

(1) In metaphor, we are constrained not to violate the image-schematic structure of the target; this entails that we are constrained not to violate whatever image-schematic structure may be possessed by nonimage components of the target.

If we add to this constraint the further hypothesis, discussed in the notes to chapter 3, that

(2) For those parts of the source and target determined to be part of the mapping, impart to the target as much of the generic-level structure of the source as is consistent with (1),

then the result is a version of what George Lakoff and I have called the invariance hypothesis.[14]

The invariance hypothesis is something above generic-level metaphor, governing generic-level metaphor and—while not accounting for every generic-level metaphor—nonetheless motivating each. It is a constraint, as discussed in chapter 3, that applies to all metaphoric connection, whether conventional or novel.

The first case in which the invariance hypothesis applies is the case of image metaphors, which we have just discussed. In that case, the target and source already contain image-schemas, and the source image-schema must be compatible with the target image-schema.

The second case in which the invariance hypothesis applies is more important. It is the case in which we must not violate image-schemas that structure nonimage components of the target. Consider the metaphor that SOLVING A PROBLEM IS JOURNEYING TO A DESTINATION. Journeying to a destination is the source domain. It contains a SOURCE-PATH-GOAL image-schema. The target domain, solving a problem, does not inherently contain an image, and so of course does not contain an image-schema associated with an image. But this does not mean that the target domain does not contain image-schematic structure. For example, solving a problem contains an order: we go through stages in solving a problem, where each stage is associated with a degree of success in solving the problem. The first stage is considering the problem. Every partial success in solving the problem puts us in a later stage of solving it. The last stage is solving the problem. Such ordering is image-schematic structure. When we map the image-schema from the source domain onto the target domain, we therefore must do so in such a way as to not to violate the ordering in the target domain. When we map the SOURCE-PATH-GOAL image-schema onto the target domain of *solving a problem*, it acquires the image-schematic structure of *journeying to a destination*. For example, we "start on" a problem just as we "start on" a journey. We "arrive" at a solution just as we "arrive" at a destination. But the way *solving a problem* acquires the image-schematic structure of *journeying to a destination* must not violate whatever image-schematic structure is possessed by *solving a problem*, namely, the temporal ordering.

A question arises here: does *solving a problem* have any order except the order given to it through this metaphor? In other words, does it make any sense to say that *solving a problem* has, independent of the metaphor, an image-schematic order that metaphor is constrained not to violate? This is a special instance of the larger and daunting question of the nature and genesis of abstract concepts. Let us begin by separating novel from conventional cases. In the novel case where the metaphor has no entrenchment, we can often see image-schematic structure in the target that the new metaphor must respect. We can invent new metaphors by figuring out the image-schematic structure of the target and finding a source that matches it. For example, if we observe that in death something goes out of existence with no return, then we can hunt about for some other event that fits this structure, such as being tossed into the garbage, and personify death unconventionally as a garbageman. The structure of the target did not come from this unconventional metaphor. As another example, consider the case in which a law student remarks that a concept of justice becomes more and more complicated over time and his classmate responds, "Yes, it's just like a traveler who acquires so much baggage as he goes along that soon he is unfit to travel." There was order in the target—states of less complexity precede in time states of more complexity—and it existed before the invention of this unconventional metaphor. The metaphor respects that order but does not impart it. In unconventional cases like these we can often see image-schematic structure existing in the target prior to the invention of the unconventional metaphor. But the evidence in the case of conventional metaphor is quite different. We cannot separate the metaphor SOLVING A PROBLEM IS A JOURNEY out from our concept of *solving a problem*. We cannot inspect what *solving a problem* would look like if we did not have this metaphor. In such cases, we can observe the fact that the metaphor respects the image-schematic structure of the target, but we may come to two different explanations of how this situation arose. In the first explanation, we assume that the image-schematic structure belonged to the target independent of the metaphor and was respected as the metaphor was formed. In the second explanation, we assume that the image-schematic structure of the target was imparted through the metaphor according to (2) above; it matches the source because it came from the source. Evidentially, the result is the same: to the extent that order is part of the mapping, the image-schematic structure of order in the source must under either explanation be compatible with the image-schematic structure of order in the target.

So far, we have considered some cases in which the source and target both have images associated with them, and one case in which the source contains an image but the target does not. Now let us consider a case in which neither source nor target inherently contains an image, namely, DEATH IS A THIEF, as in "death robbed him of his life." Suppose a disease has led to the death of a person. There is an image-schema associated with this causal structure. It consists of paths linking nodes. By virtue of this image-schematic structuring of causation, we may say that the disease "led to" death and be understood as meaning that the disease caused the death. Any metaphorical understanding of that death must not violate this image-schematic structure. Since the causal structure is image-schematic, the causal structure of the schema must not be violated by the metaphor. Suppose we understand this death metaphorically by mapping onto it the source domain for theft, as in "death robbed him of life." Then neither the source nor the target inherently contains an image, but both contain causal structure that is image-schematic, and those causal structures match. In both the source and the target, the causation is structured by the image-schema of a directed path from the cause to the effect, and the mapping does not violate that image-schematic structure.

The logic of the metaphors in these examples may seem obvious, but that is only because our use of image-schema preservation in metaphorical understanding is automatic. Actually, it is a remarkable phenomenon that we know how to work the logic of metaphorical understanding so easily and fluidly. In any specific metaphorical understanding, many components in the source domain and the target domain go unmapped, ignored, or violated. We know that in metaphorical understanding, only certain things "count" as part of the mapping, and they "count" only in certain systematic ways. But these obvious understandings of the logic of metaphor require work: they do not happen by magic. There is no little man inside our head who does all the work and gives us the answer. Any explanation of these cognitive phenomena must provide a model of how our conceptual apparatus works to determine the resultant mapping.

Consider an example that will highlight both the deceptive obviousness and the subtle intricacy of image-schematic preservation. Suppose someone says to us, "I'm half-way done with the problem," and then later tells us, "Well, I'm a third of the way done with the problem." When he gives us that second report, we know that either (1) he now believes that he has in fact had less success solving the problem than he previously thought he had achieved when he told us that he was half-way done, or (2) he now considers the problem to be much harder than he originally thought. *Why do we know this?* This inference seems obvious only because it is automatic. There is nothing obvious about why we should arrive at this understanding of the metaphoric expression. The question requires an exact answer. We arrive at this understanding because we know that the metaphoric mapping of *journeying* onto *solving a problem* must not violate the image-schematic structure of the target. The image-schema associated with a journey has a linear order, and in that order, the beginning point is before the point that corresponds to one-third of the way, which is before the point that corresponds to one-half of the way. The temporal order in which we arrive at points in the path is moreover identical to the spatial order in which these points are arranged on the path. The target domain, *solving a problem*, also contains image-schematic structure. In particular, it contains an order: success is accretive, such that a state of less success is always before a state of more success; therefore, the initial state of taking up the problem occurs before all others, and the state of having solved the problem occurs after all others. When we map the image-schematic information in the source onto the target, the image-schematic information in the target is not to be violated. Thus, the order relation between any two points on the path must be mirrored in the order relation between the two states of success onto which they are mapped. Any mapping must be such that, for any states of success c and d, and any points on the path a and b that are mapped onto c and d, respectively, c is before d if and only if a is before b. Consequently, the state of being metaphorically one-third of the way finished with the problem must be before the state of being metaphorically half-way finished with the problem, because being at the one-third point on the path is before being at the half-way point on the path. This constraint is met if we take the second report as revising backward the original estimate of the degree of success. This constraint is alternatively met if we take the first report as indicating half-success with a problem of a certain difficulty and the second report as indicating one-third success with the same problem now reconsidered to be much harder, because halfway down a short path can be shorter than a third of the way down a longer path. These two different ways of meeting the constraint give us two different readings: the speaker is revising his report of success with a problem of fixed difficulty or revising his assessment of the difficulty of the problem. These readings seem obvious to us, but their explanation is anything but obvious. We cannot begin to explain them, or indeed any reading of any text, without investigating the intricate and complicated activity of the background conceptual system that produces these readings.

ASPECTS OF IMAGE-SCHEMAS

With the invariance hypothesis now elaborated, and some examples given of why the hypothesis bears on a range of phenomena in metaphorical understanding, let us look at what kind of information seems to be contained in image-schemas. What sort of properties count for image-schemas?

Absolute size is unimportant for image-schemas. An image-schema of a circle is no different from an image-schema of a larger circle. But relative size is important. An image-schema that includes both a small circle and a large circle is different from an image-schema that includes two circles of equal size.

Movement counts. We have not only static image-schemas but also dynamic image-schemas. We have, for example, an image-schema of a dip, which consists of the dynamic image of the movement of a point tracing out a dip.

Number of entities counts, at least up to a certain fuzzy magnitude of number: that is, an image-schema of two entities is different from an image-schema of three; but we probably do not have an image-schema of 927 and if we did it would probably not be different from an image schema of 928. One image-schema associated with the event of *separation* consists of a single image-schematic entity separating into two. One image-schema associated with the event of *combination* consists of two image-schematic entities combining into one.

Interiors, exteriors, centers, and boundaries count. The following are all different image-schemas: a circle with a marked point at its center; a circle with a marked point somewhere else interior to the boundary; a circle with a marked point on the boundary; and a circle with a marked point exterior to the boundary.

Connectedness of the image counts, as does continuity. Degree of curvature counts, but only in rough fashion: The image-schema associated with *cup* need not have an exact degree of curvature; but if we flatten out the sides to the point that the image-schema begins to approach an image-schema associated with *plate*, for example, then we have not preserved the original image-schema.

Various image-schematic relations count. For example, consider our image-schemas of triangles: any triangle is similar to (has the same interior angles as) itself; if a triangle A is similar to B, then B is similar to A; and if A is similar to B and B is similar to C, then A is similar to C. All of these relations (reflexivity, symmetry, and transitivity) count in image-schema space, in the sense that we cannot change the image-schema in such a way as to violate these relations and still feel that we are left with the same image-schema. An equivalence relation is any relation that is reflexive, symmetric, and transitive. Since reflexivity, symmetry, and transitivity count, it follows that all equivalence relations count.

Certain order relations count. For example, if we have an image-schema in which vertical lines are ordered by relative size, beginning with the smallest and proceeding on to the largest, in a row, then we cannot alter that order and feel that we still have the same image-schema. This is a linear order. As an example of a different kind of order relation, called a dictionary order, consider three vertical lines ordered horizontally by relative size, followed by three circles ordered horizontally by relative size, followed by three squares ordered horizontally by relative size. We cannot transpose the middle circle and the middle line, for example, and still feel that we have the same image-schema. We in fact cannot alter the order in any way and feel that we still have the same image-schema.

It is not at all surprising that we should have a cognitive category of image-schemas, almost as if they could be characterized mathematically as elements in an image-schema space. It is not at all surprising that we should know what counts in that space. Introspection demonstrates our ease in dealing with image-schema space: consider one image-schema of two concentric circles, and another image-schema of two concentric squares. It is immediately and intuitively obvious to us how to transform one into the other, and exactly what is preserved, and exactly what is not preserved, in such a transformation. Properties of the image-schema that are not preserved are smoothness of the boundary and rough degree of curvature. Properties that are preserved are interiors and exteriors (and hence containment), connectedness, number of entities, similarity of contained and containing figure, and so on.

The invariance hypothesis is not that we cannot change image-schemas. On the contrary, we mentally transform image-schematic structure with great ease and fluidity. We know many transformations that turn one image-schema into another. The invariance hypothesis claims rather that metaphorical mapping does not violate the image-schematic structure of the target. We know when we attempt to understand one concept in terms of another that the image-schematic structure of the target must not be violated. The invariance hypothesis claims that generic-level information in the target is largely structured by image-schemas, and that to the extent it is so structured, it remains invariant under metaphorical mapping. Thus, image-schematic properties define a topology on generic-level schemas.

EXAMPLES OF INVARIANCE

Let us consider how this topological invariance operates in some metaphorical understandings. Consider the generic-level metaphor EVENTS ARE ACTIONS. One of the constraints on this generic-level metaphor is that the general shape of the target event is not to be violated. The shape of the event is defined by certain properties, such as instantaneous or extended, single or repeated, completed or open-ended, preserving, creating, or destroying entities, cyclic or not, and so on. But each of these properties is associated with an image-schema, which is why it is so natural for us to talk about the "shape" of the event. Consider, for example, a conception of death in which we think of something going entirely out of existence and not returning. That event-shape has an image-schema associated with it, namely, a single image-schematic entity disappearing. If we are to understand that event metaphorically as an event resulting from action, then the source event must, by the invariance hypothesis, have a compatible image-schema associated with it; which is to say, it must have the same event-shape. Thus the constraint on EVENTS ARE ACTIONS that the shape of the target event be preserved is just a consequence of the invariance hypothesis.

What can change in EVENTS ARE ACTIONS is the status of a cause in the target event: it can become, by means of the metaphor, an agent. But this does not involve any violation of image-schematic information. Understanding a cause as a causal agent preserves whatever image-schematic structuring of causation the target event may contain. For example, if we understand causation as directed links from causes to effects, then understanding one of those causes as a causal agent changes nothing in the image-schematic directed linkage. It changes the target, but it does not change the image-schematic structure of the target.

Consider the generic-level metaphor FORM IS MOTION. Here, invariance is obvious: the trace of a motion is a form, and that form is mapped onto the target form, so that a static form is understood as the trace that results from the motion that would have created that trace. In this mapping, paths are mapped to paths, curves to curves, turns to turns, contact to contact, and so on.

Consider the generic-level metaphor CAUSATION IS PROGENERATION. The image-schematic information associated with the conception of progeneration that this metaphor uses as source has to do with the event-shape and with causal relations: in a dynamic image-schema, one bounded interior swells in some spot and pushes that part to the boundary until the part, acquiring its own boundary, separates entirely from the original bounded interior, resulting in two bounded interiors. The moment of separation is relatively quick. The first and second entities each have unity, cohesion, boundedness, and duration. This image-schematic information is not to be violated, under the invariance hypothesis. Thus the specific instances of causation that can be understood metaphorically in terms of progeneration are only those whose image-schematic structure is not violated when we impose on the target the image-schema associated with progeneration.

Consider a particular example of THE GREAT CHAIN METAPHOR, the phrase "Still waters run deep." By means of THE GREAT CHAIN METAPHOR, we can interpret it as referring to the nature of human psychological states and behavior. I have encountered three different interpretations of this proverb that derive from THE GREAT CHAIN METAPHOR. The first is "water that looks still on the surface moves quickly deep down below the surface; just so, a person who appears calm and impassive has 'deep down' a powerfully active interior psychology." The second is "a body of water with a smooth surface looks deceptively safe on that surface but is really dangerous because only deep water has such as smooth surface; just so, a calm personal behavior and appearance look deceptively safe but are really dangerous because they are the result of a formidable interior psychology." The third interpretation, which I have heard only once, is "water that exhibits a calm surface is calm clear to the bottom; just so, someone who exhibits a calm, steady behavior is calm and steady all the way down through his interior psychology." It is truly amazing what happens in these metaphorical understandings: note that the metaphorical understandings fail to preserve crucial and dominant things, and we do not care at all. A human being becomes a body of water. The processes of human psychology and behavior become physical processes of a natural event. Expressions that we take to be indications that the person is particularly impassive about something become "stillness." And on and on. But what is preserved in the mapping is image-schematic structure. We associate with both the person and the river an image-schema of an interior and an exterior. The first and second interpretations employ the folk theory that appearance metaphorically conceals essence: the exterior is an opaque surface stopping our vision from seeing into the interior. In these two interpretations, the river's surface is understood as an opaque exterior through which we cannot see to the interior depths; the person's ostensible appearance and behavior are understood as a surface that blocks our insight into the person's "interior" psychology, as when we say, "On the surface, she seemed quite pleased, but it turned out that her inner thoughts were rather different." The third interpretation relies on the contrary folk theory that appearance metaphorically reveals essence: the interior is not available to view, but does not need to be, since the surface reveals the interior. The proverb "Still waters run deep" in all three interpretations refers to the relationship between the surface and the interior. In all three interpretations, the image-schematic structure of the source is mapped onto a conventional image-schematic structuring of the relationship between human behavior and human psychology.

I propose that the invariance hypothesis unites all metaphorical understanding. Whether new, old, conventional, novel, imagistic, basic, or generic-level, all metaphor conforms to it. From this perspective, metaphoric understanding is an extremely imaginative process, and basic metaphors, far from being rigid little automatic preformed packets that save us from having to use our imaginations, are rather cases where imaginative connections have become conventional and where mappings that are ontologically constituted by imaginative links have become, through reinforcement, entrenched.

INVARIANCE AND THE BRAIN

It is not surprising that we should map cognitively so as not to violate image-schematic information. We interact with our environments through a variety of modalities simultaneously, and we need to be able to preserve image-schematic information across all those modalities. For example, as Patricia Churchland has pointed out, our mental model of the visual field has a coordinate system and our mental model of tactile space has a different coordinate system, yet when we do something as simple as reach for a stationary visible object, we need to be able to map the coordinates of visual field space onto the coordinates of tactile space, so that the brain can tell the hand to move toward whatever coordinates in tactile space correspond to the coordinates of the location of the object in visual space.[15] Let us push this observation a little further. Suppose we want to catch a ball, or a cup falling from a shelf. What we see as a dynamic path in visual space had better correspond to a dynamic path in tactile space; otherwise we will place our hands at the wrong place, and fail to catch the object. It is possible to hear something fall in the dark and catch it. If what we hear as a path in mental auditory space did not correspond to a path in mental tactile space, we could not catch the falling object. Consider further the simple motion of putting one's fingers around the handle of a mug, to heft it. We see the space enclosed by the handle as an open interior space bounded by a ring. If the topological properties of that mug as represented in visual space did not correspond to the same topological properties in what we touch, then we would not know how to grab things; we would not be able to see what we could put our fingers through, for example. We must be able to map mentally from modality to modality in such a way as to preserve image-schematic information. The invariance hypothesis asserts that such correlation of image-schematic information extends to metaphoric projection.

The invariance hypothesis leads to an intriguing, but logically independent, hypothesis. This hypothesis is so speculative as to be supported by almost no evidence at all. The ubiquity, generality, and scope of the invariance hypothesis suggests that there might be a correspondence between topological properties at the conceptual level and topological properties at the level of neural architecture. The topology of a space, and the kinds of transformations that preserve properties expressed purely in topological terms, are extremely well understood by mathematicians, and the mathematics involved for simple topological properties such as those I have attributed to "image-schema space" is rudimentary. It may be that there is a topology to neural architecture or neural functioning. It may be that topology-preserving transformations correspond to certain neural processes. Image-schema preservation would then be a result of the way our brains are constructed: when one neuronal group pattern of connections is structured in terms of another neuronal group pattern of connections through projection, it may be that the projection occurs in such a way as to preserve image-schematic structure.

I can only guess more or less vacuously about what such processes of projection might be, but I will indulge in two representative guesses. First, the neocortex is a stack of layers, and there are many connections within layers, and relatively fewer vertical connections between layers. Perhaps when one pattern at one level activates, through these vertical connections, another pattern at another level, it does so in such a way that those vertical connections preserve image-schematic information. Here is a second guess: the neocortex is actually two stacks of layers. One, when crumpled up, is the left hemisphere, and the other, the right. These two stacks, flattened out, are roughly the mirror image of each other. And the two mirror images are connected in such a way that, fairly closely, a neuron on one side is "homotopically" connected to its mirror-image neuron on the other. Then suppose, as seems plausible, that for any pattern of neuronal activity, in no matter what configuration, the brain can induce the activation of its mirror-image pattern. Such an activation would be an isomorphism, as discussed in chapter 4. For example, for any ordered components a and b and any linear relation R that are somehow embodied in the first neuronal group pattern, there would have to be, in the mirror image, corresponding components a' and b' and a corresponding linear relation R' such that aRb if and only if $a'R'b'$. The isomorphic nature of mirror-image reflection would also preserve entities, interiors, boundaries, connectedness, and all the other properties I have attributed to image-schema space.

This guesswork hypothesis, that there is a topology of neural structure or functioning that corresponds to the topology of what I have labeled "image-schema space," is a hypothesis of eliminative materialism; that is, it suggests that certain conceptual processes can be accounted for in terms of neural processes. As such, it will be quite unacceptable to many philosophers and cognitive scientists. But the invariance hypothesis is independent of it.

Chapter 8

THE POETRY OF CONNECTIONS, II

LANGUAGE IS A VIRUS

We have worked upward along the gradients of generality and ingenuity from basic metaphors to generic-level metaphors to principles governing all metaphor. We have not yet specifically opened our study to idiosyncratic and uncommon metaphors like "Language is a virus." What can unfamiliar expressions of this sort teach us about the poetry of conceptual connection? I will begin at the small end, with metaphoric expressions that provide only the most minimal clues toward their construal.

Bare equations or similarities like "Promises are wind," "Kingdoms are clay," "Inactivity is death," "All reactionaries are paper tigers," and "Gifts are like hooks" tell us very little about how to attribute meaning to them. They explicitly indicate nothing except that some unspecified relation holds between two conceptual domains. We are not told the relation. Where the saying expresses a basic metaphor, activating the basic metaphor provides most of the meaning. But in cases where no basic metaphor does the trick, we must fall back on the principles discussed in chapter 7. This is true not only of bare equations and bare similarities, but also of bare instantiations, like "Time is a physician," "Chicago is a dungheap," "Memory is a net," "Flattery is a juggler," "Plain dealing is a jewel," and "Love is a razor." How do we understand such bare expressions?

THE NATURE OF THINGS

If we are lucky, the two concepts referred to in the equation hold places in our commonplace notion of the Great Chain, in which case THE GREAT CHAIN METAPHOR guides us. But *language*, for example, holds no clear place on the Great Chain. Nor does *virus*. What then can we use to understand "Language is a virus"? What can we use to understand "His prose is garbage," "Reactionaries are paper tigers," and "Kingdoms are clay"?

We can use conceptual instruments that are used in THE GREAT CHAIN METAPHOR but that apply more widely. Two of the dominant conceptual tools we use to understand bare analogies are the invariance principle and the commonplace notion of The Nature of Things.

The commonplace notion of The Nature of Things takes the view that being leads to doing: attributes possessed by a form of being lead to the way it behaves. By *doing* I mean not only intentional behavior but also the way inanimate and even insubstantial forms of being are thought to function. For example, clay crumbles and washes away because it is only a moderately self-adhesive material. It deforms readily in response to force because it is malleable. I call this commonplace notion of how clay behaves, and how that behavior derives from its attributes, "The Nature of Clay." In general, for anything with attributes and behavior, I will refer to the concept of what it does, and how that doing derives from its being, as its "Nature." For example, it is The Nature of a Fool to behave foolishly, because he is foolish: his being leads to his doing; his attributes lead to his behavior. Our sense that a person can act in ways untrue to his nature rests on the commonplace notion that a person has attributes that lead in the standard case to his behavior.

We attempt to understand bare equations that involve concepts not conventionally part of the Great Chain hierarchy by mapping part of The Nature of the Source onto part of The Nature of the Target. The part that we attempt to map is the image-schematic part, the part governed by the invariance principle.

Consider, for example, the bare expression "Kingdoms are clay." It expresses no basic metaphor that I know of. It indicates no part of the mapping we are to construct. But we can all understand it easily as implying that kingdoms disintegrate or deform easily, and none of us would understand it as implying that kingdoms, like clay, are to be found in the ground. We arrive at this reading by mapping the image-schematic structure in The Nature of Clay onto The Nature of Kingdom, according to the invariance principle.

Such a mapping might connect one level of attribute and behavior in the source to a different level of attribute and behavior of the target, but this mismatch does not bother us because it does not involve image-schematic structure. For example, in "Kingdoms are clay," we are not bothered that the levels of the source and target do not match: *kingdom* is a political entity and *clay* is a physical entity; *kingdom* has political causality and *clay* has physical causality; and so on. But we are concerned about causal structure, temporal structure, and event-shape. We are concerned that the aspectual shape of the behavior we associate with *clay* be mapped onto the aspectual shape of the behavior of *kingdom*.

Our commonplace notion of how something behaves and how its attributes lead to that behavior contains both specific-level information and generic-level information. For example, The Nature of Clay contains specific-level information, such as that clay dissolves to a certain degree in water, and generic-level information, such as that it maintains its structural integrity moderately well, but breaks apart over time under natural forces. This generic-level information is image-schematic information. We can now state the following principle of understanding bare analogies:

—We attempt to understand a bare analogy by focusing on the generic-level information in The Nature of the Target and The Nature of the Source. We preserve the generic-level information in The Nature of the Target and map onto it as much generic-level information in The Nature of the Source as is consistent with this preservation.

Our preference to map the *behavior* of the source onto the target can be seen in the way we understand many ordinary phrases. When we hear "She's a witch," "He's a fool," "He's a fiend," "He's like iron," "He's a steamroller," "He's a machine," or any similar phrase, we understand it in the default case as prompting us to map The Nature of the Source—its behavior and the way that behavior derives from its attributes—onto The Nature of the Target. We understand "She's a witch" to mean primarily that the person referred to *behaves* in a witchy way, not that the person referred to, for example, *looks like* a witch. To indicate that someone looks like a witch, we must say explicitly "She looks like a witch" or give some supplementary expression or gesture. In fact, "She looks like a witch" is still ambiguous as to behavior versus appearance: it can mean "From her looks, I guess that she will behave like a witch" as easily as it can mean "She resembles visually my image of a witch." In such a case, an even stronger cue may be required to direct us to appearance, as in "She looks just like a witch." But even that cue might fail to override the default expectation.

We understand "He's a broken record" as prompting us to map the generic-level information in The Nature of a Broken Record—which is to repeat—onto the person who is the target. We understand "He's like the wind" as prompting us to map generic-level information in The Nature of the Wind, which is to move quickly and apparently effortlessly, onto the person who is the target.

We understand "Time is a physician" as prompting us to map onto *time* the generic level information in The Nature of a Physician—namely, that the physician performs functions leading to healing, mending, and recovery. We understand "Religion is a disease" as prompting us to map onto *religion* the generic-level information in The Nature of Disease, namely, that it infects, debilitates, and weakens. We understand "A good face is a letter of recommendation" as prompting us to map onto *a good face* the generic-level information in The Nature of a Letter of Recommendation, namely, that it has a winning effect, opens doors, and so on. We understand "Memory is a net" as indicating that The Nature of Memory should be understood in terms of the generic-level of The Nature of a Net—namely, that it arrests and retains things. We understand "Electricity is like water" as indicating that electricity behaves like water: it "flows" along the "path" of least "resistance"; it can be "stored" in a "container" from which it can be "released," and so on.

Consider "Language is a virus," an unconventional metaphor that was once the main phrase of a not very popular song. It allegedly quotes a line in a novel by William Burroughs, "Language is a virus from outer space." The Nature of a Virus is to move from organism to organism, in a "communicable" fashion, infecting each organism as it moves along, causing similar symptoms in each infected organism. Those infected typically exhibit symptoms and typically transmit the virus to others, who consequently develop the same symptoms. To understand "Language is a virus," we map the generic-level information in The Nature of a Virus onto *language*, to arrive at the interpretation that language is something transmitted from person to person, and that those who show the symptoms of "having language" pass language on to others, who consequently develop the same symptoms. It is odd to think of language as a communicable disease, yet we have no difficulty doing so, because we possess a conceptual instrument that provides us with the requisite imaginative capacity.

There are other constructions equivalent to bare expressions of a metaphor. For example, we understand Malcolm X's metaphor "You show me a capitalist, I'll show you a bloodsucker" as a bare equation that gives us only as much information as we need to recognize it as a metaphor. We are to map onto *capitalist* the generic-level information in The Nature of a Bloodsucker.

So far, we have considered active behavior. The behavior of something is active when we situate causal agency in that entity. For example, if we press down with our thumb on clay and the clay deforms, we situate causal agency in the thumb, which we think of as having the active behavior of pressing down. Water has the active behavior of flowing along the path of least resistance. A bloodsucker has the active behavior of obtaining its sustenance by drawing it out of some vital organism. Our first preference in understanding a bare metaphor is to map the generic level of such an active behavior from the source onto the target, constrained, as always, by the invariance principle.

But we also talk about how clay *behaves* under pressure or how it *responds* to pressure. In these cases, we think of the event as actively caused by something outside the clay, and of the clay as possessing some attribute that permits the caused event to occur. This attribute is not sufficient for the event to occur, since it requires the active behavior of something outside the clay; but it is necessary for it to occur. In this fashion, the attributes possessed by a being can lead to the way it behaves in response to action from outside. I will call this its *passive* behavior.

Our concepts contain information about the typical passive behaviors of such beings, and these passive behaviors are just as much a part of The Nature of a Being as are its active behaviors. For example, our ordinary concept of glass includes the information that it is *fragile* and *brittle* and therefore that it *can be broken easily.* Here, an attribute leads to a certain kind of passive behavior: it is The Nature of Glass that its attributes—fragility and brittleness—lead to its (passive) doing—being broken easily.

Often, our concept of something includes both active behavior and passive behavior. We think of *garbage* as having attributes that lead it to offend and to be discarded. When we say of someone's prose that a certain passage is garbage, we mean that its worthlessness and foulness make it offensive (which is active) and hence to be thrown out (which is passive).

Consider "Good prose is like a window pane." The Nature of a Window Pane includes the information that its translucency (an attribute) results in an active behavior of transmitting light (and hence images) and a passive behavior of being looked through; its solidity and impermeability lead to its being used at boundaries in spots where light is to be admitted and people are to look out. It is the Nature of a Window Pane to bring us the view of whatever is on the other side. In "Good prose is like a window pane," we are to understand the target, namely, good prose, in terms of the generic level of The Nature of a Window Pane: good prose is "lucid" and presents to us "clearly" its meaning. Through the good prose we can perceive accurately and without distortion or obscurity that which is "on the other side" of the prose, namely, the meaning. This understanding coheres with an additional metaphor in which words are understood metaphorically as a surface or container, and meaning is understood metaphorically as "below" or "on the other side" of that surface. In this metaphor, the reader must metaphorically see what is on the other side in order to understand the meaning of the words.

This example raises two points. First, there is generic-level information in the Nature of the Window Pane that is not mapped onto the target because it would violate the image-schematic structure of the target and is thus ruled out by the invariance principle. It is the Nature of a Window Pane to shatter when stricken. But the Nature of Good Prose is to cohere, and not to be stricken. We therefore do not map onto the target the window pane's active behavior of shattering when it undergoes the passive behavior of being stricken.

Second, there are ostensibly different ways to understand "Good prose is like a window pane" that are functionally identical. We could analyze "Good prose is like a window pane" as an expression of the specific-level conceptual metaphor UNDERSTANDING IS SEEING: to understand the meaning of words is metaphorically to see what they have to present. We could also analyze "Good prose is like a window pane" as an expression of THE GREAT CHAIN METAPHOR: in the folk model of the Great Chain, *understanding* is a higher-order cognitive activity while *seeing* is a lower-order "bodily" activity.

We can take these different approaches because they are isomorphic. To use THE GREAT CHAIN METAPHOR is automatically to use the invariance principle and the Nature of Things. UNDERSTANDING IS SEEING—like all specific-level metaphors in which the mind is understood in terms of the body—is just a specific-level instantiation of THE GREAT CHAIN METAPHOR and is formed on the basis of the invariance principle and the Nature of Things.

Consider "All reactionaries are paper tigers." A paper tiger has, conventionally, both an active and a passive behavior: it appears ferocious and powerful but it is also easily overcome, incapable as it is of resisting force. We understand "All reactionaries are paper tigers" as mapping the generic level of this active and passive behavior onto *reactionaries*: reactionaries threaten, with ostensible power, but are effortlessly overcome or dismissed, or even ignored with impunity.

An extremely common and basic source concept can serve as a prototype of a certain generic-level Nature. For example, The Nature of Honey is to please us with its extremely pleasant taste; it is pleasant in particular ways that we know very well, but that are difficult to describe in words, a kind of sweetness and purity with a certain viscosity. When something—say, for example, a voice—is described as being "like honey," we understand the phrase by mapping onto the voice the generic level of The Nature of Honey: the voice pleases us because we perceive in it extremely pleasant qualities of sound that we understand at the generic level in terms of the extremely pleasant qualities of taste we find in honey. It is The Nature of a Flower to live naturally, and to please us through visual, aromatic, and tactile qualities. It is The Nature of a Louse to disgust us with its unsavory physical qualities. It is The Nature of a Hog to take up a great deal of space and resources. "She's a flower," "He's a louse," and "John is a hog" are all understood by mapping onto the target concept the generic level of The Nature of the Source Concept. Since this process underlies THE GREAT CHAIN METAPHOR, and since *flower, louse*, and *hog* are all forms of being on The Great Chain, it follows that these expressions are also specific instances of THE GREAT CHAIN METAPHOR.

Our conventional concept of The Nature of something does not have to match our scientific knowledge, our experiential knowledge, or our anecdotal knowledge. Holding a commonplace notion is not the same as having a belief, but more like adopting an enabling convention. For example, I possess one anecdotal concept of quicksand as occurring only in the presence of water. In this concept, quicksand is not a special kind of sand, but rather a mixture of water and plain, ordinary sand; it does not swallow large objects quickly and whole. Yet my everyday concept of The Nature of Quicksand is that it is a special kind of sand that occurs in utterly dry deserts, and that it swallows large objects whole. I believe that wolves are in fact rather shy; but my concept of The Nature of Wolves includes a ferocity that leads them to attack viciously and cruelly even when unprovoked.

Scientific conceptions are thus irrelevant to our study, except to the extent that the scientific conception has influenced our commonplace conception or vice versa. This is an extremely important point. If we look at dictionary representations of meaning, we find that the bundle of features that is meant to represent a concept is usually a list of vaguely scientific or empirical attributes. But our commonplace notions are not required to match our scientific or experiential knowledge. Objects we categorize as inanimate are not represented scientifically as having behaviors, no doubt because attributing agency to them is thought to be unscientific, a relic of pantheism or animism. But we often think of something as both inanimate and as having a behavior. It is not only beings like people, cats, and frogs that are thought of as having behaviors, but also things like skies (which rain on us), the sun (which shines), tables (which hold things up), bright colors (which strike our eye and catch our attention), and nets (which arrest and restrain). Ice, for example, is thought of as having vaguely scientific and empirical attributes: it is a physical object, inanimate, hard, cold, made of water, and so on. But it also has active and passive behavior: it melts, cools things, clinks in tumblers of liquid that it is cooling, breaks in brittle fashion, chips, and shatters.

Part-Whole Relational Structure

In mapping the generic level of The Nature of the Source onto The Nature of the Target, we are guided by the invariance principle. But there may be additional generic-level information that gets mapped, aside from The Nature of the Concept. Part-whole relational structure, which is often implicit in our knowledge of The Nature of the Concept, may also be mapped.

Frequently, we attempt to understand a bare metaphor as prompting us to map the generic level of the part-whole relational structure of the source concept onto the target. The generic level of the part-whole relational structure of a concept is image-schematic information. Consider, for example, "The receptionist is the link." To be sure, we map The Nature of a Link onto The Nature of the Receptionist. We do this without having any certain notion of what it is the receptionist might link, but no matter. We do not require that information. Implicit in this mapping of

Nature is the mapping of the part-whole relational structure associated with *link*: a link is a physical entity physically connecting two physical things, making contact with each. When we map the generic level of this part-whole relational structure onto *the receptionist*, we understand that the receptionist is a connection between two things, and that he or she connects them by dealing with them both, as an intermediary.

IMAGES

So far, we have considered cases where we map the generic level of The Nature of the Source, and the generic level of the part-whole relational structure of the source. But there is also specific-level imagistic information that often is mapped in bare analogies, as when we hear "Her eyes are like lakes," and understand it to mean that we should map onto her blue, moist, translucent eyes the image of two lakes. In mapping this detailed, specific-level imagistic detail, we must of course conform to the invariance principle. For example, we must preserve number of entities. She has two eyes, and so we must map onto our conception of those eyes two lakes. We would find the metaphor "Her eyes are one lake" radical, because it does not conform to the invariance principle (provided the physical form of her eyes is part of the mapping). One way to try to deal with this, of course, would be to eliminate physical form as part of the mapping, and take the metaphor as dealing only with The Nature of Her Eyes and The Nature of a Lake, as in "Her eyes are like a lake inviting me to dive in and explore."

Images need be neither static nor visual. The way a leaf flutters, the way honey tastes, the way the opening of Beethoven's Fifth Symphony sounds, the way water feels, the way smoke smells—all of this is imagistic information. We understand certain bare metaphors as prompting us to map such specific-level imagistic information from the source to the target.

Our preference to map from The Nature of the Source to The Nature of the Target is denied when our concept of the source does not contain a salient nature. Often, a source concept will not come readily equipped with a commonplace notion of its salient nature, but will come readily equipped with a richly detailed image. In a bare metaphor with such a source, we may try to understand the metaphor as an image metaphor, provided that it is possible for the target to have a rich image associated with it, and provided that mapping the source image onto the target image does not violate image-schematic information in the target. Consider, for example, *lake*, as compared to *wolf*. The Nature of a Wolf is a dominant part of our conventional concept of a wolf. But The Nature of a Lake is not a dominant part of our conventional concept of a lake, or at least not of mine. To be sure, if we are asked what the behavior of a lake is, we could probably give an answer, and a metaphor with explicit cues could lead us to map that behavior, as in "He became still as a lake becomes still when the wind dies." But without such cues, we would not have a clear concept of what was involved in mapping the behavior of a lake onto something. At least I would not.

Mapping one sort of information from the source onto the target does not preclude mapping other sorts. There are, for instance, cases of bare metaphor that lead us to map compositely onto the target both the generic level of The Nature of the Source and the source image. For example, in "His blows were like cannon fire," we map the dynamic image of multiple volleys of cannon fire onto the punches, and compositely map the behavior of the cannon fire—namely, its destruction of what it encounters—onto the punches. There are also cases where we map onto the target all three things: a Nature, a part-whole relational structure, and an image. Consider, as an example, "Fame is a bubble." The Nature of a Bubble is to pop soon and suddenly, and also to be popped easily. Our concept of a bubble has a static image associated with it, an image that we find beautiful and interesting and rare. Our concept of a bubble also has a dynamic image associated with the popping of the bubble: the popping is sudden and completely destructive. That image also has part-whole structure: the bubble itself is a boundary, which contains an empty interior. We can easily use all of this information in understanding "Fame is a bubble": fame vanishes soon and suddenly; fame is easily destroyed by others; fame sparkles, catching our attention; the popping of fame completely destroys it; fame is an exterior that can be perceived, but within that boundary there is nothing; and so on.

PROTOTYPES

We think of certain things as bearing a relation of prototypicality to certain attributes and behaviors, and we possess a construction in English for expressing these relations: smooth as silk, warm as wool, blind as a bat, clear as crystal, busy as a bee, dry as dust, good as gold, hot as hell, hungry as a horse, sweet as sugar, and big as a barn door. Usually when a prototype is in the source position of a bare equation, its entire Nature is involved in the mapping. But certain prototypes prototypify attributes rather than behaviors, and so we emphasize the attributes when we map, as in "John is a barn door" or "Jack is a bean pole." An interesting case arises when the prototype is prototypical of both a behavior and an attribute but we do not think of that attribute as generally leading to that behavior. For example, *bear* is prototypical of both gruff behavior and large size. For *bear*, the attribute and the behavior are linked in its Nature. But this linkage is not general: many large things behave gently or have no salient behavior, and conversely many gruff beings are not particularly large. In such a case, the use of the prototype in the source position can lead to an ambiguity, as in "John is a bear." Is he gruff, large, or both? We can legitimately wonder in such a case whether we are to map the entire Nature, or only the behavior, or only the attribute. Accordingly, such an equation almost always comes supplied with further cues provided by context or expression.

PERSPECTIVES

Sometimes, we get some help in constructing a poetic connection or in determining the utility of the connection.[1] Some metaphors, for example, include cues about individual taste or perspective. Consider, for example, "Gin is mother's milk to her." If the metaphor were simply "Gin is mother's milk," we would recognize it as a poetic connection, and understand the mapping it intends to assert, but we might disagree with it. We have the conventional knowledge that many people cannot stand the taste of gin and that even those who like gin may have acquired a taste for it with some initial difficulty. This is a general characterization of gin; we know that a general characterization might not apply in a particular case: there can be someone who has always been on friendly terms with gin, or who has become so habituated to the taste that it has become, to that individual, natural and automatic to drink gin.

Consider Wendell Berry's lines,

> The grower of trees, the gardener, the man born to farming,
> whose hands reach into the ground and sprout,
> to him the soil is a divine drug.[2]

Not all of us think of the soil as a divine drug. Many of us loathe dirt. But we can all understand how a certain person might understand *soil* analogically in terms of *divine drug*.

When a metaphor contains a cue that the conceptual connection holds only for someone who sees it from a certain perspective, we ask ourselves the purpose of that cue. In this way, a perspectival cue is like any communicative act: it has a purpose, and part of our job in understanding it is to determine its purpose. Perspectival cues have a variety of purposes:

(1) The perspectival cue can be taken as indicating the degree of utility of the conceptual connection. In "Gin is mother's milk to her," we are cued that the degree of applicability of the connection is very tightly limited. It does not apply to everyone who drinks gin, but only to this one person. A person has a relationship to his own mind that no one else can have, and from that perspective one can say, "My mind to me a kingdom is." Believers in the Lord have a different relationship to *the Lord* than nonbelievers, and each of the believers can say, "The Lord is my shep-

herd." Each of us can understand how, from the perspective of a believer, *the Lord* can be understood metaphorically in terms of *shepherd*.

(2) The perspectival cue can be taken as indicating that the perspective, and not the conceptual connection, is the principal object of the statement. Berry tells us that the cultivator experiences the soil as a divine drug. We may take this as indicating that we are to inspect and consider the perspective likely to be held by a *cultivator*, to come to a richer understanding of *cultivator*. Understanding the conceptual connection between *soil* and *divine drug* is secondary to this purpose.

(3) The perspectival cue can be taken as indicating that the reader should understand the fact of the connection for someone and the consequences of that fact. This is different from understanding the nature of the connection. We may not care, for example, how *soil* could be connected to *drug*, or how *gin* could be connected to *mother's milk*, and not care either about understanding the mentality of someone who can connect concepts in these ways, but care to know that for a certain person these things are connected and that the person will behave accordingly.

(4) The first-person perspectival cue, as in "My mind to me a kingdom is," can be taken as indicating the general case, "Each person's mind is a kingdom to that person." This differs from other perspectival cues, such as "His mind is a kingdom to him," which does not suggest the general case.

(5) The perspectival cue can be taken as indicating that we are to develop the domain involving that perspective. For example, the perspectival cue in Berry's lines can be taken as asking us to come to a richer understanding not only of the person holding the perspective, namely, the cultivator, but also of the entire domain of cultivation.

Let us consider a complicated case of a perspectival cue: "Every beetle is a gazelle in the eyes of its mother." We immediately make very clear sense of this expression, but the ease with which we do so obscures the fact that the conceptual process involved is complicated. One domain concerns animals: beetles, mother beetles, and gazelles. Within this domain, there is a being, the mother beetle, who bears a certain relationship to her offspring, and who therefore perceives her offspring in a way no one else does. But of course, we know that this expression is not just about beetles and gazelles. By means of THE GREAT CHAIN METAPHOR, we understand that the entire scenario presented here in the animal domain is a source scenario for understanding the domain of human beings.

ASPECTS, INSTANCES, AND SPECIFICATIONS

Some cues direct us to parts of concepts that are to play a role in the mapping. As we discussed in the floor plan and again at the beginning of chapter 7, our concepts are not monolithic. They have aspects. Our concept of a house, for example, has many different aspects: the home-base aspect, the shelter aspect, the compartmentalized interior aspect, the architectural style aspect, the financial investment aspect, and so on.

Let us consider the difference between two aspects of *man*. Consider "He's just a man" and "He's a real man." Those two constantly used words in colloquial Modern English—"just" and "real"—do not here specify any particular details of *man* that we are to recognize. Rather, the first serves to prompt us to consider what I will label the *weak* or *negative* or *limited* aspect of a concept, and the second serves to prompt us to consider what I will label the *strong* or *positive* or *able* aspect of a concept. "Just" and "real" do not tell us what those two aspects are; we are instead expected to know them. We are cued to such aspects by syncategorematic words—words like "just," "real," "mere," "best," and so on. These words have individual differences in the ways they work, but they have one thing in common: they rely on our knowledge of a category and evoke relative states in a category. For example, "it's just a book" relies upon our knowledge of the category *book* and indicates that the book in question has only the indispensable properties of *book* but nothing extra. We are expected to know what these properties are, and what it means to be located as a minimal instance of the category. "This is a real cup of coffee" said of an actual cup of coffee relies upon our knowledge of the category *coffee* and what it means to be an exemplar of that category.

We are expected to know that, in our conventional concept of *man*, a man has certain limitations and also certain capacities; that he is weak in some ways and strong in others; that he is negative in some ways and positive in others. "He's just a man" and "he's a real man" rely upon our knowledge of these aspects and cue us to use one of these aspects in the mapping. Many metaphoric expressions cue us to use as a source not a conventional concept but rather a conventional aspect of that concept. We are expected to know these conventional aspects.

Consider:

> Beauty is but a flower.
> Man is only a reed.
> Poetry's a mere drug.
> Woord is but wynd. (John Lydgate)
> Worldly renown is but a breath of wind.
> Age is a bad traveling companion.

These are cues to the limited, negative, or weak aspect of a source concept. Words like "but," "only," "mere," and "bad" add no specific detail to the source concept; they do not tell us anything in particular. Rather, they ask us to take the weak aspect of the source. For example, we are to consider *flower* as fragile and transitory and not as delightful and invaluable. We are to take *reed* as bending and not as waterproof. We are to take *drug* as addictive diminisher of acuity and not as opener of the doors of perception. We are to take *wind* as random, insubstantial blowing and not as violent, directed, all-powerful monsoon or hurricane, or as a whirl-wind charged with a sort of supreme dynamism.

Cues that ask us to consider the weak aspect of a concept are common not only in metaphor, but also in description and categorization, as in "An aged man is but a paltry thing," "Premature consolation is but the remembrancer of sorrow," "If I speak rather like a mere man," "The throat, being only a mere way and place of passage," and the ubiquitous "He's just a boy," "She's just a girl," "Why, she's a mere child," and "He's only a child."

There are similar cues to the strong or positive aspect of a concept:

> Time is the great physician. (Disraeli)
> Time is the greatest innovator. (Francis Bacon)
> Self-love is the greatest of all flatterers.
> Eyes are the great intruders.
> Delay is the great procuress.
> Opposition is true Friendship. (Blake)
> Praise is the best diet for us, after all.
> Hunger is the best sauce.
> Patience is the best medicine. (John Florio)
> A good conscience is the best divinity. (Thomas Fuller)
> Elbow-grease is the best polish.
> The splinter in the eye is the best magnifying glass. (Adorno)

Consider "Hunger is mere sauce," "Hunger is really good sauce," and "Hunger is the best sauce." Ostensibly, they seem different: the first ("mere sauce") asks us to consider an aspect; the second ("really good sauce") asks us to consider a kind; the third ("the best sauce") asks us to consider a particular instance. But from the point of view of metaphor, they all work in the same way. Aspects, instances, and kinds are closely related to each other by virtue of what are seen as essential properties. "Real sauce" evokes certain properties. "The best sauce" refers to something that has those properties. "Really good sauce" refers to a kind of sauce having those properties. The effect is in all cases the same.

But there are metaphors where the attribute or behavior to be used in the mapping is not wholly contained in the weak or strong aspect of a concept, and so some further specification must be given. Consider, as an example, Emerson's "Art is a jealous mistress." Emerson is asking us to understand the demands of art upon the artist in terms of the demands of a jealous mistress upon her lover. Emerson cannot simply refer to the mistress as "a bad mistress" or "a poor mistress," because we do not think of the weak aspect of *mistress* as conventionally including the behavior associated with jealousy. Therefore, Emerson must cue us to that particular behavior by directing us to a particular possible instance of the concept. The case is similar for Richard Hugo's "The day is a woman who loves you," Hamlet's reference to the world as "an unweeded garden / That grows to seed," Dryden's "Love's a malady without a cure," and Shakespeare's "Your face, my thane, is as a book where men / May read strange matters."

The lines between an aspect, an instance, and a kind are not sharp. Consider, for example, the phrase "empty bubble." Does this refer to a *kind* of bubble, a particular *instance* of the category *bubble*, or does it simply call attention to one *aspect* of our concept of *bubble*? There are many metaphors that direct us to a certain Nature that can be an aspect of a concept or merely possible for a particular instance or kind of the concept. Often, the author must make a judgment call as to whether to include explicit direction to this Nature.

As an example of this judgment call, consider the Epistle Dedicatory to the King James Bible, which in dedicating the work to Queen Elizabeth refers to her as "that bright *Occidental Star*." Typically, we think of stars as shining brightly. Dim stars are not prototypical stars. The authors of this dedication could have relied upon our knowing that The Nature of a Star is to shine, or could have relied upon our specific knowledge that the Occidental Star (Venus as the Evening Star) shines with particular intensity, yet he chose to include a specific cue to that behavior. Whether the cue is taken as emphasizing an aspect or as specifying an instance is not important. What is important is that whenever such an explicit cue is included in the noun phrase referring to the source concept, we know that what it points to must be included in the metaphoric mapping we construct.

One way to give such a cue is to use an expression of the form "*x* is the *y* of *z*," where "*y* of *z*" is conventional in its reference and *z* points to important information contained in *y*. Consider "The past is the best prophet of the future." The future is just what prophets talk about, and accordingly "prophet of the future" merely cues us to an aspect of our conventional concept of *prophet*. Consider "She's an angel of God." In our conventional knowledge, it is automatic that an angel is God's angel, and so we take the expression "of God" in "She's an angel of God" as cueing us to certain aspects of *angel*.

But the case is quite different with "Language is the mirror of the mind": mirrors do not—according to our conventional knowledge— reflect minds, or belong to minds, or in general stand in any conventional way to minds. "Mirror of the mind" is not conventional in what it refers to, and therefore presents us with a problem. I will call a phrase like "Language is the mirror of the mind" an "*xyz* metaphor." *Xyz* metaphors are a highly adaptable and virtually ubiquitous construction in the English language. Their job is to invite us to construct certain connections between concepts. They will be the first subject of our next study.

Chapter 9

THE POETRY OF CONNECTIONS, III

[A]sk yourself whether our language is complete;
whether it was so before the symbolism of chemistry and
the notation of the infinitesimal calculus were incorpo-
rated into it; for these are, so to speak, the suburbs of
our language.
—Wittgenstein, *Philosophical Investigations*

Sex is the poor man's opera.

Because of its many canals, Venice is sometimes called
the Venice of Italy.
—James McCawley

LANGUAGE IS THE MIRROR OF THE MIND

"Money is the root of all evil," "Brevity is the soul of wit," "The wages
of sin is death," "Politics is the art of the possible," "Religion is the opiate
of the masses," and "Language is the mirror of the mind" share a form
first noted by Aristotle:

> As old age (D) is to life (C), so is evening (B) to day (A). One will accord-
> ingly describe evening (B) as the "old age of the day" (D + A)—or by the
> Empedoclean equivalent; and old age (D) as the "evening" or "sunset of
> life" (B + C). (*Poetics*, 1457b)

The genitive phrase in each case specifies a concept in a way incompatible
with our default version of that concept.[1] Roots belong to plants, not to
evil. A soul is possible for a human being, but not for wit. We get wages
for work, not for sin. A mirror reflects a face, not a mind, because a face
is visible but a mind is not.

How do we understand these sayings? We might be tempted to assume
that we understand them because we have heard them used, and meaning
is use. We might say that we just know metaphoric meanings of "root,"
"wages," "soul," and so on, and that we just use these metaphoric meanings to make sense of these sayings. But that would not explain how we
understand parallel sayings that are altogether novel and even strange,
such as "Causation is the cement of the universe," "Custom is the tyrant
of mankind," "Art is the sex of the imagination," "Brevity is the soul of

lingerie," "Today is yesterday's pupil," "Vanity is the quicksand of reason," "Cunning is the dwarf of wisdom," and "Sex is the ancilla of art." It is amazing that we understand and invent such phrases so easily.

The engines of metaphor do not run on their own. Principles of metaphor operate on familiar knowledge, allowing us to understand what we do not know in terms of what we know very well. In the preceding sections of "The Poetry of Connections," we considered general principles of great scope. Here, we will examine specific knowledge of limited scope. Ultimately, we will consider ways in which these general principles and this specific knowledge interact in understanding.

BASIC SOURCE DOMAINS

Conceptual domains that we know very well serve as basic source domains for metaphoric understanding. *Eating, dress, learning, buildings, travel, combat,* and *plants* are basic source domains, grounded in our forms of life.

Consider *wealth, labor, and commerce.* Our knowledge of this basic source domain is rich and familiar, enabling us to activate detailed ranges of it at will; a mere word like "money," "price," "treasurer," or "wages" activates for us this feltwork of knowledge and relations.

Metaphors such as "The wages of sin is death" direct us to use a basic source domain—in this case *labor*—to understand the relation between two things—in this case *death* and *sin*. Such constructions are instances of a special form that I will call "*xyz* metaphor." In this construction, "*x*," "*y*," and "*z*" are noun phrases, and "*y*" and "*z*" are connected by some linguistic form, such as "of" or "to," that typically indicates some relationship between the concepts *y* and *z*. The specific knowledge we are to use in constructing a meaning for the *xyz* metaphor comes from a source domain with which *y* is associated. This source domain is usually a basic source domain.

Consider, as examples of *xyz* metaphors, the following expressions, all of which have *wealth and commerce* as their basic source domain:

> Children are the riches of poor men.
> The wages of sin is death.
> Vigilance is the price of liberty.
> Trouble is the price of progress.
> Labor is the capital of the workingman.
> Memory is the treasurer of the mind.
> A leader is a dealer in hope. (Napoleon I)
> Gratefulness is the poor man's payment.
> Evermore thanks, the exchequer of the poor. (*Richard II*, 2.3.65)

We understand these metaphors instantly, but not because they are expressions of conventional basic metaphors or generic-level metaphors. We understand them as directing us to consider the relationship between x and z metaphorically in terms of something unspecified from the y-domain. For example, "Children are the riches of poor men" directs us to consider the relationship between *children* and *poor men* metaphorically in terms of a domain containing y, namely, *riches*. To do this, we must be very familiar with the conceptual domain containing y, because the domain we are to use and the relevant useful knowledge within that domain are not mentioned in the xyz metaphor; we are given only the single word, "y."

For example, we take "Children are the riches of poor men" as directing us to understand the relation between *children* and *poor men* metaphorically in terms of some unmentioned knowledge from some unmentioned domain containing *riches*. An example of such a domain would be *wealth and commerce*. We know the possible relationships in this domain between y (riches) and the other parts of the domain. When we hear "riches of," we know the possible words that can follow. "Riches of kings," "riches of Rockefeller," or in general "riches of rich people" are possible phrases, referring in conventional ways to conventional knowledge we possess.

But in an xyz metaphor, "z" is not one of the things that can follow "y of," because we believe that y and z do not bear a relationship in some conceptual domain that we conventionally express by saying "y of z." For example, the phrase "poor men" is not something that can follow "riches of." "Riches of poor men" expresses a relationship between *riches* and *poor men* that is counter to our conventional knowledge: poor men do not have riches. We take an "x is the y of z" expression of this sort as prompting us to construct a metaphor.

> An xyz metaphor prompts us to understand the conjunction between x and z metaphorically in terms of a conceptual domain containing y. In particular, we are to find some w in our conceptual knowledge that stands in a relation to y which we can refer to conventionally by the expression "y of w," and we are to map the relation between y and w onto the conjunction of x and z.

For example, "Children are the riches of poor men" prompts us to find a w, *rich people*, related to y, *riches*, and to map the relationship between y and w, that is, between *riches* and *rich people*, onto the conjunction of *children* and *poor men*. We are to understand the relationship between *children* and *poor men* metaphorically in terms of the relationship between *riches* and *rich men*. We do this according to the general principles discussed in the previous two chapters, with the additional help that the xyz metaphor cues us to map a relation onto a relation. In mapping the

y-w relationship onto the x-z conjunction, we are guided by the invariance principle: we map onto the x-z conjunction the image-schematic information in the y-w relation.

Xyz metaphors are more varied in their appearance than we have so far considered. Not only "x is the y of z" but also "x is the y to z," "x is the y toward z," "x is the y for z," "the y for z is x," and many other constructions can prompt us to perform just the same sort of metaphoric mapping. In such cases, the xyz metaphor has the form of an equation between two noun phrases, where we can take one noun phrase ("x") as referring to some conventional concept x, but where the other noun phrase (namely, "y of z" or "y to z" or "y in z" or, in general, "yRz") is referentially weird because, if we use our conventional ways of understanding it, then it refers to something that runs counter to our conventional knowledge. We take any such equation as prompting us to construct a metaphor: we are to try to bring x and z together into a conceptual domain, and understand that domain metaphorically in terms of some conceptual domain containing y. In particular, we are to try to understand the relationship between x and z in terms of some relationship that does exist in our conceptual knowledge between y and some unmentioned w, such that the noun phrase "yRw" is not referentially weird, but expresses a conventionally known relationship between y and w.

We must distinguish between the skeletal form of the xyz metaphor and the lexical content that fills it. The skeletal form is general. The lexical content is specific, and differs from case to case. The lexical content guides us more or less specifically in each case we encounter. The skeletal form, which we know as a general construction, guides us generally, for all cases. Here, I characterize the semantics of that skeletal form, as it interacts with and is independent of the semantics of the lexical material that fills it. We all know the skeletal form, and use it to make sense of specific cases. In specific cases, we get more or less extra guidance from the lexical content.

For example, in "Money is the root of all evil," "root" is a relational noun, and strongly suggests *plant* as the unmentioned w we are to use, so that the root-plant relation is to be mapped onto the money-evil conjunction. Here, the lexical content of the xyz skeletal form gives us some guidance. But in "Vanity is the quicksand of reason," the lexical content gives us much less guidance. However much guidance the specific lexical content gives us, what we always have is the guidance given by the skeletal form itself, which is the subject here. In certain cases, virtually the only guidance we have in making sense of the xyz metaphor is our knowledge of the semantics of that skeletal form. In these cases, the particular xyz metaphor—such as "Vanity is the quicksand of reason"—contains lexical content that does not point to the metaphoric mapping. The metaphor is

not in the words. The metaphor is rather in what we do mentally to determine that a mapping is in order and to construct that mapping.

An *xyz* metaphor gives us in general almost none of the information we
need to understand the metaphor that it suggests. In general, it merely
points us in a direction. We are equipped to understand it by bringing to
bear a powerful commonplace conceptual apparatus that includes knowledge of basic source domains. We know different possible relationships
between *riches* and *rich people*: riches can be spent by rich people, riches
are valuable things to rich people, and riches bring pleasure to rich people. We seek such relationships in the *y*-domain that can plausibly be
mapped onto the *x-z* conjunction. For example, we cannot map onto the
conjunction between *children* and *poor men* the relationship that, as rich
people literally spend riches, so poor people literally spend children, because it runs counter to our knowledge: poor men do not routinely spend
their children. But we can map onto the conjunction between *children*
and *poor men* a different relationship between *riches* and *rich people*: a
poor man's children can be valuable to him, bringing him pleasure and
joy.

In achieving this understanding, we use no prefabricated basic metaphor or even a generic-level metaphor. We arrive at this understanding
imaginatively through taking a basic source domain we understand very
well, and—constrained by the invariance principle and our conventional
knowledge of the target—mapping from that basic source domain onto
the target domain. In doing this, we are constrained not to violate the
image-schematic structure of the target domain. For example, we do not
take the metaphor as meaning that poor men can put children in the bank
or buy stocks with them or offer them as collateral in a leveraged buy-out
or pay income taxes with them or bribe foreign corporations with them
or any of the many other things that rich people can do with their riches.
We know not to take the metaphor as indicating any of these things because they all violate either our conventional knowledge or the event
structures associated with the target.

Let us consider the basic source domain of *travel*, or more accurately,
of physical progress toward physical locations. Consider the following
metaphoric expressions:

> Adversity is the first path to truth. (Byron)
> Death is the end of woes. (Spenser)
> [Of a hansom] The gondola of London. (Disraeli)
> Self-respect is the gate of heaven.
> Anarchy is the stepping stone to absolute power. (Napoleon)
> Custom is the guide of the ignorant.
> It is death that is the guide of our life.

The cross is the ladder of heaven.

Logical consequences are the beacons of wise men. (T. H. Huxley)

Commonplaces are the tramways of intellectual transportation. (Ortega y Gasset)

Cheese—milk's leap toward immortality.

The bar in America is the road to honor. (William Wirt)

We understand these *xyz* metaphors as prompting us to bring *x* (for example, *The bar in America*) and *z* (for example, *honor*) into a conceptual domain that is to be understood in terms of another conceptual domain (for example, *travel*) containing *y* (for example, *road*). This requires that the domain containing *y*, and the particular knowledge we are to use from that domain, be extremely familiar to us, because again that domain and that knowledge are not mentioned; we are only given the single word, "*y*."

Consider "The bar in America is the road to honor." We know that "road to" needs some destination to follow the "to." Our specific knowledge of the relationship between a road and its destination is that the road is something we can choose to engage with in a conventional way, namely, by traveling it, and that engaging with it in the conventional way will result in a change in the relationship between ourselves and the end of the road, namely, we will be at that end. The image-schematic structure of this relationship is to be mapped onto the conjunction of *the bar in America* and *honor*: that is, the bar is something we can choose to engage with in a conventional way, and doing so will result in a change in the relationship between ourselves and honor, namely, we will be honored. In order to conduct this mapping, we must understand the target domain image-schematically in terms of a journey, and the metaphor explicitly asks us to do that. It explicitly asks us to understand the bar as a path, and honor as the end of that path. We are therefore guided to understand conventional engagement with the bar (that is, becoming a member of the bar and working as a member of the bar) as traversing that path. Understanding the bar in America as a path that we can traverse, and that leads to honor, is the result of image-schematic mapping.

In principle, we can arrive at this understanding without using a prefabricated basic metaphor or even a particular generic-level metaphor; in practice, in this case, the general principles of conceptual connection have resulted in relevant basic metaphors and generic-level metaphors that already contain the image-schematic mapping.

How do such conventional conceptual metaphors come to exist? The *xyz* form has something to teach us on this score. Suppose we have many specific target domains, each containing some means. Suppose we understand each of these means in each of these specific target domains in

terms of paths. Then the cognitive pattern inhering in all these metaphoric understandings would be the conventional conceptual metaphor
MEANS TO GOALS ARE PATHS TO DESTINATIONS, and could be used to structure yet other target domains.

Let us drop down a level in specificity. Consider two conceptual domains, JOURNEYING as the source and SOLVING A PROBLEM as the target.
Mapping the image-schema of a directed path onto this target domain in
such a way as to preserve topological structure (such as ordering) results
in mapping the destination onto the solution, the path onto the means of
solving the problem (that is, onto the mental work that one must complete in order to reach the solution), the traveler of the path onto the
mind doing the thinking, distance traveled along the path onto the degree of success in solving the problem, and so on. The result is a specific-
level metaphor, MENTALLY SOLVING A PROBLEM IS JOURNEYING ALONG
A PATH TO A DESTINATION. Repeatedly understanding mental problem-
solving in this way entrenches the specific-level metaphor, and makes it
conventional, until it becomes a basic metaphor. MENTALLY SOLVING A
PROBLEM IS JOURNEYING ALONG A PATH TO A DESTINATION is in fact a very
basic metaphor that we use frequently.

This combining of the invariance principle and the extremely specific
and textured knowledge we have of basic source domains underlies the
entire range of *xyz* metaphors. The range of such metaphors is infinite: we
can and do construct them at will, often with seeming effortlessness.

We can understand the target relationship in terms of more than one
source domain, as in Walter Lippman's "Social movements are at once
the symptoms and the instruments of progress." We can understand
more than one target conjunction in terms of a single source relation, as
in "As poetry is the harmony of words, so conversation is the harmony of
minds." We can understand *x* as a component of more than one *x-z* conjunction, as in "The idea is the old age of the spirit and the disease of the
mind." Other complex *xyz* metaphors appear in the appendix.

The cognitive process behind the "*xyz* metaphor" is not restricted to
the linguistic construction "*x* is the *yRz*" where *R* is some linguistic form,
like "to" or "of," that we take as expressing a relationship between *y* and
z. The cognitive *xyz* structure also underlies compound noun forms like
"disc jockey," "road hog," and "budget ceiling." These are abbreviated
expressions of the *xyz* metaphor. Consider "disc jockey." In this case, a
person is *x*. *y* is *jockey*. We expect *jockey* to be associated with *race horses*.
But instead, this jockey is associated with a *z*—namely, *discs* or *records*—
that does not belong to the domain of *race horses*. The person (*x*) is a
jockey (*y*) not with respect to horses (*w*) but rather with respect to discs
or records (*z*). We understand this metaphor just as we understand all *xyz*
metaphors: the relationship between *x* (the person) and *z* (discs, or rec-

ords) is to be understood metaphorically in terms of the well-known relationship between a jockey (y) and horses (w). Consider another example. A pair of dogs runs to the front door when they hear a noise outside.
They push aside the curtains that cover the glass panes in the door, and
sit looking out the glass panes at anything that goes by. They bark their
approbation, but in general stare out transfixed by more or less nothing.
The dog owner refers to this door and what the dogs see through it as
"dog TV," which is to say, television for dogs. We understand this compound noun by understanding metaphorically that this glass-paned front
door (x) is TV (y) not for human beings (w) but rather for dogs (z).
Again, y belongs to a very familiar basic source domain (television enter-
tainment); we know that television is for human beings (w); we are given
a relationship not between y and the expected w, but rather between y and
a z that is not part of the source domain containing y. English is rich in
compound nouns formed along these lines: "tax bite," "computer jock,"
"dog heaven," "card shark," "land shark," "record jacket," "record
sleeve," "fire storm," "wave train," "brain spasm," and "price war." I
have heard a large, expensive car referred to as a "land yacht." A children's program on TV is referred to as "baby crack," where crack is an
addictive drug. A vendor of aloe vera plants in a flea market says, "You
have your aloe vera, honey? That's your kitchen medicine cabinet." In
certain cases, the xyz form can become one word, like "brainwashing," as
in the phrase "Brainwashing is evil." The activity known as "brainwashing" stands to minds as washing stands to things washed.

BACKLASH ON THE UNMENTIONED CONCEPT

Occasionally, the source and target in an xyz metaphor will overlap in
their components, leading to the possibility of a "backlash" comment on
the source.[2] Consider "Children (x) are the riches (y) of poor men (z)."
The missing w is *rich men*: The children-poor men (x-z) conjunction is
the target, to be understood in terms of the source relation between
riches and rich men (y-w). But *children* is a possible component not only
of the target but also of the source: there is a natural connection not only
between poor men and children but also between rich men and children;
this allows us to read the expression as implying that rich men have sadly
violated this natural connection by allowing riches to supplant children.
This is a backlash reading; it is a comment upon the source, not the target. In particular, it is a comment on the unmentioned concept, rich
men, in the source. "Sex (x) is the opera (y) of poor men (z)" also has a
backlash reading: sex, which is a possible component not only for the
target but also for the source, has been supplanted for rich men by
opera.

Implications of *xyz* Metaphors

An *xyz* metaphor, such as "Fame is the beauty-parlor of the dead" or "Humanity is the sin of God" or even "disc jockey," gives us almost none of the information we need to understand it; it merely points us on our way toward a meaning. It mentions *y* but does not mention the domain containing *y* or the possible *w*'s to which *y* can bear a relationship in that domain, or the relationship that actually obtains between *y* and such a *w*. It does not tell us to perform a mapping. It does not tell us how to perform that mapping. In order to understand an *xyz* metaphor, we must bring to bear elaborate and detailed conceptual knowledge not referred to in the expression. This is the common situation of all language: expressions do not mean; they are prompts for us to construct meanings by working with processes we already know. In no sense is the meaning of an *xyz* metaphor or of any utterance "right there in the words." When we understand an utterance, we in no sense are understanding "just what the words say"; the words themselves say nothing independent of the richly detailed knowledge and powerful cognitive processes we bring to bear.

The construction of such meaning is, as we have seen with *xyz* metaphors, open-ended. Our understanding of an *xyz* metaphor can be skeletal, rich, or in between, depending upon our interpretive energies. It is misguided to claim that the words of the expression tell us just exactly so much, and that anything else we find in the expression is the result of our "reading meanings into" the utterance. All reading is reading in. If one stopped at "just what the language says," then one would never begin understanding at all.

Consider, as an example of this open-endedness, "Vanity is the quicksand of reason." We understand "quicksand of" as referring to some conceptual domain containing *quicksand*, in which *quicksand* bears some relation to some *w* that we can express linguistically as "quicksand of *w*." For example, stereotypically, *quicksand* is part of the *desert*, so "quicksand of *w*" might suggest to us "quicksand of the desert." In this case, we would see the metaphor as asking us to see *vanity* as part of *reason* in the way *quicksand* is part of the *desert*. While this reading is possible, and could be pushed, let us instead pursue the alternative approach in which we assume that stereotypically *vanity* conflicts with and is not part of *reason*. Then we would more plausibly take "quicksand of *w*" as evoking things that travel across the desert, such as *human beings, animals,* and *vehicles.* The implication would be that as quicksand acts on things traveling in the desert, so vanity acts on reason.

In that case, "Vanity is the quicksand of reason" would be a special instance of the more general metaphor that MENTAL PROGRESS IS JOUR-

NEYING, expressed in "Let's walk through the problem," "P = NP is the Mt. Everest of complexity theory," and "We have to work our way around that problem." How might we lock together MENTAL PROGRESS IS JOURNEYING, or the general principles of metaphoric understanding that result in this metaphor, with our knowledge of *quicksand, vanity, deserts,* and *reason* to arrive at a metaphoric understanding of the vanity-reason conjunction in terms of the quicksand-travelers relationship?

We have stereotypical knowledge that quicksand acts on travelers crossing the desert. We can use this knowledge of the source domain in a variety of finely grained ways to understand that just as quicksand catches travelers unaware, so vanity catches reason unaware; that vanity, like quicksand, is a hidden danger that can be skirted if one uses proper caution; that the danger of vanity, like the danger of quicksand, is ever-present, requiring constant precaution; that the domains of discovery over which reason wanders contain hidden traps; and so on, and on, and on, bringing to bear a great deal of very finely grained knowledge about the source domain.

We have choices in what finely grained knowledge we bring to bear. If we bring to bear the conventional but erroneous stereotypical knowledge of quicksand that it occurs where there is no water and that it swallows up victims whole, then we conceive of reason as a person quickly swallowed whole by vanity. If we bring to bear experiential knowledge that quicksand almost surely will not swallow a traveler, we might understand that reason can encounter but pass through vanity if reason simply keeps its wits and moves quickly and fluidly without becoming distracted by momentary encounters with vanity. But if reason dallies with vanity, or dallies unaware that it is in vanity, then reason might become bogged in the midst of vanity, and its progress halted. At that point, reason might call on one of its companions—love, anguish, self-loathing, nihilism—to pull it out of vanity. If none are there or can help, reason might try to extricate itself. If shrewd or properly trained, reason might succeed. If not, its motions to escape will only sink it deeper. And while vanity will almost certainly never swallow reason, reason might be caught half-submerged in vanity, unable to escape, slowly dying, constantly aware of the increasing probability of its near death. And so on and on and on.

Consider "London is the cesspool of the Empire." This *xyz* metaphor has been extracted from Arthur Conan Doyle's more elaborate version, "London, that great cesspool into which all the loungers of the Empire are irresistibly drained." This metaphor evokes two vast domains and prompts us to investigate the fine details of our knowledge of these domains. It places one foot in each of two domains: the first is *London,* the explicitly mentioned *x.* Connected with the domain of *London* is the phrase "loungers of the Empire." But this phrase is also used to modify the *y* domain, *cesspool*. This *y* domain is also explicitly mentioned, and the phrase "drained" is connected with that *y* domain. What are the possible mappings here? The loungers of the Empire, we are told, get "drained" into London. So we must map *cesspool* onto *London,* and *whatever gets drained into a cesspool* onto *loungers.* What gets drained into a cesspool? We know that the answer is *liquid waste,* which is not mentioned. So we may try to understand *loungers of the Empire* metaphorically in terms of *liquid waste.* How would we do that? There is generic-level information in our concept of *liquid waste*: it is undesirable and fluid, and the waste product of something. None of this knowledge is referred to in the expression. We understand *loungers* metaphorically in terms of *liquid waste* by understanding the loungers, at the generic level, as undesirable, fluid, and the waste products of something. Of what might they be the waste products? We might take the expression as indicating that Empire is the source of these waste products. This leads to another set of metaphoric mappings. The Empire must have waste products, so it must be a dynamic process, or a collection of processes (like a body or an industry, or a town full of industries and bodies, or a market-place full of industries and bodies and ecological systems), all of which have waste products. Such processes have crafted products, births, deaths, and so on, but certainly they have waste products. Therefore, while the Empire may have many components, it also, like all dynamic systems associated with "cesspool," must have metaphoric liquid waste products. We know that liquid waste is drained. Drainage takes place in physical environments with either natural or artificial structure that impels, by gravity or other means, the waste products toward the drain. We may take this as suggesting that, as gravity and physical structure impel liquid sewage toward the cesspool, so some component of the structure of Empire impels loungers toward London.

Let us pause to notice how much knowledge we have to bring to bear to arrive at such an understanding, even though that understanding seems automatic and effortless. The possibilities of physical structure must be mapped to the possibilities of political, societal, economic, transportational, or, in brief, Imperial structure. The mapping of physical structure onto Imperial structure entails a mapping of causality between the two domains: something in the physical structure causes liquid sewage to be impelled to the cesspool; something in the Imperial structure causes the loungers to be impelled to London.

Why should this impelling structure of Empire work on loungers but not on others? Asking this question (unconsciously) may prompt us to yet a further metaphoric understanding: as waste has no life, no power, no will to resist the flow, so too are loungers impotent to resist—much less employ—this structure of Empire. We may take ourselves as nudged toward this interpretation by the cue "irresistibly." Presumably capitalists and artists are drawn to London, but drawn, not drained. How else might loungers in an Empire be like waste products in a house, town, market, and so on? Is it that, as waste products are those things the industries and bodies have no use for, so loungers are those people that the Empire has no use for? Is it that loungers, like waste products, have nothing to contribute?

Let us stop there with this metaphoric understanding. It is clear that with the appropriate interest and energy, it could be extended to the length of a novel. The lessons we draw from the way we go about understanding such an *xyz* metaphor are:

—The invariance principle guides us. In this metaphoric mapping, paths are mapped to paths, an image-schema of causation is mapped to the same image-schema of causation, the general shape of the target event is preserved, and so on.
—We bring to bear a tremendous range of detailed knowledge, including such knowledge as the association of London with the British Empire, and its association with the work ethic and Victorian values. Vast ranges of conceptual knowledge not in the least explicit in the expression are indispensable for understanding the metaphor.
—Understanding a metaphor is often actually understanding whole systems of metaphoric mappings, involving many components in the source and the target.
—There is no natural terminus to understanding a metaphor. It is nonsense to say that the reader should stop when he has determined "just what the linguistic expression says," because the linguistic expression itself does not mean.
—The power of language lies not in words, but in the mind.

LANGUAGE IS FOSSIL POETRY

Earlier, we considered cases like "Art is a jealous mistress," "This world is an unweeded garden," and "The Queen, that bright Occidental star," where the source domain was specified in some unobjectionable way. But in certain illuminating cases the specification runs counter to our conventional knowledge. Consider "Language is fossil poetry." Many things can be fossil, but we do not think of *poetry* as one of them. Consider "Daniel Webster struck me much like a steam-engine in trousers." Many things can wear trousers, but we think a steam engine is not one of them. Such a specification runs counter to our concept of what it specifies. I will call such specifications "weird." How do we understand metaphors containing weirdly specified source concepts?

Specifying the Source with
Something That Belongs to the Target

Consider "Daniel Webster is a steam-engine." This is a bare metaphor, which we understand by means of THE GREAT CHAIN METAPHOR. We know that Daniel Webster is one form of being, a human being, and that a steam engine is a different form of being, a machine, and that our understanding of Daniel Webster metaphorically in terms of a steam-engine by means of THE GREAT CHAIN METAPHOR must bridge over exactly this distinction.

Many metaphoric expressions simply take the principal information separating the target from the source and pin it weirdly on the source, as in "Daniel Webster is a *human* steam-engine." This weird specification then emphasizes exactly that distinction which we must bridge over when we use THE GREAT CHAIN METAPHOR.

The information pinned on the source can also be something metonymic of the principal distinction separating the target from the source. For example, *wearing trousers* is metonymic of *being human*. Hence, "Daniel Webster is a steam-engine in trousers."

We take such weird specifications as emphasizing just that distinction we must bridge over in using general principles to construct a metaphoric understanding. I label such a weird specification *merely* weird, to distinguish it from *really* weird specifications that we will encounter in a moment. A merely weird specification pins something from the target onto the source. Metaphors that involve source domains that have been specified in a merely weird fashion are extremely common, and occur in phrases such as "Macaulay is a walking encyclopedia," "My big brother is a living garbage disposal," "He's a living dream," "This airplane is a flying garbage can," "He's a walking time-bomb," "Old men are walking hospitals," "She's a walking beauty parlor," "She's a computer with legs," "This car is a rolling disaster area," and "He's a human vegetable." The obese beggar Iros in the *Odyssey* is referred to as a "walking famine." Less common examples are "A minister of finance is a *legally authorized* pickpocket," "Hope is a *waking* dream," and "A father is a banker *provided by nature*."

The principal distinction on the Great Chain between Helen and Venus is mortality versus immortality. Hence "Helen is the mortal Venus." The principal distinction between a *mixed metaphor* and a *sore thumb* is that a mixed metaphor results from cognitive behavior while a sore thumb results from physical behavior. Hence "A mixed metaphor is a *cognitive* sore thumb." Understanding *Helen* in terms of *Venus* while emphasizing the mortal versus immortal contrast between them is to understand that Helen in the mortal world is the metaphoric equivalent of Venus in the immortal world. Understanding *mixed metaphor* in terms of a *sore thumb* while emphasizing the contrast of cognitive versus bodily between them is to understand that a mixed metaphor is the metaphoric equivalent in the realm of cognitive behavior of a sore thumb in the realm of bodily behavior. The case is similar for "Cynicism is intellectual dandyism."

Commonplace Transformations

We know how to transform things mentally from one state into another. Certain transformations are commonplaces. Specifications often ask us to transform a concept according to a commonplace transformation.

We have concepts not only of objects like *dog* and *table*, but also of actions like *theft* and *departure* and of events like *healing* and *death*. Many such actions and events can be thought of as *transformations*—operations that transform something from one state into another. Enlarging an area, coloring an object, rearranging flowers, coining metal, breaking a piece of pottery, freezing water, educating a mind, and getting a body into shape are all commonplace transformations.

Our knowledge of a commonplace transformation includes what it works on. Education operates on minds, not water. When we think of freezing water into ice, or of educating a mind by taking it from ignorance to knowledge, we are thinking of a commonplace transformation. A commonplace transformation is a conventional transformation as applied to the sort of thing it conventionally applies to. For example, we think of a polished stone as the result of a commonplace transformation, namely, polishing, which transforms the stone from its natural state to a polished state.

A commonplace transformation of a concept results in a specification of that concept, as follows: a commonplace transformation of some concept *x* creates some final transformed state of *x*, and we think of that final state as a specification of *x*. *Polishing* is a commonplace transformation that we think of as applying to, among other things, *stone*. The result of applying *polishing* to *stone* is *polished stone*. We think of a *polished stone* as a specification of *stone*.

This raises a curious point. At the conceptual level, an *unpolished stone* and a *polished stone* are tightly connected. This should seem bizarre: an unpolished stone and a polished stone are completely incompatible. No unpolished stone can be a polished stone and conversely. Yet we do not think of *unpolished stone* and *polished stone* as far apart. Apparently, we feel that commonplace transformations preserve some part of the essence of a concept.

Many specifications can be thought of as caused by commonplace transformations. We think of a jealous mistress as a specific kind of mistress, namely, one who is jealous, but we can equivalently think of a jealous mistress as one who *is* jealous because she has been *made* jealous. Any such transformation of a person from one affective state to another by means of some action or perception is a commonplace transformation.

Commonplace Transformations That Are
Specifications Transforming the Source into the Target

One way to understand what it means to bridge over such a distinction is to understand that some commonplace transformation transforms the source so that it is no longer separated from the target by that distinction. Consider "A rhombus is a square pushed over." *Pushing over* is a commonplace transformation that can be applied conceptually to shapes. The specification *pushed over* applies to the target, *rhombus*, but not to the source, *square*. This distinction between the target and the source is removed by applying to the source a commonplace transformation that removes the distinction.

For many of the metaphors involving sources specified with something fitting the target but not the source, it is possible to see the specification as suggesting the application of a commonplace transformation that would transform the source into the target. In "Las Vegas is the American Monte Carlo," the specification "American" fits the target, *Las Vegas*, but not the source, *Monte Carlo*; we understand that it emphasizes the principal distinction between *Las Vegas* and *Monte Carlo*: Las Vegas is American, but Monte Carlo is European. We must bridge over this distinction in constructing the metaphor. So far, so good. One way of bridging over this distinction is to take "American" as suggesting a commonplace transformation, namely, *Americanize*. We often talk of *Americanizing* non-American parts of the world. *Americanizing* them involves changing their economies, their cultural patterns, the stereotypical styles of their citizens, and so on, to bring them into line with American forms. We think of Monte Carlo as aristocratic, imbued with an atmosphere of European high culture and pretense. To Americanize it might mean to eliminate its aristocratic and cultural atmosphere, substituting instead the jumble of American demographic types coupled with vulgarity in architecture, speech, and behavior. Monte Carlo connotes old money and the psychology that goes with monetary security. To Americanize it might mean to substitute instead new money and the psychology of the lottery.

It should be clear that a commonplace transformation is not necessarily a realistic transformation. It is instead a transformation that we can apply conceptually. It is implausible that one could ever Americanize Monte Carlo (or that one would want to), but one can imagine it. One cannot actually push over a drawn square, but one can visualize it mentally as being pushed over. One cannot actually *humanize* a vegetable or a tree or a car, but conceptually, it is quite easy for us to think of humanizing such things, as we see in animated cartoons. When, in a metaphor like "He's a human vegetable," something fitting for the target but not the source is attached to the source, thereby emphasizing the distinction separating the target and the source, we know that we must bridge over that distinction to construct the metaphor. One way to understand what it means to bridge over that distinction is to understand that a commonplace transformation separates target and source.

Specifications That Are Commonplace Transformations Inappropriate for Both Source and Target

Consider "Language is fossil poetry." The specification, *fossil*, is *really weird* because it is inappropriate for not only the source but also the target. We think of a fossil as the result of a commonplace transformation, *fossilization*. But we think of this transformation as applying only to organisms and physical traces of organisms, such as bones, footprints, leaf imprints, and so on. It certainly does not apply to poetry. Therefore, we cannot think of *fossil poetry* through commonplace transformation of *poetry* in the way we can think, for example, of *fossil bones* or *fossil footprints* as commonplace transformations of the concepts *bones* and *footprints*. The commonplace transformation *fossilization* does not apply to *poetry*. Similarly, we think of various things as the results of *fossilization*, but language cannot be one of them. So, in this case, the commonplace transformation is inappropriate for both the source and the target: it cannot conventionally be applied to the source, and the target cannot be the result of applying it to anything.

Yet, in a different way, *fossilization* can apply to *poetry*. Although the specific-level information in the commonplace transformation *fossilization* cannot be applied to *poetry*, the generic level information in *fossilization* can be applied to *poetry*. A commonplace transformation has a Nature, and consequently a behavior. *Fossilization*, for example, has a Nature: it behaves in a certain way, on certain sorts of things. This Nature has both specific-level information and generic-level information. When such a commonplace transformation is inappropriately applied to a concept, we take it as a cue to apply the generic level of The Nature of the Transformation to that concept. For example, the generic level of *fossilization* is: a transformation in which the passage of long time transforms or takes the impression of part of a changing, interactive world, resulting in a rigid fixity that has none of the original freshness or changeability or capacity of what was fossilized but that bears its marks. If we apply this generic-level Nature of Fossilization to *poetry*, then the result is: a transformation or impression-taking of poetry through the passage of long time, thereby creating a rigid fixity that has none of the original freshness or changeability or capacity of poetry, but that bears its traces. We are therefore to understand language as this fixity. Language is the final state that derives from the original state, poetry, and the mechanism of this derivation is the generic level of The Nature of Fossilization. The passage of time has turned poetic inventions into a rigid language system that still bears the traces of poetry.

Really Weird Specifications and xyz Metaphors

A metaphor with a source that is specified in a really weird way may have an equivalent *xyz* form. "Language is fossil poetry," for example, is equivalent to the *xyz* form "Language is the fossil of poetry." Let us inspect the details of this equivalence. We understand "Language is fossil poetry" by taking the generic level of the commonplace transformation of *fossilization*, applying it to *poetry*, and mapping the result onto *language*. We understand "Language is the fossil of poetry" in the same way, as follows: We know that we are to map the relationship between *fossil* (y) and *that which has been fossilized* (w) onto the conjunction of *language* (x) and *poetry* (z). What is that relationship? It is that the first is the result of applying the commonplace transformation *fossilization* to the second. What is entailed in mapping that relationship onto the target? Guided by the invariance principle, we map the generic level of that source relationship onto that target conjunction: as a fossil is the result of fossilizing something, so language is the result of the generic-level fossilization of poetry. In both cases, then, we map onto *language* the result of applying the generic level of *fossilization* to *poetry*. The *xyz* version and the version involving the really weird specification are equivalent.

CONCLUSION

In this study of the poetry of connections, we have seen a high-level coherence among the principles of conceptual connection. First, we discussed basic metaphors, then generic-level metaphors that both underlie basic metaphors and enable us to understand metaphoric expressions when no basic metaphor does the trick, and then higher-order principles of metaphoric understanding that underlie all metaphoric understanding, including basic and generic-level metaphors.

We observed how we employ these higher-order principles to understand bare metaphoric expressions that are not instances of basic metaphors and that contain no cues of the sort we find in *xyz* metaphors. We found that we use these higher-order principles in conjunction with our commonplace notion of The Nature of Things.

We examined our processes for understanding a particular construction, the *xyz* metaphor: we take it as directing us to understand the *x-z* conjunction in terms of some *y-w* relation drawn from a basic source domain like *eating, dress, combat, travel,* and so on. This led to a theory of the origin of basic metaphors: a basic metaphor is the entrenched result of applying higher-order principles of metaphoric understanding to a certain basic source domain in order to understand a certain target domain.

We have taken up cases where the source domain is specified in a way that is merely weird or really weird. We understand the merely weird case—where something from the target is pinned on the source—in just the way we understand any bare metaphoric expression, save that we take the merely weird specification as cueing us to the principal distinction between source and target that we must bridge over in applying higher-order principles to arrive at a metaphoric understanding. We considered commonplace transformations as conceptual connections between two concepts where one is viewed as the initial state and the other is viewed as the transformed state. We saw that some merely weird specifications can be understood as commonplace transformations that conceptually transform the source into the target. We then took up the case of really weird specification, where a commonplace transformation that is inappropriate for both the source and target is applied to the source. We saw that we can understand such metaphoric expressions as asking us to perform a mapping at the generic level: we are to apply to the source the generic level of the transformation and map the result onto the target. We then saw that source domains that have been specified in a really weird fashion have equivalent *xyz* metaphors, where the conceptual processes involved in understanding them are isomorphic.

This book, which is meant as a start-up program for the reader's own activities, has now concluded its illustrative guided tours intended to suggest lines or modes of research open in the study of English in the age of cognitive science. They are initial laboratory experiments, provisional and topical only, offered in the hope of leading to a reconsideration of what our research into language and literature might become if we began to think of language and literature as acts of a human mind in a human brain in a human body that must make sense of its environment if it is to survive.

We have one more tour to take. It concerns not the nature of our research in the age of cognitive science, but the nature of our teaching.

Chapter 10

CULTURAL LITERACY AND
POETIC THOUGHT

To begin with, the art of jigsaw puzzles seems of little substance, easily exhausted, wholly dealt with by a basic introduction to Gestalt: the perceived object—we may be dealing with a perceptual act, the acquisition of a skill, a physiological system, or, as in the present case, a wooden jigsaw puzzle—is not a sum of elements to be distinguished from each other and analysed discretely, but a pattern, that is to say a form, a structure: the element's existence does not precede the existence of the whole, it comes neither before nor after it, for the parts do not determine the pattern, but the pattern determines the parts: knowledge of the pattern and of its laws, of the set and its structure, could not possibly be derived from discrete knowledge of the elements that compose it. That means that you can look at a piece of a puzzle for three whole days, you can believe that you know all there is to know about its colouring and shape, and be no further on than when you started. The only thing that counts is the ability to link this piece to other pieces, and in that sense the art of the jigsaw puzzle has something in common with the art of go. The pieces are readable, take on a sense, only when assembled; in isolation, a puzzle piece means nothing—just an impossible question, an opaque challenge.
—Georges Perec[1]

CLASSICAL RHETORIC gave us a view of cultural literacy with consequences not only, as we have seen, for research, but also for pedagogy—a view in which concepts are not isolated or inert pieces but rather nodes connected in a vast and marvelous pattern whose principal characteristics are dynamism and activity. For example, the information we possess that
Nothing is certain but death and taxes
is not isolated. It is connected—potentially and dynamically, in the active mind—through its distinguished status as a "commonplace," which is to

say, its status as a widely held general assertion applicable to any number of unforeseen particular cases. To know the phrase

Nothing is certain but death and taxes

is not just to recognize it, but also to know, at least unconsciously, that it is a commonplace, and to have in the mental action of employing it an understanding of the kind of concepts with respect to which it appropriately serves as a commonplace. For example, if someone says "$2 + 2 = 4$," it would in usual circumstances be inappropriate to respond "Nothing is certain but death and taxes." The proposition, as a commonplace, can be potentially linked to many other phrases, but not simply or arbitrarily. It would not in usual circumstances be an appropriate retort, for example, to "Moscow is the capital of Russia" or "I believe that God is Love," although it might serve for "He will love her forever."

This classical view of cultural literacy is inseparable from the distinguished role it accords to language as the tool for disclosing our conceptual system but more significantly for honing and developing it. A conceptual system is refined by exercise. The core of the exercise is constant and ambitious practice in speaking a mature language—practice whose criterial activity is the deployment of rhetorical tools of mind.

Invention—the working of our conceptual system—is taken to be the beginning point of rhetoric, and the root of our cultural literacy. Systematicity, links, connections—these are, for the classical rhetorician, what education must live by. Arrangement follows in importance, but arrangement focusing on the whole, on the assumption that individual phrases in discourse have meaning only to the extent that we see them as situated in the inclusive and linked discourse. Memory comes much further down the list in classical rhetoric, and is described in the *Ad Herennium* as a mere treasure-house or guardian (3.15.26).[2] Of course, memory is indispensable to cultural literacy, but nevertheless is merely subsidiary and accessory.

If a modern rhetorician were to list capabilities any culturally literate person should have, the result would of course include, as secondary and derivative, the ability to recognize a great many phrases, such as "There is a tide in the affairs of men." If we were to list the phrases that the culturally literate person should be able to recognize, that list would be open to the charge of inadequacy: anyone in the audience could protest that the list omits what he or she knows and cares about. This is a legitimate charge, but from the rhetorical view, it is a superficial and misdirected charge. To see why it is superficial and misdirected, let us look at some of the other capabilities that a rhetorician would expect of a culturally literate person:

—The culturally literate person can distinguish metaphors, category statements, identities, and definitions. For example, a culturally literate person knows to try to take "Language is a virus" but not "A nickel is a dime" as a metaphor.

—The culturally literate person can make metonymic connections, understanding for example that "Romania" can stand for "the government of Romania," as in "Romania has fallen."

—The culturally literate person can connect concepts metaphorically. If, in times of economic scarcity, a friend takes a distasteful but safe job, and offers the explanation

any port in a storm,

the culturally literate person will understand this comment whether or not it is familiar.

—The culturally literate person understands the concept of an intellectual topography and will thus understand that an argument must be carried out upon common intellectual ground. The culturally literate person will understand that the nature of the argument differs according to the ground on which it occurs: the contrary propositions "You stole it!" versus "I didn't touch it!" constitute an argument but the contrary propositions "You stole it!" versus "I only borrowed it!" constitute a very different kind of argument.

—The culturally literate person will understand and employ many common constructions expressing conceptual connection, such as the *xyz* form, exemplified by

Necessity is the mother of invention.

The culturally literate person will be able both to generate new uses of this form, as in "Adams Morgan is the Greenwich Village of Washington, D.C.," and to understand new uses of it, as when, in the 1988 presidential debate, candidate Michael Dukakis claimed that "George Bush is the Joe Isuzu of American politics." Of course, understanding these expressions requires specific information—such as that Greenwich Village is a certain part of New York City, with a certain ambience, and that Joe Isuzu is an advertising character who specializes in affable and outrageous lies. But the information does not give the understanding. The culturally literate person can arrive at that understanding not because he or she has learned these phrases through some catechism but because the culturally literate person has the capacity to work conceptual connections. The culturally literate person can link up the pieces.

—The culturally literate person will understand noun phrases like "debt ceiling," "dog TV," "baby crack," and "land yacht"—which are abbreviated *xyz* forms—regardless of whether he or she is familiar with them.

—The culturally literate person will understand commonplace transformations, such as "pushing over," as in the phrase "A rhombus is a square pushed over." The culturally literate person will recognize that "A rhombus is a square pushed over" is a definition or a description.

—The culturally literate person will understand what I have called merely weird specifications, such as "Daniel Webster is a *human* steam-engine," and also what I have called really weird specifications, such as "Language is *fossil* poetry." The culturally literate person will understand these phrases regardless of whether he or she is familiar with them.

The lesson of this short list is not that the rhetorician hopes to include in the list of cultural literacy rhetorical phrases and tropes: everybody wishes to include on such a list his or her own shibboleths. Instead, the lesson is that rhetoric sees cultural literacy not in the recognition of phrases on a list—any phrases, regardless of who loves them—but rather in capacities for systematic understanding, invention, and thought.

The culturally literate person will understand those things I have mentioned on my short list and a great many more not by virtue of having memorized them but rather by virtue of a capacity to work links dynamically in a conceptual system. This system contains a great deal of finely textured information, but does not consist just of isolated pieces of information, even many isolated pieces of information, even many medium-sized isolated pieces of information, such as isolated schemas.

It might be tempting to think that the varieties of knowledge I have listed consist of abstract skills that are formal and independent of information. We might, for example, wish to think that recognizing metaphor is an abstract skill, consisting of the application of the supposedly information-free abstract rule that a speaker who equates one concept with a different concept is speaking metaphorically. But not so. To recognize a metaphor requires not only recognizing the equated concepts but also knowing their relationship to each other and their relative locations with respect to the rest of the conceptual system. We do not recognize as metaphors the phrases "A nickel is a dime," "A mug is a tumbler," "Parsley is cumin," or "A petunia is a daisy," even though these phrases equate nonidentical concepts. Instead, we recognize each as equating concepts that are subcategories of the same basic-level category, as in the case where *daisy* and *petunia* are subcategories of the basic-level category *flower*. We prefer not to recognize a metaphor in such a case. The recognition of metaphor is thus not formal, but depends upon information, not only of the mentioned concepts but also of their "place" in our conceptual system. Indeed, an equation is not a metaphor or an analogy on its own; it is a metaphor or an analogy only with respect to the full patterning of a conceptual system.

There is no knowledge independent of a great deal of information. The split between so-called formal skills and so-called information is a mistaken split, much like the split between the jigsaw puzzle and its parts. There is no cultural literacy independent of a great deal of information, but cultural literacy does not consist of piling up information.

Let us explore a specific example of the way in which understanding and information are inseparable. To understand the *xyz* phrase

Necessity is the mother of invention

requires us to call up missing bits of information. This phrase mentions neither *child* nor the *mother-child relationship*—information we must use to understand the phrase. We must know and supply this information. The meaning of the phrase cannot be figured out formally by recognizing the words in the phrase. The same is true of the *xyz* phrase

Brevity is the soul of wit.

We must be able to supply the information that a soul is related in a certain way to a person or a body. Otherwise we will not be able to draw the metaphorical entailment that wit without brevity is—like a person without a soul—dead and lifeless.

Each form of knowledge is ineradicably dependent upon a fine texture of information. However, none consists of having information. In every case, the form of knowledge requires the use of conceptual connections that cannot be looked up in a dictionary. One cannot know the meanings of the phrases I have listed in any significant sense by looking them up. One cannot learn them in any significant sense by being told to look them up. One cannot look up conceptual patterns, but conceptual patterns are the soul of cultural literacy. One cannot learn conceptual systematicity and connectivity except by exercising one's conceptual system, usually through language. For all these reasons, the test of cultural literacy is not the ability to recognize allusions, but the ability to engage in culturally literate communication. Someone who cannot engage in the give and take of culturally literate conversation is culturally illiterate, no matter how much information he or she has memorized and can recognize.

Let us take a detailed look at the conceptual systematicity surrounding a particular piece. Take

The Grim Reaper

as a personification of Death. It may look at first blush like an isolated piece of folklore, the product of some Druid's overheated imagination, but it is in fact a mild extension of a pattern that runs deep and wide throughout our conceptual system. In this pattern, there is a metaphoric connection between our concept of a plant and our concept of a person: people are understood metaphorically as plants with respect to the life cycle. This metaphoric understanding underlies everyday expressions like "She's withering away," "He's a late bloomer," "He's a young sprout," and "He's a budding theoretician." It also underlies many poetic metaphors, such as

> Why ask my birth, Diomedes? Very like leaves
> upon this earth are the generations of men—
> old leaves cast on the ground by wind, young leaves
> the greening forest bears when spring comes in.

So mortals pass; one generation flowers
even as another dies away.

(Iliad 6, translated by Robert Fitzgerald)

In this metaphor, the death of the plant corresponds to the death of the person. As it is written in Job, "Man that is born of a woman . . . cometh forth like a flower, and is cut down." It is the metaphor behind Herrick's poem "To the Virgins, to make much of time," which begins

> *Gather ye rosebuds while ye may*
> Old Time is still a-flying:
> And this same flower that smiles today
> Tomorrow will be dying.

It is the basis of many such carpe diem poems.

This basic metaphor, that PEOPLE ARE PLANTS with respect to the life cycle, is one part of the system that allows the Grim Reaper to stand for death. There is another part, the scenario of cultivation and harvest in which grain is harvested by reapers. There is yet a third part, our commonplace notion that all individual deaths are the result of Death-in-general: everyone is subject to Death, and particular deaths are caused by Death. And there is a fourth and last part, which is complicated, and which consists of our knowledge of how to make metaphoric connections between EVENTS (that do not have agents) and ACTIONS (that do have agents). When we say, "My car decided to strand me this morning," we are understanding an EVENT (the engine not working) in terms of an ACTION (deciding to strand). I call the generic-level knowledge that allows us to understand events in terms of actions the EVENTS ARE ACTIONS metaphor. It enables us to personify.

In the case of the Grim Reaper, we use PEOPLE ARE PLANTS to map, metaphorically, the plant onto the person and the death of the plant onto the death of the person. We use EVENTS ARE ACTIONS to arrive at a complex mapping in which the action of reaping corresponds to the event of causing a human death, and the Reaper corresponds to Death-in-General.

There are constraints on EVENTS ARE ACTIONS. In general, the patterns of our thought constrain us from arbitrary connections: we cannot map arbitrarily; not just anything can be personified in any old way. We are constrained, for example, against violating the causal structure of the target. Our concept of a person—the target—contains a causal connection between Death-in-General and the individual death of the individual person; we are constrained against violating it when we personify. This is why not just any person from the scenario of cultivation will do as a personification of death. The scenario of cultivation includes an irrigator, for example, but we cannot without provoking complaint personify Death as

"The Grim Irrigator": there is a causal link between Death-in-general and the individual death of the person; there is no causal link between the irrigator and the plant death. To map the irrigator onto Death-in-general and the plant death onto the human death would be to destroy the causal link in the target.[3]

There is another part in the systematicity of our understanding of

The Grim Reaper

which has to do with why he appears grim. We commonly project our feelings about an event onto the agent whose action produced that event. Consequently, we give to a personification an appearance that evokes the feeling associated with the event he causes. If we feel that healing is a benign event and personify Time as a Healer, then Time the Healer cannot appear terrifying and malicious. Under the same constraint, we personify death as grim. There is no reason associated with harvesting to make us think of a reaper as grim. Reapers can be robust, vigorous, and full of joyful song, and there are positive images of Christ "harvesting" souls. But Death the Reaper cannot have this sort of appearance.

Similar constraints underlie every one of the other forms of knowledge I have listed. For brief example, to understand

Necessity is the mother of invention

is not just to be able to translate it into "necessity leads to invention," but also to know, unconsciously, that the metaphoric progeneration involved is of a certain sort, constrained in certain ways. There would be something jarring in the expressions "Love is the father of purity," "Murder is the mother of jail sentences," or "Death is the child of cyanide." There would be something very unusual but intriguing about "Death is the mother of beauty." We know all this because of the patterning in our thought. Memorizing translations of phrases like

The wish is father to the thought

should not count, I think, as understanding the phrases, and certainly should not count as cultural literacy. It is the *patterning* between these conceptual pieces that is the indispensable characteristic of cultural literacy.

Cultural literacy is not principally a function of our memory of a handful of phrases. Consider

any port in a storm.

This phrase is an expression of a systematic basic metaphor in our conceptual apparatus, LIFE IS A JOURNEY. We speak of "just starting out in life," "getting somewhere in life," "having lost our direction in life," and "coming to the end of the trail." These are everyday expressions of the metaphor. In this metaphor, the person leading a life is a traveler; his purposes are destinations; the means for achieving purposes are routes; difficulties in life are impediments to travel; counselors are guides; and progress is the distance traveled. The target schema, life, is understood metaphorically in terms of the source schema, journey.

This basic metaphor can be fleshed-out. We know many kinds of journeys, such as taking a walk or going by boat. In a journey by boat, a storm is a rough spot in the travel. A port is a haven from the storm. If life is metaphorically a journey by boat, then difficulties in life can be storms, metaphorically, and a situation protected from these difficulties can be a port, metaphorically. But we also know that while we are in port we are not getting any traveling done. Consequently, it is a metaphoric entailment that a person who is metaphorically "in port" is not "getting on" with life, and that someone who has been metaphorically "forced into port by the storm" may not even like the situation, aside from its safety.

All this patterning lies behind understanding

any port in a storm.

To have knowledge of what this phrase means is to be able to work these connections, at least unconsciously. These connections enable the culturally literate person to understand the phrase even if he or she has never encountered it before, because

any port in a storm

is not inert or isolated. It is part of the system that underlies any number of other phrases we might list, such as

The course of true love never did run smooth

and

Crossing the bridge when you come to it.

Let us pause to take stock. In 1981, a rhetorician no doubt would have taken all I have been saying as a workaday presentation of a classical conception of competence, although fleshed out with some modern ideas. But in 1991, the case is very different, because in the intervening decade, E. D. Hirsch, the William R. Kenan Professor of English at the University of Virginia, has formed, announced, and popularized a program for reforming pedagogy. This project—easily the most influential such proposal in my lifetime—has swept the nation. It has swept our popular media, popular consciousness, intellectual magazines, journals, professional symposia, and conferences. Championed at the outset by then-Secretary of Education William Bennett, the proposal is now widely influencing practice. It is presented fully in Hirsch's omnipresent best-seller, *Cultural Literacy: What Every American Needs to Know*, published in 1987. It has spawned an organization, the Cultural Literacy Foundation. The inclusive activity associated with Hirsch's proposal is referred to as "The Cultural Literacy Project."

Hirsch claims that Americans are sadly unacquainted with enough of the right kinds of information, and that if they were acquainted with this information, they would be culturally literate. Hirsch gives a list of this basic information in *Cultural Literacy*, a list compiled with the help of Joseph Kett and James Trefil. That list is the basis for their more expansive best-seller, *The Dictionary of Cultural Literacy*. No reader will be surprised that I have taken from the Cultural Literacy List the phrases "Nothing is certain but death and taxes," "any port in a storm," "The course of true love never did run smooth," "Crossing the bridge when you come to it," "Necessity is the mother of invention," "The wish is father to the thought," "brevity is the soul of wit," and "Gather ye rosebuds while ye may." I have taken "The Grim Reaper" from The *Dictionary of Cultural Literacy*.

Hirsch has been sufficiently disturbed by the undeniably low level of cultural literacy in our society and the crushing consequences of having a culturally illiterate citizenry to take the time to formulate and propose a remedy. But there is an inadequacy in Hirsch's program that, if unchecked, may actually render the program injurious in practice. Hirsch's program is founded upon what I think is a spurious concept of knowledge, namely, that knowledge consists of having lots of information.[4] It is true that our situation would be preferable if everybody knew everything Hirsch lists (and a great deal besides). But I believe Hirsch may have a mistaken notion of what it means to know the things on his list. Consequently, he may have a mistaken notion of what it means to teach cultural literacy. I think that classical rhetoric had it right, and that Hirsch has it wrong.

Hirsch begins his book with the sentence, "To be culturally literate is to possess the basic information needed to thrive in the modern world."[5] The basic information Hirsch lists may or may not be necessary to thrive, but acquaintance with it will not make one culturally literate. Just what is it that Hirsch thinks acquaintance with this basic information will bring us? Apparently, everything: "Only by piling up specific, communally shared information can children learn to participate in complex cooperative activities with other members of their communities."[6] Hirsch equates knowledge with information, and assumes that an acquaintance with information gives us all those powers we associate with cultural literacy. We can see this in the following representative passage, where Hirsch discusses "world knowledge":

> Professor Chall is one of several reading specialists who have observed that "world knowledge" is essential to the development of reading and writing skills. What she calls world knowledge I call cultural literacy, namely, the network of information that all competent readers possess. It is the background information, stored in their minds, that enables them to take up a

newspaper and read it with an adequate level of comprehension, getting the point, grasping the implications, relating what they read to the unstated context which alone gives meaning to what they read.[7]

There are many troubling spots in this passage, I think. First, having this information will not make a person able to comprehend, get the point, grasp the implications, attribute meaning, and so on. Second, Hirsch does not focus on conceptual patterns, which is what cultural literacy is all about. Third, Hirsch thinks that knowledge is something static that is stored in the mind and trotted out when needed. Hirsch nods briefly in the direction of the "network" of this information, but this nod is perhaps most troubling of all, since he seems to understand the essential networking as a static organization of static information rather than as an active systematicity of dynamic thought. Contrary to Hirsch's conception, concepts—bits of information—are not objects but activities. They do not have essences; they have functions. Their principal function is to be used in thought.

Let us look at a few examples of how Hirsch ignores conceptual patterns. The highest level of system in Hirsch's book is the notion of the schema. In his section on "The Psychological Structure of Background Knowledge," Hirsch claims that we make sense of fragmentary information by seeing it in terms of organizing schemas, which is true enough. Concepts like *leaf, root,* and *branch* are grouped into the schema for *tree,* and we make sense out of seeing leaves and roots and branches by projecting upon them our schema for a tree. That is the extent of patterns for Hirsch. Beyond the level of the schema, information—as Hirsch seems to present it—is arbitrary.

What makes our knowledge not arbitrary is the patterns in our conceptual structure, the sort of patterns we have discussed throughout our studies in this book. Consider the Grim Reaper. The Grim Reaper is not just an arbitrary concept, to be learned as an inert piece the way one learns the meaning of "Dutch Treat" (which is on The List). To be culturally literate is not just to know that the Grim Reaper stands for death, in such a way that one could pick out the right association in a multiple-choice test, or fill in the blank correctly on a fill-in-the-blank test. As we have seen, to be culturally literate is to possess the conceptual patterns behind the concept of the Grim Reaper, and those patterns are elaborate and powerful. One must know the basic metaphor that PEOPLE ARE PLANTS with respect to the life cycle, know the scenario of cultivation, know the commonplace notion of the general cause of individual deaths, know the very complicated way in which events can be understood metaphorically in terms of actions, know how to personify, and know all the constraints on this conceptual connectivity.

But let us look at the entry for the Grim Reaper in *The Dictionary of Cultural Literacy*:

> Grim Reaper: A figure commonly used to represent death. The Grim Reaper is a skeleton or solemn-looking man carrying a scythe, who cuts off people's lives as though he were harvesting grain.

What is missing from this entry is almost everything. A student may memorize this entry, and repeat it perfectly on a test, but that will be no indication of the student's knowledge of the conceptual patterns in which the concept of the Grim Reaper is embedded. In this dictionary entry, the Grim Reaper is presented as an arbitrary, inert, isolated bit of information, something like a jigsaw puzzle piece isolated from the puzzle into which it fits. The culturally literate person does not recognize the Grim Reaper as an arbitrary, inert, isolated bit of information, a piece without its puzzle, but rather as something that fits into a conceptual system. The culturally literate person may not be able to articulate this knowledge or bring it into consciousness, but it is powerfully there nonetheless.

Let us give a little demonstration of the existence of this unconscious knowledge. Suppose you opened the *Dictionary of Cultural Literacy*, and saw any of the following entries, each of which I have invented:

> The Starving Shepherd: A figure commonly used to represent Death. The Starving Shepherd is an emaciated basketball player who kills people as if he were standing watch over sheep.
>
> The Jaunty Electrician: A figure commonly used to represent Death. The Jaunty Electrician is a rotund philanthropist who kills people as though he were installing light switches for free.
>
> The Melodious Victim: A figure commonly used to represent Death. The Melodious Victim kills people as if he were whistling while being beaten up.
>
> The Scratching Hemophiliac: A figure commonly used to represent Death. The Scratching Hemophiliac kills people as if he were bleeding while scratching.

These fantasy entries are all ridiculous exactly because they are arbitrary with respect to our conceptual patterns. We view them as problematic or silly because we know those patterns even though we cannot articulate them. To naturalize any of these silly entries through an interpretation that transformed it into something less arbitrary would take a great deal of creative construal. By contrast, there is absolutely nothing arbitrary about the Grim Reaper as a figure for Death, but Hirsch gives no indication of any difference between a concept that participates in our conceptual patterns, like the Grim Reaper, and an arbitrary concept, like the Jaunty Electrician. The Grim Reaper is presented in the "Mythology and

Folklore" section of *The Dictionary of Cultural Literacy* as if it were just an arbitrary weird invention.

To be sure, there are fairly arbitrary phrases in our language. "Dutch Treat" is not, as far as I know, an expression of a powerful general conceptual connection.[8] It is not systematically connected (at least for me) with the rest of our concepts. It could have been "Swedish Treat" just as easily. It is fairly inert. We just have to memorize it. The same is true of "independent as a hog on ice" (whose meaning is opaque to me, although I know its use). But we do not just memorize phrases like "on the level" or "getting it off my chest" or "staff of life" or "through thick and thin" as if they were isolated. At least, we do not just memorize them as arbitrary piecemeal definitions, not if we want to understand, not if we want to be literate. Hirsch, in short, leaves out the conceptual patterns that are the heart of cultural literacy, conceptual patterns of the sort this book is exercised to uncover. Hirsch treats "The Grim Reaper" and "Dutch Treat" as if they were the same sort of concept.

If a friend does not recognize "Dutch Treat," we will not be too distressed. Perhaps he has never heard it before, or never noticed it. But take "James is the George Washington of Nosnibor." If a friend who has never heard the phrase and who moreover has never even heard of James or Nosnibor cannot make some sense of the phrase, then we will be quite distressed. If this friend fails to understand not only "any port in a storm" but any of a range of new expressions of the metaphor of life as a journey—such as "I took a detour for a while through advertising but finally got back on the road toward architecture"—then we will be even more distressed, and think that something is gravely wrong with someone we previously judged to be culturally literate. Different things on Hirsch's list have different weight, according to their connections within our conceptual system, but Hirsch does not present them as such because he does not focus on these connections.

This seems so obvious that it is difficult to say how Hirsch could have been misled, but perhaps there is an explanation. Hirsch thinks that the list he offers is a test, and he is right! Suppose we give this list to someone who has never seen it before, and he recognizes nearly everything on the list. By definition, that person will be culturally literate in Hirsch's sense, but it is highly likely that he will *also* be culturally literate in the classical sense. Such a person probably became acquainted with that information through wide reading and conversation. Such a person has additionally the systematicity of mind to enable him or her to master and remember that information in something other than a trivial sense. Such a person would probably be able to do just as well on a similar list of altogether different items. Such a person would probably be able to converse about the things on the list, hold a discussion, construct an argument. Such a person would probably have powers of invention and arrangement, the powers most important in the classical model of cultural literacy.

However, suppose we give this list to a little computer program that memorizes lists of pairs and spits back the second half of the pair when prompted with its twin. We say to the computer, "The Grim Reaper," and the computer flashes back,

> A figure commonly used to represent death. The Grim Reaper is a skeleton or solemn-looking man carrying a scythe, who cuts off people's lives as though he were harvesting grain.

The computer will do perfectly on the list, but should receive an F in cultural literacy. Suppose we give this list to a student who learns it in the sense of memorizing it. The student will do very well on the test, but may have learned virtually nothing. The list is a test—Hirsch is correct about that. But what it is testing depends upon how acquaintance with its contents was acquired. Someone who is culturally literate has acquired, as a *byproduct*, acquaintance with the list. But the converse does not hold. Someone who is acquainted with the list has not acquired cultural literacy.

Suppose I give you Hirsch's book, but you cannot read. What good will the book do you? That is an analogue of what it is like to be acquainted with the information on Hirsch's list but not to have the finely textured conceptual patterns that Hirsch does not discuss.

"Literacy" means both reading and *writing*. If you cannot write your name, you are not literate. One test of cultural literacy then would be whether someone can write in what we consider a culturally literate way. Does anyone imagine that memorizing this list will allow one to write in a culturally literate way? I do not mean write like Shakespeare. I mean simply write something that gets a set of points across in a coherent, ordered, competent manner.

There are many other tests of cultural literacy that someone acquainted with Hirsch's list might fail utterly. If you cannot read Hirsch's book, for example, you are not culturally literate. So Hirsch's book—and not just the appended list—functions itself as a test of cultural literacy. Let us have a look, then, at a few passages from Hirsch's book, and see what is involved in passing this test of cultural literacy.

At one point, Hirsch tells a story about how he is glancing out the window as he writes.[9] He says that his view is blocked by some objects—partial and fragmented bits of information—which he takes to correspond to leaves and branches and to belong to trees. His point is that we understand bits of information, such as images of leaves and branches, by seeing them as belonging to a schema, such as the schema for trees. Hirsch then quotes a paragraph including certain words that refer to places, people, and events associated with the Civil War. Hirsch then comments, "These words are like the leaves outside my window."[10]

A culturally literate person can understand this comment as meaning that just as we use schemata to organize fragmentary visual data, so we use schemata to organize bits of information mentioned in words; on the basis of a few words, we project onto the paragraph about the Civil War our schema of the Civil War. But here is the problem: there is nothing in learning Hirsch's list, or anything like it, that can give you the ability to understand Hirsch's analogical comment. Learning Hirsch's list will not enable you to read Hirsch's book, which means that you can learn Hirsch's list and still flunk the most basic test of cultural literacy.

This raises a crucial distinction. The titles on Hirsch's list, and the snippet quotations, are powerful things to have read and wrestled with and understood. Working through them in the original, in a full context, is likely to provide someone with cultural literacy. But learning to recognize them from the list is not at all the same thing. The difference between learning through the originals and learning through the list is the difference between having had a love affair and having memorized a definition of "sex."

Let us look at another passage from *Cultural Literacy*, that book which, presumably, culturally literate people should be able to understand. Hirsch argues, correctly I believe, against the formalist notions that students can be taught abstract skills independent of information. He argues that reading and writing are not a set of information-free techniques that can be taught by coaching, and argues that, consequently, reading and writing are not like baseball and skating. Hirsch writes,

> The skill idea becomes an oversimplification as soon as students start reading for meaning rather than for cracking the alphabetic code. If reading were just hitting the right alphabetic ball with the right phonic bat, or just learning "text strategies," it *would* be like baseball. We could teach everybody to groove their swings and watch for the seven different types of pitches. The trouble is that reading for meaning is a different sort of game entirely. It is different every time, depending on what the piece of writing is about. Every text, even the most elementary, implies information that it takes for granted and doesn't explain. Knowing such information is *the* decisive skill of reading.[11]

I agree that knowing the information is a decisive skill of reading, but think that Hirsch's view of what it means to know that information is a two-dimensional view. A culturally literate reader can make sense, for example, of Hirsch's analogy about reading and baseball, and understand too why Hirsch thinks the analogy invalid. The decisive element in understanding this passage is the ability to connect concepts analogically, and to make certain inferences about those connections. This cannot be looked up. Surely it is not on The List, and could not be on any List, since it is an activity, not a phrase.

Indeed, although Hirsch is quite right that there is no knowledge without detailed and specific information, he seems to have overstressed the things on his list, as if only this *particular* list of detailed and specific information can, in his conception, give us knowledge, which of course is a wrong claim to make in the first instance since no list can give knowledge. Is the information on Hirsch's list really so privileged? I think not. I do not merely want to assert that Hirsch's list is arbitrary or that it should include other or different bundles of information. These are the principal objections directed against Hirsch, but at best they are trivial and at worst they strengthen what they mean to attack since they embrace Hirsch's conception of knowledge. My objections are of a different order: (1) conceptual patterns, although always inhering in a wealth of specific information, do not depend upon any particular information, and (2) while knowing the patterns allows one to pile up information, the converse is not true. Consider

Chappaquidick was Teddy Kennedy's Waterloo.
Bimini Island was Gary Hart's Chappaquidick.
James is the George Washington of Nosnibor.

If we know the *xyz* form, and some of the information mentioned in these phrases, and have never heard them before, never seen them on any list, we can both make fair sense of them and pile up new information out of the sense we make. The indispensable element in understanding them is not acquaintance with every term. Indeed, acquaintance with every term will not give us an understanding if we are deficient in conceptual patterns. But by contrast, having the conceptual patterns will indeed let us understand these phrases, and pile up information, even if we are unacquainted with half or even more of the phrases they contain.

If we have conceptual patterns, they will of course be grounded in a great deal of finely textured information. We will then be culturally literate, in my sense. A student who has this conceptual systematicity will be able to pick up new information easily. But there is no particular packet of specific information that is indispensable to conceptual patterns. A student who lacks this conceptual systematicity will not be able to pick up new information easily, no matter how many packets of information he learns to recognize. Without conceptual patterns, the student will not be able to integrate information into a conceptual system. No matter how many bits of information such a student picks up, his literacy will be weak. An army of a million soldiers is weak if it must march single file down a single road. Adding more soldiers will not help if they can only fight one at a time.

As far as I know, no one has done any empirical work to see how well students do on this score. To test students for their capability to deal with the *xyz* form and to use it to become better informed is to test one kind of ability; to test them for their ability to recognize *x, y,* and *z* is to test something else. I have seen many tests of the latter sort, which I take to be inferior, and none of the former sort, which I take to be essential.

Are there packets of information that are indispensable to conceptual systematicity, and thus to cultural literacy? Suppose Hirsch's passage had read, "If reading were just splatting the right alphabetic ball with the right phonic splatter, or just learning 'text strategies,' it *would* be like the game of splat." Culturally literate people could make fair sense of this passage, even though they are unacquainted with the game of splat. To do so would require them to locate an appropriate general level of information about games, grounded in acquaintance with some specific information, but not necessarily in any unique game. Second, it would require them to map metaphorically between schemas, to connect the schema for sounding out words with the schema for playing a game, so that the player corresponds to the reader; splatting the ball corresponds to dealing with a letter by assigning a sound; the splatter—taken as an instrument for doing something to the ball—corresponds to phonics—taken as an instrument for decoding; splatting a ball with a splatter corresponds to assigning the right phonic sound to the letter, and so on.

But that is only the beginning of what culturally literate people would be able to understand. They would be able to see further that if this metaphor held, then learning to read would indeed be like learning this game, and consequently that teaching reading would be like teaching this game. Thus, they would be able to draw a complicated metaphoric entailment. They would then be able to understand yet further that since the metaphor does not hold (according to the author), the implications of the metaphor for reading pedagogy must be rejected.

Being able to understand all this just is what we expect of a culturally literate person. But this conceptual knowledge (as opposed to information) is just what Hirsch's project misses entirely. No amount of memorizing information can give it to students. Only practice in dealing with information can give it to students. Knowledge comes from dealing with a great deal of information; it is not constituted in any important sense by that information alone. Indeed, having the specific knowledge of baseball is not even particularly necessary for understanding Hirsch's passage. A culturally literate person, to understand Hirsch's book, needs conceptual patterns grounded in information. But he does not need to know about baseball.

Once we begin to look for the conceptual patterning that Hirsch's list presupposes but does not mention, we see it everywhere. For example, as we saw in our study of the poetry of connections, our conceptual apparatus includes knowledge of THE GREAT CHAIN METAPHOR. It underlies many of the expressions in Hirsch's list, such as

His bark is worse than his bite
Birds of a feather flock together
biting the hand that feeds one
blind leading the blind
bolt from the blue
brainwashing
break the ice
build castles in the air
The burnt child fears the fire
cast pearls before swine
chip off the old block
cold hands, warm heart
get the cold shoulder
cool one's heels
Hit the nail on the head
It's always darkest before the dawn
One rotten apple spoils the barrel
steal one's thunder
There is a tide in the affairs of men
Variety is the spice of life
You can't fit a square peg in a round hole

These snippets are not inert or isolated. All are cases where something at one level of the Great Chain is understood metaphorically in terms of something at a different level in the Great Chain according to some fairly complicated unconscious principles. A culturally literate person is at ease in understanding and using THE GREAT CHAIN METAPHOR, and that capacity is inseparable from a great deal of information. The culturally literate person need not be acquainted with any particular set of expressions of THE GREAT CHAIN METAPHOR, but will be able to generate and assimilate new expressions of it easily. That sort of patterning is missing from Hirsch's theory of knowledge, and consequently is missing from his considerations of pedagogy.

If the Cultural Literacy Project is potentially injurious to pedagogy, it is because it is a false fix to a profound problem. The great danger of the Cultural Literacy Project is that it will produce students with well-catechized third-rate minds. Catechism does not make you culturally literate. Concepts in one's conceptual system are active devices. They compete with each other to become activated in a dynamic and systematic fashion, inhibiting, reinforcing, tuning, and changing each other. They are kept up by being used. They are not static bits "stored in memory," as Hirsch describes them. They are not "stored" at all. Catechism is a pedagogy that suits a theory of concepts as inert bits stored in memory, and it suits a theory of knowledge as constituted by a list of information. If we have a different idea of concepts and knowledge—as dynamic, competitive, and systematic—then we need a different form of pedagogy, such as practice in using one's conceptual system by engaging in culturally literate forms of conversation. That is the classical model.

In actual practice among the culturally literate, bits of information do not occur on their own; they occur in units of discourse that can stand on their own, relative to the conceptual apparatus of the intended audience. The phrase "any port in a storm" does not occur on its own, but rather as embedded in a discourse whose understanding requires us to use patterns in our conceptual apparatus. This leads to a pedagogical principle, which I will call the principle of meaningful wholes: If a student is to acquire cultural literacy, the student cannot work with anything less than a unit of discourse that can stand on its own, relative to the student's conceptual apparatus. Understanding of anything less than such a unit of discourse is not effective learning. The principle of meaningful wholes is not a subject of Hirsch's project. Apparently, the pedagogy recommended by Hirsch's project actually violates the principle of meaningful wholes.

Perhaps I have misconstrued Hirsch's intention. It could be that, although he has slighted conceptual systematicity, he means for it to be taught through practice, and that I have only been misled by Hirsch's emphasis on information, his equation of information with knowledge, and his infamous List. If I have misconstrued Hirsch's intention, then I ask him to clarify to the nation that so energetically follows his lead that he did not mean to equate cultural literacy with recognizing information. The pedagogy that has actually developed from Hirsch's project is exemplified by materials like *Test Your Cultural Literacy*.[12] This book, a series of multiple-choice recognitions, contains items like:

> The incident or thing that finally causes you to lose control is
> a. "the lunatic fringe"
> b. "the last straw"
> c. "the most unkindest cut of all"
> d. "Pandora's box"[13]

In the terms of *Test Your Cultural Literacy*, the culturally literate person should be able to pick out that *b* is the right answer. I claim that the culturally literate person—while knowing that the makers of the test think that *b* is the right answer—will be able to make a good case for any of the answers, will understand implicitly why lunatics are referred to as being at the "fringe" (a metaphoric conception), will know—implicitly, unconsciously, as a result of conceptual patterns—why we say "the last straw" and not "the last anvil," and a host of other things besides. In *Test Your Cultural Literacy,* which Hirsch did not write, and in Hirsch's own *Cultural Literacy* and *Dictionary of Cultural Literacy,* cultural literacy becomes trivial pursuit.

The question is, did Hirsch intend for his project to result in publications such as *Test Your Cultural Literacy?* Does Hirsch say in *Cultural Literacy* anything that would tell us that this is not a result he welcomes?

Let us look at Hirsch's own book for an example of what sort of pedagogy he might have in mind. The example is unsettling. Early in his book, Hirsch uses a passage from *Julius Caesar.*

> There is a tide in the affairs of men
> Which taken at the flood leads on to fortune;
> Omitted, all the voyage of their life
> Is bound in shallows and in miseries.
> On such a full sea are we now afloat,
> And we must take the current when it serves,
> Or lose our ventures.

This is an excellent passage for students to have to deal with. A student who comes to understand this passage will be at least well on the way toward a sophisticated capability to connect schemas. In particular, the student will have the beginnings of the conception of life in terms of journeys and voyages, will have the beginnings of what it means to draw entailments that arise through metaphor, and will have some sense of the uses of information in persuasion. The point of reading Shakespeare is to have a mind of the sort that has dealt with reading Shakespeare, a mind with both conceptual patterns and the ability to work them, rooted of course in specific information, such as the specific information that comes from reading Shakespeare. The conceptual patterns that result will be inseparable from the information the student will have encountered, but will not in any way be reducible to that information. Only at the most trivial level is the point of reading Shakespeare to be able to recognize allusions from Shakespeare.

Unfortunately, it is just this trivial and insubstantial recognition that Hirsch takes as constituting cultural literacy. Hirsch's comment on the passage are as follows:

> My father used to write business letters that alluded to Shakespeare. These allusions were effective for conveying complex messages to his associates, because, in his day, business people could make such allusions with every expectation of being understood. For instance, in my father's commodity business, the timing of sales and purchases was all-important, and he would

sometimes write or say to his colleagues, "There is a tide," without further elaboration. Those four words carried not only a lot of complex information, but also the persuasive force of a proverb. In addition to the basic practical meaning, "Act now!" what came across was a lot of implicit reasons why immediate action was important. . . .

To say "There is a tide" is better than saying "Buy (or sell) now and you'll cover expenses for the whole year, but if you fail to act right away, you may regret it the rest of your life." That would be twenty-seven words instead of four, and while the bare message of the longer statement would be conveyed, the persuasive force wouldn't.[14]

For Hirsch, recognizing the reference saves a lot of time, and efficiency seems to be the principal issue. The phrase is thus useful principally as an abbreviation. If I read this passage correctly, in the context of Hirsch's book, then the reason Hirsch thinks the four words "There is a tide" carry a lot of information is that they are an abbreviated symbol of the passage, which carries a lot of information. And the reference, for Hirsch, is persuasive because it has the force of a pithy proverb.

This is a very feeble result. It is true that this passage is persuasive, but the reason it is persuasive is that it is based upon a strong conceptual patterning through which it is linked to many of our ways of thinking, including THE GREAT CHAIN METAPHOR: events in life are being understood in terms of natural events. Shakespeare's metaphoric understanding is not arbitrary, and it is not isolated. What gives power to the passage is its connection to conceptual patterns, which is exactly what Hirsch ignores. It may be that what Hirsch has in mind for pedagogy is a classical view, but I cannot locate such a view in Hirsch's book. Neither Hirsch's project of extensive education, in which we learn the list, nor his barely mentioned tandem project of intensive education, in which we study a few things with more attention, brings up the issue of the sort of conceptual patterns discussed here. The reason for knowing proverbs and snippets is to have a mind that can wrap itself around them and understand them, not just recognize them.

At one point in this passage, Hirsch does seem to imply the existence of an active conceptual network that consists of much more than information, when he observes that the information contained in "There is a tide" comes with a host of implicit reasons for taking the advice. This is a suggestive comment. An explanation of what implicit reasons come along and why they come along and the manner in which they come along might have led Hirsch to an appropriate recognition of the nature of that network. But if we subject Hirsch's descriptions of that network to the kind of analysis developed so far in this book, we see that his assertions and descriptions consistently express the metaphoric conceptions that IDEAS ARE OBJECTS and UNDERSTANDING IS GRASPING. This makes of the mind a mechanism. These metaphors imply that knowledge is static, that it can be possessed, that it can be stored away and brought out of storage. It does not really matter what Hirsch intended to follow from his project, because the metaphors underlying his conception lead inevitably to making lists of objects to be grasped and testing students on whether or not they grasp them. Against these metaphors, I propose a contrary set of conceptions: ideas are not objects to be grasped but rather activities to be conducted; concepts are active devices that have functions; concepts compete with each other, dynamically, and are plastic; concepts are honed through use in thought; most importantly, mind is not a storehouse; it is a process.

The last point I would like to make about the classical view of cultural literacy is that our patterns of mind are not partitioned by disciplines. The rhetorical forms of poetic thought supposedly reserved only for poets are part of everyday thought. They are ineradicable and irreducible in everyday thought. They are disclosed everywhere in our everyday language. They are not opposed to reason. On the contrary, reason and poetic thought are hypertrophies of a common imaginative capability that belongs to human beings. There was a reason that the classical view of cultural literacy involved breadth of education and the training of all parts of the mind. The workings of the mind in different subject matters, although never independent of information, are nonetheless connected through conceptual patterns, not least because all human thought occurs in a human mind in a human brain in a human body in an environment that the human being must be able to make sense of in order to survive. From the view of the systematicity of the mind, the logician should be trained in poetry and the poet should be trained in logic. The research agenda of classical rhetoric and the pedagogy of classical rhetoric thus go, we might say, "hand-in-hand," a phrase which is not on the list, but which any culturally literate person—who knows THE GREAT CHAIN META-PHOR and his body—will understand.

Lists are common in the humanities. Sometimes, the humanities just seem to consist of lists of discrete subject matters. At many times in the history of the humanities, the humanities have degenerated into a list. Certainly this occurred when the discipline of rhetoric degenerated after the Classical era, a degeneration from which our popular conception of rhetoric has never recovered, and which seems to me to have been the greatest loss that the humanities, and intellectual life in general, ever suffered. We still think of rhetoric, and of the humanities, as constituted by a list of little affectations and adornments that allow the literati to preen endlessly in the pursuit of appearing erudite.

This view of the humanities as founded on a list of some sort or other leads us to two activities, neither of them thought. The first is to wrangle over what goes into the list—an activity that presupposes that the essence of the humanities is the list and that all we can do is to scratch and gouge, like weasels fighting in a hole, for the inclusion of something in the list and the exclusion of something else.

The second activity is a school-room activity, the activity of test-taking. When knowledge consists of a list, the normal pedagogical sequence is to give a test on the list. This activity, slightly extended at each step, carries the student in the humanities from the primary grades through the Ph.D. orals, and often becomes a form of life. Much of the conversation in the humanities consists of test-taking and test-giving as a mode of social discourse. We allude to a line by Yeats—thereby testing others—and try to catch in turn their allusions—thereby taking the tests given to us. This passes in the humanities for discourse. Sometimes, it passes for scholarship.

The Cultural Literacy Project is a product of this form of life. Its underlying metaphoric conceptions that IDEAS ARE OBJECTS, UNDERSTANDING IS GRASPING, and KNOWING IS POSSESSING lead to the view that knowing is turning the world into a series of objects and being able to measure those objects. The problem with this form of life is not that the world cannot be conceived this way; it can. The problem is rather the consequence: knowledge becomes the possession of bureaucrats, the human mind is distorted into a passive client of these bureaucrats, and we are all degraded into something less than human beings. This is an intolerable state of affairs, and accounts, I think, for the attraction of deconstruction. Deconstructionists are professional antibureaucrats, their existence derived from the ambition to function as an omnipresent and indefatigable antibureaucratic virus. Cognitive rhetoric, as I have tried to develop it in this book, is a humanistic discipline, standing apart from the debate between the bureaucrats and the antibureaucrats, on the view that they have both misconceived the nature of humanistic inquiry.

Early in this book, I mentioned that the humanities suffer in both popular and intellectual culture from an eerily consistent Aristophanic caricature as a Disney World of self-absorption and harmless irrelevancy. This view of the humanities as a list, and of knowledge as codifying and fussing around with this list, and of challenge as fighting over this list, and of discourse as repackaging this list, and of inquiry as constructing a series of allusions to this list, contributes mightily to the view of the humanities as peripheral and as offering nothing to the discovery of the mind, the central intellectual activity in the age of cognitive science. It is a view that allots to the humanities no role in creation, no role in discovery, and a trivial role in pedagogy.

But what a falling off is here. In classical rhetoric, the humanities consisted of the investigation into what belongs to human beings, with the hope of *discovering* the nature of what belongs to human beings. Language and literature—seen as very tightly connected—held a central place in that investigation. Later, in the fourteenth, fifteenth, and sixteenth centuries, the humanities were also enveloped with a sense of creation and discovery. Language and literature, painting and music seemed at the center of this investigation.

The key characteristic of these great ages of the humanities was an intellectual *activity*. The list Hirsch presents is not active; it is static. The natural response to the list is not active, but reactive: to recognize it. One cannot have a user's manual to Hirsch's list, or to any of the other lists that are taken to constitute the humanities, because they do not lead to an intellectual activity, only to recognitions.

This book hopes to restart a view of the humanities as an *activity* whose practitioners endeavor to see how the humanities fit into full human life and into the entirety of mental space—not just the little surface layer of mental space in which you remember that Gloria Grahame won the academy award for best supporting actress in 1952 (*The Bad and the Beautiful*, Vincente Minnelli, director). In the activity envisaged in this book, the pursuit is not trivial. On the contrary, the goal is to discover the greatest thing we could discover, how the human mind works. This activity would require us to reconsider our notions of language and literature as acts of the human brain in a human body in a human environment. It would require us to reconsider our default concepts of the humanities, the person, the body, the brain, thinking, consciousness, concepts, language, and literature, and to do so not just once but continually, as the constitutive activity of the humanities. It is to encourage this activity that this book, this start-up program, has been written. To be sure, this activity is a tall order, but it is a worthy calling, and it is our tradition. It is an activity that belonged to the humanities at times in the past when the humanities were important. It is an activity that is indispensable, and that will be conducted in our future. Whether it will be conducted by humanists, however, we can only wait and see.

Chapter 11

ENVOI: COGNITIVE RHETORIC AND
LITERARY CRITICISM

THIS BOOK has asked us to imagine how the study of English might change if we viewed language and literature as cognitive acts. Language and literature reflect the nature of cognition. Cognition is brain activity in human bodies and is subject to the constraints of selection for fitness. This perspective sees cognitive studies as the first ground of both linguistics and criticism. It cuts against a premise engrained in us by both our tacit cultural education and our professional training—the premise that language, literature, and mind are separate objects of study.

This premise is a form, a mold. Into it we have cast the research and teaching activity of our institutions of higher learning. What comes out of the mold, like poured and hardened concrete, is an organization of academic departments that embodies this premise, transmits it through the controlling structure of our forms of professional life, and instills and enforces it through ritualistic and social mechanisms of a highly conservative nature. The premise belongs intellectually to the past, but lives with us in the institutional present, and like all institutional structures resists innovation and revision.

This premise may come automatically to the hand of the overworked literary critic who wishes to sweep aside the project of this book as extrinsic to literary criticism. Under the default concept of literary criticism, the project of this book is extrinsic since it declines to see literature as a special world to be treated with special tools designed exclusively for the investigation of literature. But that concept of literary criticism is what I most hope to change. I cannot hope to convince the critic who declines to engage this project of its indispensability. I hope that the critic who fully engages it will convince himself. To play out the future revisions of literary criticism I have in mind by conducting extended treatments of individual literary works according to the lines of cognitive rhetoric would lead to another book or perhaps even a series of books of an entirely different flavor and nature. They would be books of applied theory, not start-up programs for launching a project or discipline. They would be case studies explaining individual works and elucidating in the process three levels on which cognitive studies form the ground of criticism.

The first level is the most important and the most pervasive. It is the level of local phrasing. It is easy to show how critical analysis of any literary passage instantly encounters a thicket of cognitive rhetorical problems that it must engage at the start if it is to count as analysis. This is no surprise: half of the examples in this book are literary. We encounter such problems the moment we open any literary text. It would be easy to give demonstration after demonstration here, by taking up, for example, Shelley's "Me—who am as a nerve o'er which do creep / The else unfelt oppressions of the earth," or Blake's "The man who never alters his opinions is like standing water, and breeds reptiles of the mind," or Thoreau's "I am a parcel of vain strivings tied by a chance bond together." We might look at Ben Jonson's conceptual connection between the concept of a son and the concept of a poem: "Rest in soft peace, and asked, say here doth lie / Ben Jonson, his best piece of poetry." We might look at George Herbert's "Time is the rider that breaks youth."

We might select whatever books on my shelf here at hand are famous for the difficulty and challenge of their literary expression, such as the works of Ezra Pound, and look at "Usura is a murrain" (Canto 45) or "Death was ever a churl" ("Pan is dead"); or images such as "With ripples like dragon-scales, going grass green on the water" ("Exile's Letter") or "Sunset, the ribbon-like road lies, in red cross-light" ("Near Perigord") or "That lizard's feet are like snow flakes / τετραδάκτυλος / (pale young four toes)" (Canto 114); or perspectival cues like "O moon *my* pin-up" (Canto 84) or "The ant's a centaur *in his dragon world* " (Canto 81); or commonplace transformations like "Cloud like a sail *inverted*" (Canto 23); or *xyz* constructions like "Earth is the nurse of all men" or "Nor is the white bud Time's inquisitor" (Canto 80) or "Fear, father of cruelty" (Canto 114).

Such demonstrations are most important. Paradoxically, they might have least effect on the critic, exactly because they focus on local phrasing rather than on whole literary works. A book seems to be a whole and substantial unit, not merely to consist of a string of individual small phrases. So the critic may wish to see instead a demonstration at the level of a whole literary work.

There is a mistaken assumption here. Conceptual connections and patterns and activities in the mind are expressed at all levels, large and small. In language, the macrocosm is revealed in the microcosm and conversely, simply because all levels of language embody the same conceptual figures of thought. True, conceptual connections are manifested in individual local phrases, but they do not reside there or do not principally or exclusively reside there. They are equivalently expressed through whole works, indeed expressed through patterns of meaning that transcend whole works. While particular capacities in our language for disclosing these connections at the level of local phrasing hold interest for us in their own right, they are not primarily the focus of cognitive rhetoric; they are instead most interesting not in themselves but as windows on conceptual activity in general, which can be expressed at any level.

Let us consider briefly the level above individual phrasing. At the end of chapter 6, we touched upon the way in which an entire literary work (or even a type of literary work) can be inspired and informed globally by a controlling conceptual connection. We saw as examples the connection between a journey and self-discovery in the *Odyssey* and the connection between conversational wit and sex in *Much Ado about Nothing*. Here, let us consider three of our everyday concepts: *conversation, argument,* and *journey.* These concepts, unimaginably intricate in their detail yet supple when they go to work, are broadly powerful, and underlie a wide range of our everyday thought, speech, and behavior. Each is an object of wonder quite superior to any literary work with which we might care to compare it. Not surprisingly, these concepts and their conceptual connections often constitute the ground of entire literary works. Such entire works exist at their highest level as partial expressions and uses of these concepts. Such works are almost entirely informed by such everyday concepts. While their originality is the most noticeable thing about such works, that originality is only the smallest step beyond unoriginal concepts, and is indeed only possible as an exploitation of these concepts, with respect to which it is simple and dependent. If we could explain fully everything there is to be explained about our everyday conceptual apparatus and its operation, there would be relatively little left over in these works to be accounted for, and the accounting, while difficult, would be easy relative to the extreme difficulty of accounting for how we think.

Consider Pound's "Praise of Ysolt." I choose this poem because it is esoteric and proudly literary. Modeled on the *cansos* of the troubadours, self-consciously an artifact of willfully elite literary composition, it nonetheless exists as an exploitation of commonplace concepts. It is with respect to these concepts that it can be written and read and understood. "Praise of Ysolt" is at the largest level a conceptual metaphor: the speaker's subjectivity, his feelings, and his relation to his feelings are all understood metaphorically in terms of *conversation.* The speaker holds a conversation with his heart:

> In vain have I striven,
>   to teach my heart to bow;
> In vain have I said to him
> "There be many singers greater than thou."

This conversation is in particular an *argument* between the speaker and the heart, replete with speech acts and implicatures, logical entailments and presuppositions. Our everyday and extremely rich concepts of *conver-sation* and *argument* are the dominant unoriginal ground upon which this poem is constituted. The heart demands a song; the poet endeavors to teach his heart and soul that he cannot sing because the woman has departed; the soul sends a woman; the poet comes to see that his side of the argument must collapse because it is based on the mistaken assump-tion that the woman has departed, while in fact she resides in his heart. The speaker has indeed striven "in vain" to teach his heart and soul to bow, not in the initial sense of "unsuccessfully," but in the sense of fool-ishly and mistakenly:

> In vain have I striven with my soul
>   to teach my soul to bow.
> What soul boweth
>   while in his heart art thou?

The "thou" addresses the woman. The poet's asking the woman a question implies the existence of a conversation and thus her presence, and begins again the conversation. The woman will always be present; the conversation will always be present: they are both implied by the last line. The song too will always be present: it is also implied by the last line, which completes the song. The very argument the speaker has been con-ducting with his heart as a means of teaching his heart that he cannot deliver a song in fact delivers that song, and is appropriately named as such: "Praise of Ysolt."

"Praise of Ysolt" is quite a long poem, and its local intricacies of con-ceptual connection are not even suggested by this brief summary. But this summary should suffice to gesture toward the ways in which the unorig-inal ground that dominates this poem includes our commonplace con-cepts of *conversation* and *argument* and their metaphoric use in accord with principles of conceptual connection investigated in this book. The important point here is that our concepts of *conversation* and *argument* and our powers of conceptual connection are extremely powerful and in-tricate and we know extremely little about them. Because of our condi-tioning, it sounds simple to say that we use these concepts and these con-nections to make sense of the poem. But that use is anything but simple. It is the least simple thing about this poem. That use is the ground of this poem. The critic cannot assume that ground and proceed from it, for it is the most important, most complex, and by far the least well understood thing about this poem. We must start with this ground, admit our great ignorance of what is involved in it, and seek to explain it.

Krapp's Last Tape, down my shelf a bit, invokes the concept of conver-sation by means of tape-recorded diary entries. The replay of these re-cordings is one side of a conversation between Krapp on stage and his former voice on the tape. Krapp's voice on tape converses with his future self, and, in commenting on earlier tapes as he records, with his former self. Krapp on stage converses with his former self both by commenting on the recorded messages and by taking up the microphone to respond with a new entry. This is a use of our concept of turn-taking in conversation. We know what turn-taking is, but that knowledge is very complicated and elaborately textured; we use it constantly but no doubt could not articulate it. There is another way in which Krapp converses: he controls the tape machine. He selects which tapes to hear, which parts of tapes to hear, which parts of tapes to hear over, which parts of tapes to skip over. His life, a conversation with himself, comes to silence. *Krapp's Last Tape* is so unusual in its literariness as to seem exotic and experimental. But the unoriginal ground of this play, the commonplace conceptual knowledge that is supple enough and powerful enough to allow us to make sense of it, is the everyday concept of conversation.

Our concept of a *letter* is based upon our concept of *conversation*. Some works on my bookshelf—*Clarissa, Selected Letters of Ezra Pound, Les Lettres Provinciales,* and *Persian Letters*—are constituted with respect to the concept of *conversation.* Pascal's *Lettres Provinciales* are presented as letters to someone in the provinces from someone in Paris, and as such are understood as a sort of conversation that is one-sided in expression but whose speaker imagines the participation of the other. These letters— understood as special cases of our concept of conversation—themselves purport to quote at great length conversations. Pascal's *Lettres Provinciales* not only exploit our concept of conversation, they also, of course, marvelously and masterfully exploit our complicated concept of argument. The work as a whole is an argument, a defense of Jansenism. The conversations they quote are understood as arguments of various kinds.

That same characterization—argument as a whole containing individual passages understood through the concept of *argument*—is a way of seeing not only each play by Aristophanes, but the entire *oeuvre* of Aristophanes, contained on my shelf here in these three small green books numbered 178, 179, and 180. In chapter 5, "The Poetry of Argument," we began the analysis of the nature of our default concepts of reason and argument, and the disclosure of those concepts in everyday language. At the time, our discussion may have seemed extrinsic to literary criticism. But here we hold in our hands a collection of literary works—*Acharnians, Peace, The Clouds, The Birds,* and so on—each one of which we can understand in terms of our concept of an *argument.* If we think of just one of the plays, say *The Acharnians,* we can begin to see how complicated and multipartite our concept of argument is. *The Acharnians* is an argument for peace. It includes arguments pitting the war party against Dikaiopolis, who stands for peace and who concludes a separate treaty with Sparta. It includes ridicule of the opponents of peace. It includes imputations to them of self-interest, to make their arguments look weaker. It includes a survey of the bad consequences that follow from their policy, to diminish support for it. It includes through various skits suggestions of the possible good consequences of peace. The interpretation of the status of these skits is complicated: we must take individual skits of events happening in Dikaiopolis's front yard as microcosmic symbols or models or emblems of general peace, and weigh the characteristics of that general peace against general war. *The Acharnians* also includes argument through narrative in the story of the Megarians. It includes in the speeches of the chorus an intricate variety of types of argument, including indirect argument through commentary on skits and through reactions to other arguments. Through such means the play becomes a structural network of arguments and side arguments and nested subarguments. We take that network as constituting one whole argument, the argument of the play. *The Acharnians* deploys a wide range of distinctively different types of evidence, each with its particular weight and place, its felicity conditions and appropriateness. *The Acharnians* is an argument against war with Sparta, by which I mean that our principal conceptual tool for understanding this play is our intricate commonplace concept of argument. To be sure, the comedies of Aristophanes contain special literary forms, special dramatic forms, and special comic structures, but those forms and structures are constituted as a slight step beyond our everyday concept of argument, and that is why we can understand them.

We have often in this book seen the use of our concept of *journey* in literary constructions, and its expression in local phrases. But it is equivalently easy to show the way it informs entire literary works; exactly because the macroscopic and microscopic levels in literature express the same conceptual patterns and connections. Consider Ezra Pound's major work, the *Cantos*. Literary critics have from time to time judged this epic poem to be so experimental and failed in its experiments as to be ultimately incoherent. But from a cognitive rhetorical perspective, the *Cantos* is coherent as an elaboration of a commonplace concept, *journey*, and a commonplace metaphor, LIFE IS A JOURNEY.

Our everyday concept of *journey* is detailed, and writers of classic travel narratives—such as *Travels in Arabia Deserta*—prompt us to use it to make sense of their works. We additionally know the basic and highly productive metaphor LIFE IS A JOURNEY. When we combine LIFE IS A JOURNEY with THE MIND IS A BODY MOVING IN SPACE, we arrive at the standard metaphoric conception that LIFE IS A JOURNEY OF DISCOVERY. One particular form of discovery is SELF-DISCOVERY, giving us the metaphor LIFE IS

A JOURNEY OF SELF-DISCOVERY. There are many classic literary works conceived of as the interplay between a travel narrative and the metaphor LIFE IS A JOURNEY OF SELF-DISCOVERY. The actual journey in the travel narrative and the metaphoric journey of self-discovery become intertwined, as in *The Odyssey* or *Heart of Darkness*.

Pound's *Cantos* are fundamentally constituted through the metaphor LIFE IS A JOURNEY OF SELF-DISCOVERY, with the added twists that it is the author who is taking the metaphoric journey of self-discovery, that the self-discovery of a poet has as one of its threads the discovery of aspects of poetry, that the poet's narrative is told while the journey is in progress so that its method of composition must necessarily remain open and constantly susceptible of revision, and that the poet's evidence of his encounters and discoveries during this metaphoric journey itself has a claim to be part of the narrative. Pound is quite explicit about all of this in some of his letters. The controlling and informing ground of the *Cantos*, that which makes it possible to be written and read, is a basic metaphor: LIFE IS A JOURNEY OF SELF-DISCOVERY. That is why Pound chose to open the *Cantos* with a translation of Odysseus's journey to the underworld. The retelling constitutes a second journey, which is in some sense Pound's own: the voyager is asked by Tiresius why he has come a second time. We recall that Odysseus journeyed to the underworld in pursuit of advice, directions, vision from this guide, so that he could conduct his journey. This is the position in which Pound wishes to cast himself at the opening of the *Cantos*, as a metaphoric journeyer seeking metaphoric guidance, only in Pound's case the role of metaphoric guide is taken by cultural and literary artifacts—the rhythms of Old English, the translation of the *Odyssey* into Latin, the visions Pound thought he discovered in the works of the troubadours, the Confucian *Odes*, and so on, through the entire overwhelming list of metaphoric guides Pound sought out during his metaphoric journey.

There is a third level at which we might investigate the way in which cognitive rhetoric serves as a ground for criticism. This is a level beyond local phrasing, beyond even individual whole works. It is the level at which we conceive of literature generally. Literature can be understood as a special case of our everyday concept of conversation, in this case conversations between authors and readers. Wayne Booth has treated this conception of reading as conversation in *The Company We Keep*. It is not surprising that Booth began his career with a doctoral dissertation on Sterne's *Tristram Shandy*, a work that is ingenious in its capacity to force the reader into taking an active role in the conversation between author and reader.

We can also understand reading as journeying, with authors as guides or companions. Since guides or companions converse with us, the two conceptions of literature as journeying and as conversing can supplement each other coherently.

At the highest level of all, there is an extremely powerful and pervasive conceptual connection between our concept of *mind* and our concept of *writing*.[1] Records are understood as a sort of external memory, and memory as internal records. Writing is understood as thinking on paper, and thought as writing in the mind. By means of this conceptual connection, the written work is taken as a substitute for or even as a distillation of the author: the author's mind is an endless paper on which he writes, making mind internal writing; and the book he writes is external mind, the external form of that writing. The writing is therefore conceived of as having a voice, one that speaks to us, and to which we respond. The author is understood as the self thinking. The self is understood as an author writing in the mind. Sometimes, the self is an author writing thoughts externally on paper. This makes it extremely easy for us to talk about "putting our thoughts down on paper" and to see the author's self as contained in the writing. This makes the everyday metonymic reference to writing by its author's name—as in "Plato is on the top shelf"—seem so natural. This sort of conceptual connection—between the mind and writing—and its systematic disclosure in the shape of language is a topic whose analysis is at the center of cognitive rhetoric. It is also an utterly unoriginal, everyday, automatic connection, everywhere disclosed in everyday speech. It gives us the beginning point for much of our thinking about literature. It is a ground of much of our literary criticism. It is one of many clear ways in which the project of cognitive rhetoric underlies both literature and literary criticism. From this view, the activity of author and critic depends automatically, unconsciously, centrally, and unavoidably upon just those activities it is the project of cognitive rhetoric to analyze, even though the author and critic may not notice in consciousness that dependence.

To explore the connections between cognitive rhetoric and literary criticism in this manner is to situate agency not in some transcendent conceptual forms but rather in the full mind of the individual human author and the individual human reader who employ those forms for local purposes. It is to connect literary criticism to what it means to have a human life. It thus makes literary criticism one of the humanities.

To ground literary criticism in cognitive rhetoric is not to make literary language homogeneous, or to reduce it to the level of everyday speech; it is rather to make it human. It is only by being constituted upon commonplace conceptual patterns that provide most of the meaning to literary texts that literary texts can be for us something other than impossible questions, opaque challenges, bizarre and mute anomalies. The imagination must move in a known space; these are the conditions upon its intelligibility. The attempt to ground literary criticism in cognitive rhetoric is no other than the attempt to map that space in which the imagination moves so that we can understand the performance of imagination within it.

To have a life, a human being requires a conceptual system and a human language disclosing that system. Our easy unconscious mastery of such a system and such a language leads us to the staggering misconceptions that our everyday conceptual system and language are relatively simple, that questions about them have obvious answers, and that what is interesting and complex are those remarkable events that happen supposedly beyond our everyday conceptual apparatus and language.

We are only beginning to glimpse the marvelously intricate, complex, and efficient details of our thought and language. Our easy unconscious mastery of a conceptual system and a human language that discloses it should make us feel awe at the power of the brain, which can embody an adaptive competence that consciousness rarely sees and as yet cannot begin to account for.

To have a human life, we need dynamic concepts at various levels. We need adaptive and complicated category structures. We need image-schemas in various modalities and the capacity to put them into registration with each other. We need the ability to structure concepts image-schematically. We need maps of the body in the mind and the capacity to understand by employing those maps to help structure a great range of concepts. We need to understand compatibilities and incompatibilities across our conceptual apparatus. We need complicated concepts like *argument* and *conversation* and *journey.* We need commonplace theories like Being Leads to Doing and commonplace models like The Great Chain. We need to know the manifold intricate ways in which concepts can be connected or can be constrained in their connection. We need a great deal more than all this, and most prominently we need a masterful knowledge—almost completely unavailable to conscious introspection—of how this conceptual apparatus is disclosed in the shape of language.

This is the ground of human life, and therefore of the humanities. It is the ground—a difficult and complicated ground—of literature. It is the inevitable ground of the study of English in the age of cognitive science.

APPENDIX

EQUATIONS AND SIMILARITIES

Education is an ornament in prosperity and a refuge in adversity. (Aristotle, in Laertius)

Public opinion is the thermometer a monarch should constantly consult. (Napoleon)

A doubtful throne is ice on summer seas. (Tennyson)

Justice is like a train that's nearly always late. (Yevtushenko, tr. MacAndrew)

Correct English is the slang of prigs who write history and essays. (George Eliot)

Language is the archives of history. (Emerson)

The law is a causeway upon which, so long as he keeps to it, a citizen may walk safely. (Robert Bell)

A reactionary is a somnambulist walking backwards. (F. D. Roosevelt)

Nature is a rag merchant, who works up every shred and ort and end into new creations. (Emerson)

You're the cream in my coffee.

Man is a wolf to man.

The human heart is like a ship on a stormy sea driven by winds blowing from all four corners of heaven. (Martin Luther)

Diplomacy is the police in grand costume. (Napoleon I)

Bigotry is the sacred disease. (Heraclitus)

Fame is a magnifying glass.

Happiness to me is wine, / Effervescent, superfine / Full of tang and fiery pleasure, / Far too hot to leave me leisure / For a single thought beyond it. (Amy Lowell)

and that inverted Bowl they call the Sky. (Edward Fitzgerald)

History is a tangled skein that one may take up at any point, and break when one has unravelled enough. (Henry Adams)

Life is an incurable disease.

Life is like an onion, which one peels crying.

Life's a pudding full of plums.

Perversity is the muse of modern literature. (Susan Sontag)

Love is a tyrant sparing none.

Love is like those shabby hotels in which all the luxury is in the lobby.

Marriage is a feast where the grace is sometimes better than the dinner.

Memory is the diary that we all carry about with us. (Oscar Wilde) the past is a bucket of ashes. (Carl Sandburg)

Modesty is the only sure bait when you angle for praise. (Lord Chesterfield)

Ready money is Aladdin's lamp.

Nature is a mutable cloud which is always and never the same. (Emerson)

The whole earth is the sepulchre of famous men. (Thucydides)

Small faults indulged are little thieves that let in greater.

Man is not man, but a wolf, to those he does not know. (Plautus)

Cards are war, in disguise of a sport. (Charles Lamb)

Goodness is the only investment that never fails. (Thoreau)

Without grace beauty is an unbaited hook.

Wit is a treacherous dart.

Youth is a perpetual intoxication.

The fall of a leaf is a whisper to the living.

The sunshine is a glorious birth. (Wordsworth)

Conscience is the inner voice that tells us somebody may be looking. (H. L. Mencken)

Every junkie's like a setting sun. (Neil Young)

Patience is cold soup. (Michael Donaghy)

XYZ METAPHORS

Language is the mirror of the mind.

Brevity is the soul of wit. (*Hamlet*)

Promise, large promise, is the soul of an advertisement. (Johnson, *The Idler*)

Impropriety is the soul of wit.

Promptness is the soul of business.

Dispatch is the soul of business. (Lord Chesterfield)

Brevity is the soul of lingerie.

Variety is the soul of pleasure.

Grace is the soule of the soule. (Donne, *Sixth Sermon*)

Enthusiasm is the life of the soul.

Poetry is the breath and finer spirit of all knowledge. (Wordsworth)

Love is the life of the soul.

Self-trust is the essence of heroism. (Emerson)

Improvisation is the essence of good taste.

Work is the meat of life.

Wit is the salt of conversation.

Disappointment is the salt of life.

The sky is the daily bread of the eyes.

Time is the devourer of everything. (*Tempus edax rerum*, Ovid, *Metamorphoses*, 15.234)

Language is the dress of thought. (Samuel Johnson)

Style is the dress of thought. (Revd. Samuel Wesley)

Politeness is the outward garment of goodwill.

The forest is the poor man's overcoat.

Blood is the god of war's rich livery. (Marlowe)

Ideas and principles that do harm are, as a rule, though not always, cloaks for evil passions. (Bertrand Russell)

Folly is the cloke of knavery. (Blake)

Shame is Prides cloke. (Blake)

A faithful friend is the medicine of life.

Ill-nature is the running-sore of the disposition.

War is the health of the state.

Science is the antidote to the poison of enthusiasm and superstition. (Adam Smith)

The nurse of full-grown souls is solitude.

For man's redemption—it is ever sure— / Which God for our soul's medicine / Gave us. (*Everyman*)

Example is the school of mankind, and they will learn at no other.

Home is the school of virtue.

Ancient sculpture is the true school of modesty. (Thomas Love Peacock)

Self-reflection is the school of wisdom.

Today is yesterday's pupil. (Thomas Fuller)

The face is the index of the mind.

A man's action is only a picture-book of his creed.

Adversity is the first path to Truth. (Byron, *Don Juan*, 12. 500)

Lufthansa: The Autobahn of the Atlantic.

Civilization is the lamb's skin in which barbarism masquerades.

There is no such whetstone, to sharpen a good wit and encourage a will to learning, as is praise. (Roger Ascham)

Some television programs are so much chewing gum for the eyes.

The miserable have no other medicine / But only hope. (*Measure for Measure*, 3.1.2)

Words are the tokens current and accepted for conceits, as moneys are for values. (Bacon)

Conformity, humility, acceptance—with these coins we are to pay our fares to paradise.

The moon is a friend for the lonesome to talk to.

A tornado seems a sort of genius among storms. (Alane Rollings)

Injustice anywhere is a threat to justice everywhere. (Martin Luther King, Jr.)

Contentment is a warm sty for the eaters and sleepers. (Marco Millions)

Death is the end of woes. (Spenser)

[Of a hansom] The gondola of London. (Disraeli)

Self-respect is the gate of heaven.

Freedom is the goal of world peace.

Anarchy is the stepping stone to absolute power. (Napoleon)

Custom is the guide of the ignorant.

It is death that is the guide of our life.

The cross is the ladder of heaven.

Logical consequences are the scarecrows of fools and the beacons of wise men. (T. H. Huxley)

Commonplaces are the tramways of intellectual transportation. (Ortega y Gasset)

Cheese—milk's leap toward immortality.

Custom, the tyrant of mankind. (Plato, *Protagoras*, 337d, tr. Guthrie)

But thought's the slave of life, and life time's fool. (*Henry 4*, Part 1, 5.2.81)

Imagination is nature's equal, sensuality her slave.

The hand is the vassal of the mind.

All good moral philosophy is but an handmaid to religion. (Bacon)

Procrastination is the thief of time. (Edward Young)

Time, the subtle thief of youth. (Milton)

Money is the power of impotence.

The adjective is the most deadly enemy of the substantive.

Ignorance is the enemy of originality.

Knowledge and history are the enemies of religion. (Napoleon)

Complacency is the enemy of study. (Mao Tse-Tung)

Security / is mortal's chiefest enemy. (*Macbeth*, 3.5.32)

Taste is the enemy of creativeness.

Abuse is the weapon of the vulgar.

Solemnity is the shield of idiots.

Neutral men are the devil's allies.

Absence is the enemy of love.

Irreverence is the champion of liberty. (Mark Twain)

Conformity is the jailer of freedom and the enemy of growth. (John Kennedy)

Everyone is a prisoner of his own experiences. (Edward R. Murrow)

Public office is the last refuge of the incompetent.

Obscurity is the refuge of incompetence.

A technical objection is the first refuge of a scoundrel.

God is the immemorial refuge of the incompetent, the helpless, and the miserable. (H. L. Mencken)

Mirth is the Mail of Anguish. (Dickinson)

Children are the riches of poor men.

The wages of sin is death.

Vigilance is the price of liberty.

Trouble is the price of progress.

Labor is the capital of the workingman.

Memory is the treasurer of the mind.

A leader is a dealer in hope. (Napoleon I)

Gratefulness is the poor man's payment.

Evermore thanks, the exchequer of the poor. (*Richard II*, 2.3.65)

The love of money is the root of all evil. (1 Tim. 6:10)

Action is the proper fruit of knowledge. (Thomas Fuller, *Gnomologia*)

Freedom is the greatest fruit of self-sufficiency.

All good things which exist are the fruits of originality. (J. S. Mill)

Destiny is the product of conduct.

Property is the fruit of labor.

Great architecture is the flowering of geometry.

Generosity is the flower of justice. (Hawthorne)

Thought is the seed of action.

Billboards are warts on the landscape.

Public schools are the nurseries of all vice and immorality. (Fielding, *Joseph Andrews*)

The blood of the martyrs is the seed of the church.

Ignorance is the womb of monsters.

The cynic, a parasite of civilization. (Ortega y Gasset)

Oaths are the fossils of piety.

Pedantry is the dotage of knowledge.

Dullness is the coming of age of seriousness. (Oscar Wilde)

Walter Mondale is Ronald Reagan's natural prey.

Metaphor is the dreamwork of language. (Donald Davidson)

Politics is the art of the possible.

Nature is the art of God.

Der Aberglaube ist die Poesie des Lebens (Superstition is the poetry of life). (Goethe)

The flower is the poetry of reproduction.

Sexuality is the lyricism of the masses.

Sex is the poor man's opera.

A riot is at bottom the language of the unheard. (Martin Luther King, Jr.)

Music is the universal language of mankind. (Longfellow)

Thinking is the talking of the soul with itself.

Slang is a poor-man's poetry.

The pen is the tongue of the hand.

Uttering a word is like striking a note on the keyboard of the imagination. (Wittgenstein)

Prejudice is the reason of fools. (Voltaire)

Ridicule is the argument of fools.

Incredulity is the wisdom of a fool.

Tact is the intelligence of the heart.

Modesty is the conscience of the body.

Causation is the cement of the universe.

Suffering is the true cement of love. (Paul Sabatier)

Grammere, that grounde is of all. (William Langland)

Good order is the foundation of all things. (Edmund Burke)

Events are the shells of ideas.

a creed is the shell of a lie. (Amy Lowell)

Bread is the staff of life.

Clemency is the support of justice.

Method is the architecture of success.

There are certain simple and unavoidably cheap dishes that are the I-beams of French cookery and are not to be tampered with. (A. J. Liebling)

Anger is one of the sinews of the soul. (Thomas Fuller)

Money is the sinews of love, as of war. (Farquhar, *Love and a Bottle*)

Good company and good discourse are the very sinews of virtue. (Izaak Walton)

Then to advise how warr may best, upheld, / Move by her two main nerves, Iron and Gold / In all her equipage. (Milton, "The Vane sonnet")

The knee is the Achilles' heel of the leg. (Quoted by Douglas Hofstadter)

Conscience is the frame of character, and love is the covering for it. (Henry Ward Beecher)

Stasis is the flip-side of degradation. (Carla Harryman)

The artist is the child of his time. (Schiller)

Silence is the virtue of fools.

Convictions are mortgages on the mind.

Love is the law of heaven.

Change is the law of life.

Nature, Creation's law. (Thomas Randolph)

Custom is the principal magistrate of man's life. (Francis Bacon)

The poet is the priest of the invisible. (Wallace Stevens)

The Youth of a Nation are the trustees of Posterity. (Disraeli)

He [Professor Moriarity] is the Napoleon of crime. (Sir Arthur Conan Doyle)

History is a distillation of rumor.

Vanity is the quicksand of reason.

Thought is the labor of the intellect, reverie is its pleasure.

Poetry is the bill and coo of sex.

The artist is the lover of Nature; therefore he is her slave and her master. (Rabindranath Tagore)

The ground's the body's bride, / Who will not be denied. (Wendell
  Berry)
Art is the sex of the imagination. (George Jean Nathan)
Speculation is the romance of trade. (Washington Irving)
Tenderness is the coquetry of age.
Indignation is the seducer of thought.
Mathematics is the bell-boy of all sciences.
Sex is the ancilla of art. (Nabokov)
Justice! Custodian of the World!
Falsehood is the jockey of misfortune.
Revolutions are the toilet of a nation.
Bachelors are the bootleggers of love.
Cunning is the dark sanctuary of incapacity.
The first hour of the morning is the rudder of the day.
Ostentation is the signal flag of hypocrisy.
The crown of literature is poetry. (W. S. Maugham)
Languages are the pedigree of nations. (Samuel Johnson)
The body is the socket of the soul.
Fame is the beauty-parlor of the dead.
The adjective is the banana peel of the parts of speech.
Religion . . . is the opium of the people. (Marx)
Dan Chaucer, well of English undefiled. (Spenser)
He [Chaucer] is a perpetual fountain of good sense.
The Crown is according to the saying the "fountain of honour"; but the
  Treasury is the spring of business. (Walter Bagehot)
Virtue is the fount whence honour springs. (Marlowe, *Tamburlaine the
  Great*)
He [the King] is a fountain of honour. (Francis Bacon)
Almighty God, the fountain of all goodness. (*Prayer Book*, 1662)
He [Chaucer] is a perpetual fountain of good sense. (Dryden, *Fables*)
Christ, that of perfeccioun is welle. (Chaucer)
Beauty is the pilot of the young soul.
Home is the girl's prison and the woman's workhouse. (Shaw)
Rime, the rack of finest wits. (Ben Jonson)
[Warwickshire], the heart of England. (Drayton, "Poly-olbion")
Veracity is the heart of morality. (T. H. Huxley)
Humanity is the Sin of God.
England is the paradise of women, the purgatory of men, and the hell of
  horses. (John Florio, *Second Frutes*)
Grammar is the grave of letters.
C: Seize the short Joyes, then, ere they fade. / Seest thou that unfre-
  quented cave? D: That den? C: Love's shrine D. But Virtue's Cave.
  (Andrew Marvell)

The past is the sepulchre of our dead emotions.

Marriage is the waste-paper basket of the emotions. (Sidney Webb)

A white wall is the fool's paper.

Pure logic is the ruin of the spirit.

Learning, the destroyer of arrogance.

Cunning is the dwarf of wisdom.

The voice is the organ of the soul.

Literature is the orchestra of platitudes.

Speech is a mirror of the soul.

Language is a mirror of the mind.

Resemblances are the shadows of differences. (Nabokov)

Applause is the echo of a platitude.

Conversation is the vent of character.

Advertising is the mouthpiece of business.

Ceremony is the smoke of friendship.

The imagination is the eye of faith.

Friends are the sunshine of life. (John Hay)

Resignation is the timid side of courage.

Suspicion is the courageous side of weakness.

Love is the selfishness of two persons.

Usury is the land-shark of commerce.

Science is the topography of ignorance.

Fairyland is nothing but the sunny country of common sense. (G. K. Chesterton)

Solitude is the playfield of Satan. (Nabokov)

Philosophers are the pioneers of revolution.

Morality is the vestibule of religion.

Antiquity is the aristocracy of history.

Pride is the mask of one's own faults.

Meekness is the mask of malice. (Robert G. Ingersoll)

The times are the masquerade of the eternities.

Blushing is the color of virtue.

Simplicity is the background of good taste.

Logical consequences are the scarecrows of fools and the beacons of wise men.

Speech is the small change of silence. (George Meredith)

For sufferance is the badge of all our tribe. (*Merchant of Venice*, 1.3.111)

Avarice, the spur of industry. (Hume)

Taste is the feminine of genius. (Edward Fitzgerald)

Moderation is the languor and indolence of the soul, as ambition is its ardour and activity.

Conformity is the ape of harmony. (Emerson)

Limited domains of discourse are the E. Coli of language research. (Patrick Winston)

He's the Babe Ruth of Hungarian kayaking.

She's the Dagwood Bumstead of femmes fatales.

Mount Vernon is the Lenin's tomb of American architecture.

The House of Lords is the British Outer Mongolia for retired politicians.

Cultural literacy is the oxygen of social discourse. (E. D. Hirsch)

COMPLEX *XYZ* METAPHORS

As brevity is the soul of wit, form, it seems to me, is the heart of humor and the salvation of comedy. (James Thurber)

The imagination is the secret and marrow of civilization.

It is the very eye of faith. (Henry Ward Beecher)

Hunger is the teacher of the arts and the bestower of invention.

Wonder is the foundation of all philosophy, inquiry the progress, ignorance the end.

Industry is fortune's right hand, and frugality her left. (Thomas Fuller)

Money is power, freedom, a cushion, the root of all evil, the sun of blessings. (Carl Sandburg)

WEIRD SPECIFICATIONS

Heredity is nothing but stored environment.

Cynicism is intellectual dandyism. (George Meredith)

A mixed metaphor is a cognitive sore thumb.

A minister of finance is a legally authorized pickpocket.

A Boston man is the east wind made flesh.

What is reading but silent conversation? (Walter Savage Landor)

The car . . . [is a] mobile Walden Pond. (Edward McDonagh)

Religion is a disease, but it is a noble disease.

My love's a noble madness. (Dryden)

Architecture is inhabited sculpture. (Constantin Brancusi)

Architecture is frozen music.

Childhood is the kingdom where nobody dies. (Edna St. Vincent Millay)

Wrinkles are the deathbed wherein women bury their illusions.

Ambition is but avarice on stilts and masked.

He [Macaulay] is like a book in breeches. (Reverend Sydney Smith)

Daniel Webster struck me much like a steam-engine in trousers. (Reverend Sydney Smith)

Painting is silent poetry, and poetry is painting with the gift of speech.

Problems are only opportunities in work clothes.

Rivers are roads that move. (Pascal, tr. Trotter)

Rumour is a pipe / Blown by surmises, jealousies, conjectures. (*2 Henry IV*, 3.1.97)

A creed is an ossified metaphor.

Censure is the tax a man pays to the public for being eminent. (Swift)

The pillow is a silent Sibyl.

Anger is brief madness.

Hope is a waking dream. (Aristotle, in Laertius)

Life is a fatal complaint, and an eminently contagious one.

Love is a universal migrane. (Robert Graves)

Man's life is a warfare against the malice of men.

A father is a banker provided by nature.

Our shortcomings are the eyes with which we see the ideal. (Nietzsche)

Time is a file that wears and makes no noise.

Tolstoy is a great moralizing infant.

A historian is a prophet in reverse.

Ireland is the old sow that eats her farrow. (James Joyce)

the mortal Venus [of Helen]. (Troilus and Cressida)

The National Humanities Center is an intellectual canal-lock: you go out at a higher level than you came in.

CASES WHERE THE FOURTH TERM MUST BE MENTIONED

Love is the crocodile on the river of desire. (Bhartrihari, ca. 625) [In the *xyz* metaphor "Love is the crocodile of desire," it is unclear what the missing fourth term should be. The full metaphor supplies it: river maps to desire and crocodile to love.]

Edward Dorn [a poet] is a can opener in the supermarket of life. (Tom Robbins) [Can opener maps to Dorn and supermarket maps to life.]

COMPLICATIONS AND COMBINATIONS

The various surface forms I have discussed do not have sharp boundaries. Sharp boundaries in form would imply corresponding sharp boundaries in our concepts. But concepts do not have sharp edges. For example, it may be a judgment call whether describing a disease as "sacred" is inappropriate, or whether describing a madness as "noble" is inappropriate. Hence, it is a judgment call whether the specifications of the sources in "Bigotry is the sacred disease" (Heraclitus) and "My love's a noble madness" are weird or not. The difference between a commonplace transformation and a weird specification is also a judgment call, which depends upon how conventional one takes the change to be, as the example "modern Babylon" demonstrates. A specification of a concept is also a concept; hence there is no sharp distinction between a bare equation and an equation with a specified source, provided that the specification be not weird. An *xyz* metaphor is a particular kind of weird change, where *z* weirdly changes our model of *y*. Therefore, some weird specifications might easily be cast into *xyz* form: Emerson's "Envy is the tax which all distinction must pay" could be phrased "Envy is the tax on distinction." That each of these surface forms of metaphor has its typical function does not mean that they cannot shade into each other. All serve to invoke some sort of metaphoric mapping between two conceptual domains. They are some of the forms most used and most expected in our language. We can construct more elaborate metaphors by combining them, as in all the following cases.

XYZ AND ASPECT

Adversity is the first path to Truth. (Byron, *Don Juan*, 12.50)
Blood is the god of war's rich livery. (*Tamburlaine* 2.3.2)
Custom, then is the great guide of life. (Hume)
Fairyland is nothing but the sunny country of common sense. (G. K. Chesterton)
Freedom is the greatest fruit of self-sufficiency. (Epicurus, tr. Geer)
Hope is the great falsifier of truth.
Love is the true price of love. (George Herbert)
O sleep! O gentle sleep! / Nature's soft nurse . . . (*Henry 4*, part 2, 3.1.5)
Prosperity is the best protector of principle. (Mark Twain)
Silence is sorrow's best food.
Silence is the perfectest herald of joy. (*Much Ado about Nothing*, 2.1.316)
Some television programs are so much chewing gum for the eyes.
Sunday is the golden clasp that binds together the volume of the week.
The conduct of our lives is the true mirror of our doctrine. (Montaigne)
The greatest assassin of life is haste.
The miserable have no other medicine / But only hope. (*Measure for Measure*, 3.1.2)
There is no such whetstone, to sharpen a good wit and encourage a will to learning, as is praise. (Roger Ascham)
We must be the great arsenal of democracy. (Franklin Delano Roosevelt)
Weariness is the shortest path to equality and fraternity. (Nietzsche)
Women, as most susceptible, are the best index of the coming hour. (Emerson)

XYZ AND SPECIFICATION

A good book is the precious life-blood of a master spirit, embalmed and
treasured up on purpose to a life beyond life. (Milton, "Areopagitica")
Sleep is pain's easiest salve. (Donne)
God is the immemorial refuge of the incompetent, the helpless, the miserable. (H. L. Mencken)
Poets are the unacknowledged legislators of the world. (Shelley)
Poverty has many roots, but the tap root is ignorance. [This is not in *xyz*
form, but closely resembles the *xyz* form "Ignorance is the tap root
of poverty."]

XYZ, ASPECT, AND SPECIFICATION

The Papacy is not other than the Ghost of the deceased Roman Empire,
sitting crowned upon the grave thereof. (Hobbes)

XYZ AND WEIRD SPECIFICATION

A film is a petrified fountain of thought. (Jean Cocteau)

ASPECT AND SPECIFICATION

Marriage is but a ceremonial toy. (Marlowe)
All empire is no more than power in trust. (Dryden, *Absalom and
Achitophel*)
A gourmet is just a glutton with brains.
Human life is but a series of footnotes to a vast obscure unfinished mas-
terpiece. (Nabokov)
Goodness is the only investment that never fails. (Thoreau)

ASPECT AND COMMONPLACE TRANSFORMATION

Men are but children of a larger growth. (Dryden)

ASPECT AND WEIRD SPECIFICATION

Ambition is only vanity ennobled. (Jerome K. Jerome)

MULTIPLE EQUATIONS

Laws are sand; customs are rock. (Mark Twain)
Tragedy is a close-up. Comedy is a long-shot. (Charlie Chaplin)

All books are either dreams or swords. (Amy Lowell)
Tradition is a guide and not a jailer. (W. Somerset Maugham)
The bachelor is a peacock, the engaged man a lion, and the married man a jackass.
A kiss can be a comma, a question mark, or an exclamation point.
Imagination is like a lofty building reared to meet the sky—fancy is a balloon, that soars at the wind's will.
Knowledge is the treasure, but judgment the treasurer of wise men. (Penn)
Everyone is either a horse, a bird, or a muffin.

MULTIPLE XYZ

Industry is fortune's right hand, and frugality her left. (Thomas Fuller)

MULTIPLE EQUATIONS AND XYZ

Money is power, freedom, a cushion, the root of all evil, the sun of blessings. (Carl Sandburg)

MULTIPLE ASPECTS, SPECIFICATIONS, AND WEIRD SPECIFICATIONS

Death is but an instant, life a long torment.
Envy's a sharper spur than pay. (John Gay)
Fame is but an inscription on a grave, and glory the melancholy blazon on a coffin lid. (Alexander Smith)
Fear is an instructor of great sagacity and the herald of all revolutions. (Emerson)
God is our refuge and strength, a very present help in trouble. (Ps. 46.1)
Good is a good doctor, but Bad is sometimes a better. (Emerson)
History is a novel which did take place; a novel is a history that could take place.
Knowledge is the true organ of sight, not the eyes.
Passion, though a bad regulator, is a powerful spring.
Prosperity is a great teacher; adversity is a greater. (Hazlitt)

NOTES

1. This portrayal runs from cartoons in periodicals to editorial columns in national newspapers to satiric poems in the *Times Literary Supplement* (*TLS*). See, for example, Jeff Reid's cartoon, "Breakfast as Text." It presents a box of Post-Modern Toasties ("Like everything you've had before, all mixed up"), a box of Deconstruction Breakfast Food Product (containing a hillock of sugar, a mound of fat, and a pile of verbiage), and a box of "Foucault Flakes" (with the commentary, "But it's empty," "But of course"). A sample of the copy: "Finally, a breakfast commodity so complex that you need a theoretical apparatus to digest it. You won't want to eat it, you'll just want to read it. A literary tour de force: Breakfast as text!" (*Harper's Magazine*, August 1989, page 27). David Lehman offers a more mandarin comment in his satiric poem "Derridadaism," which follows Lorna Sage's review, "Trouble at the Theory Carnival," in *TLS*, 18–24 May 1990:

> "Philosophy?
> *Cela suffit!*
> Said the man
> Named de Man.
> J. Hillis Miller
> J. Phillis Diller.

This poem comes with four footnotes. The footnote to the title reads, "Geoffrey Hartman's term in *Saving the Text*. An alternative spelling, *Derrida(da)ism*, subversively reveals the Russian *yes* within the demotic term for father." The footnote to "Named de Man" reads, "A neglected trope, the paradigmatic palindrome deconstructs itself into a reversed binary opposition that terminates in an undecidable *aporia*; as when a pedestrian gets stuck in a revolving door (de Man's image)." Members of the profession of English have grown inured to the predictable annual satire in the *Washington Post* or the *New York Times* of the convention of the Modern Language Association as silly, its speakers as loony and inconsequential, and its presentation of what passes for research activity in our profession as worth a New Year's chuckle of amusement to anyone who has not lost his mind. Newspaper editorials are particularly fond of the devilishly efficient comic device of simply listing titles of papers at the MLA without further comment, as if no satire could rival the reality; see, for example, the editorial column "Review and Outlook" in the *Wall Street Journal*, 26 November 1990, page A10. The *New York Times Magazine*, 10 February 1991, carries an article by Anne Matthews describing the MLA convention under the title "Deciphering Victorian Underwear and Other Seminars" (pages 43, 57–59, 69). Our professional armor allows us to deflect the periodic dismissals that appear in middle-brow publications, such as John Searle's in "The Storm over the University," *New York Review of Books* 37/19 (6 December 1990): pages 34–42. Searle reassures readers that the development of our profession since poststructuralism is not "catastrophic," as many fear, but merely "silly" (page 34).

2. See M. H. Abrams, "The Deconstructive Angel," *Critical Inquiry,* 3/3 (Spring 1977): pages 425–38. See also Frank Kermode's "Prologue," in *An Appetite for Poetry* (Cambridge: Harvard University Press, 1989), pages 4–5: "Walking through the Life Sciences building at UCLA recently, I noticed affixed to a laboratory door the following words: 'Les théories passent. Le grenouille reste. —Jean Rostand, *Carnets d'un biologiste.*' There is a risk that in the less severe discipline of criticism the result may turn out to be different; the theories will remain but the frog may disappear."

3. "The Disinherited Line," *TLS*, 31 March–6 April 1989, page 341.

4. See Gerald Graff, *Professing Literature: An Institutional History* (Chicago: University of Chicago Press, 1987) for the most recent, most detailed, and most incisive treatment of our institutional history. Terminological shifts mirror the profession's shift in its concept of what it professes. The most important professional journals in the field dating from the nineteenth century have the word "language" in their titles—conspicuously, *Modern Language Association Publications* (1884), whose new series is retitled *Publications of the Modern Language Association* (1893), and *Modern Language Notes* (1888). Shortly thereafter, a new group of important journals began publication. Nearly all of these have the word "philology" in their titles. Three of the most important are the *Journal of English and Germanic Philology* (1897), *Modern Philology* (1903), and *Studies in Philology* (1906).

5. R. S. Crane, "Criticism as Inquiry; or, The Perils of the 'High Priori Road,'" in *The Idea of the Humanities,* 2 vols. (Chicago: University of Chicago Press, 1967), 2:26.

6. It is interesting to note that as late as 1930, Richard F. Jones, a professor of English, could publish an article called "Science and English Prose Style in the Third Quarter of the Seventeenth Century" in *PMLA* (45 [1930]: pages 977–1009), and that this article could be reviewed in Crane's annual bibliography of Restoration and eighteenth-century scholarship in *Philological Quarterly* by Morris Croll and by Crane himself, two distinguished professors of English (10 [1931]: pages 184–85). By 1962, when Thomas S. Kuhn published his landmark *The Structure of Scientific Revolutions* (Chicago: University of Chicago Press), English professors who published in prominent journals were no longer exploring such questions as the influence of scientific concepts on prose style.

7. The academic study of film began as commentary and history of circumstances, moved on to theory, and only afterward began to consider for films editorial questions analogous to philological questions about texts—the questions that occupied literary scholars at the inception of our profession.

8. See note 11 to this chapter, where Michael Lockwood is quoted with respect to what happens to a profession whose problems are not respected outside its walls.

9. R. S. Crane, "Shifting Definitions and Evaluations of the Humanities from the Renaissance to the Present," in *Idea of the Humanities,* 1:22. Wayne Booth,

in his introduction to *The Idea of the Humanities*, says, "I know of nothing that is quite like this canvassing of our shortcomings and opportunities as humanists, done in the light of a historical reconstruction of previous ideas about the humanities" (1:viii). Crane's essay is the inspiration for the present chapter.

10. The methods of the humanities are not determined by subject matter. R. S. Crane cites natural and social scientists who think "about their nonhumanistic subject matters [in ways that are] indistinguishable from the way of thinking which I associate with the best practitioners I have known of the humanistic arts." He also cites "humanists (in the sense of professors of the so-called humanistic subjects) . . . who have seemed to me much less humanistic in their essential ways of thinking than these scientific friends." See Crane, "The Idea of the Humanities," in *Idea of the Humanities*, 1:4.

11. Michael Lockwood, in *Mind, Brain, and the Quantum: The Compound "I"* (Oxford: Basil Blackwell, 1989)—a book that suggests that the brain must be regarded as a quantum-mechanical system, as opposed to a classical system, if we are to give "an account of the workings of the brain that is *functionally* adequate at the level relevant to psychology" (page 240)—makes a plea for academic philosophy similar to mine for the profession of English, that it engage in the signal humanistic and intellectual work of our age, the discovery of the mind:

> Academic philosophy, if it is to play a major role in the universities, cannot afford to become too inward-looking, or too narrowly preoccupied with arcane puzzles of its own devising. It must be seen to be addressing issues whose importance is capable of being appreciated, at least by scholars in other fields, and ideally by the man or woman in the street. It needs to be perceived as having a vital contribution to make to other disciplines, and to human understanding generally. Otherwise, it will become not only increasingly marginal within our culture, but deservedly so. (page 315)

12. Allen Walker Read's unpublished 1961 speech to the Linguistic Circle of Columbia University—"Can Native Speakers of a Language Make Mistakes?" (the answer he gave was "No")—expresses this dismissal.

13. See further Gregory Colomb and Mark Turner, "Computers, Literary Theory, and Theory of Meaning," in *The Future of Literary Theory*, edited by Ralph Cohen (New York: Routledge, 1988), pages 386–410, notes: pages 436–43.

14. John Ellis makes a similar comment in *The Theory of Literary Criticism: A Logical Approach* (Berkeley: University of California Press, 1974): "[T]he material from which literary texts are made is language, and they are always exploitations of the conceptual possibilities of a given language. From this it ought certainly to follow that our understanding of how language works in general, and of the particular language of the texts, must bear some important relation to our ability to analyze literary texts" (page 256). Ellis closes this book, written in 1974, with the following passage:

> In practice, linguistics has offered critics a bad critical procedure based on a poor model of scientific research, a version of the concept of style more insidious even than the critic's own, and a primitive view of the theory

of meaning and of how language functions. Yet in theory, a command both of the best available analysis of the language in which a particular text is written, and of the way in which language functions and has meaning, should be of enormous advantage to the critic. It can only be hoped that the practical situation slowly comes to resemble what in theory it might be. (page 262)

15. Schemata are skeletal organizations of conceptual knowledge. They have variables, can embed, and can represent knowledge at all levels. For a history of the development of the idea of a schema, see David E. Rumelhart, "Schemata: The Building Blocks of Cognition," in *Theoretical Issues in Reading Comprehension: Perspectives from Cognitive Psychology, Linguistics, Artificial Intelligence, and Education*, edited by Rand J. Spiro et al. (Hillsdale, N.J.: Lawrence Erlbaum Associates, 1980). Rumelhart discusses the history of the concept of a schema, from its original sense in Kant in 1787 through its use in psychology by Head in 1920 and Bartlett in 1932. The idea of a schema, or frame, will for most readers be familiar from a range of now-classic books and articles in the 1960s and 1970s. See, for example, Charles Fillmore, "The Case for Case," in *Universals in Linguistic Theory*, edited by E. Bach and R. Harms (New York: Holt, Rinehart, and Winston, 1968), pages 1–90; Robert Schank and Robert Abelson, *Scripts, Plans, Goals, and Understanding* (Hillsdale, N.J.: Lawrence Erlbaum Associates, 1977); David Rumelhart and Andrew Ortony, "The Representation of Knowledge in Memory," in *Schooling and the Acquisition of Knowledge*, edited by R. C. Anderson et al. (Hillsdale, N.J.: Lawrence Erlbaum Associates, 1977), pages 99–135; and Marvin Minsky, "A Framework for Representing Knowledge," in *The Psychology of Computer Vision*, edited by P. H. Winston (New York: McGraw-Hill, 1975), pages 211–77. See also Charles Fillmore, "Frame Semantics," in *Linguistics in the Morning Calm*, edited by the Linguistic Society of Korea (Seoul: Hanshin, 1982), pages 111–38; Erving Goffman, *Frame Analysis* (New York: Harper and Row, 1974); and Nelson Goodman, *Languages of Art*, 2d ed. (Indianapolis: Hackett, 1976). The idea of a schema or frame or script is now a commonplace in work on cognition. See D. E. Rumelhart, J. L. McClelland, and the PDP Research Group, *Parallel Distributed Processing: Explorations in the Microstructure of Cognition*, vol. 2, *Psychological and Biological Models* (Cambridge: Bradford Books, MIT, 1986), pages 20–22; and Charles Fillmore, "Frames and the Semantics of Understanding," *Quaderni di Semantica* 6/2 (1985): pages 222–53.

16. See, for example, Fillmore, "Frame Semantics," pages 111–38; and Dorothy Holland and Naomi Quinn, editors, *Cultural Models in Language and Thought* (Cambridge: Cambridge University Press, 1988).

17. See Leonard Talmy, "Force Dynamics in Language and Cognition," *Cognitive Science* 12 (1988): pages 49–100; and Eve Sweetser, *From Etymology to Pragmatics: Metaphorical and Cultural Aspects of Semantic Structure* (Cambridge: Cambridge University Press, 1990).

18. Gilles Fauconnier, *Mental Spaces: Aspects of Meaning Construction in Natural Language* (Cambridge: Bradford Books, MIT, 1985).

19. For a survey, see George Lakoff, *Women, Fire, and Dangerous Things:*

What Categories Reveal about the Mind (Chicago: University of Chicago Press, 1987). See further Mark Turner, "Categories and Analogies," in *Analogical Reasoning: Perspectives of Artificial Intelligence, Cognitive Science, and Philosophy*, edited by David Helman (Dordrecht: Kluwer, 1988), pages 3–24.

20. For an introduction, see George Lakoff and Mark Turner, *More than Cool Reason: A Field Guide to Poetic Metaphor* (Chicago: University of Chicago Press, 1989). See also George Lakoff and Mark Johnson, *Metaphors We Live By* (Chicago: Chicago University Press, 1980); Mark Turner, *Death Is the Mother of Beauty: Mind, Metaphor, Criticism* (Chicago: University of Chicago Press, 1987); and Sweetser, *From Etymology to Pragmatics*.

21. See Mark Johnson, *The Body in the Mind* (Chicago: University of Chicago Press, 1987).

22. In *The Newsletter of the Center for Research in Language* 1/3 (February 1987). For fuller summaries, see Ronald Langacker, "An Overview of Cognitive Grammar" and "A View of Linguistics Semantics," *Topics in Cognitive Linguistics*, edited by Brygida Rudzka-Ostyn (Amsterdam/Philadelphia: John Benjamins, 1988), pages 3–48, and 49–90. For a full-length account, see Ronald Langacker, *Foundations of Cognitive Grammar*, vol. 1, *Theoretical Prerequisites* (Stanford: Stanford University Press, 1987); and Lakoff, *Women, Fire, and Dangerous Things*.

23. The International Cognitive Linguistics Association offers a catalog of reprints of the most significant publications and an extended bibliography of the field, both available from Professor Dr. René Dirven, Linguistic Agency, University of Duisburg, Lotharstraβe 65, D - 4100 Duisburg 1, Germany.

24. Lord Bolingbroke's phrase is quoted in "Criticism as Inquiry" (page 31). Crane's article distinguishes criticism as inquiry from criticism as grand a priori generalization that can never sufficiently respect the nuances of its data but rather transforms its data into fodder. See *The Idea of the Humanities*, 2:25–44, especially pages 29–32. Gerald Graff quotes at length from this article, notes the fundamental importance of the questions it raises, and provides a commentary that warrants close attention (*Professing Literature*, pages 233–43).

25. Recursive function theory is a branch of formal mathematics. Like all of formal mathematics, it treats the combination and transformation of strings of meaningless symbols. See Terry Winograd, *Language as a Cognitive Process: Syntax* (Reading: Addison-Wesley, 1983), especially the sections called "Generative Linguistics—Linguistics as Mathematics" (pages 11–13) and "Current Directions in Transformational Grammar" (pages 555–82).

Generative linguistics views language as a mathematical object and builds theories that are very much like sets of axioms and inference rules in mathematics. A sentence is grammatical if there is some *derivation* that demonstrates that its structure is in accord with the set of rules, much as a proof demonstrates the truth of a mathematical sentence. Much confusion has come from the use of the word *generative*, since to many people it falsely implies that the theory is a description of how people generate sentences. A helpful analogy is to recognize that although formal mathematics provides a precise way of recognizing whether a particular proof is valid, it has no way whatever of describing how a mathematician sets out to generate it. (page 12)

Claudia Brugman points out (personal communication) that even Winograd here inadvertently uses a standard expression implying that strings of meaningless symbols are like meaningful linguistic expressions when he refers to "a mathematical sentence."

CHAPTER 3
POETRY AND INVENTION

1. One room can differ from another in an almost unlimited number of unoriginal and pedestrian ways, all of which we know without need of reflection. This is an indication of the complexity in a full knowledge of the concept *room*.

2. *Pilgrim's Progress* fleshes out this conventional metaphor elaborately, and exploits in composition with it many other conventional metaphors, such as THE MIND IS A BODY, STATES ARE LOCATIONS, and GENERIC IS SPECIFIC. A discussion of these metaphors can be found in George Lakoff and Mark Turner, *More than Cool Reason: A Field Guide to Poetic Metaphor* (Chicago: University of Chicago Press, 1989). Many of the allegorical moments in *Pilgrim's Progress* do not appear to be extensions of any conventionalized metaphor. See, for example, the Interpreter's presentation of a parlor as the heart of a man never sanctified by the grace of the gospel, the dust in the parlor as his original sin and inward corruptions, the man who sweeps the dust as the law, water as grace, and the damsel that sprinkles water on the dust as gospel. The effect of law on sin in the heart is to be understood in terms of the effect of the sweeper on dust in the house: he merely stirs it up to worse effect, unless water is first sprinkled upon it. Since neither Christian nor the reader possesses a conventionalized conceptual metaphor with this set of mappings, both Christian and the reader must rely upon the Interpreter to indicate it to them, or hazard what they know to be guesses at the significance of the sweeping scene.

3. The notion of a schema will be used throughout this book. See note 15 to the Pretext.

4. "Source" and "target" are commonly used technical terms in discussions of metaphor. See, for example, the entry on "metaphor" in the forthcoming *Oxford International Encyclopedia of Linguistics*, in which the terminology is explained. The target conceptual domain is the domain to be understood metaphorically. The source conceptual domain is the domain in terms of which the target is to be understood metaphorically. A conceptual metaphor consists of a target, a source, and a mapping between them. Conventional metaphoric expressions draw their vocabulary from the source but are taken to refer to the target, as when we take "I'm getting nowhere"—whose vocabulary is drawn from the source schema for journeys—to refer to the state of someone's life, which is the target.

5. Technically, a relation < on a set A is called an order relation (or a simple order, or a linear order) if it has the properties of comparability (for every x and

y in A for which x does not equal y, either $x < y$ or $y < x$), nonreflexivity (for no x in A does the relation $x < x$ hold), and transitivity (if $x < y$ and $y < z$, then $x < z$).

6. Aristotle writes in *The Rhetoric*, "Metaphors, like epithets, must be fitting, which means that they must fairly correspond to the thing signified: failing this, their inappropriateness will be conspicuous: the want of harmony between two things is emphasized by their being placed side by side" (*The Rhetoric and the Poetics of Aristotle*, translated by W. Rhys Robert [New York: Modern Library, 1984], book 3, chapter 2 [1405a]).

There are many grounds on which a metaphor might be judged fitting or unfitting. As Wayne Booth points out, any rhetoric text from Aristotle's to Whately's would comment that a metaphor might be judged appropriate or inappropriate in its grandeur or triviality to what is being presented, in its contribution to the ethos the speaker desires to establish, in its level of difficulty or interest for the audience, in the style of its expression, and so on. See Booth's "Metaphor as Rhetoric," in *On Metaphor*, edited by Sheldon Sacks (Chicago: University of Chicago Press, 1979): pages 47–70. I am concerned not with these forms of fitness, but rather with the conceptual fitness of a metaphor.

7. For a survey of such work, see D. Cooper's *Metaphor* (Oxford: Blackwell, 1987). Recent work on the conceptual details of metaphor includes most prominently Dedre Gentner's work on structure-mapping, which I discuss in note 21 below, and work by George Lakoff and Mark Turner, which I also discuss in note 21 below. Older work on the conceptual details of metaphor centers on the chestnut that metaphors are conceptually constrained not to be "mixed," but this claim is in general false. Often, mixed metaphors do not bother us, and often, different metaphors can cohere. For a discussion, see Lakoff and Turner, *More than Cool Reason*, especially the sections on "Composing" (pages 70–71) and "Coherence among Metaphors" (pages 86–89). Wayne Booth, on page 50 of "Metaphor as Rhetoric" (see note 6 to this chapter), gives the following example of a "mixed" metaphor that does not disturb us at all, and that may be all the stronger for being mixed. A lawyer expresses the struggle between a large utility company and a small utility company in a figure: "So now we see what it is. They [the large utility company] got us [the small utility company] where they want us. They holding us up with one hand, their good sharp fishin' knife in the other, and they sayin,' 'you *jes* set still, little catfish, we're jes going to *gut* ya.'" Booth observes later in the article that consistency would require that the catfish be told to "hang still" rather than "set still," but that this conceptual inconsistency does not bother us. I suspect that we would be rather bothered indeed if the metaphor were instead "You jes vanish, little catfish, we're jes going to gut ya" or "You jes jump back in the water, little catfish, we're jes going to gut ya" or "You jes digest, little catfish, we're jes going to gut ya" or "You jes grow older, little catfish, we're jes going to gut ya," although these metaphors are not mixed, and that we would be equally bothered if the metaphor were "You jes hold a board meeting, little catfish, we're jes going to gut ya," which is mixed. In all these cases, we hear the conceptual gears of the metaphor grind. We feel that something at the conceptual level does not fit. Something at the conceptual level has gone awry.

8. Max Black writes, "The metaphorical utterance works by 'projecting upon'

the primary subject a set of 'associated implications,' comprised in the implicative complex, that are predicable of the secondary subject." See page 28 of "More about Metaphor" in Andrew Ortony's anthology, *Metaphor and Thought* (Cambridge: Cambridge University Press, 1979), pages 19–43.

9. *Languages of Art*, 2d ed. (Indianapolis: Hackett, 1976), page 73.

10. "Metaphor as Moonlighting," in *On Metaphor*, edited by Sheldon Sacks (Chicago: University of Chicago Press, 1979), page 178.

11. Paul Ricoeur, *The Rule of Metaphor: Multi-disciplinary Studies of the Creation of Meaning in Language* (Toronto: University of Toronto Press, 1977). This is a translation by Robert Czerny of *La Metaphore Vive*.

12. There have been before now random observations that specific metaphoric mappings are unacceptable because they go awry in some way. For example, Eva Kittay and Adrienne Lehrer note that when we attempt to make sense of Donne's "The Bait," in which courtship is presented metaphorically in terms of fishing, there is one mapping that we might try out but find unacceptable because it "does not work. The 'beloved' cannot at once be the prey and herself the means of catching the prey." That observation is true, even obviously true, but no account is given of why that specific metaphoric mapping is constrained in that way, and no general constraint is given. See Eva Kittay, *Metaphor: Its Cognitive Force and Linguistic Structure* (Oxford: Clarendon, 1987), page 273; and Eva Kittay and Adrienne Lehrer, "Semantic Fields and the Structure of Metaphor," *Studies in Language* 5 (1981): pages 31–63, especially page 47.

13. Nelson Goodman implies that such constraints exist, but gives only hints about what they might be, as in,

A schema may be transported almost anywhere. The choice of territory for invasion is arbitrary; but the operation within that territory is almost never completely so. We may at will apply temperature-predicates to sounds or hues or personalities or to degrees of nearness to a correct answer; but *which* elements in the chosen realm are warm, or are warmer than others, is then very largely determinate. Even where a schema is imposed upon a most unlikely and uncongenial realm, antecedent practice channels the application of the labels. When a label has not only literal but prior metaphorical uses, these too may serve as part of the precedent for a later metaphorical application; perhaps, for instance the way we apply "high" to sounds was guided by the earlier metaphorical application to numbers (via number of vibrations per second) rather than directly by the literal application according to altitude.

See Goodman, *Languages of Art*, pages 74–75. What is missing from this enticing passage is any account of why certain choices are determinate, how antecedent practice channels the application of labels, or how prior uses serve as part of the precedent for later metaphorical application.

14. *The New English Bible* (Oxford and Cambridge: Oxford University Press and Cambridge University Press, 1970; New Testament, 1st ed., 1961), page 132 of the second series.

15. See further Lakoff and Turner, *More than Cool Reason*.

16. I ignore what seems to me a possible metonymic reading, in which Jesus, the guide, stands with respect to reference for the path.

17. We have what I will call in a moment an "image-schema" for *one* and a different image-schema for *three*. In quotidian experience and in our metaphoric conception of a target, three cannot be one. The divine is marked as transcending such constraints.

18. An image-schema, according to Mark Johnson,

> is a recurring, dynamic pattern of our perceptual interactions and motor programs that gives coherence and structure to our experience. The VERTICALITY schema, for instance, emerges from our tendency to employ an UP-DOWN orientation in picking out meaningful structures of our experience. We grasp this structure of verticality repeatedly in thousands of perceptions and activities we experience every day, such as perceiving a tree, our felt sense of standing upright, the activity of climbing stairs, forming a mental image of a flagpole, measuring our children's heights, and experiencing the level of water rising in the bathtub.

See Mark Johnson, *The Body in the Mind* (Chicago: University of Chicago Press, 1987), page xiv. The notion that we use image-schemas to structure our perceptions and conceptions is implicit in work by David Palermo; see his "The Transfer Dilemma: From Cross-Modal Perception to Metaphor," a paper presented at the Third International Conference on Thinking, Honolulu, Hawaii, 1987; "Metaphor: A Portal for Viewing the Child's Mind," in *Essays and Experiments in Honor of Charles C. Spiker*, edited by L. P. Lipsitt et al. (Hillsdale, N.J.: Lawrence Erlbaum Associates, 1988), pages 111–36; and "Knowledge and the Child's Developing Theory of the World," in *Advances in Child Development and Behavior*, vol. 22, edited by H. W. Reese (New York: Academic, 1988), pages 269–95. Ronald Langacker has since 1974 been articulating the ways in which semantic structure is based on what he calls "images," which resemble Johnson's image-schemata; see Langacker's *Foundations of Cognitive Grammar*, vol. 1, *Theoretical Prerequisites* (Stanford: Stanford University Press, 1987), and his articles "An Overview of Cognitive Grammar" and "A View of Linguistic Semantics" in Brygida Rudzka-Ostyn's anthology *Topics in Cognitive Linguistics* (Amsterdam/ Philadelphia: John Benjamins, 1988), pages 3–48, 49–80. Technically, Langacker views Johnson's "image-schemata" as a subset of Langacker's "images" (personal communication).

19. W. H. Auden, *Collected Poems*, edited by Edward Mendelson (New York: Random House, 1976), page 50, lines 9–12.

20. Larry Hardin, "A New Look at Color," *American Philosophical Quarterly* 21 (1984): pages 125–33, suggests a possible neurophysiological mechanism for cross-modal metaphor. We think of the red end of the color spectrum image-schematically as more active and the blue end of the color spectrum image-schematically as less active. In the retina, red and yellow do in fact imply heightened neural activity, while blue implies lowered activity. Suppose, Hardin suggests, that this relationship of heightened and lowered neural activity is preserved in cortical activity corresponding to color perception; suppose further that the same opponent relationship obtains for cortical activity corresponding to the perception of hot and cold, and in general for cortical activity corresponding to opponent sensations in other modalities; and finally, suppose that there is a cross-

modal polarity comparator, which can line up the polarities in different modalities. On this set of suppositions, the metaphoric connections between red and hot and between blue and cool would have a sound neurophysiological basis.

21. The image-schematic constraint hypothesized here bears a complicated relationship to Dedre Gentner's structure-mapping theory of analogy. See Dedre Gentner, "Structure-mapping: A Theoretical Framework for Analogy," *Cognitive Science* 7/2 (1983): pages 155–70, and "The Mechanisms of Analogical Learning," a paper presented at the 1986 ARI Conference on Analogical Similarity, and contained in *Similarity and Analogical Reasoning*, edited by Stella Vosniadou and Andrew Ortony (London: Cambridge University Press: 1989), pages 199–241. Gentner writes:

> The central idea in structure-mapping is that an analogy is a mapping of knowledge from one domain (the base) into another (the target) which conveys that a system of relations that holds among the base objects also holds among the target objects. Thus an analogy is a way of focusing on relational commonalities independently of the objects in which those relations are embedded. In interpreting an analogy, people seek to put the objects of the base in one-to-one correspondence with the objects in the target so as to obtain the maximum structural match. Objects are placed in correspondence by virtue of their like roles in the common relational structure; there does not need to be any resemblance between the target objects and their corresponding base objects. Central to the mapping process is the principle of systematicity: people prefer to map connected *systems of relations* governed by higher-order relations with inferential import, rather than isolated predicates. ("The Mechanisms of Analogical Learning," pages 3–4)

Gentner here hypothesizes a heuristic used in analogical understanding. It bears the following relationships to the image-schematic constraint on metaphor I propose. If relational structure is image-schematic, as it would seem to be, then the image-schematic constraint I propose entails that we are constrained not to violate the relational structure of the target. This relational corollary to the image-schematic constraint is compatible with Gentner's heuristic in just those cases of metaphor where the relational structure of the target is not violated and is also maximally involved in the mapping: such a case satisfies both the image-schematic constraint and Gentner's heuristic. In one way, the relational corollary to the image-schematic constraint on metaphor is stronger than Gentner's heuristic because Gentner's heuristic of seeking maximal structural match does not imply a constraint against violating relational structure in the target; indeed, Gentner's heuristic apparently would allow us to violate some relational structure in the target if doing so enabled us to involve more of the relational structure in an analogical match than would otherwise be possible. Violating some relational structure in the target should be welcomed according to Gentner's heuristic if it permits greater final structural match. In another way, the relational corollary to the image-schematic constraint on metaphor is weaker than Gentner's heuristic because it is merely a constraint against violating image-schematic structure in the target, and says nothing about what should be involved in the mapping, whereas Gentner's heuristic concerns exactly that. Although the image-schematic constraint and Gentner's heuristic can in some cases be compatible, the image-schematic constraint concerns many aspects of metaphor that Gentner's heuristic apparently does not. The full image-schematic constraint itself concerns all image-schematic structure, including many things (like *slowness* as part of an event shape) that are crucial to metaphor but that do not appear to fall under what Gentner would describe as relational structure. See further chapters 6 and 7.

The rudiments of the image-schematic constraint conjectured here are presented but not analyzed in Lakoff and Turner, *More than Cool Reason*, page 82, and are suggested by my discussion in *Death Is the Mother of Beauty* (Chicago: University of Chicago Press, 1987) of constraints on CAUSATION IS PROGENERATION. CAUSATION IS PROGENERATION is a generic-level metaphor, lacking a fixed target or a fixed ontological mapping. In place of a fixed mapping, it has constraints on possible mappings. Those constraints, it turns out, are special cases of the general image-schematic constraint proposed here. Lakoff, in his paper "The Invariance Hypothesis: Do Metaphors Preserve Cognitive Topology?" (given at the 1989 Duisburg Cognitive Linguistics Symposium and available from the Linguistic Agency at the University of Duisburg), phrased the hypothesis as "Metaphorical mappings preserve the cognitive topology (this is the image-schema structure) of the source domain." But this strong phrasing of the invariance hypothesis was potentially misleading, in two ways. The first way is trivial. Many components of image-schematic structure in the source are simply not involved in the mapping. For example, when we understand our boss as a crab, the image of the crab, and consequently its image-schematic structure, are simply not part of the mapping. Accordingly, that image-schematic structure in the source is not preserved by the mapping; it is not carried over to the target. (Lakoff and I implicitly explain this in chapter 4 when we discuss how the Maxim of Quantity guides us to exclude various components of the source and target from the mapping.) The second way in which the strong version is too strong is substantive: components of the source that are indeed involved in the mapping often have image-schematic structure that is not mapped onto the target. Consider LIFE IS A JOURNEY. There is a path in the source domain, and it is mapped onto the target. That path in the source has image-schematic structure. But much of this image-schematic structure is simply not mapped onto the target. For example, it is part of the image-schematic structure of the path to be fixed, to be independent of our traversal of it. Traversing the path neither creates nor destroys it. Consequently, we can meet a fork in the path, choose one fork, take a step, change our mind, step back, and take the other fork. Metaphorically, meeting a fork corresponds to coming upon alternatives. But the fixity of the fork does not map onto the fixity of the alternatives. Many of our decisions are irrevocable. Shall we boil this egg or eat it raw? Shall we marry Tom or Harry? In these cases, the rejected alternative disappears the moment we engage in the chosen alternative. If we boil the egg, we cannot then eat it raw, and if we eat it raw, we cannot then decide to boil it. Metaphorically, one of the forks is destroyed the moment we step down the other. We cannot take a step back and be again at the metaphoric fork in the road, *because the fork does not exist anymore*. The metaphoric path, unlike the source path, changes as a result of being traversed. The fixity of the path in the source, its independence of our traversal, is not mapped onto the target. The reason it cannot be mapped onto the target in these cases is that to do so would violate the image-schematic structure of the target. In the source, there is preservation, which is image-schematic structure. In the target, there is destruction, which is image-schematic structure. To map the source preservation onto the target destruction would be to violate the image-schematic structure of the target, and so we do not map that part of the image-schematic structure of the source. We see from this example that the strongest version of the constraint and the one I present above are incompatible for a range of cases. For these cases, obeying the strong version of the constraint violates the weaker version, and obeying the weaker version of the constraint violates the stronger version. It appears that the strongest version that is acceptable is: In metaphoric mapping, for those components of the source and target domains determined to be involved in the mapping, do not violate the image-schematic structure of the target, and import as much generic-level structure from the source as is consistent with that preservation. I discuss generic-level structure more fully in chapter 7.

22. Gerald M. Edelman, *The Remembered Present: A Biological Theory of Consciousness* (New York: Basic Books, 1989), page 40. See also his *Neural Darwinism: The Theory of Neuronal Group Selection* (New York: Basic Books, 1987).

23. Ambiguity allows us to imagine the image of the trees in various ways. Here, for the sake of discussion, I assume that an unbroken line of trees first climbs, then crests, then descends. Alternatively, one arm of a forest might climb in one direction while another arm descends in a different direction. In any case, we are constrained not to violate the schematic structure of the target image.

24. Ronald Langacker, *Foundations of Cognitive Linguistics*, vol. 1, *Theoretical Prerequisites* (Palo Alto: Stanford University Press, 1987), pages 144–46.

25. Dirk Geeraerts has pointed out that seeing the FORM of the trees as the trace of a MOTION is coherent with the general metonymy of the RESULT for the PROCESS; and that any metaphoric understanding of this event in terms of an action depends upon making sense of the static *situation* as the result of an *event* taking place over time. See, in relation to this, Langacker's discussion of summary scanning, cited in the previous note.

26. *A Wave* (New York: Penguin, 1984), page 1.

27. This and all the following passages from Perec are my translation (with thanks to James Arnold and Philippe Bernard for some corrections) of Perec's "Approches de quoi?" in *l'infraordinaire* (Seuil, 1989), pages 9–13.

CHAPTER 4
THE BODY OF OUR THOUGHT

1. Hermann Weyl, *Symmetry* (Princeton: Princeton University Press, 1952).

2. Since the appearance of my article on which this chapter draws, "Symmetry and Literature," *Language and Style* 19/2 (1986): pages 164–83, Mark Johnson has independently and impressively analyzed the role of the balance schema in preconceptual and conceptual thought. See *The Body in the Mind* (Chicago: University of Chicago Press, 1987), pages 74–100. I owe a great deal at many points in this chapter and in this book to Johnson's insights.

3. See George Lakoff and Mark Turner, *More than Cool Reason: A Field Guide to Poetic Metaphor* (Chicago: University of Chicago Press, 1989), pages 162–66.

4. John Wilson, "Egypt," in *Before Philosophy*, edited by Henri Frankfort (New York: Pelican, 1949), page 50.

5. Cedric H. Whitman, *Homer and the Heroic Tradition* (Cambridge, Mass.: Harvard University Press, 1958), page 252.

6. *Odyssey*, book 11, lines 170–203. Odysseus asks how Anticlea died; whether it was disease or the archer, Artemis, who slew her; of his father and his son; of whether the honor that was his still abides with his father and son or is possessed by some other man; and of his wife. Anticlea informs him that his wife is steadfast; that no other man yet possesses the honor that was his; that his son Telemachus still holds his lands and his father still tills the land, sorrowful with longing for Odysseus; and that she died not by the archer nor by disease, but through longing for Odysseus.

7. Whitman, *Homer and the Heroic Tradition*, page 255.

8. Calvert Watkins, "Aspects of Indo-European Poetics," in *The Indo-Europeans in the Fourth and Third Millennia*, edited by Edgar C. Polomé (Ann Arbor: Karoma, 1982), pages 104–20. Poetic thought, Watkins argues, is inseparable from everyday language: to analyze everyday language we must analyze supposedly poetic forms of thought. Watkins demonstrates succinctly how the analysis of poetic thought is at the center of the study of language when he shows how certain Indo-European etymologies rest upon metonymy or metaphor. In these cases, the scholar can "prove the etymology only by making explicit the poetic nature of the semantic relation between the cognates." "And the moral is simply that linguistics needs poetics, just as it needs pragmatics." (page 108)

9. Alastair Fowler surveys the use of this type of symmetry, called "ring composition" in Classical, Renaissance, Mannerist, and Baroque texts. See "Styles of Symmetry," in *Triumphal Forms* (Cambridge: Cambridge University Press, 1970). See also Alastair Fowler, editor, *Silent Poetry: Essays in Numerological Analysis* (London: Routledge and Kegan Paul, 1970). These works are concerned not with the cognitive capabilities that enable us to grasp symmetry, but rather with complicated number symmetries hidden in literary works, to be discovered only by using special critical instruments. For a survey of such numerological criticism, see R. G. Peterson, "Critical Calculations: Measures and Symmetry in Literature," *PMLA* 91 (1976): pages 367–75.

10. G. E. R. Lloyd, *Polarity and Analogy: Two Types of Argumentation in Early Greek Thought* (Cambridge: Cambridge University Press, 1966), page 92.

11. Roman Jakobson, "Concluding Statement: Linguistics and Poetics," in *Style in Language*, edited by Thomas A. Sebeok (Cambridge: MIT, 1960), pages 350–77; the quotation comes from page 373.

12. The observation that up-forward-right are superior and opposed to down-back-left is at least as old as Aristotle. For a survey of the axiology of right versus left, see Rodney Needham, editor, *Right & Left: Essays on Dual Symbolic Classification* (Chicago: University of Chicago Press, 1973).

13. Translated by Robert Fitzgerald (Garden City, N.Y.: Anchor Doubleday, 1974), book 11, lines 401ff., pages 263–64.

14. Vladimir Propp, *The Morphology of the Folktale*, translated by Svatava Pirkova-Jakobson, revised by Louis A. Wagner (Austin: University of Texas Press, 1968), page 38.

15. Justus George Lawler, *Celestial Pantomime: Poetic Structures of Transcendence* (New Haven and London: Yale University Press, 1979), page 26.

16. Ibid., page 26.

17. Ibid., page 37.

18. See Jonathan Culler, *Structuralist Poetics* (Ithaca: Cornell University Press, 1975), page 126; William Empson, *Seven Types of Ambiguity* (New York: New Directions, 1947), page 25; and Hugh Kenner, *The Poetry of Ezra Pound* (London: Faber and Faber, 1951), page 87.

19. Samuel Levin, *Linguistic Structures in Poetry* ('s-Gravenhage: Mouton, 1962). See also Jakobson, "Concluding Statement," pages 350–73.

20. Levin, *Linguistic Structures*, page 33.

21. "Linguistics and Poetics," in *Style in Language*, edited by Thomas A. Sebeok (Cambridge: MIT, 1960), page 358. For a further development of Jakobson's assertion, see Watkins, "Aspects of Indo-European Poetics," pages 104–20.

22. Levin, *Linguistic Structures*, page 33.

23. Paul Valéry, *The Art of Poetry*, translated by Denise Folliot (New York: Vintage, 1961), page 72.

24. Stephen Booth, *Shakespeare's Sonnets* (New Haven: Yale University Press, 1977).

25. Michael S. Gazzaniga and Joseph E. LeDoux, *The Integrated Mind* (New York: Plenum, 1973), page vii.

26. Patricia Smith Churchland, *Neurophilosophy: Toward a Unified Science of the Mind-Brain* (Cambridge: MIT, 1986), pages 174–93.

27. Gazzinaga and LeDoux, *Integrated Mind*, pages 9–10.

28. Churchland, *Neurophilosophy*, pages 119–20.

29. Gerald M. Edelman, *The Remembered Present: A Biological Theory of Consciousness* (New York: Basic Books, 1989), page 54.

30. Ibid., chapter 4, "Reentrant Signaling."

CHAPTER 5
THE POETRY OF ARGUMENT

1. See John E. Toews' review article, "Intellectual History after the Linguistic Turn: The Autonomy of Meaning and the Irreducibility of Experience," *American Historical Review* 92 (October 1987): pages 879–907; and William J. Bowsma, "Intellectual History in the 1980s: From History of Ideas to History of Meaning," *Journal of Interdisciplinary History* 12 (Autumn 1981): pages 279, 280, 283.

2. Locke, *Essay Concerning Human Understanding*, book 3, chapter 10; Hobbes, *Leviathan*, part 1, chapter 4.

3. Cambridge: Cambridge University Press, 1958.

4. Mark Johnson, *The Body in the Mind* (Chicago: University of Chicago

Press, 1989). Johnson argues that classical logic is the logic of metaphorical containers. See "Inference Patterns Based on Containment Schemata," pages 37–40.

5. Otto Alvin Loeb Dieter, "Stasis," *Speech Monographs* 17 (November 1950): pages 345–69.

6. Frans H. van Eemeren, Rob Grootendorst, and Tjark Kruiger, editors, *Handbook of Argumentation Theory: A Critical Survey of Classical Backgrounds and Modern Studies* (Dordrecht, Holland: Foris, 1987).

7. Dieter, "Stasis," page 346.

8. Ibid., page 352.

9. Ibid., page 360.

10. Ibid., page 352.

11. Cicero, *Topica* 25:93. Dieter, "Stasis," page 359.

12. Ibid., pages 362–63.

13. Ibid., pages 364–65.

14. Lee S. Hultzén, "Status in Deliberative Analysis," in *The Rhetorical Idiom: Essays on Rhetoric, Oratory, Language, and Drama*, presented to Herbert August Wilchelns, edited by Donald C. Bryant (New York: Russell and Russell, 1966), pages 97–123; the quotation is from page 97.

15. Dieter, "Stasis," page 359.

16. Ibid., page 361.

17. See van Eemeren, Grootendorst, and Kruiger, *Handbook of Argumentation Theory*, page 119.

18. Dieter, "Stasis," pages 362–63.

19. Ibid., page 351.

20. For example, it is not given a principal status in the *Rhetorica ad Herennium*, Quintilian's *Institutio oratorio*, or Cicero's *De oratore*.

21. Dieter, "Stasis," page 354.

22. See George Lakoff and Mark Johnson, *Metaphors We Live By* (Chicago: University of Chicago Press, 1980), page 4.

23. David Goodwin, "*Controversiae Meta-Asystatae* and the New Rhetoric," *Rhetoric Society Quarterly* (Summer 1989): pages 206–7.

24. Dieter, "Stasis," page 386.

25. Jeanne Fahnestock and Marie Secor, "Toward a Modern Version of Stasis," in *Oldspeak/Newspeak: Rhetorical Transformations*, edited by Charles W. Kneupper (Arlington, Tex.: Rhetoric Society of America, 1985), pages 217–26; the quotation is from page 221.

26. H.L.A. Hart and M. Honoré, *Causation in the Law* (Oxford: Clarendon, 1959).

27. Fahnestock and Secor, "Toward a Modern Version of Stasis," page 223:

When we consider practical applications, we can see how arguer, audience, and occasion—in short the full rhetorical situation—can actually move the effective stasis of a dispute. An argument conducted wholly in the stasis of fact or definition can actually affect its audience in the stasis of quality or even jurisdiction. If, for example, a well-known environmentalist convinces members of the Sierra Club that the number of grizzly bears is declining, an argument in the stasis of fact, he will probably have a full-fledged movement on his hands because that audience supplies an answer in the stasis of quality ("This is reprehensible") and considers itself, even defines itself, as able to act, with the jurisdiction to act. To put it another way, the hierarchical potential of the stases defines the range of effects an argument can have when context supplies what is missing in the text.

28. Hultzén, "Status in Deliberative Analysis," pages 97–123.

29. *La Nouvelle Rhétorique: Traité de l'Argumentation* (Presses Universitaires de France, 1958); translated by John Wilkinson and Purcell Weaver as *The New Rhetoric: A Treatise on Argumentation* (Notre Dame: University of Notre Dame Press, 1969). See the section on "Use and Systematization of Loci: Classical Outlook and Romantic Outlook," pages 95–99.

30. David Goodwin, "*Controversiae Meta-Asystatae* and the New Rhetoric," page 208.

31. *New Rhetoric*, page 85.

32. See Kenneth Burke, *Language as Symbolic Action: Essays on Life, Literature, and Method* (Berkeley: University of California Press, 1966); *A Grammar of Motives* (New York: Prentice-Hall, 1945); and "The Five Master Terms," in *Twentieth-Century English*, edited by William S. Knickerbocker (New York: Philosophical Library, 1946), pages 272–88.

33. Eve Sweetser, *From Etymology to Pragmatics: Metaphorical and Cultural Aspects of Semantic Structure* (Cambridge: Cambridge University Press, 1990).

34. Goodwin, "*Controversiae Meta-Asystatae*," page 216.

35. "Force Dynamics in Language and Cognition," *Cognitive Science* 12 (1988): pages 49–100.

36. Susan L. Kline, "Toward a Contemporary Linguistic Interpretation of the Concept of Stasis," *Journal of the American Forensic Association* 16 (Fall 1979): pages 96–103. See also Eve Sweetser, "Metaphorical Models of Thought and Speech: A Comparison of Historical Directions and Metaphorical Mappings in the Two Domains," *Proceedings of the Thirteenth Annual Meeting of the Berkeley Linguistics Society* (1987), edited by Jon Aske, Natasha Beery, Laura Michaelis, and Hana Filip.

37. *More than Cool Reason: A Field Guide to Poetic Metaphor* (Chicago: University of Chicago Press, 1989). See the section on "Social and Psychological Forces," pages 191–92.

38. *Body in the Mind*.

39. Sweetser, *From Etymology to Pragmatics*, page 22.

40. Steven L. Winter, "The Metaphor of Standing and the Problem of Self-Governance," *Stanford Law Review* 40 (August 1988): pages 1371–1516; the quotation is from page 1372.

41. Ibid., page 1388.

42. In chapter 4, we considered the role of this type of symmetry in the poetry of Yeats, Herbert, and Tennyson; in the general model of revenge tragedy; in the structure of plots in fairytales; and in a range of other poetic phenomena. The metaphoric understanding of argument in terms of force dynamics depends upon the prior image-schema of bilateral and oppositional symmetry.

CHAPTER 6
CONCEPTUAL CONNECTIONS

1. I am not implying here a historical or causal or sequential narrative of the sort Locke presents in 2.11.9 of the *Essay Concerning Human Understanding*. I do not mean that developmentally—in the development of the species, culture, or organism—perception of particulars precedes the introduction of categories to corral them. On the contrary, the category can exist before particulars, and indeed enable us to perceive particulars, as when having the category *screwdriver* as tipped metal rod with handle, used for turning screws, enables someone to behave in such a way that she becomes confronted with the surprising inadequacy of a hitherto undistinguished particular (a phillips screwdriver) to do the standard job.

2. This concept of generative entrenchment was suggested to me by William C. Wimsatt, who proposes generative entrenchment as an alternative to the innate versus acquired distinction in evolutionary biology. See William C. Wimsatt, "Developmental Constraints, Generative Entrenchment, and the Innate-Acquired Distinction," in *Integrating Scientific Disciplines*, edited by W. Bechtel (Dordrecht: Martinus-Nijhoff, 1986), pages 185–208. See also J. C. Shank and W. C. Wimsatt, "Generative Entrenchment and Evolution," in *Proceedings of the Philosophy of Science Association 1986*, vol. 2, edited by A. Fine and P. K. Machamer (East Lansing: Philosophy of Science Association, 1988), pages 33–60.

3. I owe this example to Donald Freeman.

4. See E. E. Smith and D. L. Medin, *Categories and Concepts* (Cambridge: Harvard University Press, 1981).

5. For explicit trees, see J. Katz and J. A. Fodor, "The Structure of a Semantic Theory," *Language* 39 (1963): pages 170–210; J. J. Katz and Paul M. Postal, *An Integrated Theory of Linguistic Descriptions* (Cambridge: MIT, 1964); J. J. Katz, *Semantic Theory* (New York: Harper and Row, 1972); and M. Ross Quillian, "Semantic Memory," in *Semantic Information Processing*, edited by Marvin Minsky (Cambridge: MIT, 1968). I would suggest that such trees are implicit in other theories, such as those found in Roger C. Schank and Robert Abelson, *Scripts, Plans, Goals and Understanding* (Hillsdale N.J.: Lawrence Erlbaum Associates, 1977); Roger C. Schank, *Conceptual Information Processing* (New York: North-Holland, 1975); Roger C. Schank, "Identification of Conceptualizations Underlying Natural Language," in *Computer Models of Thought and Language*, edited by K. M. Colby (San Francisco: Freeman, 1973); Marvin Minsky, "A Framework for Representing Knowledge," in *The Psychology of Computer Vision*, edited by P. Winston (New York: McGraw-Hill, 1973); and D. G. Bobrow and T. Winograd, "An Overview of KRL: A Knowledge Representation Language," *Cognitive Science* 1 (1977): pages 3–46.

6. See Eleanor Rosch, "Cognitive Reference Points," *Cognitive Psychology* 7 (1975): pages 532–47; "Cognitive Representations of Semantic Categories," *Journal of Experimental Psychology: General* 104 (1975): pages 192–233; "Human Categorization," in *Advances in Cross-Cultural Psychology* (New York: Academic, 1977); "Principles of Categorization," in *Cognition and Categoriza-*

tion, edited by B. B. Lloyd and Eleanor Rosch (Hillsdale, N.J.: Lawrence Erlbaum Associates, 1978), pages 27–48; "Categorization of Natural Objects," *Annual Review of Psychology* 32 (1981): pages 89–115; "Coherences and Categorization: A Historical View," in *The Development of Language and Language Researchers: Essays in Honor of Roger Brown*, edited by Frank S. Kessel (Hillsdale, N.J.: Lawrence Erlbaum Associates, 1988); E. Rosch and C. B. Mervis, "Family Resemblance: Studies in the Internal Structure of Categories," *Cognitive Psychology* 7 (1975): pages 573–605; M. Brewer, V. Dull, and L. Lui, "Perceptions of the Elderly: Stereotypes as Prototypes," *Journal of Personality and Social Psychology* 41 (1981): pages 656–70; Kathleen Dahlgren, "The Cognitive Structure of Social Categories," *Cognitive Science* 9/3 (1985): pages 379–98; B. Fehr and J. A. Russell, "Concept of Emotion Viewed from a Prototype Perspective," *Journal of Experimental Psychology: General* 113 (1984): pages 484–86; and A. C. Graesser, S. E. Gordon, and J. Sawyer, "Recognition Memory for Typical and Atypical Actions in Scripted Activities," *Journal of Experimental Psychology: Human Learning and Memory* 6 (1979): pages 503–15.

7. George Lakoff, *Women, Fire, and Dangerous Things: What Categories Reveal about the Mind* (Chicago: University of Chicago Press, 1987).

8. The literature cited above generalizes Rosch's results to many domains besides concrete objects. Let us explore certain details of these *vertical* phenomena. My analyses in this study do not depend upon the particular way Rosch *characterizes* the basic level, but rather only on the *phenomenon* of the basic level in cognition and language. Nonetheless I will give her characterization here, because some readers will appreciate the technical details. Rosch expresses the cognitive punch of the basic level in terms of *cue validity*, a term from cognitive psychology. A cue x (for example, spins webs) is a better predictor of a category y (for example, spider) the more frequently it is associated with y and the less frequently it is associated with other categories. For example, the cue validity of "spins webs" is high for the category *spider*. The cue validity of a category is the sum of the cue validities of the attributes. The basic-level category has the highest cue validity, for the following set of reasons. Above the basic level, a category has lower cue validity than the basic-level category because its members have fewer attributes in common. (This follows from the storage of most information at the basic level.) Here are the details: First, the cues not shared by members of the category above the basic level will have on average negligible cue validity for that category. Second, each shared cue may have cue validity, but there are very few such cues, and the sum of their cue validities is therefore low. Adding up the many negligible cue validities and the few high cue validities gives a summed cue validity for the category above the basic level that is still low relative to the summed cue validity of the basic level. Now let us consider categories below the basic level. A category lower than the basic level also has lower cue validity than the basic level, because it shares more attributes with contrasting categories: a given cue for a category below the basic level is likely to have low cue validity for that category because it is frequently associated with members of contrasting categories. The sum of these low cue validities is the cue validity for the category below the basic level. It is low relative to the summed cue validity of the basic

level. (Note that Rosch's characterization is likely to be rigid and unsupple, not only because it does not weigh some attributes as more or less powerful than others, but also, more generally, because the mechanics of computing cue validity are unaffected by domain of categorization.)

9. As in the case of *vertical* phenomena (see previous note), my analyses in this study do not depend on the way Rosch characterizes these *horizontal* phenomena, but again I give her characterization because certain readers will appreciate the technical details. Higher cue validity of a category means greater differentiation from contrasting categories, so the basic level, which has the highest cue validity, is the level of maximal differentiation between contrasting categories. Below the basic level, contrasting categories share relatively many attributes, making the cue validity of each cue low and consequently the cue validity of each category low, which means that contrasting categories below the basic level are less differentiated than contrasting categories at the basic level. Above the basic level, categories have lower cue validity than basic-level categories simply because members of higher categories share fewer attributes, so there are fewer significant individual cue validities to be summed into the overall cue validity of the category, hence these categories have low cue validity and are less differentiated from each other than categories at the basic level. Nonetheless, the individual cue validity of an attribute shared by members of a category above the basic level is generally high, making that individual attribute generally a strong indicator of difference.

10. There is the additional complication in understanding equations between noun phrases that a noun phrase can often be taken as attributional rather than referential. "This rope is a necessity" can be taken as equivalent to "This rope is necessary." When we take a noun phrase in an equation as attributive, we can side-step altogether the recognition of analogy, by recognizing attribution instead.

11. Gilles Fauconnier, *Mental Spaces: Aspects of Meaning Construction in Natural Language* (Cambridge: MIT, 1985).

12. It goes without saying here and throughout the book that context can drive our understanding of a given utterance in almost any direction imaginable, if it includes the right cues, and that no utterance is ever decontextualized really, but is merely moved to a different context, and that context is frequently indispensable in distinguishing categorical statements from analogical statements ("Smith is a butcher"). But context does not in all respects indicate a particular reading. To the extent that it does not, we can investigate our default principles for making sense of the utterance. And we can investigate the regularities that occur across our readings of an utterance in the full variety of common contexts.

13. Dedre Gentner, "Structure-mapping: A Theoretical Framework for Analogy," *Cognitive Science* 7/2 (1983): pages 155–70. See also Gentner's "The Mechanisms of Analogical Learning," a paper presented at the 1986 ARI Conference on Analogical Similarity, and contained in *Similarity and Analogical Reasoning*, edited by Stella Vosniadou and Andrew Ortony (London: Cambridge University Press, 1989), pages 199–241.

14. See Mark Johnson's introduction in his anthology *Philosophical Perspectives on Metaphor* (Minneapolis: University of Minnesota Press, 1981).

15. Andrew Ortony, editor, *Metaphor and Thought* (Cambridge: Cambridge University Press, 1979) contains both John Searle's article "Metaphor" (pages 92–123) and Jerrold Sadock's "Figurative Speech and Linguistics" (pages 46–63). H. P. Grice's "Logic and Conversation" appears in *Syntax and Semantics*, vol. 3, *Speech Acts*, edited by Peter Cole and Jerry L. Morgan (New York: Academic, 1975), pages 41–58.

16. Grice, "Logic and Conversation," page 53.

17. Stephen C. Levinson, *Pragmatics* (Cambridge: Cambridge University Press, 1984), pages 156–58.

18. William C. Wimsatt, "Developmental Constraints, Generative Entrenchment, and the Innate-Acquired Distinction," in *Integrating Scientific Disciplines*, edited by W. Bechtel (Dordrecht: Martinus-Nijhoff, 1986). I find Wimsatt's description of his analysis richly suggestive for the study of the development and acquisition of concepts:

> The analysis I propose captures more of the phenomena commonly linked with the innate-acquired distinction than any prior analysis, and explains their relevance in a new way, but necessitates giving up at least two claims which have been dear to advocates of that distinction, and other assertions which depend on these claims. *The first claim* (or presupposition, since it is seldom claimed explicitly), *is that what is innate must be internal to the object in question*. This has been a presupposition of making this distinction from the earliest time and is the basis for claims that innate features are in some sense independent of or unmodifiable through experience. I will argue that under appropriate conditions, information which is embodied in the environment, and enters the organism as experience, must be regarded as innate, or something close to it, and that as a result the environment can in most even moderately complex cases play a major role in the expression of the trait.
>
> The *second claim* is a more recent accretion dating from the rise of genetics in the early 20th century. This *is the reanalysis of the classical association between the innate and the hereditary into the more modern claim that to be innate is to be genetic*. Although more recent, this claim is by now hardly less firmly entrenched than the first. While I will argue that there is a (narrow) sense in which it is correct to say that to be innate is to be "coded in the genetic program," this is a misleading and unduly narrow way of pointing to the generative role of innate elements, and leads to an incorrect identification of the innate with the (biologically) genetic. In particular, it does not follow, on the account I propose, either that if something is coded in a genetic program, it is "genetically determined" or that the information which determines it is entirely in the genome. From this it follows that not all things which are biologically genetic are innate, and not all things which are innate are biologically genetic. (p. 186)

19. See "Computer Science as Empirical Inquiry: Symbols and Search," in *Mind Design*, edited by John Haugeland (Cambridge: MIT, 1981), pages 35–66,

a reprint of the Tenth Turing Award Lecture, delivered to the annual conference of the Association for Computing Machinery in 1975, and published in *Communications of the Association for Computing Machinery* 19 (March 1976): pages 113–26.

20. See David Rumelhart, "Some Problems with the Notion of Literal Meanings" in *Metaphor and Thought*, edited by Andrew Ortony (Cambridge: Cambridge University Press, 1979), pages 78–90. Rumelhart argues that "the distinction between literal and metaphorical language is rarely, if ever, reflected in a qualitative change in the psychological processes involved in the processing of that language" (page 79). Rumelhart considers two uses of "if": "If you mow the lawn, I'll pay you $5," and "If you are a senator, you are over thirty-five." The first "if" is taken as "if and only if," and the second as a simple implication. Rumelhart argues that we know which "literal" meaning to take because we seek a schema in our representation of knowledge such that the sentence can be taken as an instance of the general schema, and that this account of the general comprehension process applies to literal and figurative language alike. I would elaborate this by saying that we seek a schema *or a system of connected schemas* such that the sentence can be taken as an instance of the general schema or the general system of schemas.

21. For an introduction to functional sentence perspective, see F. Daneš, editor, *Papers on Functional Sentence Perspective* (Prague: Academia, 1974).

CHAPTER 7
THE POETRY OF CONNECTIONS, I

1. "Contemporary theories of perception, cognition, intelligence, and other mental attributes that are of particular interest to human beings tend to regard the fact that the brain resides in a body as a superfluous detail. Because the trophic theory is based on the responses of the nervous system to changing targets, it may serve to remind us that a first step in deciphering the brain is to understand the way it serves the needs of the body it tenants" (Dale Purves, *Body and Brain: A Trophic Theory of Neural Connections* [Cambridge: Harvard University Press, 1988], page 175).

2. See Mark Johnson, *The Body in the Mind* (Chicago: University of Chicago Press, 1989), page 113.

3. For a hypothesis concerning the neurobiological development of such cross-modal knowledge, see Gerald Edelman, *The Remembered Present: A Biological Theory of Consciousness* (New York: Basic Books, 1989), chapter 4, "Reentrant Signaling."

4. For extended discussions of the theory of basic metaphor, see George Lakoff and Mark Turner, *More than Cool Reason: A Field Guide to Poetic Metaphor* (Chicago: University of Chicago Press, 1989); George Lakoff and Mark Johnson, *Metaphors We Live By* (Chicago: University of Chicago Press, 1980); William Nagy's ground-breaking "Figurative Patterns and Redundancy in the Lexicon" (Ph.D. diss., University of California at San Diego, 1974); Michael Reddy, "The Conduit Metaphor," in *Metaphor and Thought*, edited by A. Ortony (Cambridge: Cambridge University Press, 1979), pages 284–324; and Eve

Sweetser, *From Etymology to Pragmatics: Metaphorical and Cultural Aspects of Semantic Structure* (Cambridge: Cambridge University Press, 1990).

5. For a full introduction to specific-level and generic-level metaphors, see Lakoff and Turner, *More than Cool Reason*.

6. Of course, as discussed in chapter 3, we can take the violation of the constraint as signifying that we are to do conceptual work on the source or target to remove the violation. See further note 3 to chapter 10.

7. It was the fact that CAUSATION IS PROGENERATION has no fixed target domain and has additionally a range of constraints on possible mappings—constraints having to do with causal structure, event-shape, and so on—that inspired the theory of generic-level metaphor. Nonetheless, CAUSATION IS PROGENERATION is not a prototypical generic-level metaphor, because its source domain is a fixed specific-level schema. For a chapter-length discussion of this metaphor, and of the ways in which constraints can apply to an infinite range of possible mappings without actually delivering or fixing a mapping, see chapter 4 of my *Death Is the Mother of Beauty: Mind, Metaphor, Criticism* (Chicago: University of Chicago Press, 1987). That discussion contains an analysis of how the general shape of the event (technically, aspectual structure) is preserved in metaphor.

8. For a chapter-length discussion of THE GREAT CHAIN METAPHOR, see Lakoff and Turner, *More than Cool Reason*, chapter 4.

9. In some cases, we conceive of a certain physical attribute as instrumental to a certain instinctual nature and behavior. In these cases, mapping the nature and behavior motivates mapping its instruments. Thus, the nature, behavior, and physical attributes can be mapped as a package. Consider "This corporation is like an octopus." The bodily structure of radiating tentacles seems to us instrumental to the behavior of encompassing. We map the behavior and its instrument, namely, the image-schema associated with radiating tentacles. We do not think of the spider's blackness as instrumental to its behavior of laying its trap and catching its prey. Consequently, in the case of the spider, the maxim of quantity excludes the spider's physical attributes from the mapping, in the absence of any cue to involve it.

10. Of course, frequently the context supplies the cue.

11. See H. P. Grice, "Logic and Conversation," in *Syntax and Semantics*, vol. 3, *Speech Acts*, edited by Peter Cole and Jerry Morgan (New York: Academic, 1975), pages 41–58.

12. See, for example, Darwin Porter's description of the Gaudí cathedral: "Its appearance is so odd that it's difficult to describe and must be seen to be appreciated, but this may give you a clue: art nouveau run rampant, ornamental figures, eight principal well-ventilated tapering towers with celestially orbed peaks fringed with balls, and lots and lots of melting gingerbread draped in a majestic batter-like ooze over a forest of stalgmites and jutting brown icicles" (*Frommer's Spain and Morocco on $40 a Day, 1989–1990* [New York: Simon and Schuster, 1989], page 277).

13. Kenneth Burke observes that Jeremy Bentham came in spite of himself to a similar conclusion:

Bentham's great contributions to the study of persuasion were made almost in spite of himself. In trying to promote ways of discussion that could truly transcend the suggestiveness of imagery, he revealed how thoroughly imaginal our thinking is. Scrutinizing the most abstract of legalistic terms, asking himself just what it meant to plead and pass judgment in terms of "legal fictions," he proposed a methodic search for "archetypes." By "archetypes" he meant the images that underly the use of abstractions. (To quote one of his favorite examples: Consider the irrelevant but suggestive and provocative images of *binding* that lurk in the term, "obligation.")

Bentham here discovered a kind of poetry concealed beneath legal jargon usually considered the very opposite of poetry. It was *applied poetry*, or rhetoric, since it was the use of poetic resources to affect judgments, decisions, hence attitudes and actions. As we noted when discussing Richards and Mead in the *Grammar*, the notion of an attitude or incipient act is ambiguous; an attitude of sympathy, for instance, may either lead into an overt act of kindness, or it may serve "liberally" as the *substitute* for an act of kindness. And since Richards stresses in the "imaginal" action of poetry its role as an alternative to the overt act, we can see how he "repoetized" Bentham's essentially rhetorical concerns. For when one thinks of poetry as the exercise of imaginal suggestiveness in areas that transcend the practical, one has again made the step from Cicero to Longinus: one admires an expression, not for its power to move a hearer towards this or that decision, but for its use of images that are "moving" in and for themselves. Once you think of the imaginal, not as inducement to action, but as the sensitive suspension of action, invitiations that you might *fear* in rhetoric can be *enjoyed* in poetry.

See "Rhetorical Analysis in Bentham," in *A Rhetoric of Motives* (Berkeley: University of California Press, 1969 [1950]), pages 90–91.

14. For a discussion of the development of this hypothesis, and some of its details, see note 21 to chapter 3.

15. Patricia Smith Churchland, *Neurophilosophy: Toward a Unified Science of the Mind/Brain* (Cambridge: MIT, 1986), section 10.4.

CHAPTER 8
THE POETRY OF CONNECTIONS, II

1. I am indebted to Claudia Brugman and Eve Sweetser for comments on the rest of this chapter.

2. Wendell Berry, "The Man Born to Farming," *Farming: A Handbook* (San Diego: Harcourt, Brace, Jovanovich, 1985), lines 1–3, p. 3.

CHAPTER 9
THE POETRY OF CONNECTIONS, III

1. The incompatibility comes from the lexical content of the form: in "He is an angel of God," x and y are compatible, as are y and z; in "A leader is a dealer in hope," x and y are compatible but y and z are not; in "Children are the riches of poor men," x and y are incompatible, and so are y and z. In this study, we inspect what happens when y and z are incompatible.

2. Gilles Fauconnier and Cathy Harris alerted me to this phenomenon.

CHAPTER 10
CULTURAL LITERACY AND POETIC THOUGHT

1. "Preamble" to *Life: A User's Manual*, translated by David Bellos (Boston: David R. Goldine, 1987), no page number. The French original is Georges Perec, *La vie mode d'emploi* (Paris: Hachette, 1978), page 15.

2. Although there are slight differences in the presentation of the parts of rhetoric in Aristotle, Quintilian, and the Ciceronian and pseudo-Ciceronian works, I am taking Cicero's summary in the *De oratore* (1.31.142–43) as representative in its division of classical rhetoric into a hierarchy of five parts: Invention (*inventio* or εὑρησις), Arrangement (*dispositio* or τάξις), Style (*elocutio* or λέξις), Memory (*memoria* or μνήμη), and Delivery (*actio* or ὑπόκρισις). Cicero writes: "All the activity and ability of an orator falls into five divisions. . . . He must first hit upon what to say; then manage and marshal his discoveries, not merely in orderly fashion, but with a discriminating eye for the exact weight as it were of each argument; next go on to array them in the adornments of style; after that keep them guarded in his memory; and in the end deliver them with effect and charm" (translated by E. W. Sutton, Loeb edition).

3. Of course, as discussed in chapters 3 and 7, we can take the violation of the constraint as signifying that we are to do conceptual work on the source or target to remove the violation—as when we think of an Irrigator as causing death by overwatering. We thereby locate a causal connection for the source which can be mapped onto the causal connection in the target, satisfying the constraint. Such construal is evidence of our knowledge of the constraint: it is only by knowing the constraint that we recognize that we are being asked to engage in such creative construal, and again only by knowing the constraint that we know when to be satisfied with the conceptual work that we have done.

4. Gregory Colomb and I analyze in detail what is mistaken with this concept in "Computers, Literary Theory, and Theory of Meaning," in *The Future of Literary Theory*, edited by Ralph Cohen (New York: Routledge, 1988), pages 386–410, notes: pages 436–43. Colomb has elaborated these ideas in "Cultural Literacy and Theory of Meaning," *New Literary History* 20/2 (Winter 1989): pages 411–64, in which he concentrates on text linguistics and the concept of a top-down grammar.

5. E. D. Hirsch, Jr., *Cultural Literacy: What Every American Needs to Know* (Boston: Houghton Mifflin, 1987), page xiii.

6. Ibid., page xv.

7. Ibid., page 2.

8. Perhaps it was once; perhaps we once shared a stereotype of the Dutch. Perhaps it was once connected to phrases like "Dutch uncle" and "Dutch courage"—archaic phrases whose meaning I have never known.

9. *Cultural Literacy*, page 48.

10. Ibid., page 53.

11. Ibid., page 112.

12. Diane and Kathy A. Zahler, *Test Your Cultural Literacy* (New York: Arco, 1988).

13. Ibid., page 147.

14 Hirsch, *Cultural Literacy*, p. 90.

Chapter 11
Envoi

1. For an extended and illuminating description of this ubiquitous common-place connection, see Jay David Bolter, *Writing Space: The Computer, Hypertext, and the History of Writing* (Hillsdale, N.J.: Lawrence Erlbaum Associates, 1990).

INDEX

Abrams, M. H., 83, 264n.2
abstract reasoning, 61
abstract skill, 219
Acharnians, The, 244
Achilles, 82
actions, 221
active behavior, 186
acts of literature, 13
aition, 113
amphisbetesis, 105, 107
analogy, 121–50, 219; bare, 185
anatomy, 27
Anaximander, 94
ancient Near Eastern art, 75
ancient Near Eastern cosmology, 94
antagonistic standing, 105
Anticlea, 77, 275n.6
Antonello da Messina, 34
aporia, 263n.1; as defined in theory of ar-
    gument, 111
apostles, 55
argument, 99–120, 218, 241; and bodily
    metaphor, 100; concept of, 247; as con-
    stituted by conflict of claims, 101; in the
    plays of Aristophanes, 243
Aristophanes, 3, 11, 237; plays of, as argu-
    ments, 243
Aristotle, 13, 54, 94, 104, 106, 118, 198,
    269n.6, 286n.2; on metaphor, 269n.6;
    Physics, 101–3
Arrangement (part of rhetoric), 217,
    286n.2
artifacts, 30
arts of language, 16
arts of reason, 12
arts of speech, 12
Ashbery, John, 62–64
aspects of beings, 161
aspects of concepts, 193, 260; weak versus
    strong, 195
assertion of proposition as standing on its
    location, 79
astasiastic claims, 110
asymmetry and breakage, 92
"At North Farm," 62–65
Auden, W. H., 58

authority, 18
author's mind as endless paper, 246
automatic and unconscious understanding,
    39
automatic aspects of thought and language,
    25, 43, 68
automorphism, 86
autonomy of syntax, 20

background conceptual system, 43, 151
backlash on unmentioned concept, 205
"Bait, The," 270n.12
balance, 70
bare analogies, equations, similarities, 183–
    85
baseball, 13
basic concepts, 26, 38; as inherently imagi-
    native, 46; study of, as ground of literary
    criticism, 39
basic conceptual apparatus, 39
basic level of categorization, 126, 219,
    280n.8
basic metaphor, 158; as connecting specific-
    level schemas, 162; definition of, 161
basic source domain, 199
basis of literature, 39
behavior: active, 186; passive, 186; prefer-
    ence to map metaphorically, 185
Being Leads to Doing, 247
Bennett, William, 223
Bentham, Jeremy, 284n.13
Berry, Wendell, 192
Bible, 196
bicycle: learning to ride, 38
bilaterality, 75–76
bilateral symmetry, 68–98
birth, 37
Black, Max, 55, 269n.8
Blake, William, 240
bodily knowledge, 41
bodily sense of spatiality, 57
bodily symmetry, 151
body, 25; and the environment, 69; errone-
    ously viewed as estranged from the mind,
    36; as mapped in the brain, 34, 151; in
    the mind 33, 40, 41; static outside of, 31